ANTI-IMPUNITY AND THE HUMAN RIGHTS AGENDA

In the twenty-first century, fighting impunity has become both the rallying cry and a metric of progress for human rights. The new emphasis on criminal prosecution represents a fundamental change in the positions and priorities of students and practitioners of human rights and transitional justice: it has become almost unquestionable common sense that criminal punishment is a legal, political, and pragmatic imperative for addressing human rights violations. This book challenges that common sense. It does so by documenting and critically analyzing the trend toward an anti-impunity norm in a variety of institutional and geographical contexts, with an eye toward the interaction between practices at the global and local levels. Together, the chapters demonstrate how this laser focus on anti-impunity has created blind spots in practice and in scholarship that result in a constricted response to human rights violations, a narrowed conception of justice, and an impoverished approach to peace.

Karen Engle is Minerva House Drysdale Regents Chair in Law, and Founder & Co-Director of the Bernard and Audre Rapoport Center for Human Rights and Justice at the University of Texas at Austin. She is the 2016–17 Deborah Lunder and Alan Ezekowitz Founders' Circle Member at the Institute for Advanced Study.

Zinaida Miller is Assistant Professor at the School of Diplomacy and International Relations at Seton Hall University.

D.M. Davis is Judge President of the Competition Appeal Court of South Africa, and a Judge of the High Court of Cape Town. He is Honorary Professor of Law at the University of Cape Town.

Anti-Impunity and the Human Rights Agenda

Edited by

KAREN ENGLE
University of Texas School of Law

ZINAIDA MILLER
Seton Hall University
School of Diplomacy and International Relations

D.M. DAVIS
University of Cape Town Faculty of Law

For Joan,
Many Thanks for years
& inspiration!
Best,
Kn

CAMBRIDGE
UNIVERSITY PRESS

CAMBRIDGE
UNIVERSITY PRESS

University Printing House, Cambridge CB2 8BS, United Kingdom

One Liberty Plaza, 20th Floor, New York, NY 10006, USA

477 Williamstown Road, Port Melbourne, VIC 3207, Australia

4843/24, 2nd Floor, Ansari Road, Daryaganj, Delhi – 110002, India

79 Anson Road, #06-04/06, Singapore 079906

Cambridge University Press is part of the University of Cambridge.

It furthers the University's mission by disseminating knowledge in the pursuit of
education, learning, and research at the highest international levels of excellence.

www.cambridge.org
Information on this title: www.cambridge.org/9781107079878
DOI: 10.1017/9781139942263

© Cambridge University Press 2016

First published 2016
Reprinted 2016

Printed in the United States of America by Sheridan Books, Inc.

A catalog record for this publication is available from the British Library.

Library of Congress Cataloging in Publication Data
Names: Engle, Karen, editor. | Miller, Zinaida, editor. | Davis, D. M. (Denys Mathias),
editor. | Bernard and Audre Rapoport Center for Human Rights and Justice,
sponsoring body. | Harvard Law School. Institute for Global Law and Policy, sponsoring body.
Title: Anti-impunity and the human rights agenda / edited by Karen Engle,
University of Texas School of Law; Zinaida Miller, Seton Hall University;
D. M. Davis, High Court of Cape Town.
Description: Cambridge, United Kingdom ; New York, NY, USA : Cambridge
University Press, 2016. | Includes papers presented at a conference held in Spring 2013 at
The Bernard and Audre Rapoport Center for Human Rights and Justice at the University
of Texas School of Law. | Includes bibliographical references and index.
Identifiers: LCCN 2016051951| ISBN 9781107079878 (hardback) |
ISBN 9781107439221 (paperback)
Subjects: LCSH: Criminal liability (International law)–Congresses. |
Impunity–Congresses. | BISAC: POLITICAL SCIENCE /
Political Freedom & Security / Human Rights.
Classification: LCC KZ7075.A58 2016 | DDC 345/.04–dc23
LC record available at https://lccn.loc.gov/2016051951

ISBN 978-1-107-07987-8 Hardback
ISBN 978-1-107-43922-1 Paperback

Contents

Contributors

Helena Alviar García
Professor and former Dean, Faculty of Law, Universidad de los Andes

Natalie R. Davidson
Postdoctoral Fellow, Minerva Center for Human Rights, Hebrew University Jerusalem

D.M. Davis
Judge, High Court of Cape Town and Judge President, Competition Appeal Court of Cape Town; Honorary Professor, University of Cape Town Faculty of Law

Karen Engle
Minerva House Drysdale Regents Chair in Law and Founder & Co-Director, Bernard and Audre Rapoport Center for Human Rights and Justice, University of Texas at Austin

Mahmood Mamdani
Professor and Executive Director, Makerere Institute of Social Research, Makerere University, Kampala, Uganda, and Herbert Lehman Professor of Government and Professor of Anthropology, African Studies and Political Science, Columbia University

Zinaida Miller
Assistant Professor, School of Diplomacy and International Relations, Seton Hall University

Samuel Moyn
Jeremiah Smith, Jr. Professor of Law and Professor of History, Harvard University

Vasuki Nesiah
Associate Professor of Practice, Gallatin School of Individualized Study, New York University

Dianne Otto
Francine V. McNiff Professor in Human Rights Law and former Director, Institute for International Law and the Humanities (IILAH), Melbourne Law School

Fabia Fernandes Carvalho Veçoso
Assistant Professor of International Relations, Federal University of São Paulo and Postdoctoral Fellow with the Laureate Program in International Law, Melbourne Law School

Acknowledgments

We first thank all the authors who have contributed to this collection. We have learned a great deal from our interactions with them and their work. And we are grateful for the enormous patience they have shown in responding to our multiple requests for revisions and updates, and for their willingness to engage with each other's work as we have sought to make an argument with the book.

We also thank the people behind two institutions who have supported this work: The Bernard and Audre Rapoport Center for Human Rights and Justice at the University of Texas School of Law and the Institute for Global Law and Policy (IGLP) at Harvard Law School. The collaboration began before we were aware of it, when IGLP's director, David Kennedy, invited one of us (Karen Engle) to give a lecture in June 2012 and the other two of us (D.M. Davis and Zinaida Miller) to serve as respondents. Karen presented the first version of what later became her chapter for this book, and we believed we had the beginnings of a good discussion. The Rapoport Center decided to continue that discussion at its Spring 2013 conference, "Impunity, Justice and the Human Rights Agenda." Most of the contributors to this collection attended that conference, as did several other discussants and presenters to whom we are grateful for their time and substantive contributions to this project. IGLP then invited us to "workshop" the papers at a proseminar in June of that year.

We are therefore extremely grateful to David Kennedy and his team for providing financial and logistical support for the proseminar and to the following people at the Rapoport Center: Co-Director Daniel Brinks, who has been involved in numerous discussions with us, including at the conference, encouraged us to publish this collection, and agreed to dedicate much of the Center's time to the editing and production of the volume; Assistant Director William Chandler, who has deftly coordinated everything from the conference to the work of student copy-editors and the final preparation of the manuscript; and Rapoport Center Scholars and Fellows – Kyle Shen, Kallie Dale Ramos, Rhiannon Hamam, Cianan Good, and Helen Kerwin – who have provided the bulk of the editing support for the project.

Hani Sayed has been an invaluable interlocutor and contributor to our discussions on anti-impunity from the beginning and we are grateful for his many insights, at the initial conference, the IGLP proseminar, and beyond. We are also indebted to Fionnuala Ní Aoláin for her very useful comments on the individual papers presented at the proseminar as well as on the project as a whole.

We are appreciative of John Berger and Sharon McCann at Cambridge University Press, as well as of three anonymous peer reviewers for their thoughtful feedback. We and our readers also benefited enormously from the excellent indexing skills of Deborah Patton.

Finally, we are each grateful to our two co-editors as well as to the friends, family, and colleagues who have stood by us throughout the production of this book. It has been a long haul that has spanned more continents and years than we originally anticipated. We hope the result vindicates the wait.

Introduction

Karen Engle, Zinaida Miller, and D.M. Davis

In the twenty-first century, fighting impunity has become both the rallying cry and a metric of progress for human rights. Criminal prosecutions are central to this fight. Whereas in an earlier era, criminal punishment had been considered one tool among many, it has gradually become the preferred and often unquestioned method not only for attempting to end human rights violations, but for promoting sustainable peace and fostering justice. The new emphasis on anti-impunity represents a fundamental change in the positions and priorities of those involved in human rights as well as transitional justice – even as it has brought these two fields together, in part through the rapid development of international criminal law. With this shift, it has become almost unquestionable common sense that criminal punishment is a legal, political, and pragmatic imperative for addressing human rights violations. This book challenges that common sense. It does so through chapters that document and critically analyze the trend toward an anti-impunity norm in a variety of contexts.

As Part I of the book demonstrates, a number of scholars before us have noted aspects of this shift toward anti-impunity. They have, however, primarily lauded the trend. For them, prosecutions are considered to be an unalloyed good: they deter future abuses, promote the rule of law, restore the confidence of citizens in government, guarantee respect for human rights, and ensure justice for victims of atrocious crimes. Even those who criticize the traditional criminal justice model or the practice of international criminal law suggest that the problems lie chiefly in efficiency and enforcement rather than in conceptualization.

Importantly, we do not contend that the anti-impunity norm has led to the consistent punishment of even traditionally acknowledged human rights violations throughout the world, nor that impunity has disappeared. To the contrary, while we generally agree that there has been a surge in attempts to

1

criminalize and prosecute certain human rights violations in at least some parts of the world, as well as a significant increase in anti-impunity talk, we are less sanguine about a commensurate increase in justice.

In various ways, the chapters in this volume suggest that a dominant emphasis on anti-impunity has qualitatively transformed human rights and transitional justice discourses, and in turn practices, particularly by narrowing their gaze to certain types of impunity. Contrary to what is suggested by the trend in scholarship, activism, and politics, we contend that the turn is not the logical, necessary, nor preferred outcome of a linear process of maturation in either field. Rather, the chapters demonstrate how this laser focus on anti-impunity has created blindspots in practice and scholarship that result in a constricted response to human rights violations, a narrowed conception of justice, and an impoverished approach to peace.

The book is structured as follows. Part I of the volume contains three chapters – authored by Karen Engle, Samuel Moyn, and Vasuki Nesiah – that trace in broad strokes a relatively unreflective turn to anti-impunity discourse among human rights and international criminal law advocates, scholars, and practitioners. While Engle and Moyn offer critical accounts of the genealogy, framing, and rhetoric of anti-impunity in human rights and international criminal law and discourse in the twenty-first century, Nesiah analyzes how the very drive against impunity has for some time functioned to facilitate and produce impunity for those countries and actors who are powerful enough to impose criminal sanctions on others. She cautions us against suggesting that there is in fact less impunity in the world, given not only its persistence, but the specific role that anti-impunity plays in supporting unequal structures of global governance.

The chapters in Part II look more specifically at the experiences and histories of particular countries. Authored by D.M. Davis, Zinaida Miller, Fabia Fernandes Carvalho Veçoso, Helena Alviar García and Karen Engle, and Natalie R. Davidson, these chapters describe and critique the operation of anti-impunity discourse in, respectively, South Africa, Rwanda, Brazil, Colombia, and Paraguay and the United States. They do so with an eye toward the ways in which some of the international trends analyzed in the first set of chapters are either contested or pursued in national contexts.

Finally, in Part III, Dianne Otto and Mahmood Mamdani explicitly offer models for approaching transition, justice, and violence that differ from the standard anti-impunity approaches critiqued in other chapters. Albeit in different ways, both Otto, through an examination of historical and contemporary people's tribunals, and Mamdani, by bringing renewed attention to the political negotiations that facilitated the South African transition, suggest the possibility of reinserting a critical politics into a realm now dominated by individualized criminal justice.

All of the chapters in the volume, regardless of the Part in which they fall, analyze the interaction between the global and local and suggest important insights into how each constructs the other. Together, they explore the rhetoric, norm, and practice of anti-impunity deployed by national governments, international and regional organizations and courts, and local and international NGOs. In the process, they raise a series of critical questions about the turn to anti-impunity in human rights and transitional justice, and the plausibility of the justifications offered by proponents of this turn. We discuss a number of key issues in some detail in this Introduction, namely: the meaning of anti-impunity and its connection to impunity; the relationship between law and politics; and the extent to which the focus on anti-impunity displaces attention to other harms, affects the histories produced about particular conflicts, and constructs or understands the meaning of victimhood.

I. ANTI-IMPUNITY AS CRIMINALIZATION

Although Engle and Moyn convincingly demonstrate an increase in the use of the phrases "culture of impunity" and "end impunity" over the course of the twenty-first century, the chapters in the book reveal different meanings of the term "impunity" and the fight against it. Thus, questions explored throughout the collection both implicitly and explicitly include: What is anti-impunity and what does it oppose? Does anti-impunity produce justice and, if so, what type of justice and for whom? What is the relationship between impunity and anti-impunity? Nesiah most thoroughly addresses this final question, although several other chapters allude to it.

Most of the chapters in the book see the turn to anti-impunity as an embrace of the idea that criminal law is the necessary and preferred response to a particular set of human rights violations and international crimes. Together, they problematize both aspects of that turn, suggesting that prosecutions might not be the best or most effective response to such harms and that a preference for criminalization might come at the cost of the consideration of other, often more structural, concerns. Several chapters caution against accepting a crude binary between anti-impunity and impunity, particularly if the latter is defined only by the absence of a criminal prosecution.

Moyn observes, largely in the context of the International Criminal Court (ICC), that the thrust of the anti-impunity movement is reflected in a new dream of individual criminal accountability as the crown jewel of international or global justice. Yet proponents of international criminal law persistently fail to justify its utility, necessity, or efficacy. Engle notes more broadly that the attachment of the human rights movement to criminal law – and the consequent equation of criminal prosecutions, justice, and human rights – has taken place with little systematic deliberation about the aims of criminal law or its pitfalls. Moreover, the turn to criminal law as a model for human rights enforcement has subsumed many earlier debates about the priority of peace or truth in relationship to justice as well as the broader critiques of penal systems that have long been voiced by human rights advocates.

The change in position over the past few years of human rights NGOs and regional and international institutions toward amnesty laws passed in moments of apparent or anticipated transition offers an example of the turn to criminal law in a number of the chapters. Engle offers a genealogy of the treatment of amnesties in the Inter-American human rights system as an illustration of a broader turn toward criminal law in human rights. Veçoso argues that the "Inter-American view on amnesty" has negatively affected contemporary law and politics surrounding amnesty in Brazil by attempting to force the country to revisit compromises reached long ago. Alviar and Engle consider decades of proposed amnesties and pardons that have emerged from peace agreements in Colombia to show that opposition to them only began around the start of the twenty-first century.

The contemporary resistance to amnesties and the related insistence on criminal prosecutions to fight impunity are often presented in contrast to the amnesties that were constitutionally upheld, and arguably granted, in transitional South Africa. Mamdani rejects this binary between Nuremberg-style criminal trials and South Africa's Truth and Reconciliation Commission (TRC), the institution that processed amnesties, contending that it wrongly assumes that the latter displaced punishment with forgiveness. He argues that the TRC was but a surrogate for the Nuremberg model, in part because it shared the underlying assumptions that responsibility is ultimately individual and criminal in nature. Through a close reading of the Constitutional Court case that unsuccessfully challenged transitional amnesties in South Africa, Davis contextualizes both the amnesties and the Court's decision in a series of political compromises that were seen as necessary for peace. Like Mamdani, he suggests that the TRC did not in fact represent a clear alternative to criminal adjudication.

Other chapters also examine mechanisms for human rights adjudication or transitional justice that appear to operate outside the retributive criminal framework, but nevertheless end up mimicking aspects of it. Davidson's chapter on the US Alien Tort Statute and Miller's consideration of the gacaca hearings in her chapter on post-genocide Rwanda demonstrate – in line with

Davis and Mamdani's argument about the TRC in South Africa – that private and customary law processes potentially contain many of the same assumptions and pitfalls as a penal response.

Although the chapters largely agree that criminal justice has, problematically, become the focus of the move toward anti-impunity, the authors do not generally abandon the critique of impunity. Some hope, instead, to highlight forms of impunity that are generally not recognized as such. Nesiah is perhaps most explicit in this aim. Through a re-reading of earlier moments in the history of war crimes tribunals, she argues that each historical moment of "anti-impunity" may be more accurately described as one gripped simultaneously by "impunity." The same victorious powers that supported the construction of war crimes tribunals often perpetrated terrible harms that no powerful individual, state, or organization targeted for punishment.

Miller as well as Alviar and Engle also draw attention to forms of impunity that exist alongside and yet are often overlooked by a strong and broad-based discourse against impunity. For Miller, the push to legitimize anti-impunity efforts against those accused of perpetrating the genocide in Rwanda has been accompanied by the evasion by the ruling party of any prosecution for its actions during and after the civil war. This pattern of partial (anti-)impunity is hardly limited to Rwanda. Alviar and Engle show how twenty-first century Colombian politics have seen the same actors call for amnesties, pardons, and alternative or reduced sentencing with regard to one non-state military group while decrying impunity with regard to another. The reality of shifting power politics and alliances (as well as logistics and pragmatic limitations) make it probable that, particularly in transitional contexts, prosecutions will be selective. The denial of that selectivity, however, has become part of what Moyn describes as a more general avoidance of justification for the anti-impunity agenda.

II. LAW AND POLITICS

There exists a long-running, well-rehearsed set of arguments over the relationship between law and politics. In this era of the "third globalization," as Duncan Kennedy has labeled it,[1] it is difficult to argue explicitly for a conception of law that altogether eschews politics in any sense of the word. Nevertheless, anti-impunity discourse is often deployed in an attempt to construct a bulwark of law against politics, insisting that it can protect the former from the latter. Much of the contemporary discourse around impunity that we see reflected upon throughout the book reinforces this distinction: international criminal courts will provide an impartial and apolitical answer to chaotic local politics; some acts are so violent and atrocious as to reach beyond politics; amnesties, at least for certain crimes, are prohibited regardless of the trade-offs in a particular context. Moreover, the argument that the targets of anti-impunity efforts are not chosen but rather universally agreed upon is itself a denial of the politics of selectivity that considers physical violence to be atrocity but economic inequality to be contestable. The people's tribunals that Otto analyzes seek precisely to expose the fallibility of legal neutrality, objectivity, and technocracy by performing justice in ways that foreground politics, struggle, and transformation.

That many of the chapters in this book expose the politics of law (international, regional, and local) in the fight against impunity reminds us of the salience of the law–politics distinction, at least in this domain. Some chapters concentrate on the politics of the very legal institutions they consider. Moyn, for example, contends that the ICC and its role cannot be detached from "great power politics." Much as Nesiah argues in her consideration of war crimes tribunals beginning in the early twentieth century, Moyn notes that the choices the ICC makes in the instigation of investigations and prosecutions are dependent upon the balance of political forces among powerful nations. Both Moyn and Engle show how support for the ICC translates into participation in extant political agendas, including in domestic struggle within states.

One of the ways in which global governance remains legitimate is by reinforcing the hierarchy between international law and national politics, even while denying it. The ICC, for example, operates on the basis of a complementarity often claimed to reflect a genuine concern for national institutions. In fact, complementarity assumes, even demands, a particular way in which states may prove their commitment to accountability, and in that sense governs the states vulnerable to its intervention. Alviar and Engle offer a concrete example of such governance, by discussing the role that the ICC has played in contemporary peace negotiations between the Colombian government and the Revolutionary Armed Forces of Colombia (FARC), including by intervening in a Constitutional Court case regarding the framework of those negotiations.

Veçoso extends this analysis to the Inter-American Court of Human Rights, by considering the effects of its anti-impunity approach on Brazilian national politics. She criticizes the Court's application of decontextualized doctrinal reasoning to invalidate Brazil's transitional amnesty law, contending that it ignored the political dynamics central to Brazilian politics and national reconciliation. Veçoso's arguments resonate with a counterfactual posed by Davis: would the South African amnesty scheme developed in 1994 be permissible in 2016? In suggesting that international law would make it difficult for

South Africa to make the same decisions today, Davis implicitly reveals the difficulties of an international doctrine that actively ignores local politics. Miller argues that in the Rwandan context, the internationalist justifications for the International Criminal Tribunal for Rwanda (ICTR) contrasted dramatically with the transformative agenda for anti-impunity voiced more frequently by the Rwandan government. Although both international and domestic actors shared a belief in the need for retributive justice, they offered two different justifications for it – one that emphasized its "anti-political" capacity and another that incorporated the fight against impunity into the new government's efforts to gain legitimacy and consolidate authority.

Other chapters highlight the relationship between law and politics by closely reading legal decisions for the political choices they betray. Engle's analysis of the Inter-American Court's decisions on amnesty shows how they, like other recent international discourses, have come to mediate earlier debates about justice versus truth and justice versus peace, largely by denying that there is any tension between criminal justice and truth or peace. Davidson reads multiple judicial opinions in the first modern case brought under the US Alien Tort Statute, *Filártiga* v. *Peña-Irala*, in which the family of a Paraguayan victim of torture successfully brought a civil suit against his torturer in the US. She shows how the US courts' rulings in favor of the Paraguayan plaintiffs presented a decontextualized portrait of a lone torturer and single act of torture, obscuring the systemic nature of torture under the Stroessner dictatorship in Paraguay as well as any role that US policy might have played by supporting that regime. If Engle and Davidson suggest that the effect of litigation is often to mask the political choices of the courts themselves, Davis offers a reading of the South African Constitutional Court's decision to uphold its transitional amnesty law as more plainly political, dependent upon the immediate context of the conditions confronting the country.

In different ways, then, many of the chapters reveal the dynamic relationships between international law and domestic politics as well as between international politics and domestic law. Whether within legal institutions or in the interactions between them, anti-impunity has become part of an ongoing struggle over the meaning of both law and politics.

III. PRODUCTION AND DISPLACEMENT OF STRUCTURAL AND ECONOMIC HARMS

One of the ways that law functions as politics is by calling our attention to some things while distracting us from others, including the productive or distributive nature of law itself. We discussed above how some of the chapters in this collection demonstrate that anti-impunity against some is often inextricably intertwined with impunity for others, even for similar offenses. Many of the chapters also argue in one sense or another that the turn to anti-impunity, with its focus on criminal remedies for certain individualized harms, has meant the masking, displacing, or obscuring of many other types of harms, particularly economic and structural ones. Indeed, the concentration on individual perpetrators rather than on the structural bases of inequality and poverty is often considered an almost inevitable consequence of the recourse to trials, even – as in Davidson's chapter – trials for private law tort claims. In addition, anti-impunity discourse is often seen not only to displace attention from inequality but also to produce it, in part by operating as a pillar of neoliberal global governance.

Engle and Nesiah raise awareness of the productive nature of criminal law practice and rhetoric. Engle, in her analysis of the reformulation of human rights advocacy around criminal law, emphasizes the central role of the strong punitive state in the construction and success of neoliberalism at the end of the Cold War. Nesiah suggests that anti-impunity practices and, importantly, ongoing rhetorical support for them, have been partially constitutive of a drastically unequal world order. Viewing the twentieth-century story as one that culminates in a cascade of justice through the work of burgeoning liberal institutions that enjoy increasing success in pursuing individual perpetrators of atrocity, she contends, obscures the continuing disastrous effects of decades of imperial land grabs, colonial and post-colonial violence, and brutal military interventions, often performed in the name of human rights and humanitarian protection.

Mamdani presents a particularly striking example in the South African context of the dynamic Nesiah identifies. He demonstrates how the TRC, by narrowing its focus to individual victims and bodily harms (as opposed to economic or political harms that were synonymous with the architecture of apartheid itself), achieved the "truly bizarre" result of listing the African National Congress and other anti-apartheid groups as among those most culpable for crimes committed under apartheid. Such a result could only be achieved by working within a framework that accepted the legality of apartheid, and thus by leaving unquestioned the fundamental political and economic violence of the system. In this case, a moment of "anti-impunity" for South African individuals represented simultaneously a moment of impunity for the apartheid system as a whole. Mamdani's argument exemplifies at the national level what Engle and Nesiah reveal more broadly: what is touted as structural transformation may in fact constitute a project of preservation and perpetuation.

At a more granular level, various chapters illustrate the ways in which a turn to prosecution and punishment displaces attention to inequality, poverty, dispossession, and economic violence, as well as to the actors or structures responsible for them. Miller argues in the Rwandan context, for example, that much of the history and legacy of inequality, structural violence, and linkages between unequal distribution and ethnic tension were eliminated from consideration in the post-genocide justice processes – nowhere more so than at the ICTR. The world of harms narrows in a world centered on retributive and punitive justice. In their analysis of contemporary peace negotiations in Colombia, Alviar and Engle illustrate how debates about criminal accountability for members of the FARC (and nominally the military) have sidelined serious deliberation about truly redistributive land reform, even though both issues will be part of any final accord. In a bit of a push against the anti-impunity trend, the FARC has managed to reach an agreement with the government that will keep its members out of jail. At the same time, FARC negotiators have agreed to an agrarian reform draft that is much less radical than the rebels had hoped and landowners had feared.

Those interested in the Colombian peace process might consider Mamdani's criticism of the South African TRC as a cautionary tale. By concentrating on perpetrators rather than beneficiaries, he contends, the TRC failed to acknowledge, let alone address, the ways in which apartheid-era violence produced and sustained a particular socio-economic order. Beneficiaries of apartheid continue to gain from the underlying socio-economic structure inherited by apartheid.

IV. THE NARRATION OF HISTORY

History, memory, and truth have been perennial sites of debate among transitional justice and human rights scholars, activists, practitioners, and policymakers. In addition to engaging in debates about whether truth creates justice or justice produces truth – debates that were, as Davis discusses, central to the South African Constitutional Court decision upholding the TRC's amnesty-granting capacity – they have also struggled over the question of which institutions and actors are best poised to produce historical accounts of the past. As anti-impunity has developed, with its emphasis on criminal trials, lawyers and judges have been given the heavy burden of narrating history through trials and judicial opinions.

Translating complex histories of conflict or complicated narratives of harm and violation through the narrow language of criminal law almost inevitably distorts them. Davidson demonstrates that this effect is not unique to criminal law, however, but is in some ways symptomatic of the litigation process itself. The complicated world of Paraguayan politics that sparked the *Filártiga* case she discusses became, through a series of advocacy campaigns and legal judgments, a story about a single, exceptionally bad actor – the enemy of all mankind – likened to the figure of the pirate in international law. For Davidson, traditional forms of litigation, even in the case of tort, promote an individualized rather than structural conception of responsibility for political violence. At all levels of litigation in the *Filártiga* case, the courts failed (albeit in different ways) to offer an accurate account of the political conditions in both Paraguay and the US that underpinned the events giving rise to the murder of Filártiga as well as the subsequent reaction of the Paraguayan government.

Miller, too, cites the limitations of relying on judicial accounts of history. A court's temporal jurisdiction can easily become a significant stricture on the history produced at trial. Even though the ICTR, especially in its first genocide conviction, offered a relatively detailed account of the history of colonialism and its relationship to the construction of ethnic categories in Rwanda, it could not address in detail issues that have been and remain salient to long-term conflict in the country, such as land distribution or historical labor practices.

Davidson, Nesiah, and Engle all reference Hannah Arendt's caution against constructing a story of singular and exceptional bad actors – a warning that applies both to the displacement effects of criminal trials and to their innate inability to tell history. Criminal trials focus by definition on individuals rather than context and on crime rather than politics. They provide little recognition of, or response to, the structural causes of the acts that form the basis of the trial, thereby distorting complex questions of accountability and justice. In her examination of mechanisms that operate outside the realm of the state (or inter-state bodies), Otto reveals their potential for producing a more nuanced history by giving profound voice to the victims. Indeed, she invokes the description of one such hearing as itself creating a "counter-history."

V. THE FIGURE OF THE VICTIM

The victim plays an ambivalent role in the anti-impunity imagination. The promotion of prosecutions often takes place in the name of the victims, even as their voices might be suppressed, limited, or distorted at trial. Post-conflict governments often claim legitimacy as representatives of prior victims – witness Rwanda or South Africa – even as governmental policy might, as Mamdani argues, marginalize many of those who survived past atrocity. The victim is thus both central and marginal, featured and featureless, a necessary representative of a horrific past and a feared brake on future transformation. Chapters in this collection explore and sometimes exemplify this ambivalence, bringing awareness to the ways in which victims are simultaneously spoken for and silenced through the turn to anti-impunity.

In the people's tribunals analyzed by Otto, victims take center stage in a manner that throws the more familiar suppression of their voices, experiences, and history into sharp relief. For Otto, the "politics of listening" made possible by the extralegal nature of people's tribunals creates a sense of collective responsibility that is largely impossible to achieve in a traditional courtroom. Otto contrasts what she calls the "atmosphere of solidarity" in people's tribunals with the practice of criminal law, which she contends places too much responsibility and blame on the individual, distorts local experience, and privileges experts over victims.

Moyn looks behind the curtain of the international fight against impunity to challenge its rhetoric of victim representation. He directs our attention to the persistent claim that prosecution and punishment are the wishes of all victims of atrocity, and points to the paucity of empirical evidence to support the claim. Like the prioritization of criminal prosecutions themselves, the idea that criminal punishment is what victims most desire has largely become common sense for many human rights advocates. Moyn's chapter suggests that more work needs to be done to study the preferences of victims, but also to understand how those preferences are structured by the ever-narrowing repertoire of ways of responding to them.

Davis cautions us about the limits of permitting the preferences of victims, however structured, to dictate modes of justice and practices of reconciliation. When the family members of Steve Biko opposed the South African amnesty law, arguing that they should at least be entitled to bring a civil claim against the Security Police members responsible for Biko's brutal murder, the South African Constitutional Court decided to follow what it saw as the needs of the country, even over the justified wishes of the family. That said, the Court nevertheless claimed it was acting in the interests of victims, since – whether or not they knew it – they would be better off with amnesty in the long run, as it would offer them the best opportunity for learning the truth of what had happened.

Mamdani offers a different register for thinking about victimization, calling for what he terms "survivors' justice" instead of "victims' justice." He suggests that the way we imagine justice on behalf of victims simply reinforces the problematic focus on the accountability of perpetrators as they are traditionally figured. As a result, victims' justice fails to take into account both the need for political community and the necessity of societal restructuring. Survivors' justice, he contends, would be based on profound reform, reconciliation, and reconstruction rather than punishment, revenge, and stability.

VI. CONCLUSION

Invoking Clifford Geertz's notion of anti anti-relativism, Engle calls at the end of her chapter for "anti anti-impunity." In putting together this collection, we share that goal of moving away from the fetishization of anti-impunity, not by advocating impunity but by attempting to bring back to the fore the national and global political contexts and stakes that have often been backgrounded by the turn to criminal law, whether in practice or rhetoric. We have only begun to outline the ways in which each of the chapters adds to that effort. But altogether, we believe, the authors in this volume make a significant move towards recovering and offering important alternative ways of conceiving justice.

NOTE

1 Kennedy argues that the "third globalization," which followed the eras of Classical Legal Thought and the Social, is characterized by a bipolar consciousness that embraces both policy arguments and a public law neoformalism that appeals to "supposedly transcendent, but also positively enacted values in constitutions or treaties." The central figure of the third globalization is the judge, who "simultaneously represents law against legislative politics domestically and sovereign politics internationally, and must answer the charge that s/he is a usurper, doing 'politics by other means.'" Duncan Kennedy, "Three Globalizations of Law and Legal Thought: 1850–2000, *The New Law and Economic Development*, eds. Alvaro Santos and David M. Trubek (Cambridge: Cambridge University Press, 2006), 19–73, 64, 71.

PART I

WHAT DOES ANTI-IMPUNITY MEAN?

A Genealogy of the Criminal Turn in Human Rights

Karen Engle[*]

Since the beginning of the twenty-first century, the human rights movement has, for many, become almost synonymous with the fight against impunity. That is, to support human rights has increasingly meant to favor criminal accountability for those individuals who have violated international human rights or humanitarian law. It has also come to mean opposing amnesty laws that might preclude such accountability. This chapter both chronicles and critiques this turn to criminal law within human rights.

Human rights advocates have garnered significant success with their relatively recent turn to criminal law. Judicial and quasi-judicial human rights bodies, international and regional human rights institutions, and international human rights law scholars have largely concluded that states are responsible for criminally investigating, prosecuting, and punishing individuals who commit war crimes, crimes against humanity, and genocide, as well as other "serious" human rights violations. They further generally agree that a state's failure to fulfill such a duty constitutes a violation of international human rights law and that, in certain instances, international criminal institutions should be created or used to punish individual perpetrators.

For the most part, scholars and advocates alike consider the ensuing increase in criminal trials for human rights violations – what Kathryn Sikkink refers to as "the justice cascade" – as a positive turn within the human rights movement.[1] While Sikkink documents human rights trials over the past three decades and recounts when and how human rights prosecutions began and developed in Latin America before spreading around the globe, no scholar – to

* This chapter appeared in a longer form as "Anti-Impunity and the Turn to Criminal Law in Human Rights" in the *Cornell Law Review*, 100(5) 1069–1128 (2015). I am grateful to the many colleagues who offered useful feedback for that version, especially D.M. Davis, Duncan Kennedy, and Zinaida Miller. This version also benefitted from the insightful comments of Cary Franklin, Karl Klare, and Frédéric Mégret.

my knowledge – has systematically analyzed the extent to which judicial and scholarly interpretation of both treaty-based and customary international law have changed over time to facilitate and justify the shift. And few have considered the effects of that turn on the human rights movement itself.

This chapter aims to begin to fill both of those gaps. Rather than charting the number or frequency of criminal prosecutions that have taken place, it follows international human rights jurisprudence and scholarly pronouncements on the state of international law to show how criminal prosecutions have come to be seen as legally required. As such, it situates contemporary international criminal legal institutions and the broad rejection of amnesty laws by regional and international human rights courts and institutions in some of the international human rights law that predated them. And it connects these legal responses to the human rights movement's explicit fight against impunity, particularly against the "culture of impunity," which only began in the early-1990s. It was then that much human rights advocacy started to move from naming, shaming, and sometimes judicially trying states for their violations of human rights to finding ways to hold individuals criminally responsible for them.

In the chapter, I question the often unsupported or even unstated assumption that the turn to criminal prosecution is a clear success for the human rights movement by suggesting some of the disabling effects of that focus. I do not simply consider what has been missed by the turn but attempt to demonstrate that, as criminal law has become the enforcement tool of choice, it has negatively affected the lens through which the human rights movement and the international law scholars who support it view human rights violations. In short, as advocates increasingly turn to international criminal law to respond to issues ranging from economic injustice to genocide, they reinforce an individualized and decontextualized understanding of the harms they aim to address, even while relying on the state and on forms of criminalization of which they have long been critical.

Relatedly, I aim to demonstrate that the turn to criminal law was not an obvious trajectory for either the human rights movement or international law. I revisit the "truth versus justice" and "peace versus justice" debates from the late-1980s through the mid-1990s, in which human rights activists and international legal scholars actively disagreed over whether justice (meaning criminal justice) should take priority over truth and peace, primarily in the context of transitional regimes. I trace how those debates were mediated over time and attempt to revive the positions that "lost" and have largely been forgotten, even though the debates occurred during the professional lives of many who remain influential in the human rights movement.

The contemporary embrace of criminal law – along with the equation of criminal prosecutions, justice, and human rights – has taken place with little systematic deliberation about the aims of criminal law or about its pitfalls. In fact, forgotten are not only the debates about justice versus peace and truth but also broader critiques of penal systems that have long been voiced by human rights advocates. I am interested in how anti-impunity and its alignment with criminal prosecutions came to be uncontested within human rights so relatively quickly and the effect that the current, increasingly rigidified, position has on possibilities for legal interpretation as well as for internal critique within the human rights movement.

Throughout, I use Amnesty International (AI), one of the oldest and most significant of the international non-governmental organizations (NGOs) on human rights, to illustrate the shift I see from the 1970s to today within human rights advocacy. Although, given its name, it almost seems too obvious to mention, *amnesty* was central to the organization's mission when it was founded in the early-1960s to organize letter-writing campaigns calling for the release of political prisoners, or those whom it adopted as "prisoners of conscience." By the early-1970s, AI had begun to work more broadly on issues of prison conditions and due process for all prisoners. Yet, since the 1990s, AI has been one of the most vocal opponents of amnesties, now for perpetrators of human rights violations rather than prisoners of conscience. It also, if somewhat reluctantly at first, has become a strong supporter of international criminal institutions.

I use AI as my primary example, in part to show that the term "amnesty" has only relatively recently been perceived as a negative term in human rights.[2] I also believe that AI's current positions on impunity and amnesty are representative of the views of other large international human rights NGOs, as well as of many domestic human rights NGOs. I occasionally refer to other such organizations but concentrate on AI as a way to study how the shift operates within one organization.

I pursue these arguments and aims as follows. Part I provides a brief overview of the trend in human rights that I identify, locating the human rights movement's shift, in part, within post-Cold War neoliberalism. Part II situates the criminal law turn in the jurisprudence of the Inter-American Court of Human Rights (IACtHR), and shows how the Court's decision to hold states accountable for the action of non-state actors (at the urging of advocates) provided an important precursor to the criminal turn. It then considers jurisprudence on amnesty, primarily though not exclusively in the IACtHR, and contrasts it with the South African Constitutional Court's early decision on the issue. It does so to trace the truth, justice, and peace debates throughout the period. Part III studies the development of international criminal institutions and how their prosecutorial goals have both influenced and largely been adopted by the human rights movement. Part IV returns to the human rights movement and contends that the movement's focus on criminalization has narrowed and distorted its view both of human rights harms and of possible remedies for them.

I. OVERVIEW OF THE ANTI-IMPUNITY TREND

From the mid-1970s through the late 1980s, the human rights movement – at least as represented by large international NGOs based in Europe and the United States – primarily concerned itself with the protection of individual civil and political rights. These NGOs mostly used naming and shaming tactics to put pressure on states to end their direct violations of human rights. They did not generally call on states to prosecute individuals who committed the violations, in large part because states – not individuals – were considered the perpetrators.

Moreover, during this period, much human rights advocacy was directed at states' criminalization of political activity and at abuses of their penal systems. When AI first began its letter-writing campaigns in 1961, it called for the release of those it deemed prisoners of conscience, invoking the rights to freedom of thought and expression.[3] As early as 1964, however, it began scrutinizing the criminal justice system's treatment of all political prisoners, even if it did not adopt, nor call for the release of, those who advocated force.[4] By 1968, it officially expanded its mandate to express concern for the treatment of all prisoners – political and "ordinary" – relying on prohibitions on torture, cruel and inhumane punishment, and arbitrary arrest and detention.[5] While AI might have found some states' criminal justice systems more suspect than others, it saw all countries as capable of abusing their penal power.[6]

Even as international and regional human rights institutions, including adjudicatory and quasi-adjudicatory bodies, emerged or expanded during the 1970s and 1980s with the aim of enforcing human rights law beyond naming and shaming, they did so to review or judge the human rights records of states. No international criminal courts or tribunals existed to try individual perpetrators. Enthusiasm for an international criminal court to try crimes ranging from war crimes to terrorism had waxed and waned among international lawyers since before the advent of the human rights movement, even as far back as the interwar period.[7] It did not gain significant momentum, however, until the mid-1990s.

As recently as 1991, the establishment of international criminal courts to try individual perpetrators seemed implausible to many human rights advocates, as did large-scale domestic criminal adjudication. As Argentine legal theorist Carlos Nino put it in his article in the *Yale Law Journal* that year, after suggesting that an international criminal forum would be preferable to a requirement that transitional states engage in domestic prosecutions: "[I]t may be idealistic to hope for the establishment of [international criminal] courts in the present state of international law; but it is no less realistic than to hope that the international community, through external political pressure, will enforce the duty to prosecute past human rights abuses."[8] Of course, we now know that neither was as far out of reach as Nino expected.

As Cherif Bassiouni notes, although an international criminal court still seemed a distant possibility up until 1992, events in the former Yugoslavia and in Rwanda generated broad-based support for international prosecutions of war crimes, which was manifested in the United Nations Security Council resolutions establishing the ad hoc tribunals for the former Yugoslavia in 1993 and Rwanda in 1994. That support paved the way for the 1998 Rome Conference that adopted the treaty establishing the International Criminal Court (ICC).[9]

That the Security Council was able to agree on the establishment of international criminal tribunals with regard to the former Yugoslavia and Rwanda was also, of course, largely due to the end of the Cold War and reflected the end of the stalemate that the Security Council had faced for decades between its five permanent members. To be sure, an international criminal response first functioned as a compromise in the former Yugoslavia when states were still unable to agree on military intervention. And in Rwanda, international criminalization was largely seen as a necessary response to an unfortunate problem that the United Nations should have averted to begin with. Nevertheless, the Security Council's choice of international criminal tribunals in the early-1990s corresponded with a move to criminal law in other areas as well.

The rise of neoliberalism that accompanied the end of the Cold War, for instance, often called for a strong punitive state, even while relaxing government control in many other areas.[10] Criminal law played an important role in economic restructuring and rule of law projects throughout the world. Allegra McLeod explores in detail the United States' increased exportation of its own criminal justice model throughout the 1990s to combat transnational crime. Noting that then-Senator Kerry "repeatedly declared that transnational crime was 'the new communism, the new monolithic threat'" and that it was up to the United States to lead the crusade against it, she contends that "[b]attling transnational crime became a vehicle to organize US global engagement in the post-Cold War period."[11] The exported model favored retributive justice, and its spread corresponded to the rise of prison rates in the United States.

In the early 1990s, the focus and approach of the human rights movement also began to change in ways that coincided with, and perhaps fueled, the increased attention to and faith in criminal justice systems – domestic, international, and transnational. During that time, human rights advocates began to see the threat of impunity in much the way then-Senator Kerry understood the threat of transnational crime. AI's 1991 "policy statement on impunity" is exemplary of the term's usage:

> Amnesty International believes that the phenomenon of impunity is one of the main contributing factors to ["persistent patterns of gross human rights violations" that "are still occurring in many countries throughout the world"]. Impunity, literally the exemption from punishment, has serious implications for the proper administration of justice … International standards clearly require states to undertake proper investigations into human rights violations and to ensure that those responsible are brought to justice.[12]

Note that in this quotation, impunity is not simply a failure to remedy human rights violations; it is a unique cause of them. AI repeated this language in numerous country reports during this period.[13] Such impunity, of course, might occur from a state's failure to investigate human rights violations; or it might result from explicit decisions not to prosecute abuses of human rights, such as through amnesty laws. Advocates began to oppose both, increasingly decrying the "culture of impunity," a term that had rarely been used before 1991. (See Figure).

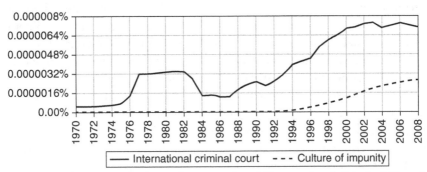

FIGURE References to "culture of impunity" and "International Criminal Court" (1970–2008)[14]

Seeing impunity as cultural suggests deeply entrenched attitudes that can only be changed over time. While one could imagine multiple ways to respond to that culture,[15] the stage was being set for individual criminal responsibility to emerge as the primary and even legally necessary response to it. Criminalization appealed to human rights advocates working on a variety of different issues. Many women's human rights proponents, for example, supported what Elizabeth Bernstein labels "carceral feminism," particularly in their attempts to address sex trafficking and sexual violence.[16]

In the next two Parts, I consider some of the ways in which individual criminal responsibility became central to the human rights effort. Domestic and international human rights NGOs as well as regional and international institutions, including human rights courts, eventually concluded that the protection of international human rights and humanitarian law (which increasingly overlapped) required criminal accountability at both domestic and international levels.

II. DOMESTIC PUNISHMENT AS INTERNATIONAL HUMAN RIGHTS REMEDY

When we think of international criminal law, we generally have in mind international criminal institutions. As I discuss in Part III, one of the aims of the ICC is to put pressure on states to prosecute individuals domestically. In this Part, I consider how international human rights law also attempts to affect domestic criminal prosecutions. That is, although it has received relatively little attention, since the late-1980s (several years before the ICC seemed likely), much human rights law has aimed to pressure states to respond criminally to human rights violations through what Alexandra Huneeus has recently termed "the quasi-criminal jurisdiction of the human rights courts," or "international criminal law by other means."[17]

I concentrate here on the development of the jurisprudence of the IACtHR, in particular on when, why, and how it has held states accountable for the criminal investigation, prosecution, and punishment of human rights violations, including by invalidating amnesty laws. I aim to show that, if inadvertently, the IACtHR's early case law set the stage for the human rights movement's anti-impunity emphasis, normalizing the turn to criminal law inside and outside of the Inter-American system. Its influence can be seen, for example, in both the European and African human rights regimes, as well as in the United Nations. I also aim to demonstrate how, along the way, the IACtHR's jurisprudence and the human rights advocacy it both followed and spurred crafted decisions and arguments to make the conclusions seem less contested than they were. To consider the extent to which there were differing opinions on the importance of impunity and the meaning of impunity and justice, I also discuss in some detail a 1996 South African Constitutional

Court decision that has escaped significant direct criticism, even though it reached a result quite different from that of the IACtHR.

A. Break-down of the Public/Private Distinction

In recent years, the IACtHR has struck down amnesty provisions in many different countries, and it is there that its anti-impunity stance is most clear. Yet, the roots of that line of cases extend to the Court's earliest jurisprudence, which is known for its progressive move to break down the public/private or state action/inaction divide. In this section, I consider that early case law, reading it in particular for how it set the stage for the Court's jurisprudence on amnesty.

In 1988, the IACtHR handed down *Velásquez-Rodríguez* v. *Honduras*, its first decision in a contentious case. In that case, the Honduran government denied responsibility for the disappearance of a political activist, although it put forward little by way of defense. Rather than requiring that the applicant prove direct state action, the Court found that state accountability did not rest on only direct state involvement. Indeed:

> [a]n illegal act which violates human rights and which is initially not directly imputable to a State (for example, because it is the act of a private person or because the person responsible has not been identified) can lead to international responsibility of the State, not because of the act itself, but because of the lack of due diligence to prevent the violation or to respond to it as required by the Convention.[18]

According to the Court, the state therefore possessed "a legal duty to take reasonable steps to prevent human rights violations and to use the means at its disposal to carry out a serious investigation of violations … to identify those responsible, to impose the appropriate punishment and to ensure the victim adequate compensation."[19]

At the time, human rights advocates and legal scholars heralded the decision as a defining moment for human rights law. Theodor Meron, for example, in a lecture on state responsibility shortly after the decision was rendered, read it as a response to the difficulty of attribution in human rights law:

> If we want international human rights law to become an authentic branch of international law, equal to all other branches of international law, we must create a conceptual structure in which we can invoke the same principles of state responsibility as in other fields of international law. The basic requirement here is that we should be able to invoke the same principles of attribution.[20]

Dinah Shelton, who would later become a member of the Inter-American Commission on Human Rights, commented that, because of the Court's willingness to interpret the American Convention on Human Rights to attribute state responsibility to state inaction, the Convention "provides guarantees for individual rights that are lacking in US constitutional law."[21] And, in a 1993 report, AI referred to the judgment as "the most far-reaching pronouncement to date of the principle of state responsibility."[22]

When the women's human rights movement began to take off in the late-1980s and early-1990s, largely with a focus on violence against women in the so-called private sphere, it saw *Velásquez-Rodríguez* as signaling a paradigmatic shift. In particular, a number of scholarly articles at the time cited the case as path-breaking for the women's human rights movement's attempts to break down the public/private distinction in international law.[23]

Given that I identify *Velásquez-Rodríguez* as a significant precursor to the turn to criminal law, it is important to point out that, despite its announcement of the state's obligation to punish, the Court explicitly distinguished itself from a criminal tribunal. The decision explained:

> The international protection of human rights should not be confused with criminal justice. States do not appear before the Court as defendants in a criminal action. The objective of international human rights law is not to punish those individuals who are guilty of violations, but rather to protect the victims and to provide for the reparation of damages resulting from the acts of the States responsible.[24]

Somewhat paradoxically, the Court asserted this distinction to lower the Commission's burden of proof. Because the Honduran government failed to provide evidence in support of a defense on the merits, the Court accepted as true the Commission's rendition of the facts, a move it acknowledged would be unlikely to satisfy the requirements of a criminal prosecution.[25]

Perhaps because it had in mind a clear distinction between itself and a criminal court and because it had little faith in the Honduran government's willingness or ability to investigate the case, the IACtHR did not order the state to engage in criminal prosecution. Instead, it ordered Honduras "to pay fair compensation" to the victim's next-of-kin.[26] In cases beginning in the mid-1990s, however, including in some countries where there was little reason to trust the police and prosecutors to engage in fair investigation, prosecution, and punishment, the Court began affirmatively to require that states initiate criminal investigations against individual perpetrators.[27] And, as Huneeus shows in great detail, over time it has become increasingly common for the IACtHR, as well as other human rights adjudicatory and quasi-adjudicatory bodies, to order, or at least exhort, states to engage in criminal proceedings at the remedial stage.[28]

Of course, the piercing of the public/private or state action/inaction divide did not necessarily require a criminalization approach. One could hold the state accountable without ordering it to prosecute individuals. Indeed, as I have already suggested, this turn to criminal law was a somewhat curious move in the context of a human rights movement that had, up until that point, largely focused on the punitive state as part of the problem.

While the IACtHR's early jurisprudence played a formative role in the turn to criminal law, it was also part of a larger trend. For example, the Vienna Declaration and Program of Action, stemming from the 1993 UN World Conference on Human Rights, emphasized anti-impunity through provisions such as one stating that "States should abrogate legislation leading to impunity for those responsible for grave violations of human rights such as torture and prosecute such violations, thereby providing a firm basis for the rule of law."[29] Indeed, in 2013, when the United Nations High Commissioner for Human Rights reflected on the twenty years since the Vienna Declaration, one of its three main accomplishments she identified was "its impact on the fight against impunity."[30]

The issue had also been on the mind of the United Nations Sub-Commission on Prevention of Discrimination and Protection of Minorities since at least 1991, when it requested that Louis Joinet undertake a study on the impunity of perpetrators of civil and political human rights violations.[31] The final report, issued in 1997 and often referred to as the Joinet Report, stated that countries have an obligation "to investigate violations, to prosecute the perpetrators; and, if their guilt is established, to punish them."[32] Further, it concluded that "[a]mnesty cannot be accorded to perpetrators before the victims have obtained justice by means of an effective remedy."[33] As we see in the following section, that connection between the obligation to punish and the prohibition on amnesty was soon to be made by the IACtHR.

B. *Invalidation of Amnesty Laws*

Today, few human rights NGOs, courts, or scholars defend the legality of amnesties, at least those amnesties that do not exclude, at a minimum, war crimes, crimes against humanity, genocide, and "serious" violations of human rights. Yet, many of these same groups, institutions, and even scholars tolerated, and sometimes even endorsed, certain types of amnesties not that long ago. Argentine human rights scholar and advocate Juan Méndez, for example, had long opposed amnesties in Latin America. In 2000, as a member of the

Inter-American Commission on Human Rights, he successfully argued before the IACtHR that Peru's amnesty law violated the American Convention on Human Rights.[34] That same year, however, he acknowledged that the amnesty process employed by transitional South Africa in the mid-1990s had met the requirements of international law.[35] In 2012, a little over a decade later, he wrote that, due to its "rapid evolution," international law would no longer support "the South African-style 'conditional amnesty' … if it covered war crimes, crimes against humanity (including disappearances), or torture."[36]

Méndez's interpretation of the international law on amnesties is one that is commonly found in the writings of human rights scholars, international institutions, and human rights courts. Although they are in the minority, a few scholars today maintain that nothing in international law prohibits a state from granting amnesty, including in at least some of the categories listed above, or that the question is at least unsettled.[37] They generally base their analysis on international humanitarian law and, as I explain more fully below, have had relatively little impact on human rights jurisprudence.[38]

As Méndez suggests, the prominence of his current view on the illegality of amnesties is relatively recent. Notwithstanding the Vienna Declaration's 1993 call on states to repeal legislation that would grant impunity to those who have committed grave human rights violations and to prosecute such crimes,[39] the issue of whether truth commissions, international criminal institutions, or even amnesties offer the greatest promise for responding to mass atrocities was seriously debated among human rights advocates during the late-1980s and mid-1990s. In what were often referred to as the "truth versus justice" and "peace versus justice" debates, "justice" referred to criminal prosecutions, and many considered that truth and peace might be incompatible with criminal punishment, in part because immunity (if not impunity) might be necessary to get perpetrators to reveal the truth or agree to a peaceful transition of government.

In the remainder of this section, I consider how this change in attitude and doctrine occurred and suggest that it worked in tandem with a shift in perspective on the relationship between truth and peace, on one hand, and justice, on the other. I begin with the 1996 decision by the Constitutional Court of South Africa upholding the amnesty provisions of the country's 1995 Act to promote national reconciliation. I use the decision to illustrate the not uncommon understanding at the time that criminal prosecutions were in conflict with goals of truth and peace, as well as forgiveness. I then turn to the jurisprudence of the IACtHR, which has ruled against the state in every case in which amnesty laws have been challenged. I demonstrate that, while the IACtHR also shares the goals of truth and to a certain extent peace (though not forgiveness), it sees criminal punishment as central – rather than opposed – to the achievement of those goals. Following my analysis of these contrasting approaches, I discuss how the IACtHR jurisprudence has migrated to other human rights regimes, including the European Court of Human Rights and the African Commission on Human Rights. Finally, I discuss that, despite a growing consensus among human rights advocates and judges against amnesties, they nevertheless persist.

1. Truth, Peace, and Forgiveness versus Justice: South Africa and Beyond

In 1995, in accordance with its 1993 interim Constitution, South Africa passed its Promotion of National Unity and Reconciliation Act, which established the Truth and Reconciliation Commission (TRC).[40] Among its purposes, the Commission was meant to facilitate "the granting of amnesty to persons who make full disclosure of all the relevant facts relating to acts associated with a political objective."[41] The Act extinguished criminal and civil liability for individuals who were granted amnesty and shielded the state and others from civil and vicarious liability.[42] In *Azanian Peoples Organization (AZAPO)* v. *President of South Africa*, an organization representing the Black Consciousness Movement and the families of several prominent anti-apartheid victims challenged the constitutionality of the Act.[43] They argued that the amnesty was inconsistent with Section 22 of the interim Constitution, which provided that "[e]very person shall have the right to have justiciable disputes settled by a court of law or, where appropriate, another independent or impartial forum."[44]

In its 1996 decision in *AZAPO*, the Constitutional Court upheld the legislation. In doing so, it deployed rationales based on truth, peace, and forgiveness. D.M. Davis and Mahmood Mamdani in their chapters in this volume demonstrate many political compromises behind the South African transition. Davis identifies them in the *AZAPO* decision while Mamdani considers those in the peace negotiations preceding the establishment of the TRC. Without disagreeing with their analyses, I here take the Court at its word, as I attempt to glean the understandings of peace, truth, and forgiveness it conveys.

With regard to truth, the Court explained:

> That truth, which the victims of repression seek so desperately to know is, in the circumstances, much more likely to be forthcoming if those responsible for such monstrous misdeeds are encouraged to disclose the whole truth with the incentive that they will not receive the punishment which they undoubtedly deserve if they do.[45]

The Court did not deny, then, that perpetrators deserved punishment, but it saw punishment and truth as incompatible and elevated the latter in the interest of all victims, including the applicants in the case who sought the opposite result. The Court continued: "Without that incentive there is nothing to encourage such persons to make the disclosures and to reveal the truth which persons in the positions of the applicants so desperately desire."[46]

Similarly, the *AZAPO* decision emphasized that peace and prosecution were in conflict. It saw the amnesty provision as central to the Constitution's "historic bridge between the past of a deeply divided society characterised by strife, conflict, untold suffering and injustice, and a future founded on the recognition of human rights, democracy and peaceful co-existence and development opportunities for all South Africans, irrespective of colour, race, class, belief or sex."[47] Indeed, the Court explained, "but for a mechanism providing for amnesty, the 'historic bridge' itself might never have been erected." The Court continued:

> If the Constitution kept alive the prospect of continuous retaliation and revenge, the agreement of those threatened by its implementation might never have been forthcoming, and if it had, the bridge itself would have remained wobbly and insecure, threatened by fear from some and anger from others. It was for this reason that those who negotiated the Constitution made a deliberate choice, preferring understanding over vengeance, reparation over retaliation, *ubuntu* over victimisation.[48]

The amnesty process was thus key to both building and maintaining a peaceful transition.

In addition to facilitating truth and peace, the Court considered that amnesty led to forgiveness.[49] Forgiveness had been central to the transitional aims of the National Unity and Reconciliation Act.[50] As Archbishop Desmond Tutu explained its function in the foreword to the final report of the Truth and Reconciliation Commission when it was issued in 1998: "Having looked the beast of the past in the eye, having asked and received forgiveness and having made amends, let us shut the door on the past – not in order to forget it but in order not to allow it to imprison us."[51] In its own discussion of forgiveness, the Court saw it as important to victims, perpetrators, and the nation as a whole:

> [W]hat might unfold are objectives fundamental to the ethos of a new constitutional order. The families of those unlawfully tortured, maimed or traumatised become more empowered to discover the truth, the perpetrators become exposed to opportunities to obtain relief from the burden of a guilt or an anxiety they might be living with for many long years, the country begins the long and necessary process of healing the wounds of the past,

transforming anger and grief into a mature understanding and creating the emotional and structural climate essential for the "reconciliation and reconstruction" which informs the very difficult and sometimes painful objectives of the amnesty articulated in the epilogue.[52]

Thus, for both the Constitutional Court and the legislation it upheld, amnesty served important instrumental and moral functions for victims as well as perpetrators.

This understanding of a dichotomous relationship between justice (meaning criminal justice), on one hand, and truth, peace, and forgiveness, on the other, could be found in most debates about and reflections on the issue of amnesty at the time. Both those who supported and those who opposed amnesties generally accepted that they had to choose between these conflicting aims.[53] Even those who were ambivalent about whether amnesty should be granted in particular circumstances generally conceded that one or all of the truth, peace, and forgiveness trilogy might have to be sacrificed for justice – or vice versa.[54]

Over time, however, most human rights advocates, institutions, and courts began to reject the dichotomies, seeing prosecutions as necessary to truth, and often to peace. (As I discuss below, forgiveness largely dropped out of the picture.) Consequently, the truth versus justice and peace versus justice debates waned. This shift in approach can be found in IACtHR decisions striking down amnesty laws as well as in the United Nations human rights documents and policies eschewing amnesty laws on which the Court often relies. Although others have recited the IACtHR jurisprudence on the legality of amnesties in judicial decisions and legal scholarship, I focus on them here with an eye toward their attempted mediation of the dichotomies that were relied upon in *AZAPO*.

2. Justice as Facilitating Truth and Perhaps Peace and Forgiveness: The Jurisprudence of the Inter-American Court of Human Rights

In a series of cases between 2001 and 2012, the IACtHR found amnesty laws in Peru, Chile, Brazil, Uruguay, and El Salvador to be incompatible with the American Convention on Human Rights. In the first few cases, the Court relied partly on the language of the Vienna Declaration and Program of Action referenced earlier.[55] As time went on, though, it also began to resurrect *Velásquez-Rodríguez* to support its position, even though it is unlikely that anyone was thinking about amnesty when *Velásquez-Rodríguez* was decided.[56] While from today's vantage point the Court's reasoning and conclusions might appear natural, the decisions were not uniformly anticipated, partly as a result of many of the debates mentioned above.

Indeed in the early-1990s, the Inter-American Commission, which refers cases to the IACtHR, issued resolutions stating that amnesty laws in Argentina, El Salvador, and Uruguay violated the American Convention. Despite the Commission's negative treatment of these laws, when the South African Constitutional Court decided *AZAPO* in 1996, it referred favorably to the amnesty and truth-seeking practices in Argentina and El Salvador as well as in Chile.[57] That same year, the Inter-American Commission began to oppose amnesty more explicitly, stating in two resolutions regarding Chile that amnesties that foreclose prosecution and punishment for "serious" human rights violations violate the American Convention.[58] Yet the Commission did not refer any of the cases on the legality of amnesty to the Court in the 1990s, likely because it was well aware that its conclusions were contested.

By 2000, however, the landscape had changed. In that year, the Commission brought a case against Peru to what it hoped would be a receptive Court and argued that the country's amnesty law violated the American Convention. The Commission was successful, and the Court's 2001 decision in that case, *Barrios Altos* v. *Peru*, is considered momentous for its finding that self-amnesty laws are "manifestly incompatible with the aims and spirit of the [American] Convention [of Human Rights]."[59] The Court followed earlier, arguably creative, interpretations of the Convention by the Commission to find specific violations of Article 8, setting forth the right to a fair trial for criminal defendants, and Article 25, recognizing the right to judicial protection, or to recourse "to a competent court or tribunal for protection against acts that violate [an individual's] fundamental rights."[60] By the time the Court's decision was handed down, impunity had become a clear target of the human rights movement, and it thus is fitting that the Court articulated its opposition to self-amnesty laws on the ground that they "lead to the defenselessness of victims and perpetuate impunity."[61] Each subsequent challenge to an amnesty law afforded the Court the opportunity to expand that decision's reach.

In 2006, in *Almonacid-Arellano* v. *Chile*, the IACtHR struck down Chile's amnesty law, which was not technically a self-amnesty law because it applied in principle to political opponents as well. The Court found, however, that the amnesty functioned as self-amnesty "since it was issued by the military regime to avoid judicial prosecution of its own crimes" and therefore violated the Convention.[62] At the same time, the Court suggested that its holding might not be limited to self-amnesties.

In 2010, in *Gomes Lund* v. *Brazil*, the Court considered the Brazilian amnesty law, which was not a self-amnesty law both because it had been legislatively adopted and because it applied to members of the guerrilla groups as well as state actors.[63] The Court nevertheless found the law in violation of the Convention, expanding its previous holdings: "In regard to [arguments] by the parties regarding whether the case deals with an amnesty, self-amnesty, or 'political agreement,' the Court notes ... that the non-compatibility with the Convention includes amnesties of serious human rights violations and is not limited to those which are denominated, 'self-amnesties.'"[64]

Having made both the source of amnesty laws and the question of whom they apply to irrelevant, the Court seemingly seamlessly invalidated the Uruguayan amnesty law in 2011, in *Gelman* v. *Uruguay*. There the Court cited its own precedent and international law more generally in support of its broad holding that "amnesty laws are, in cases of serious violations of human rights, expressly incompatible with the letter and spirit of the [American Convention on Human Rights]."[65] In fact, Uruguay had argued that its case required unique treatment because, unlike any other country in the world, Uruguay had held two popular referenda – in 1989 and in 2009 – in which voters rejected the opportunity to repeal the law.[66] The Court reinforced its view that the source of the law was irrelevant, stating: "[T]he protection of human rights constitutes a[n] impassable limit to the rule of the majority, that is, to the forum of the 'possible to be decided' by the majorities in the democratic instance ..."[67]

In 2012, the IACtHR handed down its most recent decision on amnesties. In its decision in *Massacres of El Mozote & Nearby Places* v. *El Salvador*, the Court entered new doctrinal terrain.[68] The challenged amnesty was passed in the early-1990s, not necessarily as a part of, but definitely in the context of, the peace agreement that ended the internal armed conflict in the country.[69] While the Court could simply have decided the case based on its previous reasoning invalidating amnesties as a matter of human rights law, doing so might have been read to conflict with international humanitarian law which, as I noted above, some have argued might permit amnesties. It therefore used the opportunity to interpret the 1977 Additional Protocol II to the 1949 Geneva Convention, applicable to non-international armed conflict. According to a concurring opinion in the case, the Court incorporated "international humanitarian law elements to produce an interpretation that harmonized with the obligations established in the American Convention."[70]

Article 6(5) of Protocol II states that "[a]t the end of hostilities, the authorities in power shall endeavour to grant the broadest possible amnesty to persons who have participated in the armed conflict."[71] It is the main legal provision on which those who defend the legality or uncertain legal status of amnesties rely.[72] Indeed, the South African Constitutional Court had interpreted the provision to favor amnesty in the *AZAPO* decision.[73]

The IACtHR's unanimous opinion in *El Mozote* interpreted Article 6(5) to exclude amnesties that preclude the investigation and prosecution of war crimes, such as the December 1981 military massacres in El Mozote and nearby communities at issue in the case.[74] Although there have been ongoing debates over the meaning of that provision,[75] the judgment made no reference to them. Moreover, the sole support it offered for its interpretation is the study of the International Committee for the Red Cross (ICRC) on customary international humanitarian law, with which some scholars disagree.[76] The Court thus created human rights case law on the meaning of Protocol II, finding El Salvador's amnesty law incompatible with it, at least to the extent that the amnesty law covers individuals who have committed war crimes or crimes against humanity. It then found the state responsible for violations of the American Convention and other American treaties for its failure to provide an "effective remedy to guarantee the rights of access to justice and to know the truth by the investigation and eventual punishment of those responsible."[77]

As the Court has deepened and broadened its jurisprudence on amnesty laws through this line of cases, it has attempted – with the possible exception of a concurring opinion in *El Mozote*, which I discuss in some detail below – to mediate the tension that the South African Constitutional Court and early human rights and transitional justice advocates saw between truth and justice and peace and justice. It has done so in large part by finding that criminal investigation and punishment are required for truth and, if to a lesser extent, peace.

A. TRUTH The "right to truth" has done much of the work in attempting to ameliorate the tension between truth and justice. Each of the amnesty cases has afforded the Court an opportunity to state its view of the right to truth, as each raised at some level the question of the relationship between access to truth and the prohibition on amnesty. Even as the Court has felt its way on the questions about the source of the right to truth (whether it is an "independent right," as was urged by representatives in the *El Mozote* case, or "subsumed" in certain articles of the Convention, as was first stated in *Barrios Altos* and expanded by later case law), it has continually asserted that truth and criminal justice, far from being in opposition, are in line with each other. As such, unlike the Constitutional Court of South Africa, it has avoided having to choose between the two.

Three understandings of the relationship between criminal trials and truth emerge in the IACtHR's jurisprudence. First, the Court suggests that truth is one of the purposes of criminal investigations and prosecutions. As the judgment in *Barrios Altos* puts it:

[T]he right to the truth is subsumed in the right of the victim or his next of kin to obtain clarification of the events that violated human rights and the corresponding responsibilities from the competent organs of the State, through the investigation and prosecution that are established in Articles 8 and 25 of the Convention.[78]

Similar language appears in *Almonacid-Arellano* as well.[79]

Second, the Court, especially in more recent cases, makes clear that it considers amnesty provisions to be in violation of the right to truth. It references and follows United Nations documents to identify a right to truth and, once that right is established, to consider the implications for amnesty of such a right. Accordingly, both the *Gomes Lund* and *Gelman* decisions state that "amnesties and other analogous measures contribute to impunity and constitute an obstacle to the right to the truth in that they block an investigation of the facts on the merits."[80] Moreover, citing the Office of the United Nations High Commissioner for Human Rights, they conclude, based largely on the right to truth, that amnesties are incompatible with states' obligations under "various sources of international law."[81]

Finally, the Court rejects the possibility that truth commissions without criminal prosecutions might fulfill the right to truth. While not disparaging the existence or creation of truth commissions, the Court's decisions make clear that such commissions "do not substitute the obligation of the State to establish the truth and ensure the legal determination of individual responsibility by means of criminal legal procedures."[82] Rather, the state has the obligation to open and expedite criminal investigations to determine the corresponding responsibilities.

Thus, as the right to truth has developed jurisprudentially – largely at the urging of human rights advocates – criminal prosecutions have come to be seen as essential to that right. Unlike in *AZAPO*, truth and criminal justice now fit hand-in-glove.

B. PEACE In the early amnesty cases, the Court mostly avoided addressing the relationship between peace and justice. To the extent that it did consider the issue, it seemed to accept, much like the Constitutional Court of South Africa in *AZAPO*, that the two might conflict. Yet it reached the opposite result, choosing the prohibition on amnesty over peace.[83] It nevertheless insisted (in line with "a growing sector of doctrine and also the Inter-American Court") that such "forgive and forget provisions 'cannot be permitted to cover up the most severe human rights violations, violations that constitute an utter disregard for the dignity of the human being and are repugnant to the conscience of humanity.' "[84] The Court's positive reference in *Almonacid-Arellano* to the United Nations Secretary-General's position that "all peace agreements approved by the United Nations can never promise amnesty for crimes against humanity"[85] suggested a similar view; in instances in which they are not both achievable, criminal justice is preferable to peace.

At least until *El Mozote*, more recent cases by the IACtHR have explicitly questioned the sharp distinction between peace and criminal justice. Indeed, both *Gomes Lund* and *Gelman* refer to "the false dilemma between peace and reconciliation, on the one hand, and justice on the other," and favorably reference the report on amnesties by the United Nations High Commissioner on Human Rights for its statement that:

> The amnesties that exempt from criminal sanction those responsible for atrocious crimes in the hope of securing peace have often failed to achieve their aim and have instead emboldened their beneficiaries to commit further crimes. Conversely, peace agreements have been reached without amnesty provisions in some situations where amnesty had been said to be a necessary condition of peace and where many had feared that indictments would prolong the conflict.[86]

The High Commissioner's reconciliation of criminal justice and peace avoids a difficult choice, and its sentiment is often heard among opponents of amnesty. Even were amnesty to bring peace, many claim, it would not be a "lasting peace."[87]

Such a position also made its way into the 2010 Kampala Declaration, adopted unanimously at the Review Conference of the International Criminal Court, as an agreed-upon assumption of states parties. The preamble declares that "there can be no lasting peace without justice and that peace and justice are thus complementary requirements."[88] The very next paragraph states that "justice and the fight against impunity are, and must remain, indivisible."[89]

That said, to the extent that amnesties continue to be defended, peace is generally the justification that is given. Recall that the decision in *El Mozote* was unanimous. Nevertheless, the Court's president authored a concurrence signed by a majority of the judges, which suggests that the peace argument continues to have some traction. In the opinion, Judge García-Sayán acknowledges the tension that sometimes occurs "between justice and the ending of the conflict"[90] and states that "armed conflict and negotiated solutions give rise to various issues and introduce enormous legal and ethical requirements in the search to harmonize criminal justice and negotiated peace."[91]

Although the opinion states that the aim of peace processes should be "to ensure that the combatants choose peace and submit to justice," it also recognizes that there might be a need to consider devising "alternative or suspended sentences," taking into account "the degree of responsibility for serious crimes and the extent to which responsibility is acknowledged and information is provided about what happened."[92] Truth-telling and identification of perpetrators seem essential, but criminal punishment – if not investigation – might ultimately give way to, or at least be balanced by, peace. Indeed, perhaps the greatest doctrinal innovation of Judge García-Sayán's opinion is its statement that "international human rights law should consider that peace is a right and that the State must achieve it."[93] By elevating peace from a realpolitik consideration to a right, he puts it squarely back into the realm of the Court's legal deliberation: "[T]aking into consideration that none of those rights and obligations is of an absolute nature, it is legitimate that they be weighed in such a way that the satisfaction of some does not affect the exercise of the others disproportionately."[94]

Some proponents of the legality of at least certain forms of amnesty have cited the concurrence favorably. Not surprisingly, it has been referenced in relation to the peace processes in Colombia and Northern Ireland, both countries in which some form of amnesties or reduced sentences are being debated.[95] And, as Alviar and Engle tell us in their chapter in this volume, Judge García-Sayán, just before retiring from the Court, essentially endorsed the alternative sentences proposed for certain Colombian guerrillas as a part of a long-negotiated peace process.

To the extent that the concurring opinion suggests an exception, it seems to be a rather narrow one that would in fact apply to few amnesties or forms of similar relief to date. Indeed, it makes it clear that it does not apply to any of the amnesties the Court has considered in the past. Yet by re-recognizing the tension between peace and justice and suggesting that peace might be a right to be balanced against other human rights, it at least opens the possibility for bringing some of the debate over amnesty back into human rights law and discourse.

c. forgiveness Recall that the South African Constitutional Court in *AZAPO* saw the power of forgiveness, claiming that it was good for perpetrators and victims alike, as well as for the nation. In the debates over amnesty in Latin America during the same time, forgiveness was also sometimes invoked as a justification for amnesty.[96] Yet, only one opinion by the IACtHR has addressed forgiveness in the context of amnesty: a concurring opinion by Judge Cançado Trindade, who was one of the judges on the Court most opposed to amnesty even before *Barrios Altos*. That opinion, in *Almonacid-Arellano*, stands in contrast to the perspective in *AZAPO*. As with the IACtHR's position on peace in *Gomes Lund* and *Gelman*, the opinion attempts to reconcile criminal justice and forgiveness rather than seeing them in opposition.

Judge Cançado Trindade's opinion offers a skeptical view of forgiveness as a rationale for amnesty. It refers to forgiveness (along with "achieving 'national reconciliation' through the revelation of the 'truth'") as a "pretext" for the grant of amnesty.[97] It then describes forgiveness as an individual matter, stating that it "cannot be imposed by a decree law or otherwise; instead, it can only be granted spontaneously by the victims themselves."[98] Speaking of the victims in the case, the opinion surmises that "in order to [forgive], they have sought justice."[99] While the contention that forgiveness must be an individual, not a national, matter is not new,[100] Judge Cançado Trindade has added to that concept here by suggesting that if forgiveness is to take place, criminal justice is the means by which it will generally do so.

It is not surprising that the IACtHR does not discuss forgiveness. It was not a rationale offered by the various states in the cases the Court has considered, at least according to the Court's rendition of the states' arguments. Moreover, among human rights advocates, even the more general questioning of the punitive model of justice on the ground that forgiveness might offer unique value for both victims and perpetrators (which criminal justice would impede) has largely disappeared.

3. The Influence of the Jurisprudence of the Inter-American Court of Human Rights on Other Jurisdictions

The IACtHR has clearly taken the lead on jurisprudence on amnesties. At least parts of the line of cases reviewed above have often been cited in other regional human rights courts and commissions as well as in domestic jurisdictions outside of the Americas. For example, both the African Commission on Human and Peoples' Rights (notwithstanding AZAPO) and the European Court of Human Rights (ECtHR) have used the IACtHR decisions to find amnesty laws incompatible with their respective conventions.[101]

The consideration of amnesty laws in the European human rights system has generally arisen in a different context from that found in the American system. While the Inter-American claimants in the cases I have considered are family members of victims whose cases have remained uninvestigated and unprosecuted due to amnesty laws, claimants in the European cases include criminal defendants who contend that their human rights (usually due process rights) have been violated because an amnesty granted to them has not been respected.[102] The European Convention organs have rendered six decisions that explicitly involve amnesty laws, including one decision by the Grand Chamber of the ECtHR.[103] In part because of the different way that amnesty emerges in each case, the judgments are much more disparate than those of the IACtHR, with some decisions accepting the legality of amnesty laws.[104]

The 2014 Grand Chamber judgment in *Marguš* v. *Croatia* is the most recent and authoritative of the European Court jurisprudence on the matter.[105] The applicant, former Croatian military commander Fred Marguš, challenged his 2007 conviction for war crimes committed in the early 1990s. Because initial charges brought against him had been discontinued in 1997 under the application of Croatia's General Amnesty Act, he contended his 2007 trial violated his right against double jeopardy, enshrined in Article 4 of Protocol No. 7 to the European Convention.[106] Against the urging of a number of judges who wrote concurring or partially dissenting opinions to say that the Grand Chamber's decision should have been based solely on the interpretation of Protocol No. 7 (as the lower chamber had done in ruling against Marguš), the majority of the Grand Chamber considered whether the amnesty law itself, as applied to the crimes for which Marguš was tried, violated other provisions of the European Convention, namely the right to life and the prohibition of torture found in Articles 2 and 3.[107] In doing so, it reviewed the state of international jurisprudence on amnesty laws, looking in depth at the jurisprudence of the IACtHR, including the Court's judgment in *El Mozote*.[108] It cited that jurisprudence for its "firm[] stance" against amnesties,[109] one paragraph before finding that "[a] growing tendency in international law is to see such amnesties [for grave breaches of fundamental human rights] as unacceptable because they are incompatible with the unanimously recognised obligation of States to prosecute and punish grave breaches of fundamental human rights."[110] It then concluded that, because Croatian authorities were acting in compliance with their obligations under Articles 2 and 3 of the Convention, the proscription of double jeopardy in Protocol No. 7 is not applicable.[111]

Although the Grand Chamber arguably left open the possibility that amnesties might be permissible in certain circumstances, "such as a reconciliation process and/or a form of compensation to the victims" (which it found were not present in the case in hand),[112] most of the decision belied that possibility. In fact, the Court positively referenced the IACtHR's interpretation of Article 6(5) of Additional Protocol II of the Geneva Conventions which, as noted earlier, is controversial among scholars.[113] Moreover, the Grand Chamber's decision to consider Articles 2 and 3 arguably sets up future claims by victims contending that amnesty laws violate states' duties under those provisions.

4. The Persistence of Amnesties and of Human Rights Opposition to Them

Notwithstanding increased condemnation of amnesties and the attempts by human rights advocates and courts to ameliorate the tensions between justice and truth and justice and peace, both formal and informal amnesties continue to be granted in much of the world.[114] Even the United Nations, though it had stated it would not participate in peace accords that grant amnesty, in fact did so in the well-known example of the 1999 Lomé Agreement in Sierra Leone, which it later and somewhat embarrassingly repudiated.[115]

Various explanations have been given for the persistence of amnesties, including – ironically – that they might be a response to the increasing threat and trend of prosecution.[116] Louise Mallinder notes, for example, that the number of newly enacted amnesties peaked in 2003, the year following the beginning of the ICC.[117] Their persistence also suggests that amnesty continues to be a demand of many parties to negotiated peace agreements, which might explain why the most recent decisions of the IACtHR and ECtHR (perhaps with Colombia and Northern Ireland, respectively, in mind) contain the recognition that peace processes might call into question absolutist rules on the prohibition of some forms of amnesty or at least on the requirement of criminal punishment.

Not only have amnesties continued to appear in peace agreements but even some countries in which amnesty laws were not a direct result of such agreements continue to be reluctant to repeal their laws. Indeed, both Brazil and Uruguay have in many ways acted in defiance of the IACtHR's rulings invalidating their amnesty laws.

Perhaps most famously, Brazil has explicitly refused to comply with the IACtHR's decision in *Gomes Lund*, relying instead in part on a 2010 decision of the Brazilian Federal Supreme Court that upheld the amnesty law (while the case was still pending before the IACtHR).[118] As its minister of human rights stated in 2012, Brazil considers the amnesty law to be part of the "process of national reconciliation" and it "will not get involved in the debate on the amnesty law, either domestically or at the international level."[119] In October 2014, the IACtHR again criticized Brazil. In a compliance resolution on *Gomes Lund*, it reaffirmed that Brazil's amnesty law is in violation of its international commitments, perpetuating "impunity for grave human rights violations in open disregard of the decisions of this Court and international human rights law."[120]

Notwithstanding the IACtHR's clear statement in its original decision in *Gomes Lund* that a truth commission alone would be insufficient to comply with its ruling, Brazil established such a commission in November 2011.[121] The truth commission initially generated mixed responses within the country. Both victims and military officers referred to it, respectively, as a "sham" and a "threat."[122] Human rights advocates saw it as but one step toward, rather than as a substitute for, prosecutions.[123]

In December 2014, many human rights advocates were pleasantly surprised when the truth commission released its final report.[124] Not only did the report increase the numbers of individuals identified as dead or disappeared but it also named the perpetrators of those human rights violations.[125] And, in its explicit consideration of amnesty, it endorsed the IACtHR's position on amnesty and international law, calling for the prosecution of those responsible for grave violations of human rights during the twenty-one years of dictatorship.[126]

The Brazilian government has been supportive of many parts of the report, with then-President Roussef stating upon its release that "[w]e hope this report prevents ghosts from a painful and sorrowful past from seeking refuge in the shadows of silence and omission."[127] The current minister of human rights stated that the government has begun to implement 12 of 29 of the truth commission's recommendations, but that the other 17 (presumably including the recommendations on prosecutions) would need to be dealt with through collaboration between different branches of government.[128] Several human rights organizations (from Brazil, Argentina, and the United States) have since aired the issue at a hearing before the Inter-American Commission on Human Rights, calling on Brazil to implement all of the report's recommendations. They explicitly called upon the state to determine the "legal responsibility ... of the government agents who caused the serious human rights violations that occurred in the period investigated" by the truth commission.[129]

In October 2011, after much debate and previous failed attempts, Uruguay adopted new legislation that effectively repealed its amnesty law.[130] Yet, in February 2013, the Supreme Court struck down part of the new law as unconstitutional, based on its failure to respect the statute of limitations for what it labeled common crimes of the dictatorship (versus crimes against humanity) and because of its *ex post facto* effect.[131] As in Brazil, some lower courts have found ways around the Supreme Court's ruling,[132] but the issue of amnesty continues to be both contentious and unresolved.

In addition, the newly elected president of Uruguay, Tabaré Vázquez, who had also been president between 2005 and 2010, launched a truth commission on March 1, 2015 – his first day in office – to "research and compile a comprehensive work on the crimes committed by the state during the right-wing military dictatorship (1975–1983), most notably the forced disappearances of people."[133] Nevertheless, human rights activists in the country have expressed skepticism about the commission, claiming that the result could be "a luxurious burial" of the investigations.[134]

During these periods of defiance of the IACtHR's decisions, both Brazil and Uruguay have had presidents who are ex-guerrilla members and former political prisoners.[135] Yet, neither President Rousett nor President Mujica, who preceded (and succeeded) Vázquez, promoted criminal trials for past abuses.[136] In contrast, nearly all human rights NGOs inside and outside of the countries oppose amnesties because they are seen to facilitate impunity. As one news article stated with regard to Uruguay, the Supreme Court's decision and related developments "were unsurprisingly met by a wave of international condemnations, including by Amnesty International, the UN High Commissioner for Human Rights, the Center for Justice and International Law and the Inter-American Commission on Human Rights."[137]

If human rights NGOs spend an enormous amount of time and resources in their efforts to repeal amnesty laws in countries like Brazil and Uruguay, those in countries where the laws have long been repealed continue to spend an inordinate amount of energy prosecuting human rights violators. In Argentina, for example, prosecutions first began shortly after the fall of the dictatorship in 1983.[138] The passage of the "Full Stop" law at the end of 1986 put an end to investigations and prosecutions, and the "Due Obedience" law of 1987 granted immunity to all members of the military, except those in positions of command, for crimes committed during their dictatorship.[139] Both laws were repealed in 2003, paving the way for prosecutions to begin again.[140] Over a decade later, criminal prosecutions remain an important if not exclusive focus of major human rights organizations such as Abuelas de Plaza de Mayo, Madres de Plaza de Mayo, and Asamblea Permanente por los Derechos Humanos.[141] While other human rights organizations, like Asociación Civil por la Igualdad y la Justicia and Centro de Estudios Legales y Sociales, might have a broader mandate, they do not appear to disagree on the question of amnesty or impunity.[142]

III. INTERNATIONAL CRIMINAL LAW AND THE HUMAN RIGHTS AGENDA

Even as some human rights advocates and international and regional institutions began to put pressure on states to prosecute international human rights and humanitarian law violations in domestic courts, they also recognized that states would not always be able or willing to do so. As we saw in Part I, there had long been periodic support for an international criminal court and, with the end of the Cold War, it became more of a realistic prospect.

Thus, when the United Nations Security Council was unable to agree on military intervention in the former Yugoslavia, it voted in May 1993 to use its Chapter VII powers in an unprecedented way – to establish the International Criminal Tribunal for the former Yugoslavia (ICTY).[143] Although controversy ensued over whether the Security Council had the power to establish such a tribunal,[144] many human rights advocates almost immediately claimed it as a human rights project.

In fact, the ICTY was established one month before the Vienna World Conference on Human Rights.[145] The conflict in Yugoslavia and the response of the ICTY had an obvious impact on the conference. Not only did the Vienna Declaration and Program of Action contain provisions calling for domestic prosecutions and opposing amnesty but it also promoted the development of international criminal institutions, "stress[ing] that all persons who perpetrate or authorize criminal acts associated with ethnic cleansing are individually responsible and accountable for such human rights violations, and that the international community should exert every effort to bring those legally responsible for such violations to justice."[146] Further, it "encourage[d] the International Law Commission to continue its work on an international criminal court."[147]

Notwithstanding the alignment in Vienna between human rights and international criminal institutions, Amnesty International – in line with its concerns for due process and its long-term interest in the rights of those imprisoned – expressed some initial reservations about the ICTY. It soon made clear, however, that the tribunal matched AI's "fundamental aims" to "have the full truth made known about violations of human rights and humanitarian law, and to end impunity for the perpetrators."[148] AI thereby articulated a relatively early view of the position that truth and justice are reconcilable. Still, AI saw the tribunal as a "stopgap" measure, and called for a commitment to a permanent international criminal tribunal to end impunity.[149] It supported the establishment of the International Criminal Tribunal for Rwanda (ICTR) a little over a year later on the same basis – as a step on the way to the ICC. Apparently satisfied with the procedural fairness guarantees of the institutions, it continued to encourage the development of international criminal law, including the ratification of the Rome Statute and the referral of cases to the ICC.[150]

AI was not alone among human rights NGOs in its support of an international criminal tribunal for Rwanda. In its 1994 extensive report on the Rwandan genocide, written before the Security Council passed the resolution establishing the ICTR, human rights NGO African Rights called for the need to "put the culture of impunity on trial."[151] The centrality of international criminal law to the fight against impunity was made clear by 1998, with the adoption of the Rome Statute establishing the ICC.[152] The preamble states that the ICC's goal is "to put an end to impunity for the perpetrators" who commit "the most serious crimes of concern to the international community as a whole."

Even though AI early on expressed due process concerns about international criminal tribunals and offered a justification for them based on the facilitation of truth through criminal justice mechanisms, the truth, peace, forgiveness, and justice debates did not generally make their way into the discourse around the development of international criminal institutions. In fact, international criminal tribunals were often seen as a way to avoid at least the peace concerns engendered by the prospect of domestic trials. Recall, for example, that Carlos Nino preferred the creation of an international criminal court to the implementation of a legal duty on transitional governments to prosecute their previous regimes.[153] The latter, he contended, "is too blunt an instrument to help successor governments who must struggle with the subtle complexities of re-establishing democracy."[154] He also believed that "[v]iolations of human rights belong with crimes such as terrorism, narcotics-trafficking, and destabilizing democratic governments, in a category of deeds which may, because of their magnitude, exceed the capacity of national courts to handle internally."[155]

While the ICTY and ICTR were given primary jurisdiction over the crimes they cover, the ICC was established to be "complementary to national criminal jurisdictions."[156] That is, cases involving the same conduct that has been or is being investigated or prosecuted at the domestic level are inadmissible unless the state in which the investigation took place is "unwilling or unable genuinely to carry out the investigation or prosecution."[157] Many scholars and practitioners have read complementarity as a means for the ICC to put pressure on states to prosecute human rights violations, which they generally see as a positive aspect of the Court.[158] To the extent that it does exert such pressure, however, I would contend that it faces some of the issues that have resulted from similar pressure by human rights courts. That is, it relies on the criminal apparatus of the same regime that has enabled, if not directed, the actions of the perpetrators who were themselves a part of the state. It also potentially works against the goals of recently transitioned governments who are reluctant to prosecute for fear of upsetting a fragile peace. Still, most of the attention on the ICC is not about its potential effects on domestic prosecutions but about the work it does once it exercises jurisdiction.

In considering investigations and prosecutions of the international tribunals and the ICC's exercise of jurisdiction, human rights advocates have at times been critical of the inner workings of the tribunals and courts. Yet, the primary criticism is that prosecutors or judges have not gone far enough. Advocates question, for example, decisions to omit or reject certain charges or the use of prosecutorial discretion.[159] With regard to the latter, human rights advocates and scholars alike sometimes express concern that prosecutors – who are meant to be allied with the fight against impunity – engage in selective (and what is seen as political) prosecution.[160] This issue often emerges in the context of the ICC, with human rights advocates calling for addressing selectivity by *increasing* the number and geographical sites of prosecutions – by indicting someone from outside Africa, most notably.[161]

I do not mean to suggest that no one has offered more fundamental critiques of international criminal law. To the contrary, some international relations scholars have contended that international criminal law – whether through international institutions or the assertion of universal jurisdiction – often fails to attend to realpolitik interests.[162] And both traditional and critical public international law scholars have argued that international courts or the institutions supporting them have under- or over-reached in a variety of ways.[163]

My concern is that these scholarly critiques have had little impact on the practice of human rights advocates. In a piece describing what she calls "[t]he tragedy of international criminal justice activists," Sarah Nouwen contends that for many advocates who have equated criminal prosecutions and justice, the distributional consequences that some critics have delineated are considered to be largely beside the point.[164] That is, the activists respond to the idea that their good intentions might cause harm by insisting that "justice must be done irrespective of its consequences."[165] Similarly, Samuel Moyn discusses how, in the face of criticism, supporters of the ICC generally refuse to provide explicit justifications for their institution, often assuming that doing "something" is better than doing "nothing."[166] While these representations of disregard for consequences are undoubtedly accurate for some, I believe that a more common approach is to deny such consequences altogether. The Kampala Declaration's statement that peace and justice are complementary,[167] for example, attempts to ameliorate the tension between peace and justice precisely so as not to have to articulate a choice between the two. The same could be said of much of the IACtHR's jurisprudence, particularly with regard to its reconciliation of truth and justice.

Whether through the denial of adverse consequences or of their significance to justice, the correspondence between criminal prosecution and human rights has become so ingrained that expressing opposition to any particular international prosecution is sometimes seen as anti-human rights. Early discussions over whether the United Nations Security Council should refer the case of Syria to the ICC reflected this dynamic. In January 2013, over fifty countries signed a letter penned by the Swiss government to the Security

Council that, while recognizing international criminal jurisdiction as complementary, encouraged the Security Council to address the failure of Syria to exercise its national responsibility to ensure accountability for crimes against humanity. The letter called upon "the Security Council to act by referring the situation in the Syrian Arab Republic as of March 2011 to the International Criminal Court (ICC) without exceptions and irrespective of the alleged perpetrators."[168] Sweden was the only European Union (EU) country that did not sign the letter, apparently for pragmatic reasons. As the country's foreign minister explained: "It would put Assad in a headlock and make him less flexible, because we'd be telling him 'your only option is to fight to the death.' "[169]

Reinforcing Nouwen's observation that there is no space for pro-justice advocates to attend to such potential consequences, Human Rights Watch's spokesperson in the EU responded to Sweden's failure to sign the letter by calling it "a sad day for Swedish foreign policy."[170] The lead to a story written in a Swedish newspaper about the decision began: "Sweden was the lone EU member state to opt out of [the] petition ... disappointing human rights observers who claim the move is 'un-Swedish.' "[171] The story went on to interview members of different parties, with the foreign affairs spokesperson of the Christian Democrats making clear the connection between being Swedish, pro-human rights, and pro-international prosecution: "Of course Sweden should be exerting pressure. We usually fly the flag for human rights."[172] The Swedish example demonstrates a critical change: debates over the value and consequences of, or alternatives to, prosecution no longer take place *within* the human rights movement. Instead, advocates have come to see human rights as incompatible with a reluctance to pursue an aggressive anti-impunity stance through criminal justice mechanisms.

IV. CONCERNS ABOUT THE TREND

The purpose of this chapter thus far has been to identify, describe, and understand some of the reasons for the criminal turn in human rights law and advocacy. I have aimed to demonstrate in particular how the IACtHR and the United Nations have attempted to mediate the justice versus truth and peace debates and have bolstered their anti-impunity stance in the process. I also have hoped to show more generally the ways in which the human rights movement has become aligned with the prosecutorial side of international and domestic criminal law.

Clearly the human rights movement has been engaged in other types of work over the same years that it has become invested in anti-impunity rhetoric and activity. Yet, the fight against the culture of impunity – with impunity narrowly defined as foreclosing the option of criminal punishment – has not only taken up a significant amount of the human rights movement's space; it has helped shape the direction of human rights advocacy as well as that of both international human rights and international criminal law.

While some might disagree with my assessment of the trajectory of the human rights movement, others would likely agree with the analysis but nevertheless contend that the correspondence between anti-impunity, criminal law, and human rights is a positive development. Indeed, as we have seen, many have argued that the international legal recognition of a duty to prosecute at the domestic level and the expansion of international criminal institutions have marked huge progress for human rights and humanitarian law (even as they have blurred – or perhaps attempted to harmonize – the two fields, sometimes quite intentionally as in *El Mozote*). Human rights law and humanitarian law are at last seen as enforceable.

As my description of the trend has already suggested, I have serious misgivings about the criminal turn. I am concerned not only about the significant time and resources that have gone into building criminal institutions but also about how the existence of international criminal institutions and the possibility of, even demand for, domestic prosecutions have helped shape and limit human rights aspirations. I sketch below some of my critiques around four main themes: individualization and decontextualization, conceptions of economic harm and remedy, alignment with the state, and the production of history. Some are aimed at ways in which the turn to criminal law changes the movement in negative ways, while others show how it reinforces pre-existing biases within the human rights system.

A. *Individualization and Decontextualization*

The criminal law lens often reveals a simple picture of a world infused with a few bad actors, even monsters. Hannah Arendt brought this danger to our attention long ago: we convince ourselves that if we remove the bad actors, we deal with evil.[173] That view affects the human rights movement's understanding of the world and affects its strategies and ability to attend to underlying structural causes of human rights violations. In obscuring state responsibility, it misses the ways in which bureaucracy functions – even through individual actors – to perpetuate human rights violations. It also misses the multiple ways in which even well-meaning people act both criminally and non-criminally, inside and outside of state structures, to produce and reproduce injustice.

Martti Koskenniemi argues that international criminal law's individualization, and the depoliticization that comes with it, is deliberate. Referencing the chief prosecutor's explicit statement that only the individual, not the Serb nation, was on trial in the case against Slobodan Milošević at the ICTY, he contends that "[t]he effort to end the 'culture of impunity' emerges from an interpretation of the past – the Cold War in particular – as an unacceptably political approach to international crises."[174] This refusal to take into account context, however, distorts the very search for "truth" on which human rights advocates base their defense of the trials. As Koskenniemi puts it, "the meaning of historical events often … can be grasped only by attention to structural causes, such as economic or functional necessities, or a broad institutional logic through which the actions by individuals create social effects."[175]

Individualization not only narrows historical inquiry and downplays the role of the state but it also "may even serve as an alibi for the population at large to relieve itself from responsibility."[176] Robert Meister argues that the same logic applies to the human rights movement itself which, due to its focus on evil and its sense that it has accomplished justice, fails to see the ways in which it and those with whom it aligns are often complicit in creating and continuing conditions of gross structural inequality.[177]

Both a cause and manifestation of decontextualization and depoliticization is that international human rights and humanitarian law increasingly treat state and non-state actors to a given conflict alike. The primary issue often becomes which side has committed what atrocities, without concern for the *cause* of the conflict or its ideological content. Nearly every armed conflict today involves what we might term "human rights-fare," with each side accusing the other of atrocities worthy of international attention, if not intervention. To respond, human rights advocates must often deny any political position with regard to the conflict.[178]

Of course, that human rights advocates do not claim to take a political position does not mean that they do not. When they push to indict and obtain custody of certain leaders or, as in Kenya, even of candidates for office,[179] they play a significant role in the politics of the country. They also problematically side with governments, such as with Uganda in the case of the Kony indictment and other self-referrals by states.[180] And, as already suggested, they often refuse to consider seriously the ways in which the exertion of power by international criminal institutions might block other political solutions.

As the political context gets lost, domestic and international attention often turns to questions of how to make war more humane, rather than how to prevent it or respond to underlying inequities that might lead to it. *Jus ad bellum* has thus taken a backseat to *jus in bello*.[181] More importantly, perhaps, attention is deflected away from an analysis of the multiple ways in which the Global North is complicit in military conflict in the Global South. The United

States, for example, has been and continues to be the primary supplier of arms to numerous governments involved in ongoing conflicts.[182]

B. Conceptions of Economic Harm and Remedy

Advocates of economic and social rights have often challenged the dominance of civil and political rights within human rights law and advocacy. For years, they have pushed to make economic and social rights more justiciable at the domestic and international levels, with mixed success.[183] Many now often concentrate their efforts on holding corporations criminally or civilly liable, as the slate of cases against corporations in the United States under the Alien Tort Statute attests.[184] Even though their goal might sometimes be to weaken corporate power so as to protect a broad range of rights, they often state their claims in terms of civil and political rights so as to make them more justiciable or more publicly compelling.[185]

The turn to criminal law in this context arguably perpetuates biases against economic restructuring already inherent in the human rights framework. Regardless of the extent to which economic and social rights are justiciable, they are still pursued within a neoliberal system. Given that neoliberalism depends upon and reinforces criminal law, in part to protect private property rights, the cards are stacked against any attempt to use criminal law to challenge neoliberalism. The aim of advocates is therefore to prevent excesses, rather than to restructure. They do not, for example, focus on changing property, contract, corporate, or tax law in their efforts to reduce corporate power.

It is also difficult to pursue economic reparations in the criminal justice context. For many years, economic reparations were seen as an alternative, or at least supplement, to criminal justice. The former tended to be the domain of truth and reconciliation commissions while criminal legal institutions were exclusively punitive. As criminal institutions began to be seen as necessary to transition, those who argued for reparations often pushed for courts to be able to award them. They achieved some success with the inclusion of a provision in the Rome Statute that allows the ICC to issue reparations that include financial compensation.[186] While economic remedies are important for most victims, their award is generally dependent upon a finding of guilt and a proven "'but/for' relationship between the crime and the harm."[187] Given the selectivity of criminal prosecutions, the granting of these types of reparation is relatively arbitrary. Moreover, although the Court lists the return of "lost or stolen property" as a possible form of reparation,[188] the remedy leaves little room for the significant redistribution of property that might be needed to attend to long-standing inequalities.[189]

C. Alignment with the State

When local human rights NGOs spend time and resources promoting prosecutions, they often align themselves with the state. From feminists advocating for the enforcement of anti-trafficking legislation to indigenous groups helping to strategize and participate in the prosecution of former military leaders who targeted them for extermination, human rights advocates are often dependent upon the very police, prosecutorial, and even adjudicatory apparatuses of which they have long had reason to be suspicious.

Human rights advocates also participate in the governance of the state when their advocacy encourages states to overreach in their investigations, prosecutions, and punishments. As Frédéric Mégret and Jean-Paul S. Calderón have noted in a recent piece on the neopunitivism they see in the jurisprudence of the IACtHR, "[t]here will inevitably be cases where responsibilities cannot be identified, a case beyond reasonable doubt cannot be mounted, or suspects cannot be apprehended."[190] They express a concern I share that "[t]o suggest that these cases manifest a failure of the state to comply with its duty to offer a remedy could quickly lead to a culture of 'results' that could have catastrophic consequences for the rights soundness of the criminal justice system."[191]

An example of such a focus on results can be seen in the Mexican government's response to international pressure mounted on it to investigate and prosecute those responsible for the murders of women in Ciudad Juárez. The state falsely arrested, detained, and tortured a number of individuals, many of whom lacked the resources to challenge the accusations against them.[192] A 2005 study of femicides in Mexico by the Latin American Working Group Education Fund (LAWGEF) reported strong evidence for false imprisonment in approximately one-sixth, and the use of physical or psychological torture to coerce confessions in nearly one-half, of the murder cases in which the state had detained a suspect.[193] Given Mexico's widespread use of pre-trial detention[194] and its practice of considering a femicide case "resolved" for official reporting purposes once a suspect is in custody,[195] wrongful arrest and detention offer a particularly expedient means for officials to alleviate concerns surrounding impunity for human rights violations.

This concern about overreach is not only about penal systems that do not meet formal rule of law requirements. As discussed in Part I, many penal systems in the world have undergone a neoliberal makeover – often as a direct result of explicit exportation of United States criminal justice, aimed largely at transnational crime.[196] That criminal justice project has favored large-scale incarceration and eschewed criminal justice reform initiatives – from carceral abolition to restorative justice.[197] Thus, at the same time that "justice" came to mean "criminal justice" in human rights advocacy, "criminal justice" largely came to mean incarceration in the United States and in its exported models. The possibility for imagining alternatives has therefore arguably been eroded at two different levels.

The alignment of human rights advocates with the carceral state cannot help but affect the extent to which the human rights movement is able to mount a serious criticism of mass and brutal incarceration and the biases we see in nearly every penal system in the world. Moreover, advocates might be less likely in general to be critical of governments that seem finally to be attempting to remedy past wrongs, even if through the penal system. In line with several of the previously stated concerns, advocates might also begin to conceive of the broader issues they promote as criminal issues, as though their victories in punishing a few bad actors could address centuries of biases based on race, class, and gender, thus relieving pressure on the state to attend to structural issues of distribution.

D. The Production of History

With institutional resources focused on anti-impunity, anti-impunity often becomes the primary objective for the collection of documents, archives, and video. Increasingly, archival materials are collected with their relevance for criminal trials in mind.[198] Beginning with Hannah Arendt, a number of scholars have criticized the use of criminal trials to narrate history.[199] My concern here is slightly different, though. If the collection and preservation of the historical record is guided by its legal admissibility or relevance, much of the story might be lost.[200]

Criminalization also affects the issue of access to more general archives that already exist. Those in control of such archives might be less forthcoming in collecting incriminating materials or in granting access to those materials if they believe they might be used for criminal prosecution or even civil claims. They might thereby forego "truth" in order to avoid liability.[201]

V. CONCLUSION

In this chapter, I have both shown and questioned the human rights movement's attachment to the fight against impunity and its uses of criminal law in the process. I have taken a position against a strong anti-impunity focus, with a critical look at the implications of connecting human rights remedies to criminal law. Being against anti-impunity is not the same as being for impunity. Rather, my anti anti-impunity stance is much like the "anti anti-relativism" proposed by Clifford Geertz in his famous 1984 lecture. I quote from that lecture below, replacing "cultural relativism" with "impunity":

> A scholar can hardly be better employed than in destroying a fear. The one I want to go after is [cultural relativism impunity]. Not the thing itself, which I think merely there, like Transylvania, but the dread of it, which I think unfounded. ... To be more specific, I want not to defend [relativism impunity], which is a drained term anyway, yesterday's battle cry, but to attack [anti-relativism anti-impunity], which seems to me broadly on the rise and to represent a streamlined version of an antique mistake.[202]

My aim is to encourage human rights advocates to imagine a world in which the culture of impunity is not their principal opponent. As with relativism in 1984, few would actually argue for impunity today, such that anti-impunity often "concoct[s] the anxiety it lives from."[203] In fact, as I have suggested above, anti-impunity is more often than not today the battle cry of each side to any given conflict. As such, it provides a way for all sides to avoid overt discussion of distribution, even while deploying in their political struggles the criminal justice system, a potentially potent weapon of which the human rights movement has long been critical.

NOTES

1 Kathryn Sikkink, *The Justice Cascade. How Human Rights Prosecutions Are Changing World Politics* (New York: Norton, 2011), 5.

2 As recent debates over immigration reform in the United States demonstrate, "amnesty" has come to have negative connotations in other arenas as well. See Linda S. Bosniak, "Amnesty in Immigration: Forgetting, Forgiving, Freedom," *Critical Review of International Social & Political Philosophy* 16, no. 3 (2013): 344–365, 352–353.

3 See "The Forgotten Prisoners by Peter Benenson," *Amnesty International USA*, accessed April 28, 2015, www.amnestyusa.org/about-us/amnesty-50-years/peter-benenson-remembered/the-forgotten-prisoners-by-peter-benenson; Wendy H. Wong, *Internal Affairs: How the Structure of NGOs Transforms Human Rights* (Ithaca: Cornell University Press, 2012), 208 n.4. See generally United Nations General Assembly, *Universal Declaration of Human Rights* (G.A. Res. 217A (III), 1948).

4 Amnesty International, *Annual Report*, June 1, 1964–May 31, 1965, 7, May 31, 1965, www.amnesty.org/en/library/info/POL10/001/1965/en. After much internal debate surrounding Nelson Mandela, whom AI had earlier adopted as a "forgotten prisoner," AI decided that while it would advocate for fair and prompt trials for all political prisoners, it would only campaign for the unconditional release of those who had not advocated violence. Ibid., 3, 7. See also Nelson Mandela, *Long Walk to Freedom: The Autobiography of Nelson Mandela* (New York: Back Bay Books, 1995), 612.

5 Wong, *Internal Affairs*.

6 For example, Amnesty International's 1973 "Report on Torture," which discusses the use of torture in criminal justice systems, states: "torture, now used not only

for extracting information but as a method of political control, is a world-wide
phenomenon which is on the increase." Amnesty International, *Report on Torture*,
1, January 1, 1973.

7 For discussion of various draft statutes and codes of crime that were produced in
the post-World War II era, between the 1950s and 1970s, and the effect of the Cold
War on the establishment of international criminal jurisdiction, see M. Cherif
Bassiouni, "The Making of the International Criminal Court," *International
Criminal Law, Volume III: International Enforcement*, ed. M. Cherif Bassiouni
(New York: Martinus Nijhoff Publishers, 2008), 117–122.

8 Carlos S. Nino, "The Duty to Punish Past Abuses of Human Rights Put into
Context: The Case of Argentina," *Yale Law Journal* 100, no. 8 (1991): 2619–2640,
2638–2639.

9 Bassiouni, *International Criminal Law, Volume III*, 122–132. The focus of the
ad hoc tribunals on war crimes caused a shift in terms of the scope of the
ICC, which had been revived as a project in the late 1980s to respond to drug
trafficking. In the end, it was given no jurisdiction over drug trafficking, but
covered genocide, crimes against humanity, war crimes, and the crime of
aggression. Ibid.

10 For discussion of the neoliberal turn within the United States, see generally
Jonathan Simon, *Governing Through Crime: How the War on Crime Transformed
American Democracy and Created a Culture of Fear* (New York: Oxford University
Press, 2007). For discussion of the emergence of the penal state in Latin America,
see generally Markus-Michael Müller, "The Rise of the Penal State in Latin
America," *Contemporary Justice Review* 15, no. 1 (2012): 57–76.

11 Allegra M. McLeod, "Exporting U.S. Criminal Justice," *Yale Law & Policy Review*
29, no. 1 (2010): 83–164, 104–105.

12 Amnesty International, "Policy Statement on Impunity," *Transitional Justice: How
Emerging Democracies Reckon with Former Regimes, Volume 1*, ed. Neil J. Kritz
(Washington, DC: United States Institute of Peace Press, 1995), 219.

13 See, e.g., Amnesty International, "Chile: Members of Security Forces Charged in
Connection with 'Disappearance' of Mapuche Indians in 1974," 2, February 1, 1992,
www.amnesty.org/en/library/info/AMR22/002/1992/en; Amnesty International,
"Colombia: A Further Exchange of Views with the Colombian Government," 13–
14, December 1, 1991, www.amnesty.org/fr/library/info/AMR23/069/1991/en [here-
inafter Amnesty International, Colombia]; Amnesty International, "El Salvador:
Observations and Recommendations Regarding the Commission of Truth," 11,
May 31, 1992, www.amnesty.org/en/library/info/AMR29/006/1992/en.

14 This N-gram demonstrates a steady and significant increase in usage of the term
"culture of impunity" between 1991 and 2008. The line roughly mirrors that of references to the International Criminal Court during the same period. See generally
Jean-Baptiste Michel et al., "Quantitative Analysis of Culture Using Millions of
Digitized Books," *Science* 331, no. 6014 (2011): 176–182. It also roughly coincides
with the rise in actual international, domestic, and foreign human rights prosecutions. See Sikkink, *The Justice Cascade*, at 138 fig. 5.1.

15 Even AI, despite its strong position against impunity, stated in many of its reports
in the early 1990s that it took "no position on the granting of official amnesties
or pardons once the truth about the individual abuses has been brought to light

through investigations and those responsible have been convicted." See Amnesty International, "Colombia," at 13.

16 Elizabeth Bernstein, "Militarized Humanitarianism Meets Carceral Feminism: The Politics of Sex, Rights, and Freedom in Contemporary Antitrafficking Campaigns," *Signs: Journal of Women in Culture & Society* 36, no. 1 (2010): 45–72, 47. For a discussion of the history of the turn to criminal law in the United States feminist movement during the same period, particularly among those she identifies as dominance feminists, see Aya Gruber, "The Feminist War on Crime," *Iowa Law Review* 92, no. 3 (2007): 741–833; Aya Gruber, "A 'Neo-Feminist' Assessment of Rape and Domestic Violence Law Reform," *Journal of Gender, Race & Justice* 15, no. 3 (2012): 583–615.

17 Alexandra Huneeus, "International Criminal Law by Other Means: The Quasi-Criminal Jurisdiction of the Human Rights Courts," *American Journal of International Law* 107, no. 1 (2013): 1–44, 1–3. See also Frédéric Mégret & Jean-Paul S. Calderón, "The Move Towards a Victim-Centric Concept of the Criminal Law and the 'Criminalization' of Inter-American Human Rights Law: A Case of Human Rights Law Devouring Itself?," *35 Years of the Inter-American Court of Human Rights: Theory and Practice, Present And Future*, eds. Yves Haeck, Clara Burbano Herrera, & Oswaldo Ruiz Chiriboga (Cambridge: Intersentia, 2015), 419–442.

18 *Velásquez-Rodríguez* v. *Honduras*, para. 172 (Inter-American Court of Human Rights, 1988).

19 Ibid. at para. 174.

20 Theodor Meron, "State Responsibility for Violations of Human Rights," *American Society and International Legal Procedure* 83 (1989): 372–385, 377.

21 Dinah Shelton, "Private Violence, Public Wrongs, and the Responsibility of States," *Fordham International Law Journal* 13, no. 1 (1989): 1–34, 3.

22 Amnesty International, "'Disappearances' and Political Killings: Human Rights Crisis of the 1990s – A Manual for Action: Chapter G-5: Bringing the Perpetrators to Justice," *amnesty.org*, October 1993, accessed May 17, 2013, www.amnesty.org/download/Documents/188000/act330601993en.pdf.

23 See, e.g., Andrew Byrnes, "Women, Feminism, and International Human Rights Law – Methodological Myopia, Fundamental Flaws or Meaningful Marginalisation?" *Australian Yearbook of International Law* 12 (1988–89): 205–240, 229; Margareth Etienne, "Addressing Gender-Based Violence in an International Context," *Harvard Women's Law Journal* 18 (1995): 139–170, 157 n.97; Elizabeth K. Spahn, "Waiting for Credentials: Feminist Theories of Enforcement of International Human Rights," *American University Law Review* 44, no. 4 (1995): 1053–1083, 1064 n.34.

24 *Velásquez-Rodríguez* v. *Honduras* at para. 134.

25 Ibid. at paras. 135–138.

26 Ibid. at para. 194(5).

27 See, e.g., *Caballero-Delgado and Santana* v. *Colombia, para. 72(5)* (Inter-American Court of Human Rights, 1995); *Loayza-Tamayo* v. *Peru*, para. 192(6) (Inter-American Court of Human Rights, 1998); *Paniagua-Morales et al.* v. *Guatemala, para. 181(6)* (Inter-American Court of Human Rights, 1998).

28 Huneeus, "International Criminal Law by Other Means," 2.

29 United Nations General Assembly, _Vienna Declaration and Programme of Action_, para. 60 (A/CONF.157/23, July 12, 1993), www.refworld.org/docid/3ae6b39ec.html [hereinafter Vienna Declaration].

30 See Navi Pillay, Opening Statement by Ms. Navi Pillay United Nations High Commission for Human Rights at the 22nd Session of the Human Rights Council, February 25, 2013, www.ohchr.org/en/NewsEvents/Pages/DisplayNews.aspx?NewsID=13031&LangID=e. The other two accomplishments were "its role in advancing women's rights" and "its swiftly realized recommendation to create the [High Commission]." Ibid.

31 See UN Commission on Human Rights, Sub-Commission on Prevention of Discrimination and Protection of Minorities, Question of the Impunity of Perpetrators of Human Rights Violations (Civil and Political), para. 1 (U.N. Doc. E/CN.4/Sub.2/1997/20, June 26, 1997), www.refworld.org/docid/3boof1a124.html.

32 Ibid. at para. 27. The report also sees itself as a follow-up to Vienna, stating that it "comes under the general heading of the Vienna Programme of Action." Ibid. at para. 6.

33 Ibid. at para. 32.

34 See _Barrios Altos_ v. _Peru_, para. 21 (Inter-American Court of Human Rights, 2001) (indicating that the Commission appointed Juan Méndez as one of its two delegates).

35 See Garth Meintjes & Juan E. Méndez, "Reconciling Amnesties with Universal Jurisdiction," _International Law FORUM du droit international_ 2, no 2. (2000): 76–97, 88.

36 Juan E. Méndez, "Foreword," _Amnesty in the Age of Human Rights Accountability: Comparative and International Perspectives_, eds. Francesca Lessa & Leigh A. Payne (Cambridge: Cambridge University Press, 2012), xxiii.

37 See, e.g., Mark Freeman, _Necessary Evils: Amnesties and the Search for Justice_ (Cambridge: Cambridge University Press, 2009), 32; William Schabas, _Unimaginable Atrocities: Justice, Politics, and Rights at the War Crimes Tribunals_ (New York: Oxford University Press, 2012), 177–188; Mark Freeman & Max Pensky, "The Amnesty Controversy in International Law," eds. Lessa & Payne, _Amnesty in the Age of Human Rights Accountability_, at 42, 44; Max Pensky, "Amnesty on Trial: Impunity, Accountability, and the Norms of International Law," _Ethics & Global Policy_ 1, no. 1–2 (2008): 1–40, 8–11; Michael P. Scharf, "The Amnesty Exception to the Jurisdiction of the International Criminal Court," _Cornell International Law Journal_ 32, no. 3 (1999): 507–527, 521; Transitional Justice Institute, _The Belfast Guidelines on Amnesty and Accountability_, 38 (2013), http://peacemaker.un.org/sites/peacemaker.un.org/files/BelfastGuidelines_TJI2014.pdf.

38 One such group of scholars, which includes Freeman and Schabas, wrote an amicus brief in a case before the ECtHR Grand Chamber, which I discuss later in this chapter, to respond to the initial panel's statement that international law increasingly considers amnesty for international crimes to be prohibited. The scholars "urge[d] the Grand Chamber to adopt a more legally sound and nuanced approach that recognizes the uncertain picture presented by custom as well as the weaknesses in the claim that there is any support for the prohibition of amnesty in treaty law." Brief for Third Party Interveners at 8, _Marguš_ v. _Croatia_ (European Court of Human Rights, 2014). The brief primarily focuses on international humanitarian

law and, strikingly, does not once mention the European Convention on Human Rights and Fundamental Freedoms. For elaboration on the position of this group of scholars, see Transitional Justice Institute, *The Belfast Guidelines*.

39 Vienna Declaration at para. 60.

40 South African Interim Constitution of 1993, postamble; Promotion of National Unity and Reconciliation Act of 1995, art. 2 (South Africa).

41 Promotion of National Unity and Reconciliation Act of 1995, art. 3(1)(b).

42 Ibid. at art. 20(7).

43 *Azanian Peoples Organization (AZAPO) and Others v. President of the Rep. of S. Afr.*, 4 SA 672 (South African Constitutional Court, 1996) [hereinafter AZAPO]. The plaintiffs included the family of anti-apartheid activist Steve Biko, who was tortured and died while in police custody in 1977. Biko had been one of the primary theorists of and advocates for Black Consciousness. For more information on AZAPO, see http://azapo.org.za/azapohistory/azapo-and-bcma-historical-background/. For more information on Biko, see Steve Biko, *I Write What I Like*, ed. Aelred Stubbs, 3d ed. (Chicago: University of Chicago Press, 2002). For discussion of judicial opinions by both the High Court and Constitutional Court, see Antje du Bois-Pedain, *Transitional Amnesty in South Africa* (Cambridge: Cambridge University Press, 2007), 29–37.

44 See AZAPO at paras. 7–8.

45 Ibid. at para. 17.

46 Ibid.

47 Ibid. at para. 3, n.1 (quoting South African Interim Constitution of 1993, postamble).

48 Ibid. at para. 19.

49 See ibid. at para. 17 (noting that amnesty "begins the long and necessary process of healing the wounds of the past, transforming anger and grief into a mature understanding and creating the emotional and structural climate essential for the 'reconciliation and reconstruction'").

50 See "Explanatory Memorandum to the Parliamentary Bill," Department of Justice and Constitutional Development, www.justice.gov.za/trc/legal/bill.htm ("[The National Unity and Reconciliation Act] is based on the principle that reconciliation depends on forgiveness and that forgiveness can only take place if gross violations of human rights are fully disclosed.").

51 Truth and Reconciliation Commission, *Truth and Reconciliation Commission of South Africa Report, Volume 1* (1998), 22, www.justice.gov.za/trc/report/finalreport/Volume%201.pdf.

52 See AZAPO at para. 17.

53 But see Naomi Roht-Arriaza, "State Responsibility to Investigate and Prosecute Grave Human Rights Violations in International Law," *California Law Review 78*, no. 2 (1990): 449–513, 481–482 (providing an early effort to tie prosecution to truth: "Prosecution constitutes an important avenue for recounting because it puts the state's resources at the service of truth-telling and because it identifies those responsible …").

54 See, e.g., Martha Minow, *Between Vengeance and Forgiveness: Facing History after Genocide and Mass Violence* (Boston: Beacon Press, 1998), 10; Stanley Cohen, "State Crimes of Previous Regimes: Knowledge, Accountability, and the Policing of the Past," *Law & Social Inquiry* 20, no. 1 (1995): 7–50, 43; Nino, "The Duty

to Punish Past Abuses of Human Rights Put into Context," 2620; Scharf, "The Amnesty Exception," 507; José Zalaquett, "Balancing Ethical Imperatives and Political Constraints: The Dilemma of New Democracies Confronting Past Human Rights Violations," *Hastings Law Journal* 43 (1992): 1421–1438, 1432–1433.

55 See *Barrios Altos*, para. 4 (Cançado Trindade, J., concurring). See also *Gomes Lund* v. *Brazil*, para. 153 (Inter-American Court of Human Rights, 2010) (noting that the Vienna Declaration emphasized that states "should derogate legislation that favors the impunity of those responsible for serious humans rights violations"); *Gelman* v. *Uruguay*, para. 202 (Inter-American Court of Human Rights, 2011).

56 See *Gomes Lund* at para. 137 (stating, with reference to *Velásquez-Rodríguez* that "[s]ince its first judgment, this Court has highlighted the importance of the State's obligation to investigate and punish for human rights violations"); *Massacres of El Mozote and Nearby Places* v. *El Salvador*, para. 144 (Inter-American Court of Human Rights, 2012) (citing *Velásquez-Rodríguez* when discussing a state's legal obligation to prevent and punish human rights violations).

57 See *AZAPO* at paras. 22–24.

58 Douglass Cassel, "Lessons from the Americas: Guidelines for International Response to Amnesties for Atrocities," *Law and Contemporary Problems* 59, no. 4 (1996): 196–230, 215–217 (discussing *Garay Hermosilla* v. *Chile*, paras. 77, 105–09 (Inter-American Commission on Human Rights, 1996); *Meneses Reyes* v. *Chile*, paras. 76, 103–08 (Inter-American Commission on Human Rights, 1996)).

59 *Barrios Altos* at para. 43. In 2006, the Court issued another decision finding Peru in violation of the Convention for failing to make efforts to locate the disappeared or to initiate proceedings against those thought to be responsible for a 1992 massacre. See *La Cantuta* v. *Peru* (Inter-American Court of Human Rights, 2006). In a separate concurrence, Judge Sergio García-Ramírez summarized the "Inter-American view on self-amnesty." Ibid. at paras. 1–8 (García-Ramírez, J., concurring). For further discussion of *La Cantuta*, see Fabia Fernandes Carvalho Veçoso's chapter in this volume, 118–215.

60 Organization of American States, *American Convention on Human Rights* (9 I.L.M. 673, 1970); *Barrios Altos* at para. 42. The Court also found violations of Articles 1(1) and 2 of the Convention, which include general provisions on states' obligations to respect and ensure all rights in the Convention, including through legislation. Ibid. The state of Peru did not contest the Commission's argument applying these provisions, and the Court therefore simply accepted them in this case. Its articulation can be found in earlier Commission decisions. See, e.g., *Garay Hermosilla* at para. 53; *Alicia Consuelo Herrera* v. *Argentina* (Inter-American Commission on Human Rights, 1992).

61 *Barrios Altos* at para. 43.

62 *Almonacid-Arellano* v. *Chile*, para. 120 (Inter-American Court of Human Rights, 2006).

63 *Gomes Lund* at para. 134–136. For a detailed discussion of this case, see Veçoso's chapter in this volume, 118–215.

64 Ibid. at para. 175.

65 *Gelman* at para. 226.

66 The referendum failed in 1989 by roughly 13 points and in 2009 by roughly 5 points. Ibid. at paras. 147, 149. Some argue that many voted against repeal in 2009, not

because they favored impunity but because, since 2005, President Tabaré Vásquez, a former Tupamaro and the first president elected from the left-wing Frente Amplio, had – unlike any other president – been approving the launching of investigations under a loophole in the 1986 law. For a discussion of some of the ways he did so, see Louise Mallinder, *Impunity, Accountability and Public Participation: Uruguay's Evolving Experience of Amnesty Laws* (2010), 96–100, http://works.bepress.com/louise_mallinder/1. Vásquez ended his five-year presidential term in 2010, but was elected to become president once again beginning in March 2015. For further discussion of the *Gelman* case and of the history of debates around amnesty in Uruguay, see Karen Engle, "Self-critique, (Anti)politics and Criminalization: Reflections on the History and Trajectory of the Human Rights Movement," *New Approaches to International Law: The European and American Experiences*, eds. José María Beneyto & David Kennedy (The Hague: T.M.C. Asser Press, 2012), 41–73, 61–67.

67 *Gelman* at para. 239.

68 *Massacres of El Mozote & Nearby Places* v. *El Salvador* (Inter-American Court of Human Rights, 2012).

69 See ibid. at paras. 288–89.

70 Ibid. at para. 16 (García-Sayán, J., concurring).

71 *Protocol Additional to the Geneva Conventions of 12 August 1949, and Relating to the Protection of Victims of Non-International Armed Conflicts (Protocol II)*, art. 6(5), (1125 U.N.T.S. 609, 1977).

72 See, e.g., Freeman & Pensky, "The Amnesty Controversy in International Law," at 44 ("The majority of national courts that have applied Article 6(5) have used it as a legal basis to validate or uphold amnesties covering serious crimes."); Brief for Third Party Interveners, *Marguš* v. *Croatia*, at 2–3.

73 *AZAPO* at para. 30.

74 *Massacres of El Mozote* at paras. 285–87.

75 For additional discussion around Article 6(5) and its interpretations, see Schabas, *Unimaginable Atrocities*, at 178–180 (reviewing the literature that has been written on Article 6(5)).

76 *Massacres of El Mozote* at para. 286 n.461. The Court cites – as a "Cf." – Rule 159 of the ICRC's study, which provides that "[a]t the end of hostilities, the authorities in power must endeavor to grant the broadest possible amnesty to persons who have participated in a non-international armed conflict, or those deprived of their liberty for reasons related to the armed conflict, with the exception of persons suspected of, accused of or sentenced for war crimes." The ICRC thus maintains that Article 6(5) cannot be construed to allow amnesty for individuals guilty of war crimes or crimes against humanity. For an argument that state practice and *opinio juris* do not support the ICRC's interpretation of the provision or its claim about the status of customary international law on amnesty, see Kieran McEvoy & Louise Mallinder, "Amnesties, Transitional Justice and Governing Through Mercy," *The Sage Handbook of Punishment and Society*, eds. Jonathan Simon & Richard Sparks (London: SAGE Publishers, 2013), 434, 440–441.

77 *Massacres of El Mozote* at paras. 299, 301.

78 *Barrios Altos* at para. 48.

79 *Almonacid-Arellano* at para. 148 ("[T]he right to know the truth is included in the right of victims or their next of kin to have the harmful acts and the corresponding

responsibilities elucidated by competent State bodies, through the investigation and prosecution provided for in Articles 8 and 25 of the Convention.").

80 *Gomes Lund* at para. 151 (citing Office of the UN High Commissioner for Human Rights, Rep., *Right to the Truth*, para. 20 (U.N. Doc. A/HRC/5/7, June 7, 2007)) ("Accordingly, a direct connection is made between the right to the truth and such measures as amnesties or other juridical arrangements of comparable effect, since these measures not only promote impunity: they also pose a major obstacle to efforts to uphold the right to the truth by inhibiting the conduct of full inquiries."). Identical language appears in *Gelman* at para. 199.

81 *Gomes Lund* at para. 151 (citing Office of the UN High Commissioner for Human Rights, *Rule-of-Law Tools for Post-Conflict States: Amnesties*, V (U.N. Doc. HR/PUB/09/1, 2009)). Identical language appears in *Gelman* at para. 199.

82 *Gomes Lund* at para. 297; see *La Cantuta* at para. 224; *Massacres of El Mozote* at para. 298, 316.

83 See, e.g., *Barrios Altos* at para. 11 (García-Ramírez, J., concurring).

84 Ibid. at para. 11 (García-Ramírez, J., concurring) (quoting *Castillo-Páez* v. *Peru*, para. 7 (Inter-American Court of Human Rights, 1998) (García-Ramírez, J., concurring)).

85 *Almonacid-Arellano* at para. 107 (citing UN Secretary-General, *The Rule of Law and Transitional Justice in Conflict and Post-Conflict Societies*, para. 10 (U.N. Doc. S/2004/616, Aug. 23, 2004)). The Court quotes identical language in *Gomes Lund* at para. 150; *Gelman* at para. 198.

86 *Gomes Lund* at para. 151; *Gelman* at para. 199 (quoting Office of the UN High Commissioner for Human Rights, *Right to Truth*).

87 For further discussion of the use of such language in the Colombian peace process, see Alviar and Engle's chapter in this volume, 216–254.

88 *Kampala Declaration*, preamble (RC/Decl.1, 2010), www.icc-cpi.int/iccdocs/asp_docs/Resolutions/RC-Decl.1-ENG.pdf.

89 Ibid. For a detailed discussion and critique of the position that amnesty is not permitted under the Rome Statute of the ICC or international law more broadly, see Schabas, *Unimaginable Atrocities* 37, 177–198.

90 *Massacres of El Mozote* at para. 22 (García-Sayán, J., concurring).

91 Ibid. at para. 26.

92 Ibid. at para. 30. See also ibid. at para. 31 (noting that "[r]eduction of sentences, alternative punishments, direct reparation from the perpetrator to the victim, and public acknowledgment of responsibility are other ways that can be considered").

93 Ibid. at para. 37.

94 Ibid. at para. 38.

95 With regard to Colombia, see, e.g., International Crisis Group, *Transitional Justice and Colombia's Peace Talks* (2013), 8, 18–22, www.crisisgroup.org/en/regions/latin-america-caribbean/andes/colombia/049-transitional-justice-and-colombia-s-peace-talks.aspx. The Belfast Guidelines similarly reference the decision. See Transitional Justice Institute, *The Belfast Guidelines*, at 30. According to the web page on which they are published, the Belfast Guidelines resulted in part from the debate about "promoting reconciliation and facilitating truth recovery" through amnesty in Northern Ireland, among other countries. Louise Mallinder & Tom Hadden, "The Belfast Guidelines on Amnesty and Accountability,"

www.transitionaljustice.ulster.ac.uk/TransitionalJusticeInstitute.htmAmnesty-
GuidelinesProject.htm.

96 See, e.g., José Zalaquett, "Balancing Ethical Imperatives and Political Constraints" (discussing Zalaquett's position at the time).

97 *Almonacid-Arellano* at para. 4 (Cançado Trinidade, J., concurring).

98 Ibid.

99 Ibid.

100 See, e.g., Coalition of NGOs, "About the Coalition of NGOs Concerned with Impunity for Violators of Human Rights," *Social Justice* 16, no. 1(1989): 135–142, 140 ("In response [to the argument about reconciliation], we quote a saying from Latin America: only the victims can forgive.").

101 See, e.g., *Zimbabwe Human Rights NGO Forum* v. *Zimbabwe*, paras. 204, 206, 211 (African Commission on Human and Peoples' Rights, 2006); *Ould Dah* v. *France* (European Court of Human Rights, 2009); *Marguš* v. *Croatia*, paras. 60–66, 138 (European Court of Human Rights, 2014) (Grand Chamber). For an example of a domestic court that has cited the Inter-American Court cases to find unconstitutional part of its amnesty law, see *Basnet and Pokharel* v. *Government of Nepal & Ors.*, 069-WS-0057 (Supreme Court of Nepal, 2014).

102 Of course, as in *Velásquez-Rodríguez* and many other IACtHR cases, victims and their family members do bring cases before the ECtHR alleging that the state has failed to investigate human rights violations. See, e.g., Huneeus, "International Criminal Law by Other Means," 15–27 (discussing cases of disappearance in Russia). One of the ECtHR's four cases explicitly involving amnesty laws was brought by a family member. See *Dorado* v. *Spain* (European Court of Human Rights, 2012), http://hudoc.echr.coe.int/sites/eng/pages/search.aspx?i=001-110236. The only case before the European Commission to consider the application of an amnesty law was also brought by a family member. See *Dujardin* v. *France* (European Commission on Human Rights, 1991).

103 One of the decisions was rendered by the European Commission, while the others were from the European Court. One decision is no longer valid because the Grand Chamber agreed to hear the case under Article 43 of the European Convention, and rendered a subsequent decision. See Convention for the Protection of Human Rights and Fundamental Freedoms, art. 43(2) (213 U.N.T.S. 221, 1950).

104 Cases that suggest a permissive approach to amnesty are *Dujardin* ("The State is justified in adopting, in the context of its criminal policy, any amnesty law it might consider necessary, with the proviso, however, that a balance is maintained between the legitimate interests of the State and the interests of individual members of the public ...") (regarding French amnesty law in New Caledonia, passed as part of self-determination agreement) and *Tarbuk* v. *Croatia*, para. 50 (European Court of Human Rights, 2012), http://hudoc.echr.coe.int/sites/fra/pages/search.aspx?i=001-115166 (upholding Croatia's right to impose General Amnesty Act and denying claim for monetary compensation for time imprisoned prior to its passage). Decisions finding the application of amnesty laws to violate the Convention are *Ould Dah* v. *France* ("The obligation to prosecute criminals should not therefore be undermined by granting impunity to the perpetrator in the form of an amnesty law that may be considered contrary to international law.")

(upholding France's application of its universal jurisdiction statute to Mauritanian accused of torture, despite amnesty law in Mauritania covering his acts) and *Marguš v. Croatia* (European Court of Human Rights, 2012); *Marguš v. Croatia* (European Court of Human Rights, 2014) (Grand Chamber). Because the Court ruled that *Dorado* v. *Spain* was inadmissible due to failure to demonstrate new information or evidence (para. 41) or "genuine connection" (para. 36) between a Franco era death/disappearance and any ongoing unresolved investigative process, it did not address the issue whether the Spanish amnesty was in violation of the European Convention.

105 *Marguš* (Grand Chamber).
106 Ibid. at paras. 139–141.
107 *Marguš* (Grand Chamber), at paras. 124–128.
108 Ibid. at paras. 60–66.
109 Ibid. at para. 138.
110 Ibid. at para. 139.
111 See ibid. at paras. 140–141.
112 Ibid. at para. 139.
113 Ibid. at para. 131. Shortly after the decision, Fionnuala Ní Aoláin commented: "The density of soft law is hardening on the position that amnesties should not be granted to persons who have committed such grave violations of human rights and international humanitarian law." Fionnuala Ní Aoláin, "European Court of Human Rights Rules on Amnesty and Double Jeopardy," *Just Security*, June 10, 2014, http://justsecurity.org/11112/ecthr-double-jeopardy/.
114 See, e.g., Louise Mallinder, "Amnesties' Challenge to the Global Accountability Norm? Interpreting Regional and International Trends in Amnesty Enactment," *Amnesty in the Age of Human Rights Accountability*, eds. Lessa & Payne (Cambridge: Cambridge University Press, 2012), 80–81, 87–90 (noting that amnesty enactments have persisted globally since 1979, although since 1999, amnesties have been more likely than not to exclude international crimes); see also Tricia D. Olsen, Leigh A. Payne, & Andrew G. Reiter, *Transitional Justice in Balance: Comparing Processes, Weighing Efficacy* (Washington, DC: United States Institute of Peace Press, 2010), 99 (arguing that an increased focus on criminal accountability has not been accompanied by a decline in the number of amnesties).
115 For a discussion of the Lomé agreement, the United Nations' role in it and in its repudiation, and the subsequent conflicting decisions by the Sierra Leone Truth and Reconciliation Commission and Special Court for Sierra Leone as to its legality, see William A. Schabas, "Amnesty, the Sierra Leone Truth and Reconciliation Commission and the Special Court for Sierra Leone," *U.C. Davis Journal of International Law & Policy* 11 (2004): 145–169. Since 1999, in instances in which truth commissions have considered the possibility of granting or recommending amnesties for serious crimes, the United Nations has explicitly refused to cooperate. Priscilla B. Hayner, *Unspeakable Truths: Transitional Justice and the Challenge of Truth Commissions*, 2d ed. (New York: Routledge, 2011), 105 (discussing Timor-Leste and Kenya).
116 See, e.g., Kathryn Sikkink, "The Age of Accountability: The Global Rise of Individual Criminal Accountability," *Amnesty in the Age of Human Rights*

Accountability, eds. Lessa & Payne (Cambridge: Cambridge University Press, 2012), 21 (suggesting that amnesties may reflect the "growing influence of international criminal law"); Ronald C. Slye, "The Legitimacy of Amnesties Under International Law and General Principles of Anglo-American Law: Is a Legitimate Amnesty Possible?," *Virginia Journal of International Law* 43 (2002): 173–247, 175 (arguing that the "increased use of amnesties is ... less a reflection of our increased tolerance of impunity and more of an indicator of the growing force of the international human rights movement and international criminal law").

117 Mallinder, "Amnesties' Challenge to the Global Accountability Norm?," at 81.

118 For detailed discussion of this case, see Veçoso's chapter in this volume, 118–215.

119 International Justice Desk, "Brazil Nixes International Debate of its Amnesty Law," *Radio Netherlands Worldwide*, May 22, 2012 (on file with author). In Brazil, as in other countries during times in which amnesty laws existed, there have been attempts to circumvent the amnesty law by initiating prosecutions for ongoing crimes, such as forced disappearance and kidnapping, or other crimes that fall outside the temporal scope of the amnesty. In March 2012, for example, federal prosecutors in Brazil charged a former colonel, Sebastião Curio Rodrigues de Moura, with aggravated kidnapping. The court initially dismissed the charges on the grounds that he could not be tried due to the amnesty, but the court accepted the charges on appeal. See Guerrilha do Araguaia, "Justiça Federal Aceita Denúncia Contra Major Curió," *Veja*, August 30, 2012, http://veja.abril.com.br/noticia/brasil/justica-do-para-aceita-denuncia-contra-major-curio. Similar prosecutions have gone forward more recently, despite defendants' claims that the statute of limitations prevented them. See Human Rights Watch, "Brazil: Panel Details 'Dirty War' Atrocities," December 10, 2014, www.hrw.org/news/2014/12/10/brazil-panel-details-dirty-war-atrocities (discussing the cases of Col. Carlos Alberto Brilhante Ustra and of Alcides Singillo).

120 See *Gomes Lund et al. v. Brazil, Resolution Supervising Compliance with Judgment*, para. 19 (Inter-American Court of Human Rights, 2014).

121 Law No. 12.528 (Brazil 2011).

122 See John Otis, "Brazil's Truth Commission Under Fire from Military and Torture Victims," *PRI's The World*, October 30, 2012, www.pri.org/stories/2012-10-30/brazils-truth-commission-under-fire-military-and-torture-victims.

123 See Amnesty International, "Brazil: Uncovering the Past; President Dilma Names Truth Commission Members," May 11, 2012, www.amnesty.org/en/news/brazil-truth-commission-signals-long-overdue-justice-past-crimes-2012-05-11 (describing the creation of the Brazilian truth commission as a "landmark event," but adding that "the findings of this newly formed Commission will further the vital efforts of the Public Ministry in initiating criminal prosecutions against suspected past violators").

124 Relatório Final da Comissão Nacional da Verdade, December 10, 2014, www.cnv.gov.br.

125 Simon Romero, "Brazil Releases Report on Past Rights Abuses," *New York Times*, December 10, 2014, www.nytimes.com/2014/12/11/world/americas/torture-report-on-brazilian-dictatorship-is-released.html.

126 See Relatório Final da Comissão Nacional da Verdade, at 966–967. See also Romero, "Brazil Releases Report on Past Rights Abuses"; Human Rights Watch, "Brazil: Panel Details 'Dirty War' Atrocities."

127 Romero, "Brazil Releases Report on Past Rights Abuses."

128 Roldão Arruda (in interview with Ideli Salvatti), "Governo já Segue Recomendações da Comissão da Verdade, Afirma Ministra," *Estadão*, February 4, 2015, http:// politica.estadao.com.br/blogs/roldao-arruda/governo-ja-segue-recomendacoes-da-comissao-da-verdade-afirma-ministra/.

129 Conectas, "National Truth Commission in the OAS: Organizations call for the Implementation of Recommendations and Request Monitoring by IACHR," March 24, 2015, www.conectas.org/en/actions/justice/news/31810-national-truth-commission-in-the-oas.

130 Law No. 18.831 (Uruguay 2011); Press Release, "Cámara de Representantes, Diputados Aprobo Restablecimiento de la Pretension Punitiva del Estado," October 27, 2011, www.parlamento.gub.uy/palacio3/scroll2/printscrolldb.asp?Id Comunicado=4173&Cuerpo=D.

131 Pierre-Louis Le Goff & Francesca Lessa, "Uruguay's Supreme Court of Injustice," *Argentina Independent*, March 21, 2013, www.argentinaindependent.com/socialis-sues/humanrights/uruguays-supreme-court-of-injustice/.

132 For a discussion of the lower court decisions, see Francesca Lessa & Pierre-Louis Le Goff, "'Breaking the Wall of Impunity' in Uruguay," *Al Jazeera*, May 6, 2013, www.aljazeera.com/indepth/opinion/2013/05/20135592150620600.html; see also Francesca Lessa & Pierre-Louis Le Goff, "Elusive Justice in Uruguay," *Al Jazeera*, February 13, 2014, www.aljazeera.com/indepth/opinion/2014/02/elusive-justice-uruguay-201426154329630301.html.

133 "Uruguay: President-Elect Vázquez Announces Dictatorship Truth Commission," in News, February 19, 2015, http://inserbia.info/today/2015/02/uruguay-president-elect-vazquez-announces-dictatorship-truth-commission/.

134 "Huidobro Fue el Único Jerarca Silbado en Plena Ceremonia," *El País*, March 2, 2015, www.elpais.com.uy/informacion/huidobro-unico-jerarca-silbado-ceremo-nia.html ("The commission has generated skepticism in those who work on the themes of human rights because they believe the result could be a 'luxurious burial' of the investigations.") ("Esa comisión genera escepticismo en actores que han trabajado en el tema derechos humanos por considerar que el resultado puede ser 'un entierro de lujo' de las indagatorias.").

135 Specifically, Uruguay's immediate past president, José "Pepe" Mujica, is an ex-guerrilla fighter with the Tupamaros and was also incarcerated for his guerrilla efforts. See Simon Romero, "After Years in Solitary, an Austere Life as Uruguay's President," *New York Times*, January 4, 2013, www.nytimes.com/2013/01/05/world/americas/after-years-in-solitary-an-austere-life-as-uruguays-president.html. Former Brazilian President Dilma Rouseff was a guerrilla fighter who was tortured throughout her imprisonment. See Simon Romero, "Leader's Torture in the '70s Stirs Ghosts in Brazil," *New York Times*, August 4, 2012, www.nytimes.com/2012/08/05/world/americas/president-rousseffs-decades-old-torture-detailed.html.

136 Mujica first ran for president at the same time as the 2009 referendum on repeal of the amnesty law. He is said to have reluctantly supported the referendum, but only at the end of his campaign. Although he eventually accepted the IACtHR's

ruling through an executive decree and through support of the amnesty law's legislative repeal, he did so only after having thwarted initial attempts by the legislature to repeal the law several months earlier. Jo-Marie Burt et al., "Civil Society and the Resurgent Struggle Against Impunity in Uruguay (1986–2012)," *International Journal of Transitional Justice* 7, no. 2 (2013): 306–327, 318–322. He also encouraged Uruguayans not to focus on the brutality of the past.

137 Le Goff & Lessa, "'Breaking the Wall of Impunity' in Uruguay"; Center for Justice & International Law, "CEJIL Denuncia Sentencia de la Suprema Corte de Justicia," February 25, 2013, www.cejil.org/comunicados/cejil-denuncia-sentencia-de-la-suprema-corte-de-justicia; Organización de los Estados Americanos, "Anexo al Comunicado de Prensa Emitido al Culminar el 147 Período de Sesiones," April 5, 2013, www.oas.org/es/cidh/prensa/comunicados/2013/023A.asp.

138 Emilio Fermín Mignone et al., "Dictatorship on Trial: Prosecution of Human Rights Violations in Argentina," *Yale Journal of International Law* 10, no. 1 (1984): 118–150, 118.

139 Law No. 23492, Ley de Punto Final (Argentina 1986); Law No. 23.521, Ley de Obediencia Debida (Argentina 1987).

140 For discussion of the "Full Stop" law, its complement, the "Due Obedience" law, their 2003 repeal, and subsequent developments, see Human Rights Watch, "World Report 2012: Argentina," accessed April 28, 2015, www.hrw.org/world-report-2012/argentina; see also Christine A.E. Bakker, "A Full Stop to Amnesty in Argentina: The Simón Case," *Journal of International Criminal Justice* 3, no. 5 (2005): 1106–1120 (describing the judicial and legislative downfall of the "Full Stop" law and the "Due Obedience" law).

141 See, e.g., Asamblea Permanente por los Derechos Humanos, "Protección otorgada a Hooft, el Jurado de Enjuiciamiento de Magistrados lo absolvió," April 29, 2014, www.apdh-argentina.org.ar/proteccion-otorgada-a-Hooft-sobre-jurado-de-enjuiciamiento.

142 That said, there are some scholars who are critical of the Argentine Supreme Court, the IACtHR, and the Argentine human rights movement for their "neopunitivism." They argue that the prosecutions violate prohibitions against double jeopardy, as well as other due process rights. See, e.g., Daniel R. Pastor, "La Deriva Neopunitivista de Organismos y Activistas Como Causa del Desprestigio Actual de Los Derechos Humanos," *Jura Gentium*, 2006, www.juragentium.org/topics/latina/es/pastor.htm; Nicolás Guzmán, "El Neopunitivismo en la Jurisprudencia de la Corte Suprema de Justicia de la Nación y de la Corte Interamericana de Derechos Humanos: Un Pronóstico Incierto para el 'Ne Bis In Idem' y la Cosa Juzgada," *Jurisprudencia Penal de la Corte Suprema de Justicia de la Nación*, ed. Leonardo G. Pitlevnik (Buenos Aires: Hammurabi, 2008), 257.

143 See United Nations Security Council, *Resolution* 827 (S/RES/827, 1993).

144 The ICTY rejected the challenge to its own legality in its first judgment, *Prosecutor v. Tadić*, Decision on the Defence Motion on Jurisdiction, Case No. IT-94-1 (International Criminal Tribunal for the Former Yugoslavia, 1995).

145 See United Nations Security Council, *Resolution* 827 (S/RES/827, 1993); see also Office of the High Commissioner for Human Rights, World Conference on Human Rights, June 14–25, 1993, Vienna, Austria, accessed April 8, 2015, www.ohchr.org/EN/ABOUTUS/Pages/ViennaWC.aspx.

146 Vienna Declaration at para. II-23. At another point, it expressed "dismay at massive violations of human rights especially in the form of genocide, 'ethnic cleansing' and systematic rape of women in war situations" and "reiterate[d] the call that perpetrators of such crimes be punished and such practices immediately stopped." Ibid. at para. I-28.

147 Ibid. at para. II-92.

148 Amnesty International, "Weekly Update Service," November 15, 1993, www.amnesty.org/download/Documents/188000/nws110151993en.pdf; see also Amnesty International, "Former Yugoslavia: Moving Forward to Set Up the War Crimes Tribunal for the Former Yugoslavia," 7, April 30, 1993, www.amnesty.org/en/library/info/EUR48/003/1993/en ("The war crimes Tribunal could be one step towards breaking the cycle of impunity and gross human rights violations in the former Yugoslavia, but only if it is taken seriously by governments and the UN. There is still a real danger that this initiative will be no more than an empty political gesture. Amnesty International will continue its work to ensure that the Tribunal actually prosecutes and convicts perpetrators of gross human rights violations and rigorously complies with all internationally accepted standards for fairness and justice.").

149 Amnesty International, "Moving Forward to Set Up the War Crimes Tribunal for the Former Yugoslavia," 7.

150 See, e.g., Amnesty International, "The International Criminal Court Fact Sheet 2: The Case for Ratification," July 31, 2000, www.amnesty.org/en/documents/IOR40/003/2000/en/.

151 African Rights, *Rwanda: Death, Despair and Defiance* (London: African Rights, 1994), 724.

152 Rome Statute of the International Criminal Court.

153 Nino, "The Duty to Punish Past Abuses of Human Rights Put into Context", 2638–2639.

154 Ibid., 2638.

155 Ibid., 2638.

156 Rome Statute of the International Criminal Court, art. 1

157 Ibid. at art. 17(1)(a). Article 17(1)(b) applies the same exception to cases where states have investigated but not prosecuted due to unwillingness or inability. Article 17(1)(c) excepts those cases in which the individual has been tried, but in which the proceedings were conducted for the purpose of shielding the individual from international criminal responsibility or in a way that was otherwise inconsistent with bringing the person to justice. Ibid. at arts. 17(1)(c), 20(3). For arguments that Article 17 is often misread and misunderstood in general pronouncements about the meaning of complementarity, see Sarah M.H. Nouwen, "Fine-tuning Complementarity," *Research Handbook on International Criminal Law*, ed. Bartram S. Brown (Cheltenham: Edward Elgar, 2011), 206; Darryl Robinson, "The Mysterious Mysteriousness of Complementarity," *Criminal Law Forum* 21, no. 1 (2010): 67–102.

158 See, e.g., Jann K. Kleffner, *Complementarity in the Rome Statute and National Criminal Jurisdictions* (New York: Oxford University Press, 2008); William W. Burke-White, "Proactive Complementarity: The International Criminal Court and National Courts in the Rome System of Justice," *Harvard International Law Journal* 49, no. 1 (2008): 53–108. Whether and how the ICC has in fact served as

a catalyst to increased domestic prosecution requires a complex country-specific analysis, as Sarah Nouwen has demonstrated. See Sarah Nouwen, *Complementarity in the Line of Fire. The Catalysing Effect of the International Criminal Court in Uganda and Sudan* (Cambridge: Cambridge University Press, 2013).

159 Human rights advocates expressed concern, for example, over the narrow scope of charges brought at the ICC against Thomas Lubanga Dyilo, who was eventually convicted of the conscription of child soldiers. See "Joint Letter from Human Rights Watch et al. to Luis Moreno Ocampo, Chief Prosecutor, ICC," August 1, 2006, www.hrw.org/news/2006/07/31/dr-congo-icc-charges-raise-concern. After the first pre-trial hearing to confirm the charges that had been brought against Lubanga, they criticized the court for not including charges for murder, torture, and sexual violence. Ibid. Similarly, the Democratic Republic of Congo Association of Defense of Human Rights described the charges as "feeble when compared to the crimes committed." "DRC: ICC Begins Hearings in Case Against Militia Leader," *Integrated Regional Information Networks (IRIN)*, November 9, 2006, www.irin-news.org/report/61518/drc-icc-begins-hearings-in-case-against-militia-leader.

160 See, e.g., William A. Schabas, "Victor's Justice: Selecting 'Situations' at the International Criminal Court," *John Marshall Law Review* 43, no. 3 (2010): 535–552, 549–550 (arguing ICC selectivity is inherently political); Joint Letter from Human Rights Watch et al. to Luis Moreno Ocampo, Chief Prosecutor, ICC; Julie Flint & Alex de Waal, "Case Closed: A Prosecutor Without Borders," *World Affairs*, Spring 2009, www.worldaffairsjournal.org/article/case-closed-pros-ecutor-without-borders (noting concern among Africans that the ICC "may be turning criminal prosecution into a selective political instrument"). For discussion of the Rome Conference debate on prosecutorial discretion, see Alexander K.A. Greenawalt, "Justice Without Politics? Prosecutorial Discretion and the International Criminal Court," *New York University Journal of International Law & Politics* 39, no. 3 (2007): 583–694, 590–593.

161 For an example of this position, see Human Rights Watch's report on the tenth anniversary of the Court in 2012, which is aptly titled "Unfinished Business." Human Rights Watch, *Unfinished Business: Closing Gaps in the Selection of ICC Cases* (2011), 46–47, www.hrw.org/sites/default/files/reports/icc0911webwcover.pdf.

162 See, e.g., Jack Snyder & Leslie Vinjamuri, "Trials and Errors: Principle and Pragmatism in Strategies of International Justice," *International Security* 28, no. 3 (Winter 2003/04), 5–44, 5 ("[A] strategy that many [human rights NGOs] favor for achieving this goal – the prosecution of perpetrators of atrocities according to universal standards – risks causing more atrocities than it would prevent, because it pays insufficient attention to political realities").

163 For a critical, third-world approach, see Antony Anghie & B.S. Chimni, "Third World Approaches to International Law and Individual Responsibility in Internal Conflicts," *Chinese Journal of International Law* 2, no. 1 (2003): 77–103 (criticizing the ICTY for its imposition by the Security Council, for its unwillingness to consider NATO actions in Kosovo, and for its undemocratic expansion of international criminal law doctrine). For a list of sources that "touch upon or approach international criminal law from a critical perspective," see *Bibliography, Critical Approaches to International Criminal Law Research Network*, www.caicl.net/bibli-ography/.

164 Sarah M. H. Nouwen, "Justifying Justice," *The Cambridge Companion to International Law*, eds.James Crawford & Martti Koskenniemi (Cambridge: Cambridge University Press, 2012), 327–351, 327, 337.

165 Ibid. at 338.

166 Samuel Moyn's chapter in this volume, 68–94. Frédéric Mégret made a similar argument over a decade ago at a much earlier point in the ICC's history, when he noted that "[p]roponents of a strong ICC often seem to join arguments with the moral fervour of the neophyte, at times providing no better reason as to why the ICC might come into being than the fact that it should." Frédéric Mégret, "Three Dangers for the International Criminal Court: A Critical Look at a Consensual Project," *Finnish Yearbook of International Law* 12 (2001): 195–247, 196.

167 See *Kampala Declaration*, preamble, discussed above.

168 Letter from Thomas Gürber, Deputy Permanent Representative, Permanent Mission of Switzerland to the UN, to Mohammad Massod Khan, President of UN Security Council, 2, January 14, 2013, www.news.admin.ch/NSBSubscriber/message/attachments/29293.pdf.

169 "Sweden Rules Out Taking Syria's Assad to the ICC," *The Local*, January 16, 2013, www.thelocal.se/45642/20130116.

170 Ibid.

171 Ibid.

172 Ibid.

173 See Hannah Arendt, *Eichmann in Jerusalem: A Report on the Banality of Evil* (New York: Penguin, 1963). For a similar but more contemporary argument, see Vasuki Nesiah, "The Specter of Violence that Haunts the UDHR: The Turn to Ethics and Expertise," *Maryland Journal of International Law* 24, no. 1 (2009): 135–154.

174 Martti Koskenniemi, "Between Impunity and Show Trials," *Max Planck Yearbook of UN Law* 6 (2002): 1–35, 13. He continues: "Indeed, this is precisely what the Prosecutor in the Milosevic trial, Carla del Ponte, said she was doing in The Hague in February 2002. The (Serb) nation was not on trial, only an individual was." Ibid.

175 Ibid., 13–14.

176 Ibid., 14.

177 See generally Robert Meister, *After Evil: A Politics of Human Rights* (New York: Columbia University Press, 2011).

178 This dynamic has been seen in the various disclosures and debates about atrocities committed by both sides in Syria. Even before the 2013 chemical weapons attacks, AI began to chronicle, based on interviews and video evidence, alleged war crimes committed by armed opposition groups in Syria. It then called upon those groups to stop all human rights violations, upon governments to condemn such violations and upon the United Nations Security Council to refer the situation to the ICC. See Amnesty International, "Syria: Summary Killings and Other Abuses by Armed Opposition Groups," March 14, 2013, www.amnestyusa.org/pdfs/summary_killings_by_armed_opposition_groups.pdf. Both the reporting of abuses and the call for the situation to be referred to the ICC to consider crimes on all sides allowed for, even required, claims of neutrality.

179 During the March 2013 elections, both Kenyan Presidential candidate Uhuru Kenyatta and his running mate William Ruto had been indicted by the ICC. For an analysis of the likely impact of the indictments on the election from February of that year, see Gabrielle Lynch & Miša Zgonec-Rožej, "The ICC Intervention in Kenya," February 2013, www.chathamhouse.org/sites/files/chathamhouse/public/Research/Africa/0213pp_icc_kenya.pdf. On December 5, 2014, the ICC prosecutor withdrew the charges against Kenyatta. See *Prosecutor v. Uhuru Muigai Kenyatta, Notice of Withdrawal of the Charges Against Uhuru Muigai Kenyatta*, ICC-01/09-02/11 (International Criminal Court, 2014), www.icc-cpi.int/iccdocs/doc/doc1879204.pdf.

180 In addition to advocating for the indictment of Kony, whose name gained international recognition after a video titled Kony 2012 went viral, human rights activists have been working with the Ugandan military to attempt to capture him. See Elizabeth Rubin, "How a Texas Philanthropist Helped Fund the Hunt for Joseph Kony," *The New Yorker*, October 21, 2013, www.newyorker.com/news/news-desk/how-a-texas-philanthropist-helped-fund-the-hunt-for-joseph-kony.

181 For a comparison of international legal challenges to United States atrocities committed during the Vietnam War and those committed during the war on terror, the former based on *jus ad bellum* and the latter on *jus in bello*, see Samuel Moyn, "From Antiwar Politics to Antitorture Politics," *Law and War*, eds. Austin Sarat, Lawrence Douglas & Martha Umphrey (Stanford: Stanford University Press, 2014). This perspective is in contrast to that voiced by a number of scholars shortly after the invasion of Afghanistan and Iraq, when it seemed there was a new turn to *jus ad bellum* justifications for war. See, e.g., Steven R. Ratner, "Jus ad Bellum and Jus in Bello After September 11," *American Journal of International Law* 96, no. 4 (2002): 905–921.

182 See, e.g., Richard F. Grimmett & Paul K. Kerr, "Conventional Arms Transfers to Developing Nations, 2004–2011," *Congressional Research Service*, 2012, 2–4 (noting that the developing world [defined as including countries in Asia, the Near East, Latin America, and Africa while excluding the United States, Russia, European nations, Canada, Japan, New Zealand and Australia] is the primary focus of foreign arms sales activity and that, as of 2011, the United States ranked first in arms transfer agreements with and arms deliveries to developing countries).

183 For an analysis of the effects of justiciable education and health rights in a variety of domestic courts around the world, see *Courting Social Justice: Judicial Enforcement of Social and Economic Rights in the Developing World*, eds. Varun Gauri & Daniel M. Brinks (Cambridge: Cambridge University Press, 2008).

184 Arguably, the United States Supreme Court ruling for the defendants in *Kiobel v. Royal Dutch Petroleum Co.*, 133 S.Ct. 1659 (2013) might lead to more, rather than fewer, attempts to hold corporations accountable in criminal or tort law. Global Diligence, a group of international criminal lawyers who advise corporations on human rights risk, wrote the following shortly after the decision:

> What the Kiobel ruling does not do is to de-rail the entire business and human rights movement. ... On the contrary, victim groups and NGOs are likely to re-double their efforts in seeking to hold businesses accountable. Within the US, class action trial lawyers will continue to push cases of

alleged corporate complicity in human rights violations overseas. ... Other victims will undoubtedly be dissuaded from launching an action in the US courts, but they will look to other jurisdictions for satisfaction. The courts of certain European countries – such as the UK, France and the Netherlands – may be more receptive to hearing claims of corporate complicity in extra-territorial human rights violations ... There may also be further pressure on the International Criminal Court to hold senior company executives accountable for complicity in international crimes where there is credible evidence to do so ... although extending the jurisdiction of the ICC to legal as well as natural persons does not appear likely in the immediate future.

Alex Batesmith, "The Kiobel Ruling: Big Business Wins the Battle but Not the War – and How All Companies Will Be Under Increasing Scrutiny in the Future," *Global Diligence*, April 19, 2013, www.globaldiligence.com/the-kiobel-ruling-big-business-wins-the-battle-but-not-the-war-and-how-all-companies-will-be-under-increasing-scrutiny-in-the-future.

185 Consider two cases involving Shell Oil's exploitation of oil reserves in Ogoniland, one against the corporation under the United States' Alien Tort Statute and the other against the state of Nigeria under the African Convention on Human and Peoples' Rights. Compare *Kiobel* v. *Royal Dutch Petroleum Co.*, 133 S.Ct. 1659 (2013) ("Petitioners, Nigerian nationals residing in the United States, filed suit in federal court under the Alien Tort Statute ...") with *The Social and Economic Rights Action Center & the Center for Economic and Social Rights* v. *Nigeria* (African Commission on Human & Peoples' Rights, 2001) ("The communication alleges that the military government of Nigeria ... caused environmental degra-dation and health problems resulting from the contamination of the environment among the Ogoni People."). Even though the latter case was brought intentionally to highlight the economic impact of the activities of Shell and the Nigerian-owned oil company in the region (given that economic and social rights are included in the African Commission's jurisdiction), the plaintiffs and the commission alike arguably emphasized the civil and political rights violations by the Nigerian mil-itary against those who protested Shell's activities. See *The Social and Economic Rights Action Center*, at para. 10.

186 Rome Statute of the International Criminal Court, art. 75. For further elaboration of the conditions for and types of reparations (including collective as well as indi-vidual), see Rules of Procedure and Evidence of the ICC, rule 97(1), ICC-ASP/1/3 www.icc-cpi.int/en_menus/icc/legal%20texts%20and%20tools/official%20journal/Documents/RPE.4th.ENG.08Feb1200.pdf; *Prosecutor* v. *Thomas Lubanga Dyilo*, Decision Establishing the Principles and Procedures to be Applied to Reparations, ICC-01/04-01/06 (International Criminal Court, 2012), www.icc-cpi.int/iccdocs/doc/doc1447971.pdf.

187 *Lubanga Dyilo* at para. 250.

188 Ibid., at para. 224.

189 For a discussion of the failure of reparations to address land inequality in the con-text of reparations awarded by domestic courts in Rwanda, see Zinaida Miller, "Effects of Invisibility: In Search of the 'Economic' in Transitional Justice," *International Journal of Transitional Justice* 2, no. 3 (2008): 266–291, 279–280.

190 Frédéric Mégret and Jean-Paul S. Calderón, "The Move Towards a Victim-Centric Concept," at 18.
191 Ibid.
192 See Sean Mariano García, *Scapegoats of Juárez: The Misuse of Justice in Prosecuting Women's Murders in Chihuahua, Mexico* (Washington, DC: Latin America Working Group Education Fund, 2005).
193 Ibid., 12 (citing *Informe Especial de la Comisión Nacional de los Derechos Humanos Sobre los Casos de Homicidios y Desapariciones de Mujeres en el Municipio de Juárez, Chihuahua* (1998), www.cndh.org.mx/sites/all/fuentes/documentos/informes/especiales/2003_HomicidioDesapariciones.pdf).
194 Richard M. Aborn & Ashley D. Cannon, "Prisons: In Jail, But Not Sentenced," *Americas Quarterly*, Winter 2013, www.americasquarterly.org/aborn-prisons (showing country-by-country pretrial detention rates in the Americas, and assessing their cost); Guillermo Zepeda Lecuona, *Los Mitos de la prisión preventiva en México*, 2d ed. (New York: Open Society Justice Initiative, 2010), www.opensocietyfoundations.org/reports/myths-pretrial-detention-mexico (showing that more than 40 percent of all suspects are incarcerated while awaiting trial, and contesting the reasons commonly given for such detention).
195 García, *Scapegoats of Juárez*, at 13.
196 See generally McLeod, "Exporting U.S. Criminal Justice."
197 For some of McLeod's imagined alternatives, see Allegra M. McLeod, "Confronting Criminal Law's Violence: The Possibilities of Unfinished Alternatives," *Unbound: Harvard Journal of the Legal Left* 8 (2012–2013): 109–132.
198 For an example of the ways such concerns about admissibility and relevance are addressed, see Kathleen O'Neill, Della Sentilles & Daniel M. Brinks, *New Wine in Old Wineskins? New Problems in the Use of Electronic Evidence in Human Rights Investigations and Prosecutions*, www.crl.edu/sites/default/files/attachments/pages/Rapoport-E-evidence-report.pdf.
199 See Arendt, *Eichmann in Jerusalem*. For a contemporary discussion of the crafting of historical narrative through international criminal trials, see Richard Ashby Wilson, *Writing History in International Criminal Trials* (New York: Cambridge University Press, 2011).
200 Of course it could be argued that the focus on criminal trials has led to increased funding for preserving archival materials so that, even if limited, at least records are kept. Moreover, even archives that are limited to legally relevant materials have proven useful to historians. See, e.g., Robert M.W. Kempner, "Review, The Nuremberg Trials as Sources of Recent German Political and Historical Materials," *American Political Science Review* 44, no. 2 (1950): 447–459.
201 Leora Bilsky describes, for example, how the release from legal liability provided by a class action settlement encouraged the opening of corporate archives in Germany, enabling historians to research business cooperation with the Third Reich. Leora Bilsky, "The Judge and the Historian: Transnational Holocaust Litigation as a New Model," *History & Memory* 24, no. 2(2012): 117–156, 136–138.
202 Clifford Geertz, "Distinguished Lecture: Anti Anti-Relativism," *American Anthropologist* 86, no. 2 (1984): 263–278, 263.
203 Ibid., 265.

2

Anti-Impunity as Deflection of Argument

Samuel Moyn[*]

The rise of "anti-impunity" as both a normative ideal and a mobilizational goal is surely one of the most striking developments in the broad evolution of the global human rights movement in the last couple of decades. Anti-impunity treats accountability as an overwhelmingly important feature of how conflicts are resolved, and within that preference goes further to prioritize criminal punishment of perpetrators of mass atrocity crimes. Indeed, though no one calls for "ending impunity" for all crime in domestic circumstances – in part out of prophylactic concessions to the threat of over-enforcement and in part to make room for excuse and mercy – that slogan for international affairs has become one of the unique ethical signatures of our time. The reason, an intuitive one, is that there ought to be zero tolerance for this most outrageous class of infractions. And it is also this class that states have chosen to internationalize as punishable when domestic justice fails, explaining both the importance and prestige of international criminal law.

Yet as Karen Engle shows in her chapter in this collection, there is considerable irony in this development. The human rights movement emerged in opposition to imprisonment; its early calls were for "amnesty." As a result, it is surprising that it is now so focused on throwing people in jail. "Amnesty International is dead against amnesty," one recent Ugandan observed mordantly of this irony, as outside actors to local politics brought the fight for accountability from abroad. "They work day and night to kill amnesty."[1]

* This chapter originated in a talk at Yale Law School on the occasion of Luis Moreno Ocampo's inaugural Gruber Distinguished Lecture in Global Justice in January 2013, with thanks to Owen Fiss for hosting, and incorporates some prose from that version, "Towards Instrumentalism at the International Criminal Court," *Yale Journal of International Law Online* 39 (2014): 55–65. I am grateful to Karen Engle and especially Zinaida Miller for helpful comments, and David Froomkin for critical research assistance. Most of all, I am undyingly thankful to Sarah Nouwen for helping me finalize my arguments.

Human rights had originally been a movement that deployed a supposedly pure morality as activists faced down state terror, rather than brought international governance to bear to create new forms of power in inevitably messy ways. The rise of anti-impunity was therefore a dramatic and transformative event.[2]

Even so, it has been typical to present the quest to "end impunity" as the uncontroversial fulfillment of a long-nurtured but long-postponed demand – though it turns out no one ever used the phrase "end impunity" in English until about 1986.[3] The truth, however, is that individual criminal accountability, while hardly exhausting the field of human rights, looms large in it in ways that should be more surprising than they are. In a recent book, Kathryn Sikkink shows that a norm of individual criminal accountability – having disappeared after Nuremberg and associated post-World War II processes – emerged in Latin America after dictatorship and then rose fast and traveled far after the Cold War's end.[4] Among other things, it has become central to global governance in the form of the International Criminal Court and its complementarity regime, intended to provide prosecutions for especially flagrant crimes when national jurisdictions fail.[5] But the ICC stands out as much for what it symbolizes as for what it really is: the new dream of individual criminal accountability as a central feature – perhaps the central feature – of our current vision of international or global justice.

This chapter examines the *rhetoric* of anti-impunity, particularly in the Global North, mainly among professional activists and lawyers, supported by a large segment of the public and a fair (though everyday decreasing) share of scholars. It takes up anti-impunity in its most signature domain, international criminal law in general and the ICC in particular. But it is clear that in all of these domains, the rhetoric of anti-impunity has become powerful in part through its denial that it is a controversial scheme in need of argumentative justification – in spite of the fact that it is historically surprising in its aims, even within the short time horizon of the international human rights movement. Drawing upon and synthesizing a now longstanding and rich counterpoint literature, the chapter offers an anatomy of how international criminal accountability and especially the ICC are routinely justified, or more accurately, *not* justified.[6] "Standing idly by," in the favored phrase, is not the sole option besides punishment in the face of atrocity crime, let alone other forms of injustice that haunt the world. For of course, the alternative to anti-impunity (or any other agenda) is not doing nothing; it is doing something else. International criminal law is neither the "last resort" nor the "only hope."[7] If alternatives beckon besides inaction, it is time for advocates of the anti-impunity agenda to drop its initial and current framing as needing no

defense. Sikkink refers to the rise of the norm of individual criminal accountability as a "justice cascade." But the truth is that its explosion in our world
involved the prioritization of *one definition of justice.*[8] It is now time to wonder
whether that decision occurred in competition with, and potentially at the
expense of, others.

The aim of this chapter, however, is preliminary and forensic. It is neither
to support nor to indict either the anti-impunity agenda or the International
Criminal Court, which serves as my privileged example both because it is the
most culturally visible contemporary instantiation of the quest to "end impunity" and because it provides an exemplary (if not always representative) case
to think through argumentative and rhetorical strategies that have crystallized.
The focus is on discourse because *talk matters.* Beyond generating hopeful
talk, the ICC has done so little in its first decade, for understandable reasons,
that there is little besides talk to analyze. Yet talk is powerful. I argue that it
is ironic that discourse concerning international criminal law in general and
the ICC in particular has long had its predominant real-world consequence
in forestalling inquiry into the expectable and real results of the turn to anti-
impunity. The chapter studies the effects of discourse in order to call for more
discourse about effects.

I begin, in the first section, by laying out an explicitly instrumentalist framework of analysis, one that puts a premium on legal and institutional aims and
their fulfillment. As part of this framework, the variable *internal* purposes of
criminal prosecution, whose goals, long familiar within domestic criminal law
and running from incapacitation to rehabilitation, obviously matter. But my
framework also insists on a high bar of *external* criteria of justification for
political trials – external, that is, to the usual goals of criminal processes from
incapacitation to rehabilitation – that the current form of the human rights
agenda should elicit. Sometimes the ICC is defended on Hannah Arendt's
narrow grounds that the blackest crimes, though beyond the capacity of law,
simply require retributive punishment. However, it is more often assumed or
stated with little or no argument that the anti-impunity agenda serves a much
broader range of ends, which are rarely specified and never investigated.

Appealing to Arendt's theoretical rival Judith Shklar, I ask what goals anti-
impunity is supposed to advance in theory and consider whether there is reason to believe it advances them in fact. Regardless of whether these aims are
internal or external to the criminal process, or whether the latter includes a
broader but still constrained project of short-term transition or more grandiose
expectations of social and global justice, there is a striking absence of articulacy in the current human rights movement about them. And where there is
a failure to articulate aims, not surprisingly, there will be a failure to inquire

how best to serve them – or, indeed, whether they are being served at all. Finally, in serving its enumerated aims, the general project of criminalization and the particular institution of the ICC, must verifiably avoid serving *other* purposes that are less savory, such as connivance with the hierarchical power structures of contemporary global governance. Or, to the extent they abet structural or other injustice, the benefit of doing so must clearly outweigh the harm. The insistence that "ending impunity" needs no defense blocks inquiry into the agenda's plausible goals and imaginable effects.

The chapter turns next to the regnant forms of discourse – rhetorical strategies that I call promotion, professionalism, and preservation – that tend to rule that inquiry out. After this survey, the chapter takes up the limitations of Sikkink's exceptional recent attempt to adopt instrumentalism without interfering with a promotional account of the new "justice." I conclude with a description of a newly ascendant form of justificatory discourse: victims' justice. Though never entirely absent, it has surged since Fatou Bensouda became ICC prosecutor four years ago, and began to insist that the Court's core justification – for example, against the objection that it exclusively targets weak African politicians – is that victims want its justice. But in some respects this discourse takes a serious step backwards even relative to extant deflection: it claims that *someone else* than its own agents and sponsors already provides the rationale for the Court. And yet the honorable imperative to serve victims is not straightforward and self-interpreting, but should open up a pluralistic debate about possible legal and institutional responses to horror. A victim-centric discourse, ascendant today, further and indefinitely postpones this immediate need.

It is time for doubts, not so much about the overall validity of the enterprise (yet), whether when it comes to the general trend of the "justice cascade" or the rise of the ICC in particular, but about the absence of discourse about goals and effects in mainstream circles due to the assumption that its validity goes without saying. It may seem strange to focus on strategies of argument (or their absence), as a preliminary to the necessary empiricism for which my own argument calls. But so far the most powerful effect of anti-impunity is *rhetorical* in general and *hortatory* in particular, deflecting the need for argumentative justification of the current priorities of the human rights movement. If this need is not met, the passage of time will leave anti-impunity indefensible – as it sometimes appears to be now – precisely because it has avoided justifying its priorities.

I. INSTRUMENTALISM IN CRIME AND PUNISHMENT

Many consider Hannah Arendt the leading philosopher foreseeing and explaining the importance of the belated rise of international criminal justice in our time. She acknowledged that atrocities involved a "guilt worse than crime," and inquired into the moral agency that in modernity could allow such horrendous results. Nonetheless, she fully supported Adolf Eichmann's punishment. The point of international criminal law, she wrote disarmingly at the end of *Eichmann in Jerusalem*, otherwise an often ironic book, is simple. "Hence, to the question most commonly asked about the Eichmann trial: What good does it do?, there is but one possible answer: It will do justice."[9] But justice does not come in the singular: there are always plural versions of it to consider, and choosing one may rule out aspects of another. Presumably Arendt meant retributive justice – but is that it?

As time passes, it has become clear that there is another theorist, writing at the same time as Arendt, who deserves more of our attention: Judith Shklar. She assumed that the definition of justice was not a matter of self-evidence or consensus. And so she advocated an open discussion of comparative outcomes.[10] Her insights for these purposes were twofold. First, the trials with which international criminal law are concerned are "political trials," in the sense defined by Otto Kirchheimer: proceedings in which the organizer of the event has implicit or explicit aims beyond the ordinary workings of the criminal justice system.[11] Given their intersection with global politics, Shklar assumed, war crimes trials were necessarily political trials of this kind. This did not mean that political trials are unjustifiable, she hastened to clarify, only that their justification must occur by way of their political implications, which always make them far more than a humdrum legal process. "Doing justice" in such cases is never separable from the full range of its political consequences. Second, the trials therefore have to be judged politically based on the defensibility and plausibility of the results they bring about. Shklar's approach is part of a larger family of thought known as legal instrumentalism – a view that treats law, and in this case international criminal law, as a means to an end. Some have claimed that instrumentalism is hegemonic today in legal thought; even if so, however, it is a striking latecomer to the philosophy of international criminal law.[12]

The generalized slogan "ending impunity" suggests that it is *self-evidently* and *unfailingly* a good thing to mount such political trials. Shklar doubted it. Writing in the early 1960s, Shklar applied her perspective to the post-World War II trials of Nuremberg and Tokyo. She claimed that the main problem was not following the law, which in any event ran out in the case of postwar trials where so much law was made up from scratch, but changing the world for the better. The decision to prosecute did not self-evidently do so; for example, Shklar doubted it had any valuable effect in the East Asian proceedings.[13] And among the variety of aims that prosecutors announced or that observers assigned to Nuremberg, she insisted, some were reasonable and others were extravagant or retrograde. The fact that Nuremberg was a "farce" (Shklar's provocative term) or a "liberal show trial" (in Mark Osiel's later and well-known phrase) did not mean it could not be a good thing. But if it was, the reasons had to be specified. Nuremberg assisted, she thought, in the reeducation of German officialdom, laying the basis for a decent society in the future.[14]

If one were to apply Shklar's instrumentalism to international criminal law generally, however, the first problem would be the identification of possible ends for prosecution and punishment. (Her exclusive interest in setting up a decent society after horror, while creditable on its own, did not amount to a general theory of imaginable ends.) And a place to start is provided by the traditional aims of criminal law. These certainly do include retribution: Arendt's "doing justice." But they incorporate a number of other aims: incapacitation, deterrence, pedagogy, and rehabilitation.[15]

It might seem comparatively simple to grant success with respect to retributive justice in the ICC's two convictions so far – except that so many people feel that Thomas Lubanga is not paying his debt either for all of his crimes (for example, sex crimes) or even for those for which he was found guilty (given his fourteen-year sentence).[16] But success at meting out retributive justice is success at hurdling a low bar anyway. It has often been claimed, and more often believed (or suspected), that more is at stake in the ICC's work that would allow or force us to ask about other and broader outcomes. It is also fair to grant the ICC some part of the credit for the incapacitation of criminals, with the large provisos that in many cases a trial becomes possible not because of ordinary arrest – certainly not by the ICC's non-existent constabulary – but because of the prior and independent loss of political stature by the accused. This is one reason that Omar al-Bashir of Sudan is not yet incapacitated: not so much because he has not yet stood trial in The Hague as because independent political circumstance has not yet removed him from power. It may even be the case that, in the short term and perhaps indefinitely, local political actors are strengthened against domestic incapacitation from ICC indictment: consider not just Bashir, but also Uhuru Kenyatta and William Ruto in Kenya.

But like retribution, incapacitation is only one among several possible aims of the quest to punish, and in fact a minor one given that in these cases it is politics rather than law that actually deprives the accused in international criminal processes from the capacity to commit atrocity. Yet after ten years, it is still completely mysterious whether the ICC goes further, whether with respect to internal or external criteria. Internal criteria of criminal law might include specific deterrence affecting the actors who have committed atrocities (especially when politicians are accused in the course of a war), general deterrence to reach potential actors or other sorts of crime, or expressive pedagogy that would forge public norms about the right and wrong.[17] Yet the ICC's achievements in these areas remain unclear. The same is close to true of the entirety of the turn to anti-impunity since the end of the Cold War. The work of Sikkink and others on the earliest Latin American experiences remains exceptional, and the lack of serious inquiry into the ICC's effects, exacerbated by a more general paucity of data, remains staggering given the default optimism surrounding the rise of anti-impunity.[18] As with the ICC in its fledgling career so far, it is much easier to grant the rise of anti-impunity instrumental success when it comes to retribution and incapacitation than with respect to other internal aims of the criminal law – though even these are dubious.

But much more important, I believe, it is unclear what *external* purposes international criminal law is intended to serve and how well it is doing so or could do so. Nor is there anything like sufficient discussion, a few critical scholars aside, of purposes it might serve unwittingly. Anti-impunity has been celebrated as potentially advancing a wide variety of positive outcomes. For example, ICC President Sang-Hyun Hong claimed in 2012 that the institution "is about much more than just punishing the perpetrators. The Rome Statute and the ICC bring retributive and restorative justice together with the prevention of future crimes."[19]

To the rare extent aphasia about purposes has not reigned, observers have assumed some relationship between prosecution and regime transition as the most likely instrumental value of the criminalization of atrocity crime. More specifically, the relation between prior national tribunals and the establishment of democracy has been routinely asserted in the massive literature on "transitional justice."[20] It is often claimed not simply that there is a legal "duty to prosecute," but also that it is (unfailingly?) a politically good thing to shoulder it, at least up to the point that reckoning with the past through accountability protocols threatens instability.[21] While often asserted, however, there is to my knowledge no evidence suggesting that accountability leads to the outcomes of strengthened democracy, particularly when a pluralistic set of options (most famously, truth commissions) beckons after atrocity, rather than prosecution alone. In spite of this glaring absence, the relatively confined circumstances of transition to liberal democracy are hardly the sole forum of effect routinely granted to prosecutions. Indeed, much more grandiose assumptions about their transformative results, particularly in the domain of social justice – admittedly by the mobilizational base rather than the elite leadership of the movement to end impunity – are commonly made about it.

Sometimes, most remarkably, "ending impunity" is treated as a near synonym of "global justice," another phrase on the rise across the same era.[22]

The lack of clarity about aims hardly means that the rise of anti-impunity is useless, let alone counterproductive. But it does suggest that the long potential list of internal and external aims of international criminal law requires much more discerning and disaggregated examination than it has hitherto received, and that advocates of punishment must defend their agenda with respect to the advancement of one, some, or all of those aims. There may be broad theoretical reasons that punishment is likely to advance democratic transition, to take only the most frequently cited relationship, or there may be reasons to suspect that the link holds only when narrow and specific conditions are fulfilled. A wide variety of other factors may impinge on whether the claimed results of an instrumentally chosen prosecution do in fact accrue. Finally, the rise of anti-impunity, both as a general matter and in specific cases, may intentionally or unwittingly abet *other* results. For example, many worry – and rightly so – that the ICC confirms the centrality of great power politics through its processes of UN Security Council authorization, becoming a court that ratifies a global order in which "punishment" is generally a threat for statesmen and henchmen who are powerful at home but weak in the international order.[23] The charge illustrates the value of an instrumental view of international criminal law: all of its instrumental results, and each of the ends that it enables, have to be taken into account to judge its meaning.

II. PROMOTION, PROFESSIONALISM, PRESERVATION

Despite the critical need for an assessment, there is almost no serious talk about what purposes anti-impunity is supposed to serve or whether it is successful in doing so, aside from occasional passing remarks and the research of a few empirical political scientists (to which I return below). Sooner or later, one question has pride of place: Does the anti-impunity agenda make a difference (and for better or worse)? If this question is not asked, let alone answered, the chief reason is that, compared to the instrumentalist inquiry into contexts, purposes, and outcomes, other ways of talking about international criminal law continue to predominate.

In particular, there are three other, prior, and more familiar discourses that hamper what ought to be this crucial inquiry. For the sake of alliteration, I call them the promotional, professionalizing, and preservative discourses, in contrast to the political one. The promotional discourse deploys reverential praise for the epoch-making novelty of accountability protocols (and the ICC in particular). The professionalizing discourse reflects the essential but often single-minded task of rule-interpretation and doctrine-mongering. Finally, those wielding a preservation discourse argue for the tactical sheltering of the Court from the ordinary conditions of inquiry and judgment, on the ground that it needs time and space to build strength and relevance. The priority and preeminence of these approaches limit or eliminate an instrumentalist evaluation of anti-impunity and particularly of the ICC.

Promotionalism has been extraordinarily predominant when it comes to accountability. It is characterized by a rhetorical strategy celebrating the "justice cascade" as so self-evidently good as to need no defense. "If we fail to support the ICC and its noble cause," Deputy Secretary-General of the United Nations Ashe-Rose Migiro noted recently, "we fail humanity" (as opposed to the particular agenda of one part of it).[24] The promotional idea presents the rise of accountability, not least in the high-profile ICC, as a moral achievement *in spite of* and *against* politics – or at least political interests narrower than those of humanity as a whole. Interferences with anti-impunity – as in the successful Kenyan resistance – are politics, but the Court itself has none.[25] For this reason, the details of its performance are commonly subordinated to the fact that its role has been scripted at all.

To be fair, every institution and project generates and requires a promotional account of itself. Every international criminal lawyer needs a "faith."[26] The promotional view is tempting especially in the early years of an institution. In fact promotion makes intuitive sense because there are obvious reasons to celebrate: the justice cascade has barely begun to roar, and the ICC to start its work. When asked whether the French Revolution had succeeded, Zhou en-Lai allegedly responded that after two centuries, it's still far too soon to tell.[27] That makes it rather unwise to draw any sort of balance sheet on the accountability norm, certainly as a global matter. The ICC is indeed an exceptionally surprising development, so humane in its explicit purposes as to make awestruck gratitude (or is it self-congratulation?) the natural response. No one can doubt that it is just for the ICC to hold evil men – and now an evil woman, Simone Gbagbo – to account for their atrocity crimes, which is indeed an essentially unprecedented development, even if it turns out to be only for the sake of the internal and narrow goal of retributive justice.

Whatever its truth and utility, however, promotion might now take up too much time, since ongoing institutions can't rest content with celebrating their existence alone; they need to be judged for the specifics of their work. Consider the parallel of the domestic criminal law. Suppose I worried in some hypothetical society that the criminal law seemed a scandal of selective justice and racialized opprobrium.[28] The promotional response that criminal law is self-evidently good (especially by comparison to doing nothing), though potentially true, would hardly be a compelling excuse. Similarly, Henry Hart once justified criminal law as an alternative to the generalized violence of vigilantism. It is reminiscent of Justice Robert Jackson's famous claim in his opening statement at Nuremberg that the Allies had magnanimously but also prudentially chosen to "stay the hand of vengeance" – as if the main law of relevance was criminal law, as if the sole alternative to law were violence, and as if that law itself is not violent. Yet even assuming the empirical truth of Hart's or Jackson's supposition about the inevitably worse consequences of not providing criminal accountability – which goes back to Aeschylus in our tradition – it is simply mistaken to think that the specter of the blood-dimmed tide of vendetta could ever justify the *specific form* of justice our criminal law provides. Certainly it could not do so for long. The main flaw of promotion, in other words, is that of all promotional discourses. It does not tell us what the criteria of success or what our other options are. Thus, though rhetorically understandable for leaders and members of the worldwide movement for anti-impunity, promotion is simply unpersuasive so long as we don't know what kind of justice accountability provides, how much, and with what opportunity costs.

Trailing promotion, the other main form of discourse about the ICC is professional or professionalizing; it follows from the work global courts give lawyers as vocational experience, from careers in the system to summer internships – "tribunal-hopping" as a "post-conflict justice junkie."[29] The professional sociology of law has a familiar set of discursive effects: in this case, the specific form of intellectual analysis that the ICC has crystallized around itself is a more or less familiar form of doctrinalism.[30]

As with promotionalism, the rise of professionalism is perfectly justifiable and predictable. It is justifiable because international criminal law, like any body of law, explicitly hews out a key role for legal professionalism; for lawyers, accountability affords cases to try; for judges, opinions to write; for law students, clerkships, and internships; for all of the above, the sort of meaningful life that comes from fulfilling clearly moral tasks consistent with mainstream respectability. Saving the world and serving humanity is no longer – as in the early human rights movement – a choice to be counterculturally marginal but instead is one to be respectably professional.[31] It is predictable because professionalism for the foreseeable future is the dominant option of our legal world. Precisely because the creation of work contexts for improvisational courts could have taken some other form, it is a testament to how powerful the forces have been to make its professional discourse sound like just one more domain of legal practice or of legal analysis. But the turn to professionalism, along with its equation with the priority of doctrinal analysis, also has specific consequences for how the court is typically discussed and defended.

For teachers in the legal academy, "international criminal law" provides grist for the academic mill. From the Nuremberg and successor trials to the ad hoc tribunals, there are a lot of cases to collate and lines of authority to sift. And there are problems of first impression that current events provide. Some of these, such as whether "specific direction" of assistance in atrocity is required in order to be culpable of aiding and abetting, concern above all the meaning of precedent and the evolution of judge-made law.[32] Others, especially given the novelty of the ICC and the paucity of its jurisprudence, concern treaty interpretation: how the Rome Statute bears on Saif al-Gaddhafi's disposition (whether the ICC has jurisdiction to try him over Libya's objection), for example, or how to interpret the treaty's Article 12(3), which applies only to states, in view of Palestine's invocation of it and desired access to international criminal justice. And surely lawyers, particularly given their traditional doctrinal skills, are needed to solve those problems as ones of rule and doctrine requiring expertise rather than as those of politics and morality demanding open-ended debate.

The professionalizing approach is definitely more sober than the promotional approach, in part because buttoned-up sobriety is the condition of professionalism. But the professional tack is not without its own shortcomings. It tends to bracket how improvisational – including in its rules and doctrines – the accountability jurisprudence it volunteers to formalize and rationalize has been. This is particularly the case when it comes to the ICC, which came nearly out of nowhere and, beyond the earlier Nuremberg and ad hoc tribunal precedents concerning substantive crimes, essentially started from scratch (with a carefully negotiated treaty even so). Several casebooks have been constructed already around "International Criminal Law" to induct newcomers into the field. Yet these texts seem barely to register that international criminal law revolves around anything but a settled domain or institution, but rather has been made up from scratch on short notice in a permanently political environment.[33]

Of course, generations of critical scholarship have revealed how unsettled law always is and eroded the boundary between law and politics. But when it comes to international criminal law in general and the ICC in particular, it is striking how easily the domains have turned to a familiar doctrinalism. Compared to domestic law, the gaps, conflicts, and ambiguities are so plain to non-partisan observers, and the blurriness – if not nonexistence – of any distinction between law and politics is so undeniable, that it might even be a heroic achievement that legal analysis on these matters could so quickly resort to form. But one might equally contend that the professionalizing approach risks exacerbating the vice of exclusionary focus on doctrine that is a tolerable or even desirable part of professionalism in other sectors because the need to have a larger debate about the politics of the field just seems less pressing. International criminal law broadly – and increasingly ICC practice in particular – adopted a crucial legitimation strategy: it crystallized in a form fundamentally open to colonization both by strategies of professional advancement for respectable careers and by styles of intellectual discourse known as doctrinalism. And in doing so, it bred the conditions for a much larger number of supporters than it might otherwise have had.

A third approach tends to postpone the difficult calculus of political judgment: preservation. It has special applicability to the ICC since, more even than local and temporary tribunals, it is frequently regarded by its more sophisticated defenders as a promising but beleaguered enterprise that needs all possible support, rather than nagging criticism, to achieve permanence in the international order. Recent threats that Kenya might even withdraw from the Rome treaty have prompted fears of institutional fragility to rise to new levels, but these fears have accompanied the institution, consciously or unconsciously, from its inception.[34] Observers who recognize the severe limitations of promoting and professionalizing nevertheless strategically defer, during an initial period of institution-building, what political analysis is supposed to be about: critical distance for the sake of contextualized judgment of outcomes. On the preservative view, the ICC is a fledgling cause that needs to be sheltered from the ordinary conditions of inquiry. It is vulnerable precisely because its ultimate implications are ostensibly so threatening to the world of power.

Preservers make the promotional or professional move for strategic reasons rather than out of deep conviction. Many of those who at first seem promoters or professionals turn out be preservers when challenged or pushed. In collegial private conversation, they will say that it is only by talking *as if* the ICC were a suprapolitical breakthrough or an already normalized professional field that it can become institutionally stable. Similarly, many people claim – at least in the hallway – that ICC actors like Luis Moreno Ocampo (the ICC's first prosecutor) are self-conscious political actors concerned above all with the institutional viability of the Court. Yet the same individuals routinely make claims similar to a 2010 statement by Ocampo: "I apply the law without political considerations."[35] Though such a statement is obviously false, it has been tolerated for a long time on a preservationist rationale.

Of the extant forms of discourse, it is the preservative one that seems most precarious after the first ten years of the court's existence. The difficulty the preserver faces is straightforward: it is not really clear how long the clock runs on the strategy. Perhaps some of the obvious threats to the Court's long-term viability – not only its budgetary woes but the logistical imperatives that have so protracted adjudication – are worth discussing, if quietly. After all, in the scheme of things, they are subject to imaginable institutional fixes. Alterations in prosecutorial strategy and casebuilding, prompted by the Lubanga trial's verdict or its controversies over intermediary witnesses, or by the acquittal of Mathieu Ngudjolo, may fall into the same category.[36] The same may be true of the ICC's failure in Kenya, though there its inability to access and control witnesses when heads of state or other strong actors are in power seems like a hard nut to crack.

However, compared to difficult problems to solve it is simply utopian to wish away other features of the persistence and visibility of politics in the international criminal justice project. Some political realities, that is, ruin the calculation of short-run tradeoff for long-term gain on which the preservative gambit is based. Unlike a healthy domestic criminal regime, which long ago achieved at least some functional systemic autonomy (or at least the generally shared belief in such autonomy), the work of the ICC will never be fundamentally detached from great power politics. All are agreed that the politics of initiation of court scrutiny of "situations" when the UN Security Council is involved (and even more, as in Syria today, when it is not involved), are too vivid a reality to suppress or forget. And the activities and choices of the Office of the Prosecutor increasingly are fodder for open political discussion, if only by some scholars. And if so, even the image of detachment from "politics" that domestic law and legal institutions have acquired seems unavailable to the ICC, because the visibility of great power conflict in which the court is self-evidently embroiled will remain too glaring for familiar myths ever to accrue. A dilatory strategy simply will not erase these realities; passing time and institutional momentum on their own will not do the trick. The prosecutor recently protested inaction of both the United Nations Security Council and some ratifying states when it comes to Bashir. After changing Bashir's case to inactive status, Bensouda voiced frustration that the ICC charges hardly interfered with his travel schedule in Africa and beyond.[37] But she did not publicly reflect on what it said that ineffective shaming of leading and even weaker states was the only tool at her disposal to seek apprehension of a man whom her office had begun investigating thanks to a great power referral in the first place.

In fact, the first ten years of the Court's operation – particularly when Security Council action is taken into account – suggest that the clock has run out on the preservative approach. Unless they really believe that promotion and professionalism are sufficient, preservationists should move more hastily to some sort of political defense of the ICC in both its current and imaginable forms. Admittedly, the preservative approach is usually premised on the assumption that even the narrowest goal of bringing local strongmen to justice is likely to face serious enemies who require caution and management to be contained. But it is also sometimes believed – except of course among American international lawyers, who routinely justify their country's guarded relationship to the ICC regime – that the danger international criminal law poses to the greatest and most unbridled power in the world means keeping the threat surreptitious while it builds to full strength.[38] But if one concludes (as I do) that the ICC has so far chiefly been threatening only to some elites in some weak states, and not without utility for elites in both strong and weak states, then it is unclear why sheltering the Court would make sense. This skepticism is especially relevant to assessing outcomes because it seems to be the major externality of the ICC that it serves an unjust and hierarchical interstate order even as it pursues petty despots, warlords, and henchmen for individual accountability.[39] (The United States is perhaps the one actor explicitly committed to evaluating the ICC instrumentally, when its tasks intersect the country's foreign policy aims, and the Court does not threaten its own geopolitical role. But its own instrumental calculus is unlikely to serve as a general defense of the ICC for the rest of the world.)

In response to the ongoing commotion around Palestine's desire to bring its grievances to the court, Kevin Heller, one of the leading and most astute and learned analysts of international criminal law, stepped out from his usual professionalism, making his preservative agenda exoteric. "[I]t would be suicidal," he wrote, "for the ICC to wade into the most politicized conflict in history – virtually guaranteeing that the United States would revert to its previous hostility and that all of the Court's other work would be ignored by the media and the international community. The Court's long-term legitimacy is more important than any individual investigation, no matter how deserving of investigation a situation might be."[40] The specific judgment might be intelligible – though it does leave open the problem of why only this conflict is "politicized" enough to present excessive risks for the Court. (What does it tell us about the world that others apparently are not?) But even bracketing that concern, the preserver has to be asked: if the overwhelming imperative is to shelter the Court only insofar as it does nothing to irritate the truly powerful, what is it being sheltered from?

III. TAKING DEFLECTION TO A HIGHER LEVEL

Silence about ends prevails, interrupted only by passing remarks about what they are and certainty that they are being met. Widespread and deflective

forms of discourse obviate real analytical clarity. There are two exceptions to
these generalizations. One is the old and intermittent worry – for advocates it
is typically regarded as surpassed – that "justice" (defined as criminal accountability) interferes with peace.[41] With regard to the ICC, it surfaced during the
negotiations in northern Uganda and, famously, during the Darfur killings.
The possibility that pursuing justice would sacrifice peace came up as well
in the short period of months in 2011 after the UN Security Council referred
Libya to the ICC and before Moammar Qaddafi was executed by the side
of the road. Most recently, it reappeared in half-hearted justification for why
Bashar al-Assad has not been subject to ICC scrutiny even once the Security
Council targeted his use of chemical weapons against civilians.[42]

The intermittent relevance of the peace versus justice framing for thinking
about the Court may seem like an acknowledgment of the obviously political
role of the ICC; moreover, it may suggest that the political cat has never been
in the bag, in spite of the prominence of the discourses catalogued above.
Actually, however, the peace versus justice debate was probably flawed from
the start, for it treated the ICC as a purely legal and non-political enterprise
that some external political imperative might occasionally need to trump. Far
from undermining the alleged autonomy of international justice and law from
politics, the peace versus justice debate presupposes that autonomy. It does
not tell us what political ends are to be served by "justice," and it treats "peace"
as an external concern to justice.

In part for this very reason, the exception of rigorous instrumentalism that
empirical political scientists offer to common rhetorical evasions which unite
a wide variety of other observers – from journalists to lawyers to scholars – is
much more important to confront. Sikkink's path-breaking book provides an
accomplished and convenient case study of the extent to which exceptional
political scientists have achieved more satisfactory justificatory strategies.
Sikkink creditably focuses on empirical results of the rise of anti-impunity,
in part out of fatigue with "tiresome arguments with colleagues," notably
American conservatives who have made it a practice to snipe at liberal inter-
nationalism for decades, and accordingly now make the latter's legal priorities (including the commitment to end impunity) a focus.[43] To her immense
credit, however, Sikkink responded to conservative attacks on human rights,
as well as the disciplinary norm of political scientists to avoid folk wisdom and
unsubstantiated hope, by doing empirical work herself. "There was clearly a
need to bring in more data, to stop speculating, and to start testing some of
these propositions," Sikkink remarks of her own path beyond promotion.[44]

Yet the devil is in the details of any empirical demonstration, including
Sikkink's ultimately reassuring finding that the rise of criminal accountability

for atrocity crimes "makes a difference."[45] Even though she entitled her study *The Justice Cascade*, Sikkink acknowledges that "justice" means "so many things to different people that trials inevitably fall short of expectations," a theme I will take up below since many observers think criminal accountability is easy to justify by appealing to victims, disregarding the irreparability of their losses and the plurality of their demands. Sikkink begins, in forthright recognition of this fact, by deciding to measure outcomes based on what she calls "the common denominator [victims] share with scholars, policy makers, and practitioners," which is the narrower effect of prosecuting past atrocity crimes on the criminal behavior itself, rather than broader outcomes such as "democratization."[46]

Sikkink's criteria for evaluating success are particularly revealing once she establishes this narrower ambit of consequences – which I called "internal" above – to distinguish them from a broader set of desirable outcomes beyond the criminal domain. Sikkink rules out two sets of criteria as overly optimistic and based on unfair standards for success that no existing movement could hope to match. The first is what she calls "comparisons to the ideal," that is, whether the rise of prosecutions perfectly fulfill expectations of their consequences within the criminal process. The second is what Sikkink calls "counterfactual reasoning," which occurs when analysts measure what criminal prosecutions achieve compared to what expectably might have happened in their absence. According to Sikkink, the trouble with both is that it is controversial to determine what the alternative universe would look like – and the counterfactual scenario often simply allows projection of higher ideals, even though it is doubtful they would have been fulfilled in some alternative world either. Sikkink rejects the first form of establishing criteria as too utopian and the second as too speculative; instead, she uses a third model of evaluation, which she terms "systematic comparative empirical research." For example, a country that fulfilled the internal criteria for success through prosecutions deserves praise, more so than a country that refused to pursue prosecutions at all. With her co-author, Hunjoon Kim, Sikkink built an empirical database that, she contends, measurably shows that countries that prosecute atrocity crimes are likelier to avoid them in the future. In addition, she finds that prosecutorial countries influence neighboring countries to decrease atrocities; she posits some combination of deterrent and pedagogical effects to explain these findings. "I don't say that these prosecutions met my ideals of justice," Sikkink remarks, "but simply that countries that used them appear to be better off."[47]

Sikkink's empirical research responds very creditably to a call for articulacy about aims and inquiry into their fulfillment. She takes the debate far beyond the rhetorical syndromes enumerated above. In fact, it was in response to such calls for articulacy and inquiry that Sikkink first turned to the project and learned the techniques of empirical substantiation, suggesting that "skepticism" is a continually productive response to promotion. It also implies a pleasing division of labor in the future between one set of scholars and practitioners who professionalize through doctrine and another set who insist on broader academic and perhaps public deliberation about ends and their fulfillment. Of course, such empirical demonstrations that some institution made a marginal difference are open to numerous objections. For example, while rebutting the cynical worry that prosecutions made things worse, Sikkink's research so far seems to establish that, in fact, the rise of anti-impunity made extremely modest differences in global human rights outcomes, with improvements largely localized to Latin American cases.[48] Even according to Sikkink herself, her study of national tribunals does not simply carry over to the ICC (and it would be surprising if it did).

Cutting across her own calls for modesty and measurement in establishing criteria and investigating their fulfillment, however, is a prior chapter in Sikkink's book suggesting that it is difficult for observers to avoid "comparison to the ideal." It is obvious why: the minor though important use of anti-impunity for narrowly defined ends within the criminal domain, like the modest advancement of those ends in measureable outcomes, simply does not fit with the promotional attitude toward prosecutions that Sikkink otherwise supports. In a more geographically specific chapter, therefore, Sikkink credits the prosecutorial turn in Latin America with a much broader range of positive consequences, notably in stabilizing or encouraging democratic transition, dissipating violent conflict, and strengthening the rule of law across the board. All of this is very curious, since Sikkink's own evidence clearly shows that it was the end of the Cold War that allowed prosecutions to take off.[49] Yet she does not mention that geopolitical changes rather than "prosecutions" were by any reckoning the threshold condition for these transformations. And along with that geopolitical change, the justice cascade of criminal prosecutions occurred as a flood of other possibilities – which were not always counterfactual – was dammed up.[50] People of good faith can debate whether the overall balance sheet is positive, but Sikkink's own work shows that there is no way to avoid contending sets of ideological expectations with which evaluation of specific legal institutions is inevitably bound up. In summary, Sikkink's very attempt to become an instrumentalist reinstates promotionalism.

IV. WHAT DOES A VICTIM WANT?

The spike of appeal to victims' interests at the ICC requires separate and final treatment, for it occurred more recently than the rise of promotion, and indeed updated that approach precisely by claiming to transcend it, in the face of nagging intuitions of institutional crisis. Of course, attention to victims was an insistent form of discourse without which the origins of human rights are unintelligible, and several later developments such as the focus on acknowledgment of suffering in transitional justice depended on it.[51] Even against this baseline, however, Fatou Bensouda took it a massive step further.

Bensouda, who recently assumed the role of chief prosecutor at the ICC, immediately offered a stirring defense of the existence, and African focus so far, of her institution: it serves victims. "I am a victim-oriented person," she told the *New York Times*. "I like to see that the victims know they have a voice."[52] Similarly, her normal response to queries about the still exclusively African caseload of the court is that it is not the institution's fault that the victims are there. "Indeed, the greatest affront to victims of these brutal, unimaginable crimes – women and young girls raped, families brutalised, robbed of everything, entire communities terrorised and shattered – is to see those powerful individuals responsible for their sufferings trying to portray themselves as the victims of a 'pro-Western, anti-African' court," she remarked to *New African*. "Our focus is on individual criminal behavior against innocent victims. ... The Office of the Prosecutor will go where the victims need us. No one will divert me from the course of justice!"[53]

The appeal to victims often resembles promotional discourse, implying as it does that callous disregard of those hurt by war and politics is the sole alternative to the Court's work. Yet at a minimum, the victims discourse reaches beyond promotionalism by offering up *someone other* than the Court's supporters to provide justification. Bensouda's remarks have given new weight to the argument that identifying with victims necessarily means supporting anti-impunity (as well as to the converse suggestion that doubts about impunity result from a failure of empathy). So have the recent threats to the ICC from African statesmen, whom Westerners oppose not in their own names but in reference to what victims want.[54] But this response is, while moving, inadequate, and contributes to the reign of aphasia around the rise of anti-impunity.[55]

The victims discourse assumes that historical injury has a straightforward and unique complement: criminal prosecution of perpetrators, with the particular institutions that have emerged to do so, in the ways they are working now (with possible monetary restitution in the future). Even if criminal prosecution should in most cases be pursued, especially against perpetrators of atrocious crimes, citing the preferences of victims is a strange way to reach that result. Victims once stereotypically wanted revenge. Indeed, one of the oldest justifications of law in the first place, to replace privatized blood feud with public moral censure, is that criminal processes are a necessary *alternative* to what victims want. As if Aeschylus had never been, the assumption today is that victims want legal prosecution. Yet as with the deflection strategies explored above, it is fundamentally implausible to cite a general rationale for some sort of justice as a justification of the particular kind of justice that exists; it is even more egregious to use such a general rationale to justify the specific institutions that we have. It is for this reason that appealing to what victims want is an evasive tactic in the current controversy over institutional selectivity. Even were it empirically true that African crimes in recent years have been worse than in other regions, they are not the only ones. In what sense could it matter (if it is true at all) that African victims focus uniquely on criminal retribution, if victims elsewhere get none?

That victims may *not* prioritize criminal prosecution is an even more important rejoinder to the deflection strategy centering around victims. Today, victims mutely serve international criminal justice as tools of rhetorical evasion while being denied the opportunity to voice their entire set of aspirations, as if the role of "bearing witness to atrocity" now widely supplied in judicial proceedings exhausted their use.[56] The truth is that victims typically want a wide variety of things, even when they list or even prioritize criminal prosecution, ranging from petty revenge to social to cosmic justice. And many political projects have promised to answer the cries of "the wretched of the earth." Serving victims is, in fact, a potentially sordid way of establishing legitimacy. Many prior moral and political projects, from Jesus's defense of the meek to Karl Marx's redemption of humanity, claimed to meet the needs of victims long before the age of the ICC dawned; their prior existence and controversial records should make appeals to serving victims difficult rather than easy to credit. That justification by way of victims so easily substitutes for argument about particular institutions and their specific work may even say more about our inability to identify with victimhood than it does about our ability to do so. That is, it illustrates more the popularity of the vision of justice currently reigning in elite spaces – just as the assumption that Christianity and communism would serve humanity once did – rather than any real attempt to empathize with others. And it is surely no accident that the most usual victims for whom Bensouda and others speak are children, whose voice in the international system is simultaneously most actually silent and most frequently ventriloquized for various causes.[57]

Sikkink illustrates well the tenacity of the assumption that victims want criminal accountability (and in a particular form) while also deflecting a broader inquiry into the range of other things they might desire. She generously cites a study of villagers in Northern Uganda who were terrorized by the Lord's Resistance Army (whose leader, Joseph Kony, is under ICC indictment). "Their main priorities," Sikkink acknowledges, "were health care, peace, education, and livelihood. Only 3 percent mentioned 'justice' as their top priority." Her response to this finding is that statistics are refractory and ambiguous, depending utterly on how the data are interpreted, as if this observation did not have major implications for her own reliance on quantitative empirical work. "In the same survey," she explains, "70 percent of respondents said it was important to hold people accountable for human rights violations and war crimes, and 59 percent said that the LRA leaders should be put on trial. It is difficult to interpret these findings as clearly indicating that people in northern Uganda don't care about justice or that legal accountability is an unwelcome Western imposition."[58] Sikkink takes the finding that some number of people said they wanted accountability *alongside and within a constellation of other and more important aims* as sufficient to establish her cause, and immediately moves on. The possibility that grassroots victims may not desire what transnational legal and some political elites suddenly want in the era of anti-impunity, and certainly not by itself, is barely allowed to interfere with standard operating procedure.

V. CONCLUDING REFLECTIONS

Judith Shklar did not entirely dismiss formal and especially procedural legality. But for her, what distinguished Andrei Vyshinski (the Soviet prosecutor who staged the Moscow purge trials but also pitched in at the Nuremberg trials) was not so much that prosecutors at other political trials were not showmen. Rather, the difference is that Vyshinski had bad political causes. According to Skhlar, it is possible for political trials to have good ones. She insisted, for this reason, that the burden is not merely to set up a formal legal system but also to engage in discourse about what makes specific aims valuable in a given political context – and about how valuable they really are. The beginning of wisdom about the accountability norm, as about the ICC in particular, is to acknowledge that it is a political enterprise, and moreover never an autonomous one, for it intersects with other extant political agendas, especially in domestic struggle within states and great power politics in the global "order."[59]

All things considered, anti-impunity should invite not mindless allegiance, but exploration of what it is trying to do and actually achieving, compared with hypothetical alternatives with which it competes or which it even rules out. There is dawning recognition of this fact. In a recent speech to the youth NGO "Invisible Children" in her first public remarks as United States ambassador to the United Nations, Samantha Power insisted that it is the "real-world scoreboard" that counts.[60] Shklar's point, of course, was that it was crucial first of all to define the available games so as to decide which one to play. To be sure, to complain of aphasia and to indict misdirection is hardly to undermine any extant agenda or institution. And it is also, *a fortiori*, hardly to justify some other plan. But demands that the critique of impunity actually identify an extant alternative or supply a theoretical one do not make very much sense. Even were such demands impossible to fulfill, it would not undermine the critical analysis of the search for impunity, and would not save it the trouble of explaining itself in the face of that indictment.

Sikkink, mentioning that one of her interlocutors insisted that the capitalist system, rather than some petty despot, should have been tried in the name of accountability, calls for observers to be more explicit in the alternatives they imagine.[61] If it is fair to insist as much, it could not save defenders of anti-impunity, as her own work helpfully proves, from the trouble of specifying the (typically more minimal) effects they are seeking and whether they are succeeding in producing those effects. In any case, restricting inquiry to empirical evaluation of where history has in fact gone and ruling out consideration of where else it might go is to deprive our ethical imagination of its most stimulating catalyst. The rise of anti-impunity, so often celebrated as a breakthrough, should want its rationale to be that it is better than available and possible alternatives, not something defensible only *faute de mieux*. To offer a modest call for such explanation, in view of the impressive (though selective) rise of accountability in our time, can also be a first step into the search for something else, should the explanation never come – or should it prove wanting when it does.

NOTES

1 Cited in Sarah M.H. Nouwen, *Complementarity in the Line of Fire: The Catalysing Effect of the International Criminal Court in Uganda and Sudan* (New York: Cambridge University Press, 2014), 214.
2 For this general framework, see Samuel Moyn, *The Last Utopia: Human Rights in History* (Cambridge, Mass.: Harvard University Press, 2010), especially chapter 4 and epilogue.
3 See http://bit.ly/1qAW4TO.
4 Kathryn Sikkink, *The Justice Cascade: How Human Rights Prosecutions Are Changing World Politics* (New York: W.W. Norton, 2011). For deep background to

the post-1980s revival, on which there is as yet no serious history, the best work is now Mark Lewis, *The Birth of the New Justice: The Internationalization of Crime and Punishment, 1919–1950* (New York: Oxford University Press, 2014).

5 See the chapter by Vasuki Nesiah [Chapter 3] in this volume.

6 See especially Immi Tallgren, "The Sense and Sensibility of International Criminal Law," *European Journal of International Law* 13, no. 3 (2002): 561–595.

7 For the first phrase, see "Kenya and the International Criminal Court," *New York Times*, November 10, 2013, SR10. For the second, Elizabeth Evenson, "Justice for Kenya Stumbles at the ICC," *Policy Review*, December 2013, accessed January 25, 2014, www.policyreview.eu/justice-for-kenya-stumbles-at-the-icc/.

8 See especially Sarah M.H. Nouwen and Wouter G. Werner, "Monopolizing Global Justice: International Criminal Law as a Challenge to Human Diversity," *Journal of International Criminal Justice* 13, no. 1 (2014): 151–176, written from a similar perspective as mine.

9 Hannah Arendt, *Eichmann in Jerusalem: A Report on the Banality of Evil*, rev. ed. (New York: Viking, 1964), 254.

10 Judith N. Shklar, *Legalism* (Cambridge, Mass.: Harvard University Press, 1963), later republished with a new preface and currently available as *Legalism: Law, Morals, and Political Trials* (Cambridge, Mass.: Harvard University Press, 1986). For more recent need to attend more carefully to the otherwise strictly retributive aims of international justice, see Andrew K. Woods, "Moral Judgments and International Crimes: The Disutility of Desert," *Virginia International Law Journal* 52, no. 3 (2012): 633–681.

11 See Otto Kirchheimer, *Political Justice: The Use of Legal Procedure for Political Ends* (Princeton: Princeton University Press, 1961).

12 The most famous work of legal instrumentalism is Rudolf von Jhering, *Der Zweck im Recht*, 2 vols. (Leipzig: Breitkopf & Härtel, 1877–1883), in English as *Law as a Means to an End*, trans. Isaac Husik (Boston: Boston Book Company, 1913); for the worried claim of instrumentalist prevalence, see Brian Tamanaha, *Law as a Means to an End: Threat to the Rule of Law* (Cambridge: Cambridge University Press, 2006).

13 Shklar credited Nuremberg for boggling the mind of German lawyers and "officialdom" and thus restoring the legalism she considered a part of decent liberal societies; but East Asia, in her view, had no legalism to restore so other strategies of response were more appropriate. For further detail, see Samuel Moyn, "Judith Shklar versus the International Criminal Court," *Humanity* 4, no. 3 (Fall 2013): 473–500, where I argue that recent histories of postwar Germany confirm Shklar's analytical perspective precisely because they undermine her guess and our expectation that prosecutions played a role in the transition to liberal democracy that occurred.

14 Shklar, *Legalism*, 160; Mark J. Osiel, *Mass Atrocity, Collective Memory, and the Law* (New Brunswick: Transaction Publishers, 1999), 65.

15 Henry M. Hart, Jr., "The Aims of the Criminal Law," *Law and Contemporary Problems* 23, no. 3 (Summer 1958): 401–441.

16 *The Prosecutor v. Thomas Lubanga Dyilo*, ICC-01/04-01/06-2842 (2012).

17 In passing remarks, it seems clear that general deterrence is the most often cited reason beyond retribution for international trials. Amnesty International, for example,

characterized the Lubanga verdict as "an important milestone that should give pause to those who think they can commit crimes with impunity." Angela Chang, "Milestone Verdict on Child Soldiers: Will Kony Be Next?," *Amnesty International Human Rights Now Blog*, March 14, 2012, accessed January 25, 2014, http://blog. amnestyusa.org/africa/milestone-verdict-on-child-soldiers-will-kony-be-next/. Similarly, Radhika Coomaraswamy, UN special representative for children and armed conflict, said the verdict would "reach warlords and commanders across the world and serve as a strong deterrent." Mike Corder, "Congo Warlord Thomas Lubanga Convicted of Using Child Soldiers," *The Independent*, March 14, 2012.

18 On certain fronts, it seems fairly daunting to suppose the ICC has made any discernible difference. Mark Kersten, for example, writes that "deterrence hasn't worked in the Central African Republic – like at all. It has been almost ten years since the CAR government referred itself to the ICC. Former DRC President Jean-Pierre Bemba is on trial for his alleged responsibility for war crimes and crimes against humanity committed in the CAR. But the ICC's intervention hasn't prevented – or really had *any* effect – on the country's slide into political violence and slaughter. Making matters worse, it is exactly the types of crimes that the ICC has focused on – sexual violence, mass displacement, executions of civilians and the use of child soldiers – that characterize the current violence in the CAR." Mark Kersten, "The ICC in the Central African Republic: The Death of Deterrence?," *Justice in Conflict*, December 11, 2013, accessed January 25, 2014, http://justiceinconflict.org/2013/12/11/the-icc-in-the-central-african-republic-the-death-of-deterrence/.

19 Remarks, Opening Session of the 7th Consultative Assembly of Parliamentarians of the International Criminal Court and the Rule of Law and World Parliamentary Conference of Human Rights (2012), quoted in "ICC President tells World Parliamentary Conference 'ICC brings retributive and restorative justice together with the prevention of future crimes,'" *International Criminal Court*, December 2012, accessed January 15, 2014, www.icc-cpi.int/en_menus/icc/press%20and%20media/press%20releases/news%20and%20highlights/Pages/pr860.aspx.

20 It was of course no accident in this regard that Luis Moreno Ocampo had won renown for participating in Argentine transition and retroactive criminal prosecution before becoming ICC prosecutor. He himself asserted the relationship between his new court and transition, even though the ICC so far rarely acts in the aftermath of regime change, as in the Argentine and other Latin American cases. See Luis Moreno Ocampo, "Transitional Justice in Ongoing Conflicts," *International Journal of Transitional Justice* 1, no. 1 (2007): 8–9.

21 See for instance Juan Méndez, "In Defense of Transitional Justice," *Transitional Justice and the Rule of Law in New Democracies*, ed. A. James McAdams (Notre Dame: Notre Dame University Press, 1997); Diane F. Orentlicher, "Settling Accounts: The Duty to Prosecute Human Rights Violations of a Prior Regime," *Yale Law Journal* 100, no. 8 (1995): 2537–2615; Naomi Roht-Arriaza, *The Pinochet Effect: Transnational Justice in the Age of Human Rights* (Philadelphia: University of Pennsylvania Press, 1995); and Naomi Roht-Arriaza and Javier Mariezcurrena, eds., *Transitional Justice in the Twenty-First Century: Beyond Truth versus Justice* (Cambridge: Cambridge University Press, 2006).

22 For one of sundry examples of this conflation, see a talk by prominent human rights activist Geoffrey Robertson. Geoffrey Robertson, "Ending Impunity: The

Quest for Global Justice," *Youtube.com*, November 21, 2011, accessed January 25, 2014, www.youtube.com/watch?v=kROj5QMoi2Y.

23 For the ICC as a tool of great powers, see David Bosco, *Rough Justice: The International Criminal Court in a World of Power Politics* (New York. Oxford University Press, 2014), and my review, "Who Guards the Guardians?," *Wall Street Journal*, January 22, 2014, A17.

24 Cited in "Support for Ending Impunity for International Crimes Must Grow," *UN News Centre*, December 12, 2011, accessed January 25, 2014, www.un.org/apps/news/story.asp/www.unaids.org/en/story.asp?NewsID=40703. See also Adam Branch, "What the ICC Review Conference Can't Fix," *African Arguments*, March 11, 2010, accessed December 9, 2015, http://africanarguments.org/2010/03/11/what-the-icc-review-conference-can%E2%80%99t-fix/.

25 "Our members view the efforts of Kenya and other African governments to excuse, defer or exempt heads of governments from prosecution as a serious political threat to the integrity of the Rome Statute and ICC, to victims, to witnesses and to the NGOs that support them," noted William Pace, convenor of the Coalition for the International Criminal Court recently. "Political attacks on the Court, especially when it first came into existence, were overcome and we are committed to protecting it from this one." "ICC Must Be Defended from Political Interference," *Coalition for the International Criminal Court*, November 28, 2013, accessed January 25, 2014, www.iccnow.org/documents/CICCPR_Closing_ASP_2013.pdf.

26 David S. Koller, "The Faith of the International Criminal Lawyer," *NYU Journal of International Law and Politics* 40 (2008): 1019–1069.

27 It was recently revealed that Zhou did not actually say this, but the words long attributed to him were wise all the same. Richard McGregor, "Zhou's Cryptic Caution Lost in Translation," *Financial Times*, June 10, 2011, accessed January 25, 2014, www.ft.com/cms/s/0/74916db6-938d-11e0-922e-00144feab49a.html#axzz2rRrV1XN3.

28 Cf. Michelle Alexander, *The New Jim Crow: Mass Incarceration in the Age of Colorblindness* (New York: New Press, 2010).

29 Elena Baylis, "Tribunal-Hopping with the Post-Conflict Justice Junkies," *Oregon Review of International Law* 10 (2008): 361–390.

30 See Mikkel Jarle Christensen, "Academics for International Criminal Justice: The Role of Legal Scholars in Creating and Sustaining a New Legal Field," iCourts Working Paper Series (2014), available at http://papers.ssrn.com/sol3/papers.cfm?abstract_id=2539048.

31 See also Sarah M.H. Nouwen, "Justifying Justice," in James Crawford and Martti Koskenniemi, eds., *Cambridge Companion to International Law* (Cambridge, 2012).

32 See, e.g., Janine Natalya Clark, "'Specific Direction' and the Fragmentation of International Jurisprudence on Aiding and Abetting: Perišić and Beyond," *International Criminal Law Review* 15, no. 3 (2015): 411–451; Case Note, "Special Court for Sierra Leone Rejects "Specific Direction" Requirement for Aiding and Abetting Violations of International Law – *Prosecutor* v. *Taylor*, Case No. SCSL-03-01-A, Judgment (Spec. Ct. for Sierra Leone Sept. 26, 2013)," *Harvard Law Review* 127, no. 6 (2014): 1847–1854.

33 See, e.g., Beth van Schaak and Ronald C. Slye, *International Criminal Law and Its Enforcement* (New York: Foundation Press, 2010); David Luban et al., eds., *International and Transnational Criminal Law* (New York: Aspen Publishers, 2009).

34 "[F]ailure [in the Uhuru Kenyatta prosecution] could spell doom for the dream of global justice…. If the case against Kenyatta were to collapse, the ICC would lose what little authority it still has and would become a tool as useless as it is costly. And it isn't just a matter of the court's survival: The long-cherished dream of global justice seems on the verge of failure." Erich Follath, "'Big Mama' and the Massacre: ICC's Reputation at Risk in Kenya," *Der Spiegel* (online), July 26, 2013, accessed January 25, 2014, www.spiegel.de/international/world/reputation-of-icc-on-the-line-in-case-against-kenya-president-kenyatta-a-913090.html.

35 Luis Moreno Ocampo, *Keynote Address to Council on Foreign Relations* (February 4, 2010).

36 This is the general spirit of the casenote by Diane Marie Amann, "International Decisions: *Prosecutor v. Lubanga*," *American Journal of International Law* 106 (2012): 809–817.

37 See, e.g., "ICC Chief Prosecutor Shelves Darfur War Crimes Probe," *The Guardian*, December 14, 2014; "Fatou Bensouda: South Africa 'Had to Arrest Omar al-Bashir," *Al Jazeera Online*, June 27, 2015, accessed December 9, 2015, www.aljazeera.com/programmes/talktojazeera/2015/06/fatou-bensouda-africa-arrest-omar-al-bashir-150626132631885.html.

38 See, e.g., Harold Hongju Koh, "International Criminal Justice 5.0," *Yale Journal of International Law* 38, no. 2 (2013): 525–542, 535: "[P]lease do not misread our skepticism of certain institutions as hostility to the bedrock norms and values of international criminal justice."

39 See Bosco, *Rough Justice*.

40 Cited in Mark Kersten, "Frustrations over the ICC and Justice in Palestine," *Justice in Conflict*, November 11, 2012, accessed January 25, 2014, http://justiceinconflict.org/2012/11/30/frustrations-over-the-icc-and-justice-in-palestine/. For the broader theoretical point that more talk is needed, though he makes it only for prosecutorial discretion, see James A. Goldston, "More Candour about Criteria: The Exercise of Discretion by the Prosecutor of the International Criminal Court," *Journal of International Criminal Justice* 8, no. 2 (2010): 383–406.

41 For more on the peace versus justice debate and its trajectory, see Karen Engle's chapter in this volume [Chapter 1], and Nouwen, "Justifying Justice."

42 See Ian Black, "Bashar al-Assad Implicated in Syria War Crimes, says UN," *The Guardian*, December 2, 2013, accessed January 19, 2016, www.theguardian.com/world/2013/dec/02/syrian-officials-involved-war-crimes-bashar-al-assad-un-investigators (indicating that the US, UK, and France opposed an ICC referral as it might jeopardize Syria's attendance at the Geneva II peace conference the next year).

43 Sikkink, *Justice Cascade*, 132, reporting the views of Jack Goldsmith, Stephen Krasner, and Jack Snyder. For further evidence of a salutary turn to instrumentalism, see Yuval Shany, ed., *Assessing the Effectiveness of International Courts* (New York: Oxford University Press, forthcoming).

44 Sikkink, *Justice Cascade*, 135.

45 In this respect Sikkink's work is part of the so-called "empirical turn" in international law, on par with Beth Simmons's renowned empirical demonstration that human rights treaties make some difference. See Gregory Shaffer and Tom Ginsburg, "The Empirical Turn in International Law Scholarship," *American Journal of*

International Law 106, no. 1 (January 2012): 1–46; Beth A. Simmons, *Mobilizing for Human Rights: International Law in Domestic Politics* (Cambridge: Cambridge University Press, 2009); and for my parallel skepticism about the low-level hope attached to human rights treaties compared to other imaginable possible ends, "Do Human Rights Treaties Make Enough of a Difference?," *Cambridge Companion to Human Rights Law*, eds. Conor Gearty and Costas Douzinas (Cambridge: Cambridge University Press, 2012).

46 Sikkink, *Justice Cascade*, 162–163.

47 Ibid., 167.

48 See the chart in ibid., 181.

49 Ibid., Part I.

50 For further thoughts on Sikkink's historical framing, see Samuel Moyn, "Of Deserts and Promised Lands," *The Nation*, February 29, 2012, reprinted in Moyn, *Human Rights and the Uses of History* (New York: Verso, 2014). For a different presentation of Latin America's Cold War history than in Sikkink's anodyne description of its syndrome of "weak democracy," but with full allowance for its violent past, see, for example, Greg Grandin and Gilbert M. Joseph, eds., *A Century of Revolution: Insurgent and Counterinsurgent Violence during Latin America's Long Cold War* (Durham: Duke University Press, 2010).

51 In the history of international criminal law, the Eichmann trial is normally given credit for the innovation given how profoundly prior proceedings like Nuremberg had marginalized live witnesses in general and atrocity victims in particular. But for a more general picture of the rise of victimhood, see Didier Fassin and Richard Rechtman, *The Empire of Trauma: An Inquiry into the Condition of Victimhood*, trans. Rachel Gomme (Princeton: Princeton University Press, 2009).

52 Rick Gladstone, "A Lifelong Passion Is Now Put to Practice in the Hague," *New York Times*, January 19, 2013, A7.

53 Mercy Eno, "Fatou Bensouda: 'We Are Not Against Africa,'" *New African*, September 11, 2012, accessed January 25, 2014, www.newafricanmagazine.com/features/politics/fatou-bensouda-we-are-not-against-africa.

54 In a typical recent expression of the view that justice must mean individual criminal accountability, and insistence that it is what everyone (in Africa, especially) wants, consider Human Rights Watch head Kenneth Roth's plangent response to the Kenyan disturbance: "The court's future now rests to a large extent on the battle being waged between African leaders with little interest in justice and those Africans, including many activists and victims, who see an end to impunity for mass atrocities as essential for Africa's future. One can only hope that the welfare of African people takes precedence over the perceived interests of African leaders." Kenneth Roth, "Africa Attacks the International Criminal Court," *New York Review of Books* 61, no. 2 (February 6, 2014), accessed January 25, 2014, www.nybooks.com/articles/archives/2014/feb/06/africa-attacks-international-criminal-court/.

55 See Sarah Kendall and Sarah Nouwen, "Representational Practices at the International Criminal Court: The Gap between Juridified and Abstract Victimhood," *Law and Contemporary Problems* 76, no. 3–4 (2014): 235–262.

56 See, e.g., James Dawes, *That the World May Know: Bearing Witness to Atrocity* (Cambridge, Mass.: Harvard University Press, 2007) or Eric Stover, *The Witnesses: War Crimes and the Promise of Justice in the Hague* (Philadelphia: University of

Pennsylvania Press, 2005); for further critical reflections, see Samuel Moyn, "Bearing Witness: Theological Origins of a New Secular Morality," *The Holocaust and Historical Methodology*, Dan Stone, ed. (New York: Berghahn Books, 2012).

57 "This is their day," actress and activist Angelina Jolie noted in response to the Lubanga verdict she heard as a member of the audience, referring to the children in whose name she spoke, "where these children will feel there is no impunity for what happened to them, for what they suffered." Quoted in Corder, "Congo Warlord Thomas Lubanga."

58 Sikkink, *Justice Cascade*, 133, citing Berkeley-Tulane Initiative on Vulnerable Populations, "When the War Ends: A Population-Based Survey on Attitudes about Peace, Justice, and Social Reconstruction in Northern Uganda," (December 2007).

59 See also Sarah Nouwen and Wouter Werner's valuable attempt to inject a "political" dimension into the discussion, which focuses more on how the ICC functions according to a logic of hostility in the international system. See Sarah M.H. Nouwen and Wouter G. Werner, "Doing Justice to the Political: The International Criminal Court in Uganda and Sudan," *European Journal of International Law* 21, no. 4 (2010): 941–965. See also a typological survey of definitions in Samuel Moyn, "Concepts of the Political in Twentieth-Century European Thought," *Oxford Handbook to Carl Schmitt*, Jens Meierhenrich and Oliver Simons, eds. (forthcoming).

60 "What matters are results – everything else is just noise," Power remarked. "Invisible Children could have gotten self-satisfied that 2 million people watched its Kony 2012 video and that they were thrust into the limelight, globally. But this new generation understands that the video is not what matters; the number of Twitter followers is not what matters. These are just means to an end; indeed Invisible Children is just a means to an end. It's just an organization with a cause. What matters is the real world scoreboard." Ambassador Samantha Power, US Permanent Representative to the United Nations, *Remarks at the Fourth Estate Leadership Summit*, August 10, 2013, accessed January 25, 2014, http://usun.state.gov/briefing/statements/213034.htm.

61 Sikkink, *Justice Cascade*, 165.

3

Doing History with Impunity

Vasuki Nesiah*

Histories of human rights have emerged as a popular genre of scholarship in a variety of disciplines.[1] An array of scholars has offered both celebratory and critical accounts of the development of human rights. They jockey over the origin point of the human rights project but generally agree that, over time, human rights has expanded in scope and power.[2] These narratives regarding human rights and the inexorable movement forward toward greater normative recognition, wider policy significance, and deeper institutionalization in law and practice pitch a pre-history to the role of human rights in the current moment.[3] In no arena is this claim more resonant than in relation to the history of anti-impunity. The birth of the International Criminal Court (ICC) two years into the new millennium was heralded by efforts to treat that institution as the logical endgame of a strengthening struggle against impunity in different parts of the globe.

Let us first look quickly at three examples of works published around the turn of the new millennium that illustrate the scholarly narratives of a historical crescendo toward anti-impunity that was seen to have climaxed with the ICC. First, in 1996, Naomi Roht-Arriaza argued that, in contrast to an earlier culture of impunity, in recent years international legal developments were directed at efforts "to reaffirm and expand on duties to investigate, prosecute, and compensate, and to be critical of amnesties that preclude any of these things."[4] Second, in 2000, Gary Bass argued that what I call here "anti-impunity efforts" have a longer pedigree that begins in the aftermath of the Napoleonic wars. With a primary interest in the twentieth

* My thanks to the editors of this volume for their insights and suggestions. I am also grateful for the opportunity for dialogue about this paper with other contributors to this volume at the author meetings for this book, and with participants at the ICES seminar in Colombo, Sri Lanka in March 2015 when I presented this paper. Particular thanks to Radhika Coomaraswamy for her comments on the paper in Colombo.

century, Bass's book offers a story of liberal states advancing a series of institutional experiments to prosecute war crimes.[5] He draws a line from the early and tenuous moves of the post-World War I period to the post-World War II trials of Nuremberg to what he describes as the "Hague" period, where the international tribunals and the ICC help fuel anti-impunity efforts internationally. Finally, in 2001, Kathryn Sikkink and Ellen Lutz spoke of a "justice cascade," tracking prosecutions of human rights abusers in different countries, in what they described as an incremental but definitive shift toward a normative consensus to fight impunity.[6]

In contrast to these claims about the momentum and directionality of the arc of human rights history, this chapter argues that the historical story is much messier. Considering the history of impunity and anti-impunity primarily through critical engagement with Gary Bass's ambitious history of war crimes tribunals, I make two arguments. First, the heightened attention to the fight against impunity has all but eclipsed the intertwined history and legacy of impunity that has accompanied every attempt at international justice. Second, the particular ways in which international justice and anti-impunity have been framed have reproduced and reinforced a structure of global governance premised on exploitation and inequality. Moments of anti-impunity against perpetrators of international crimes are also moments of impunity for injustices committed by systemic inequality. The forces of impunity and anti-impunity are co-travelers and, in the moments examined in this chapter, these apparently contradictory forces are partly in symbiosis.

I. WAR CRIMES AND THE ARC OF HISTORY

In *Stay the Hand of Vengeance: The Politics of War Crimes Tribunals*,[7] Bass seeks to establish the long history of war crimes tribunals and efforts toward such tribunals on the international stage. In so doing, he is particularly concerned with interpreting these efforts as a struggle for humanist idealism in international relations and he claims a close nexus between these initiatives and liberal states. "In a world where impunity is the rule," Bass reads these efforts as a rejection of impunity for accountability and a rejection of vengeful war for tribunalized justice.[8] Accordingly, I read Bass's book as a history of the turn to anti-impunity, a turn signified by the increasing embrace of war crimes tribunals and international criminal justice. His is not a story of the forces of justice moving forward with clarity of purpose and definitive institutional force;[9] rather it is a story of justice "lurching forward" unevenly and incrementally, emboldened at some points and compromised at others, but with forward momentum nevertheless. There are two struggles in Bass's account: an internal struggle within liberal states for the better angels to triumph over the Kissingeresque realists and an external struggle with "illiberal" states.[10] With a direction and force forged through those battles, Bass claims there has been a "reaction to continued impunity" and a long movement toward "a well-institutionalized international forum where such cases can be heard" that has been gradually, if fitfully, gaining momentum through criminal justice projects that have followed wars and prolonged conflicts over the past century.[11] In contrast to writers such as Sikkink, he is much more focused on state actors rather than non-state actors and on the international stage rather than domestic battles. Yet these are largely complementary projects with differences in emphasis.

Bass's narrative exemplifies the broader "justice cascade" story about the historical momentum of anti-impunity, described sometimes as a reaction against impunity, at other times as the pursuit of accountability, and most often as an embrace of legalism and international justice.[12] *Stay the Hand of Vengeance* is magisterial in its telling of a global history of war crimes tribunals, while also being impressively detailed in its granular tracing of how decisions were debated and struggled for within the diplomatic and jurist community of "liberal" states (and in particular, the United States). He sees these tribunals as poster children for victors' justice in the best sense of liberal legalist "justice": the decision to combat impunity through trials while forgoing summary execution of enemy perpetrators. Bass presents war crimes tribunals as alternatives to both vengeance and impunity, institutional paeans to due process and liberal legalism.[13] In Bass's telling, liberal states' idealistic commitment to "international justice" is strongest when it is focused on crimes against its own citizens, and in that sense the anti-impunity commitment is not immune to nationalist self-interest considerations.[14] Nevertheless, Bass dismisses accusations of "western double standards" out of hand as merely the cynical efforts of [former Yugoslavian President Slobodan] Milošević and others to make "comprehensiveness" the enemy of international justice.[15]

In advancing my alternative reading of the historical arc of criminal justice, I look at three moments where Bass describes efforts for international criminal accountability. These are the moments he labels Constantinople,[16] Nuremberg,[17] and The Hague.[18] The book itself tells a longer history,[19] but these are three of the most significant chapters in the book and speak to the historical arc of his narrative regarding the gradual and fitful – but nevertheless determinedly ascendant – anti-impunity imperative. Constantinople, Nuremberg, and The Hague appear as way stations for the human rights train.

The efforts to establish individual accountability for war crimes become critical catalysts (or "high points" in the Bass narrative) for anti-impunity energies. The stakes of each of these moments need to be understood as bricks in the edifice of global governance and its promise of cosmopolitan humanist history, not as instances of heroic struggles against mass crimes. That edifice may involve a range of significant historical factors, including imperial land grabs, the empowerment of "liberal states," the mythologies of justice that attend multinational judicial institutions, and the entrenching of the global economic power of the Global North. Thus, re-reading each of Bass's foundational moments, I argue first that the very same state actors credited with international justice efforts were amongst those which also helped entrench impunity for their own actions. The same processes that established limited accountability in some realms also helped legitimize impunity in other realms. The concern focuses not only on whose actions remain unseen and unpunished through tribunals and courts, but also which actions remain invisible and unaccountable. Thus, I argue that the focus on anti-impunity for war crimes does the work of distracting from (and thereby, in some cases, aiding) other agendas that are part of the different articulations of empire at each of these historical conjunctures. For many states, the real stakes may not have been criminal justice but various alternative projects, including particular territorial, economic, and governance agendas that moved forward without opposition partly because post-war criminal justice measures got equated with justice as such. The focus on war crimes and short, intense periods of extraordinary violence normalizes systematic abuses and ordinary or "slow violence."[20] Moreover, the war crimes prosecution of some contributes to the legitimacy of international legal institutions in ways that distract from the impunity enjoyed by others for war crimes - usually those (often in "the Global North") who benefit most from international law.

Stay the Hand of Vengeance speaks to an overlapping consensus among scholars such as Lutz, Sikkink, and Roht-Arriaza on the empowerment of anti-impunity forces in the present moment.[21] While they see the current moment as one in which the forces of anti-impunity are clearly ascendant, they do not claim that the forces of impunity are decisively defeated. For instance, Bass notes that over the course of the century, the forces of anti-impunity gained more power and influence in shaping the course of international criminal justice institutions – but each anti-impunity initiative he describes pushed against competing interests and agendas.[22] This very struggle is offered as testament to the heroism of liberal legalism's soldiers and the remarkable historical momentum against impunity on the battleground of international criminal justice. Thus, when the International Center for Transitional Justice convened an online debate in early 2015 on whether the struggle for anti-impunity was being derailed, even the articulation of this concern functioned as a rallying point for those who resolved to march forward with renewed vigor.[23] In the words of the United Nations High Commissioner for Human Rights, Zeid Ra'ad Al Hussein, "the road to victory is long and strewn with obstacles. We have come a long way already in the fight against impunity," and accountability measures "that would have been unthinkable only a decade ago" have been advanced in recent years.[24] Thus, as Bass would frame it, the arc of history bends closer to accountability as the "cause of international justice has been lurching forward on all fronts."[25]

In contrast to these developments, many cite earlier moments when impunity was the order of the day. When Pol Pot, Augusto Pinochet, Ríos Montt and Hissène Habré left power, there were few prospects of holding them accountable through criminal prosecutions. The mainstream of the human rights movement is largely celebratory about the move to criminal prosecutions. Many see this trend as a progressive realization of human rights by vindicating the rights of victims and speaking truth to power.[26] Sikkink, who popularized the terminology of a "justice cascade," notes that criminal prosecution of heads of state and former heads of state for human rights abuses "represents a very new development in world politics. Only 30 years ago, it was virtually unheard of, almost unimaginable, for a national or international tribunal to hold state officials criminally accountable for human rights violations."[27] In a similar vein, Naomi Roht-Arriaza notes that for much of the twentieth century, impunity was the dominant norm: "Although some legal obligations to investigate, prosecute, and punish perpetrators or compensate victims already existed, until the 1990s the issue was not on the agenda of either the human rights community or states."[28] For instance, she notes that "blanket pre-conviction amnesties"[29] were common in Latin America in the 1970s and 1980s. It is against the backdrop of rampant impunity that the "progress narrative" about the move to anti-impunity is advanced.

While those engaging with the human rights field are largely celebratory about this narrative, there are – as many of the chapters in this volume illustrate – important voices advancing a more heterodox relationship to the turn to criminal prosecutions. Some argue that criminal justice should not crowd out a more holistic, multi-faceted approach to transitional justice. They see justice as involving truth-seeking, reparations, memorialization, and a host of other dimensions of transitional justice that are not captured by the narrowly legalized approach of criminal prosecutions.[30] Others are concerned that the transitional justice framework is itself too narrow and that transitional justice in general, and criminal justice in particular, may crowd out, defer, or displace distributive justice concerns and other priorities.[31] Yet others argue that the ascendency of international criminal justice risks overwhelming national criminal justice processes.[32] Moreover, there have been critics of the criminal justice model who have been concerned that the courtroom's focus on perpetrator guilt can distort and diminish the complex questions of accountability and justice that attend mass human rights abuse. Hannah Arendt's analysis of the Eichmann trial offers perhaps the most well-known articulation of this concern.[33]

Others, including Adam Branch and Mahmood Mamdani, have been particularly critical of actions by the ICC in places such as Darfur and Uganda on the theory that framing issues in terms of prosecutions and criminal justice simplifies politically complex situations in ways that have far-reaching adverse consequences.[34] Those more skeptical of the turn to criminal law may not necessarily disagree with the analysis of Bass, Sikkink, and Roht-Arriaza that there is a movement toward fighting impunity for human rights abuses. However, they have a different assessment about whether this direction should be applauded and advanced.

Finally, Richard Falk and others condemn the historical claims of the anti-impunity narrative because they involve a double standard that ignores the impunity of the West while simultaneously applauding anti-impunity efforts by the West.[35] These double standards were seen to track military victors and losers following the World Wars and more determinedly trace North-South lines today. As William Schabas puts it: "Why prosecute post-election violence in Kenya or recruitment of child soldiers in the Democratic Republic of the Congo, but not murder and torture of prisoners in Iraq or illegal settlements in the West Bank?"[36] As I elaborate further in this chapter, my concerns with the Bass-style anti-impunity histories goes beyond the double-standard charge; nevertheless, I share the concerns of Falk, Schabas, and others who suggest that focusing only on anti-impunity may distract from a history of impunity – one with distinctive and repetitive geopolitical and distributive patterns over time. The work of Falk and others challenge the mythologies of liberal states and vindication of the progress narratives of liberal cosmopolitanism that claim a victory for humanity each time an international criminal tribunal is established.[37]

In the following sections, I seek to re-historicize "the justice cascade" by situating it alongside systemic impunity and by reframing it not as a story of human rights but as one of global governance. Each moment that has been described as a part of a turn toward anti-impunity has also been the occasion of astonishing impunity for international crimes. Indeed, in the decades that followed the end of the Cold War, there was a simultaneous scaling up of both a "criminal law" and an "anti-criminal law" turn. For example, while international criminal law institutions proliferated, universal jurisdiction was practically shut down.[38] There was, in other words, an intensification of policies, institutional innovations, and legitimating language in both directions; sometimes the very crusaders of anti-impunity were also the champions of impunity.[39] Moreover, as the "double standards critics" suggest, the bi-directionality is not random: if there were victors' and losers' lines that explained Nuremberg, there are North-South lines of allegiance and geopolitical power that explain who are the targets of anti-impunity efforts by the ICC today.[40]

These specific patterns of bias and double standards regarding impunity are critical to foreground, but this focus is inadequate to explain the structural contradictions of global governance that the impunity/anti-impunity trends exemplify. For this we also need to understand and unpack the preoccupation with anti-impunity to situate it in the architecture of global governance. What kind of work is being done by the claim that there is a turn to anti-impunity? How does this focus expand or consolidate the dominant structures of global governance? The anti-impunity conversation as a whole may sometimes function as a historical decoy. It can contribute to a narrative of progress that assumes universal benefits from anti-impunity and deter a critical interrogation of the work done by the focus on international crimes. Such an interrogation can probe the genealogy of that focus and its consequences. Bookending two world wars and the Cold War, this focus helped consolidate a victor's story about the meaning of those same wars, while also generating a space of legitimacy for the post-war world order. To help illuminate these dynamics, this chapter situates the framing of impunity in Constantinople, Nuremberg, and The Hague in relation to developments such as territorial acquisition and international financial institutions. Suturing those developments to the story about liberal legalist pieties (and attendant hierarchies and maldistributions between liberal and illiberal states and their citizens) offers a window into the politics of empire. Empire may well have provided fertile ground for those pieties, while those pieties themselves contributed to the normative scaffolding upholding empire.

II. A HISTORY OF STRUGGLE REGARDING IMPUNITY

The larger story Bass tells is of more than a century of struggle against impunity progressing in fits and starts. Some efforts were more successful than others, but gradually momentum has built to ensure more successes than failures and a more settled common sense of anti-impunity commitments defining international institutions and informing the global commons. Thus, he settles on an optimistic note that "human rights and accountability have become almost an expected part of the Western agenda ... after so many reversals and failures in modern history, one may be forgiven for temporarily dropping the habitual gloom."[41]

A. *Constantinople*

Bass begins his story of Constantinople in the waning days of World War I where claims regarding Ottoman and German atrocities culminated in a focus on the Armenian genocide.[42] In the aftermath of World War I, the discussions at the Paris Peace Conference empowered the Allies to pursue war crimes trials on two fronts: at Leipzig via the Treaty of Versailles and in Constantinople via the Treaty of Sèvres. The former was focused primarily on German perpetrators with some debate regarding the appropriate forum for the trial of Kaiser Wilhelm II (who had escaped to the Netherlands), and the latter focused primarily on the leadership of the Ottoman empire in its waning days for crimes that occurred simultaneously with, but outside, the immediate dynamics of World War I. Bass describes how the Peace Conference established a multi-national Commission of Responsibilities that was tasked with addressing questions of criminal accountability and a prosecution agenda.[43] Interested in the particular role of "liberal states," Bass notes that although the Commission was staffed by representatives of all of the Allies, from the beginning of the process it was the British who were most invested in individual criminal accountability.[44] The Commission of Responsibilities drafted provisions for the trials called for by the Treaty of Sèvres between the Ottoman Empire and the Allies.[45] Given its early invocation of "crimes against humanity," the Commission described the mandate of the Treaty as a focus on both "the laws and customs of war" and "the laws of humanity," thus calling for prosecution of both "war crimes" and "crimes against the laws of humanity" that took place during the period of the war.[46] Bass applauds the invocation of crimes against humanity for yoking universalist empathy to prosecutions: "Britain's universalist indignation found its expression in legalism: a demand that the Young Turks be held individually criminally accountable."[47] The Turkish Grand Vizier, foreign ministers, justice ministers, and other senior officials were taken into custody and awaited trial. However, eventually these efforts fell apart for reasons that range from geopolitical horse-trading to the Turkish civil war to questions of evidence. If it had succeeded, Bass says wistfully, this "might have been Nuremberg."[48]

In Bass's rendering, this is a story in which the Allies, and in particular the British, made a valiant effort to fight impunity even prior to the actual signing of the Treaty of Sèvres in August 1920. While some key figures had already fled to Germany, a number of arrests were made and a martial court began operating in Constantinople from 1919–1920. Judgments were handed down and those found guilty were sentenced to long-term imprisonment or given the death penalty. The courts martial were eventually halted, Bass says, because of political backlash in Turkey and the weakness of the Turkish judicial system. The whole process became politicized by all sides with some trials used for partisan gain, some prisoners released in response to nationalist pressure, and the executed celebrated as martyrs. British investment in the Turkish trials eroded and they shifted their attention to the Malta International Court that was to be set up by the Treaty of Sèvres. In fact, the British arranged for the transfer of prisoners from the martial court in Constantinople to British custody in Malta, and began processing their cases anew in anticipation of an international court established by the peace treaty between the Allies and the Ottomans.

Bass's account describes the British as high-minded adherents to legalism, committed both to accountability for the Armenians but also to due process so that the approach to the trials evidenced political will and exemplified judicial propriety. British plans ran aground for a number of reasons that Bass recounts, some having to do with the trials themselves, and others having to deal with larger political dynamics.[49] Thus, for a range of reasons, national, regional, and global, the follow-up to Constantinople did not take place as envisioned and the Malta tribunal was never established. Bass considers the Constantinople affair (and to a lesser extent the companion effort in Leipzig that resulted from negotiations that emerged from the Treaty of Versailles) to have been an early effort against impunity. While the Turkish martial court was flawed and its work foreshortened, and the tribunal at Malta never materialized, Bass sees the British engagement with this process as an important effort within the larger movement of international justice. He repeatedly cites the category of "crimes against humanity" that became codified in 1945 as having been birthed in this earlier moment.[50] Similarly, he argues that British efforts toward accountability for violations against the Armenians reflected a universalist approach to criminal justice. For Bass, this universalist impulse is a critical element of liberal states' capacity for cosmopolitan humanism and the key to understanding that potential in the register of ethics rather than politics.

What is striking about Bass's discussion of impunity and the Constantinople moment is that he pays little attention to impunity for war crimes by the Allies – crimes that are many, varied, and well-documented. From the summary execution of prisoners of war[51] to the use of poison gas, the British and many (if not all) of the Allies were in clear violation of international law on many fronts. Yet there was little attention paid to these abuses. Indeed, in the case of Britain, war crimes and colonial violence were interlinked. Gases used in the battlefield against German soldiers, and then against the Bolsheviks, were later used against rebels in Afghanistan by the British Raj.[52] The World

War I trials were understood not as anti-impunity efforts but as victors' justice not only by many Germans and Turks but even by some of the Allies.[53]

In many ways, the most interesting dimension of the Constantinople and Leipzig war crimes processes is their role as decoy, clouding the fact that the real action was the land grab that was enabled by the military defeat of the Central powers. Lenin famously condemned World War I as a war that was driven by territorial greed.[54] Indeed, the Allies occupied German colonial territories within days of the war beginning. By 1918, Britain had acquired or dominated all German colonial territory and the Peace of Versailles further clarified the dispossession of Germany's territorial reach within Europe.[55] France took control of Alsace-Lorraine, and many German territorial domains were placed under League of Nations protectorate.

Even more significant were the partition of the Ottoman Empire and a redistribution of those territories to Allied control. In the early years of the war, Britain and France, with the support of czarist Russia, made a secret agreement (the "Asia Minor Agreement") clarifying their ambitions for the spoils of the Ottoman Empire. The Bolsheviks ultimately exposed the agreement after the 1917 revolution.[56] This unveiling of imperial motivations may have resulted in embarrassment to the Allies but it did not interfere with the impunity the latter enjoyed. Following the 1918 Armistice of Mudros, the Allies occupied Constantinople even before the end of the war and began planning for the dismemberment that could enable a post-Ottoman cartography.[57] The Treaty of Sèvres provided for terms that were hugely detrimental to Turkey, with all financial control being taken over by the Allies and a range of territorial reallocations, most notably the creation of the Mandate system, with provision for British control over Iraq and Palestine and French control over Lebanon and Syria.[58]

Bass's discussion of Constantinople as reflecting a high-minded universalist solidarity with the Armenians ignores the underside to the Allies' imperial investment in the defeat and discrediting of the Ottoman leadership. This investment helped enable the expansion of British and French territorial holdings and political influence over hugely expanded empires. Yet a focus on anti-impunity and war crimes does important work in seeking to legitimize the post-war conduct of the Allies distracting from everything else that took place in the aftermath of war, including the partitioning of the Ottoman territory amongst themselves. The assertion of moral authority helped grease the wheels of colonial political authority exercised through the mandate system.[59] The focus on "extraordinary" crimes and genocide also crowds out what was then ordinary: the routinized large-scale violence of empire.[60] Thus the Constantinople affair was not only a pivot for the simultaneous operation of impunity and anti-impunity, it also conveys that the struggle over impunity was itself a fig leaf for the expansion and consolidation of European empire.

B. Nuremberg

Nuremberg looms large in the history of anti-impunity efforts.[61] The trials are presented as performatively enacting the Allies' moral authority in the defeat of fascism. Nuremberg is the linchpin that helps connect the cosmopolitan humanist dots from Constantinople to The Hague and places that connection on a progressive narrative of an international law increasingly focused on the fight against impunity and the forces of global criminality. In Bass's narrative, Constantinople represented the World War I moment of a burgeoning universalism and the accompanying notion that humanity had a common stake in the conduct of war and peace. For him, this is the moment from which we can invoke humanity in applauding transnational solidarities and condemning crimes that were so egregious as to be considered crimes against humanity. Yet these anti-impunity intentions did not materialize in robust prosecutions of World War I war crimes. It is this gap between intent and legal action that was corrected with Nuremberg. Bass describes Nuremberg as a triumph against all odds. Indeed, when Roosevelt and Churchill met in Quebec to discuss policy for the war's end, they both signed a statement agreeing to summarily execute Nazi leadership.[62] For Bass, the shift from executions to trials is a shift from vengeance to liberal legalism that pulls the aftermath of World War II into the human rights history books. Bass describes the change in policy as one that emerged through a series of "David against Goliath" battles fought in the realms of public opinion,[63] policy making,[64] and international diplomacy[65] to become "the most significant tribute that power has ever paid to reason."[66]

Bass seeks to do several things in his depiction of the Nuremberg court as the unlikely hero of the postwar settlement. Most significantly, he wants to cast criminal prosecutions as an astonishing achievement of universalist ideals which emerge through an epic struggle against numerous obstacles and wide-ranging opposition. Anti-impunity represents, in this narrative, the best of the American system's cosmopolitan promise. Quoting Stimson's advocacy as an effort to reform Germans "with the Bill of Rights and the Supreme Court," Bass describes it as a "trial proposal" that emerges from "the Constitution, the holy of holies in American domestic politics."[67] It is a humanist vision that perseveres against the forces of evil but also against those with a lesser commitment to ensuring individual accountability for that evil, even when the victims are not one's own compatriots.

In addition to a celebration of Nuremberg in its own historical context, Bass's broader narrative is also interested in laying the case for historical continuity through the progress made by liberal states in world affairs. From Constantinople to Nuremberg, the mantle of liberal idealism shifts from Britain to the United States as the voice of progress in a universalist struggle against impunity. Bass describes progress as difficult and gradual but with an unmistakable direction, making him heavily invested in situating Nuremberg in the trajectory launched in Constantinople. He locates the impulse to prosecute crimes against humanity as emerging from the ashes of World War I, and celebrates Nuremberg as the next step in the progress of anti-impunity forces. Bass notes repeatedly that this step forward is not to be taken for granted. It was not inevitable; Nuremberg was the majestic achievement of high-minded commitment to legalism despite the lesser resolve of allies and fellow travelers.

If we step back from Bass's optimistic endorsement, the post-war moment looks slightly different. Indeed, with clear parallels to Constantinople, Nuremberg and Tokyo emerge not only as symbols of the struggle against impunity, but as icons of impunity facilitating the equation of victors' justice with justice as such.[68] The London Charter, or the Charter of the International Military Tribunal as it is officially titled (and to which Bass gives the Americans the central role in establishing), details the mandate and procedure of the Nuremberg trials. It was signed by the Allies on August 8, 1945, sandwiched between the US bombing of Hiroshima on August 6 and Nagasaki on August 9. The fact that these three events took place in the same week renders it less than persuasive that this was a choice of anti-impunity over impunity, of American liberal legalism over vengeance, or even, in the words of Robert Jackson, of reason over power.[69] Rather, it suggests that anti-impunity and impunity are intricately related.

There are many different ways in which to understand this relationship. Perhaps most prominent is a view that this linkage is key to the notion of exceptionalism that fuels American empire[70] even where the notion of America as an imperial power is either denied[71] or understood as benevolent when deployed in the service of democracy and liberty.[72] More than any other country in Bass's story, the United States is the definitive liberal state advancing and embodying human rights ideals. These contradictions may not simply be dimensions of American empire, but may well be more central to liberalism and the world order which it birthed: From the nation-state[73] and international law;[74] from human rights[75] and "humanitarian reason."[76] This "dark side of virtue"[77] may be central to the foundational concepts of liberalism and their institutional embodiment. Indeed, this may be the geopolitical projection of the psychological construction of selfhood, where splitting the domain of impunity and the domain of anti-impunity is also a negotiation between those two domains and the actors relevant to each.[78]

What is most relevant for the argument here is that the anti-impunity reach of Nuremberg (not to mention Tokyo) was carefully delimited. The London Charter not only sidestepped its brothers Hiroshima and Nagasaki, it also ignored a host of allegations about Allied war crimes that had taken place over the duration of the war.[79] These crimes included civilian air raids such as the bombing of Dresden by the British and Americans,[80] wartime rapes by occupying Russian soldiers in Berlin, the killing of German prisoners of war in Dachau, and many more acts of torture, ill treatment, and killings of both civilians and enemy combatants.[81] The London Charter designates the court's subject matter jurisdiction as crimes against peace (a precursor to the modern crime of aggression), war crimes, and crimes against humanity. However, the Charter also indicates that this is not a "universalist" approach to these crimes: rather, the Tribunal was established "for the trial and punishment" of persons committing these crimes only when they are "acting in the interests of the European Axis countries."[82] Thus, the statement of the Court's jurisdiction is simultaneously an act of anti-impunity as well as an act of impunity.

Significantly, Bass's narration of the Nuremberg story focuses primarily on the development of an American post-war policy on trials and the negotiations amongst the Allies that led to the London Charter. There is very little on the actual trials themselves, and he pays no attention to the specifics of the cases or what Jackson, in his summation, described as the "trials' mad and melancholy record."[83] The establishment of the court emerges as sufficient achievement for anti-impunity. However, and as with Constantinople, there is value in taking Nuremberg outside the debate about the pros and cons of anti-impunity efforts to understand its significance, because here too we can see the impunity conversation is a footnote to a larger project. In particular, there is value in looking at the work done by Nuremberg in the post-war global landscape: a performative enactment of exceptionalism for a world audience (one which continues to be performed to this day)[84] to amplify the moral authority claimed by the Allies in shaping the post-war world order. Already, the framing of the war effort itself as a fight for democracy and liberty distracted from the embarrassment of colonialism, not only on the global stage but also in various national theaters.[85] However, going forward, what would prove even more significant would be Nuremberg's place in the architecture of global governance.

The narrative of Nuremberg as an ode to liberal global governance is an anthem to the post-war world order and its claim to universalist legitimacy. Perhaps this is why even the details of the trials are ignored by Bass: the institution of the court itself satisfies the anti-impunity project. It contributes to the endorsement of the position of the Allies as arbiters of a new world order in which their military victory is entrenched not only through the design of the Security Council but also through the international financial institutions (IFIs) established in that same period. The United Nations and the Security Council were established in October 1945. Only a few weeks later, in November 1945, the Nuremberg trials got underway. The next month, the International Monetary Fund was established.[86] The momentous international institution-building that took place in the last three months of 1945 is, of course, deeply linked. Elizabeth Bogwardt has argued that Nuremberg, Bretton Woods, and the United Nations were the closely linked three-part institutional architecture designed to empower America in post-war global governance.[87] Bogwardt describes this brave new world as an achievement bringing to life the blueprint of the 1941 Atlantic Charter that expressed the United Kingdom's and United States' joint interests. In the Atlantic Charter, the Anglo-American alliance declared that "[a]fter the final destruction of Nazi tyranny," it aimed "to see established a peace which will … afford assurance that all the men in all the lands may live out their lives in freedom from fear and want," thereby employing various euphemisms which linked the agenda of fighting the Nazis with the military and economic agendas of the Allies.[88]

The most significant implication of the story of the three interlinked post-war institutional projects resituates Nuremberg in the wider landscape of global governance in relation both to "peace and security," as well as to trade and political economy. This allows us to see a different kind of continuity with the role of the ad hoc tribunals and the ICC: not in legitimizing specific struggles against impunity but in legitimizing the dominant structures of global governance. If Nuremberg provided closure for World War II in ways that fed into a redemptive history endorsing the post-war settlement, then arguably the Hague institutions had a parallel function in the aftermath of the Cold War.

C. The Hague

The Hague is the venue for the final saga in Bass's argument that there has been a fight against impunity over the course of the last century. Bass's primary preoccupation in this chapter is the war in the former Yugoslavia and the establishment of the International Criminal Tribunal for the Former Yugoslavia (ICTY) in response to that war. He sees liberal states as punching below their weight in world affairs and wishes they had taken a more aggressive role to "stop the slaughters."[89] Having abdicated this responsibility, he sees criminal prosecutions holding Milošević, Tadić, and others responsible for the slaughter as critical: "Legalism will never make up for the lives lost but legalism is all we have now."[90]

Bass also sees the work of the ICTY as a kind of gateway drug to the "tribunalization of justice," including both the International Criminal Tribunal for Rwanda (ICTR) and the ICC.[91] If this tribunalization has been gradually gaining momentum, then it is at The Hague where we finally get to the point of no return. Not only have the forces of anti-impunity racked up more points in the win column than the loss column in the courtroom; they have also succeeded in creating a new normative common sense in the world of international law and policy. The story of the ascendance of criminal prosecutions in The Hague is less a flashy three-month spell of global institution-building and more an extended effort to change hearts, minds, and foreign policy priorities.

As noted earlier, in his discussion of Nuremberg, Bass is content to ignore the trial details and describe the establishment of the institution of the Court as itself a strike against impunity. In contrast, in his discussion of the Hague era, Bass is much more focused on the granular unfolding of the ICTY trials where the struggle against impunity continues in the course of the trials themselves. From discussions about legal strategy in the Office of the Prosecutor, to the challenges of gathering evidence in mass graves, to questions of budget and salaries, to the challenge of detaining the indicted. in Bass's narrative of the Hague period, these are all different battles in the larger war against impunity. The (perhaps unconscious) contrast between the Nuremburg and The Hague narratives is striking and tells its own story about how these initiatives fit within their larger historical moment. Thus, Bass's description of The Hague is less "a mad and melancholy record" of genocidal horrors and more a record of activists inside and outside Hague institutions taking on the negotiation of bureaucratic hurdles and political jostling.[92] While Nuremberg bejewels a narrative of high purpose, Bass's story about the ICTY pulls it into a narrative about the hard slog of emerging from the Cold War to push toward a new institutional turn to international criminal justice, and a new normative turn toward anti-impunity in more and more contexts.

The ICTY proved to be the first post-Cold War battleground for this push; according to Bass, the new normative turn was achieved by fighting against the headwinds of competing foreign policy priorities on the part of "liberal states," and indifference, or even active embrace of impunity, by "illiberal" ones. Thus, in this inaugural post-Cold War tribunal, the double standard is not between victors and non-victors – as at Nuremburg – but between liberal and illiberal, which, in turn, becomes the zoning principle of moral, political, and juridical power on the post-Cold War global stage.[93] Anti-impunity initiatives benefit not only from the liberal triumphalism associated with Cold War victory laps but also from having Washington Consensus discourses such as "good governance" and "failed states" as fellow travelers. All of these factors come together in helping to normalize the double standard and empower liberal states and their civil society allies as especially qualified to give content to the idea of anti-impunity.[94]

It is a telling window into the historical moment that, unlike the story Bass tells about Constantinople and Nuremberg, a distinctive dimension of his Hague story is that Western states do not have the same decisive role in defining the agenda; rather, they lead from behind. As Bass narrates it, the real architects of the anti-impunity institutions in The Hague are zealous human rights advocates. In some cases these are organizations such as Human Rights Watch; in others, they are individuals in powerful positions such as Cherif Bassiouni or Madeline Albright. In the 1990s – the decade that launched the Hague period – states, even liberal states, lost their glow. Neoliberal discourse became hegemonic and the heroes of human rights became individuals and civil society organizations – "social change" entrepreneurs compatible with the neoliberal logics of that decade.[95] When the United Nations was slow to fund the Tribunal, entrepreneurial Tribunal staff turned to the MacArthur and Soros Foundations for funds.

The United Nations emerges in this drama as more obstructionist than helpful: slow, bureaucratic, and uncommitted to fighting impunity, it is dragged into supporting the ICTY kicking and screaming. Bass argues that liberal states have a mixed record[96] but ultimately, even if they were not able to prevent the atrocities that accompanied the dismemberment of the former Yugoslavia, Bass celebrates them for generating awareness of those atrocities and for building the requisite political will to hold to account those responsible.

Moreover, Bass sees forward movement for the future. While the ICTY is the last big institutional project he addresses, he is heartened that the ICTY was followed by the establishment of the ICTR, the courts in Sierra Leone and Cambodia, and the passage of the Rome Statute and the creation of the ICC. These developments, it is suggested, are evidence that the indictment-by-indictment effort finally got traction in the struggle to stay the hand of vengeance and give deference to international criminal tribunals.

Perhaps in keeping with Bass's deference to a more chastened role for liberal states in the anti-impunity struggles of the Hague moment, in this last section of the book he is also ready to cede some ground to the "double standards" critics – as long as he can still redeem the progress narrative of liberal cosmopolitanism. Thus, when he cedes "double standards" vis-à-vis "liberal" states, he rests the concession on criticizing the fact "that some victims count more than others" and that the Americans or the British are slower to act on behalf of the Rwandans or the Bosnian Muslims than if American or British citizens were at risk.[97] He skirts around the notion that perpetrators in "liberal" states act with impunity and narrows his discussion of perpetrators from powerful states to Russia or China[98] – countries he condemns as patrons of impunity who could, at most, be cajoled into supporting, or at least not obstructing, institutional developments in international criminal justice. In the case of the United States, he is keener to manage charges of US double standards as ones that are not fundamentally threatening to the broader historical movement toward anti-impunity. While he laments the USA not becoming a party to the ICC, he is also eager to explain this as something other than impunity in relation to its own actions. He does this by arguing that the Bush administration's fears about frivolous charges against the United States were not unfounded, and asserts that a "tribunal that could pass and enforce judgments against all countries, weak and strong" could be manipulated by nationalists of Milošević's ilk.[99] Most significantly, he isolates United States atrocities in the Vietnam-era as aberrations and applauds a "country whose military deserves praise for teaching its soldiers the laws of war."[100]

Bass's effort to narrow the discussion of US war crimes to Vietnam functions as an exculpatory narrative regarding a range of other theaters of war, be they direct or indirect engagements, ranging from Nicaragua to the first Gulf War, Angola to Guatemala, Indonesia to El Salvador, or even the Kosovo bombings themselves. Moreover, Bass's citations to policy makers such as Kissinger or military personal such as McNamara and Kerrey keeps the focus on individuals with bad records – bad apples, not bad structures.

The contours of the anti-impunity conversation so celebrated in the Hague era performs and legitimates an accountability discourse centered on individual culpability for international crimes rather than the structural arrangements of trade and aid that facilitate conditions of life and debt that should be criminal. Indeed, even the individualizing focus of Hague era anti-impunity efforts narrow the gaze to the local rather than the transnational: the petty warlord recruiting children to fight resource wars and their proxy battles rather than the global corporate CEO profiting from those same resource wars and exploited child combatants.

These asymmetries in the criminal prosecution of international crimes are, however, beside the point in some respects. The concern here is not about a non-comprehensive legalism but a concern about who benefits from narrowing the conversation to the terrain of international criminal law, the monstrous perpetrators it ensnares, and the definitions of accountability and atrocity it generates. In the current "Hague" period, the discursive economies and institutional projects of anti-impunity became incorporated into the dominant logics of global governance. Central to this project is the empowerment of the notion of liberal states as being (even when politically driven and inconsistent) on the side of the angels in the larger arc of anti-impunity trends – a side that is on the right side of history and progress and better suited for leadership in global governance. In addition to international criminal law, contemporary global governance entails a number of related projects that range from nation-building to humanitarian intervention to "counter-terrorism." Central to the imagination and regulation of violence in these different realms is greater impunity for structures and policies facilitating the dominant forces of global governance. It is this broader trend insulating the dominant global order from accountability – which is to say, ensuring impunity – which is twinned with the turn toward anti-impunity in international criminal law.

III. CONCLUSION

This paper has focused on Bass, but the issues it raises are hardly specific to his thesis. As discussed earlier, a range of scholars support the claim that there has been a distinctive turn to anti-impunity over the last two decades. Moreover, many also draw a path from Nuremberg to the ICC in establishing the importance of prosecution. Some speak of domestic law, as opposed to Bass's preoccupation with international tribunals, but they all tell markedly parallel stories regarding the historic momentum of anti-impunity.

The ambitious century-long scope of Bass's anti-impunity narrative, and the intertwined role of legal argument and political maneuvering in his portrayal of international courts, makes him a particularly valuable interlocutor in engaging with claims about the direction of international law. Bass sees a unidirectional arrow from Constantinople to Nuremberg to The Hague. Strategic jostling by key political players on the international stage, the gradual development of a global human rights consciousness, international institutions, and the professional activists who staffed them all play a role in ensuring this arrow stayed its course. In Bass's story, although the anti-impunity arrow may shoot straight ahead in some periods, while lurching forward unsteadily in others, the directionality is one of liberal states becoming more "liberal" and matching their political behavior to their political ethics.

In contrast to Bass's account, we have foregrounded arrows whizzing in other directions, including toward impunity. Arrows nominally traveling in opposing directions may, in fact, work in tandem – for example, when an anti-impunity narrative regarding international crimes helps to legitimate grounds for impunity (be it for other war crimes or for "routinized" crimes that are generated by, or embedded in, the dominant order). Moreover, at various historical junctures the significance of international criminal tribunals may not lie in their anti-impunity work but in dynamics that pertain to other dimensions of international politics. These range from the transnational land grabs for the territories formerly controlled by the Ottoman Empire that accompanied Constantinople, to the establishment of the IFIs and related institutions alongside Nuremberg, to structural adjustment, humanitarian intervention, and the many faces of post-Cold War global governance projects which have emerged alongside the Hague prosecutions. Significantly, in all these contexts, anti-impunity projects may have legitimized the dominant global order in the name of liberal political ethics and therefore helped entrench impunity in other realms.

In my counter-account, I have highlighted how the domain of anti-impunity initiatives in international criminal law has been limited to certain demarcated zones – primarily war crimes, crimes against humanity, genocide, and crimes of aggression (and their canonical definitions) – while there has been wide impunity for atrocities such as exploitative terms of international trade which enable and condition socio-economic abuses. Similarly, my counter-narrative has drawn attention to the ways in which the mantle of legitimacy that is vested in claims to anti-impunity has authorized companion agendas by association and delegitimized challenges to the dominant order as ones that risk empowering war criminals and criminal regimes. In other words, the dominance of the narrative that there is a turn to anti-impunity is itself doing work that I have aimed to unpack and critique.

Through this extended critical engagement with Bass, this chapter has sought to situate the notion of "anti-impunity," not as a trans-historical high-minded ideal that travels from Constantinople to The Hague, but as one that has had particular and contested backstories with specific political stakes in each of these moments of "tribunalizing justice." By foregrounding the structures and interpretive disputes that attend invocations of anti-impunity, we can look at what work "anti-impunity" is actually doing in relation to specific contexts – whether in the post-Ottoman scramble for territory at the end of World War I or in the narrowing of the human rights agenda to accountability only for extraordinary as opposed to ordinary violence, or for individuals rather than structures. Only a situated analysis of the social context and political dynamics of invocations of anti-impunity will allow us to understand the meaning of what an institution such as the ICTY does beyond the four walls of its courtroom, including who it benefits and who it hurts. In this way, questions of political economy, distribution, and redistribution become central to how we interpret anti-impunity initiatives and situate their relationship to global governance as a whole.

For many who describe and celebrate the anti-impunity turn, it is not only an effort to empower international criminal law as we know it, but also a claim about the value of legalism and the possibility of divorcing law from politics. International law (like all law) is seen to achieve greater legitimacy if it is less subject to political maneuvering. This is a familiar line of justification from advocates of the ICC who applaud the Court as a historically momentous stride against impunity because "it has accelerated moves away from politics and towards ethics in international relations."[101] The celebrants of the "anti-impunity" narrative do not claim that law is divorced from politics. Rather, and significantly, they reduce the political to the realm of realpolitik[102] and see liberal states as driven by some combination of cosmopolitan humanist ethics and statist interest in its own citizenry. For instance, scholars such as Bass situate the ICTY as emerging from a combination of NATO states politicking over their own interests and a push by human rights activists (in and outside those same governments) for an ethical response. This framing does enormous work as a redemptive narrative celebrating liberal pieties and preemptively immunizing liberal states so that "it is possible to see liberal states pursuing a foreign policy that is in the interests of humanity."[103] In contrast, this attempt to rehistoricize international criminal tribunals can also be understood as an effort to parochialize concepts such as impunity or anti-impunity but most importantly, to parochialize the invocation of "the interests of humanity."[104]

NOTES

1 See, e.g., Manu Bhagavan, *India and the Quest for One World: The Peacemakers* (New York: Palgrave Macmillan, 2013); Jenny S. Martinez, *The Slave Trade and the Origins of International Human Rights Law* (Oxford: Oxford University Press, 2012); Samuel Moyn, *The Last Utopia: Human Rights in History* (Cambridge, MA: Harvard University Press, 2010); Lynn Hunt, *Inventing Human Rights: A History* (New York: W.W. Norton, 2007); Gary Bass, *Stay the Hand of Vengeance: The Politics of War Crimes Tribunals* (Princeton: Princeton University Press, 2000).

2 For instance, Lynn Hunt pegs the origin moment in the 1700s and Samuel Moyn places it in the 1970s, but both tell a story that leads in significantly parallel lines to the present moment. By and large, for both of them this is a story about the movement of ideas and political movements across the Atlantic, from Europe to the United States and back again. Hunt, *Inventing Human Rights*, and Moyn, *The Last Utopia*.

3 As Moyn notes, in providing "backstories to the vogue of human rights" these histories risk distorting "the past to suit the present." Samuel Moyn, "On the

Genealogy of Morals," *The Nation*, March 29, 2007, accessed June 3, 2015, www.thenation.com/article/genealogy-morals. That said, not all of these scholars see their primary agenda as a history of human rights; however, their narrative of that history is critical to the intervention they seek to advance. For instance, Bass explores the twentieth century history of war crimes tribunals to marshal arguments for his debate with other international relations theorists about why liberal states have advocated war crimes tribunals; Bhagavan explores the mid-twentieth century to make an argument about the influence of the Nehru government in shaping the institutionalization of human rights within the UN. Moyn explores the history of human rights in the USA and Europe in the 1970s to make an argument about the politics of human rights. Bass, *Stay the Hand of Vengeance*; Moyn, *The Last Utopia*; Bhagavan, *India and the Quest for One World*.

4 Naomi Roht-Arriaza, "Combating Immunity: Some Thoughts on the Way Forward," *Law and Contemporary Problems* 59, no. 4 (1996): 93–102, 95.

5 For Bass liberal states are driven by a political idealism in domestic affairs that seeps into their international relations, and the history of war crime tribunals offers a potent window into this idealism. He notes "Liberal states commonly see their foes not as mere enemies but as war criminals deserving punishment." Bass, *Hand of Vengeance*, 35.

6 Ellen Lutz and Kathryn Sikkink, "The Justice Cascade: The Evolution and Impact of Foreign Human Rights Trials in Latin America," *Chicago Journal of International Law* 2, no 1 (2001): 1–34

7 Bass, *Hand of Vengeance*.

8 Ibid., 329.

9 As Bass tells the story, liberal states have a high-minded commitment to anti-impunity but these noble ideals are not upheld consistently. Liberal states will not compromise the safety of their own citizens. Moreover, when the victims of war criminals are not their own citizens but foreigners, they may be slower off the start line. Ibid., 28–36.

10 As exemplified for instance by Nuremberg in contrast to Stalin's prescription for mass executions. Ibid., 186.

11 Ibid., 328–29.

12 I rely primarily on the language of anti-impunity and struggles against impunity throughout this chapter to underscore how Bass's analysis is in conversation with the themes of this book.

13 "... liberal ideas make liberal states take up the cause of international justice, treating their humbled foes in a way utterly divorced from the methods practiced by illiberal states." Bass, *Hand of Vengeance*, 18.

14 Ibid., 28

15 Ibid., 329

16 Ibid., 106–46.

17 Ibid., 147–205.

18 Ibid., 206–276.

19 Bass's narrative is anchored by five historical moments that he links to the cities that were the stage for the initiatives he describes: St. Helena, Leipzig, Constantinople, Nuremberg, and The Hague. Given the space limitations, this chapter engages only with Bass's argument re: Constantinople, Nuremberg, and The Hague.

20 I borrow the term "slow violence" from Rob Nixon but use it to reference all long-term structural violence and not just the environmental degradation that Nixon highlights. Rob Nixon, *Slow Violence and the Environmentalism of the Poor* (Cambridge, MA: Harvard, 2011).

21 There are of course important differences on the specifics of their stories – for instance, in the relative significance of state and non-state actors, of the NATO states and the states of the Global South, etc. – and their interlocutors.

22 Citing a whole range of examples from the ICC to the hybrid tribunals to domestic accountability efforts, he concludes that "There are enough signs of progress that, after so many reversals and failures in modern history, one can be forgiven for temporarily dropping the habitual gloom." Bass, *Hand of Vengeance*, 324.

23 "Is the International Community Abandoning the Fight Against Impunity?," *International Center for Transitional Justice*, February 9, 2015, accessed June 3, 2015, www.ictj.org/debate/impunity/opening-remarks.

24 Zeid Ra'ad Al Hussein, "Despite Setbacks, Fight Against Impunity Continues," *International Center for Transitional Justice*, February 9, 2015, accessed June 3, 2015, www.ictj.org/debate/article/despite-setbacks-fight-against-impunity-continues.

25 Bass, *Hand of Vengeance*, 324.

26 For discussions of the evolution of this trend, its endorsement in human rights and international criminal law, and its claims to speak for victims, see Karen Engle's and Samuel Moyn's chapters in this volume.

27 Kathryn Sikkink, "The Justice Cascade: Human Rights Prosecutions and Change in World Politics," *University of Pennsylvania Center for International Politics Speaker Series 2009–10* (2010): 1–67, 1, accessed June 3, 2015, https://bc.sas.upenn.edu/system/files/Sikkink_04.08.10.pdf.

28 Roht-Arriaza, "Combating Impunity," 93.

29 Ibid., 94.

30 For example, Christoph Safferling argues that we may have unrealistic and problematic expectations for what criminal justice can achieve in responding to mass human rights violations. Christoph Safferling, "Can Criminal Prosecution be the Answer to Massive Human Rights Violations?," *German Law Journal* 5 (2004): 1469–1488.

31 Mahmood Mamdani urges that framing the issues in the legalistic terms of victims and perpetrators may distract us from the distributive justice issues that could be apparent when we look at human rights issues in terms of victims and beneficiaries. Mahmood Mamdani, *When Victims Become Killers: Colonialism, Nativism and the Genocide in Rwanda* (Princeton; Princeton University Press, 2001). See also Vasuki Nesiah and Alan Keenan, who argue that the individualizing dimensions of a legalistic response misrepresents and distracts from the structural and systemic dimensions of human rights abuse in ways that have maldistributive effects. Vasuki Nesiah and Alan Keenan, "Human Rights and Sacred Cows: Framing Violence, Disappearing Struggles," *From the Margins of Globalization: Critical Perspectives on Human Rights*, ed. Neve Gordon (Lanham, MD: Lexington Books, 2004). See also chapters in this volume by Helena Alviar and Karen Engle, Karen Engle, and Zinaida Miller.

32 For example, Elena A. Baylis points to the important work that national courts can do and urges that this not be deprioritized in the turn to international criminal justice. Elena A. Baylis, "Reassessing the Role of International Criminal

Law: Rebuilding National Courts Through Transnational Networks," *Boston College Law Review* 50, no. 1 (2009): 1–85.

33 Hannah Arendt, *Eichmann in Jerusalem: A Report on the Banality of Evil* (New York: Penguin Books, 1992). Recently, Thabo Mbeki and Mamdani have argued along similar lines about the limits of courts in dealing with the complex, context-specific lines of responsibility that accompany civil wars where no parties are wholly innocent or wholly guilty. Thabo Mbeki and Mahmood Mamdani, "Courts Can't End Civil Wars," *New York Times*, February 5, 2014. See also Natalie Davidson's chapter in this volume.

34 See Mamdani, Victims Become Killers, and Adam Branch, "Uganda's Civil War and the Politics of ICC Intervention," *Ethics and International Affairs* 21, no. 2 (2007): 179–198.

35 See Richard Falk, "Opposing Impunity for Geopolitical Criminality," *Foreign Policy Journal*, April 6, 2015, accessed May 26, 2015, www.foreignpolicyjournal.com/2015/04/06/opposing-impunity-for-geopolitical-criminality/. See also *Genocide, War Crimes and the West: History and Complicity*, ed. Adam Jones (London: Zed Books, 2004).

36 William Schabas (in interview by *World Politics Review* editors), "Global Insider," *World Politics Review*, March 19, 2013, accessed May 26, 2015, www.worldpoliticsreview.com/trend-lines/12798/global-insider-ten-years-in-icc-s-acquittal-rate-is-extraordinarily-high.

37 For instance, we may see the work of the ICTY as doing different kinds of work, including helping effect the distinction between liberal/illiberal states that would feed into notions of failed states that became central to post cold-war global governance projects. Anne-Marie Slaughter offered a prominent defense of this distinction in "International Law in a World of Liberal States," *European Journal of International Law* 6, no. 1 (1995): 503–538.

38 Bass advocates for war crimes tribunals as an antidote to universal jurisdiction. Bass, *Hand of Vengeance*, 328–329.

39 Bass himself manifests this when celebrating the ICC while expressing sympathy for US arguments for not becoming a signatory. Bass, *Hand of Vengeance*, 326.

40 For instance, it was efforts to address the impunity of US and Israeli officials that was the critical catalyst in the defeat of universal jurisdiction. See ibid.; Falk, "Opposing Impunity."

41 Bass, *Hand of Vengeance*, 324.

42 Bass says the British began pressuring the Turks to make arrests of those responsible for atrocities against the Armenians even before the war ended. Ibid., 117, 119.

43 Ibid., 100. See also Commission on the Responsibility of the Authors of the War and on Enforcement of Penalties, *American Journal of International Law* 14, no. 1/2 (Jan.–Apr., 1920): 95–154.

44 Bass, *Hand of Vengeance*, 80–82.

45 The Commission also helped draft provisions of the Treaty of Versailles that called for the arrest and trial of a designated list of German officials for war crimes in tribunals established by the Allies. After negotiations with the post-war German government, the forum of prosecution was shifted to Leipzig and the German judicial system. While the Allies' initial list contained almost a thousand names, eventually only a dozen were brought to trial and the Leipzig war crimes trials faded into obscurity as flawed and failed experiments.

46 The notion of crimes against humanity is prefigured in the 1915 Allied Joint Declaration; a Declaration that is little recognized but significant in the history of anti-impunity efforts for the first mention of crimes against humanity and the precursor to its codification in Nuremberg and its mainstreaming in contemporary international criminal law. Sévane Garibian, "From the 1915 Allied Joint Declaration to the 1920 Treaty of Sevres: Back to an International Criminal Law in Progress," *The Armenian Review* 52, no 1/2 (2010): 86–103, 90. When the war-time "warning" of 1915 finds its way into the prosecution provisions of the post-war Treaty of Sèvres, Bass describes the effort to try Ottoman officials "as a striking display of British idealism and universalism" since it focused not only on strikes against British but also a condemnation of crimes against Armenians that drew on "a liberal concept of universal rights." Bass, *Hand of Vengeance*, 106.

47 Ibid., 107.

48 Ibid., 107.

49 The British had to confront significant due process issues. Many of those imprisoned were identified through faulty lists; there was little forensic evidence even against those who were alleged to be guilty and it looked unlikely that they could develop cases that could produce convictions. Perhaps most significant, Churchill was much more interested in using the Turkish prisoners in Malta for leverage in obtaining the release of British prisoners in Turkish custody. The prisoner swap took place – and took the place of the tribunal. Ibid., 136–143.

50 Ibid., 116.

51 See, for example, discussion of the Baralong incidents where the British summarily executed German survivors of a submarine attack in Heather Jones, *Violence against Prisoners of War in the First World War: Britain, France and Germany, 1914–1920* (Cambridge: Cambridge University Press, 2013), 86–87.

52 James W. Hammond Jr., *Poison Gas: The Myths Versus Reality* (Westport: Greenwood Press, 1999), 13.

53 The USA famously withdrew its participation in the Allies' call for an expansive war crimes tribunal with jurisdiction directed at key Germany officials because President Woodrow Wilson and Secretary of State Robert Lansing thought that an exercise in victors' justice would engender German resentment and trigger a backlash that could destabilize the post-war settlement. Ibid., 93, 99–104.

54 "... the war of 1914–18 was imperialist (that is, an annexationist, predatory, war of plunder) on the part of both sides; it was a war for the division of the world, for partition and repartition of colonies and spheres of influence of finance capital, etc." Vladimir Lenin, "Imperialism, the Highest Stage of Capitalism," *The Lenin Anthology*, ed. Robert Tucker (New York: WW Norton, 1975), 204–276, 206.

55 Treaty of Peace between the Allied and Associated Powers and Germany [Treaty of Versailles] (June 28, 1919), http://avalon.law.yale.edu/subject_menus/versailles_menu.asp.

56 Asia Minor Agreement [Sykes-Picot Agreement], Britain-France (May 16, 1916), www.lib.byu.edu/index.php/Sykes-Picot_Agreement.

57 Paul C. Helmreich, *From Paris to Sèvres: The Partition of the Ottoman Empire at the Peace Conference of 1919–1920* (Columbus, OH: Ohio University Press, 1974).

58 Ibid.

59 For a discussion of the colonial logics of the mandate system, see Anthony Anghie, "Colonialism and the Birth of the International Institutions: Sovereignty, Economy and the Mandate System of the League of Nations,"*New York University Journal of International Law and Politics* 34, no. 3 (2002): 513–634.

60 For instance, in April 1919, even as the last phrases of the Treaty of Versailles were being negotiated (to be signed in June 1919), the British killed several hundred non-violent protestors within a few minutes in what has become known as the Amritsar massacre. Derek Sayer, "British Reaction to the Amritsar Massacre 1919–1920," *Past & Present* No. 131 (1991): 130–164. In the ensuing decades, even apart from such incidents or organized violence, millions of Indians died in famines as Indian grain was exported to Britain. These incidents signal the normalized dispensability of the colonized that is cemented by colonial logics of governance – governance that fails to interrupt the moral economies of anti-impunity invoked at Versailles, or British sympathy for Armenian victims of Turkey.

61 Significantly, Tokyo is referenced by Bass but largely ignored, as his primary pre-occupation is Nuremberg trials. This is the fate of Tokyo in most human rights histories.

62 Ibid., 151.

63 When the American public was surveyed, summary executions against the German and Japanese leadership trumped all other options in public opinion polls. The legalistic response became celebrated and framed in patriotic rhetoric regarding the American commitment to law only after the trials had begun. Indeed, for many, it was only after they were completed. Ibid., 169.

64 Bass pays much attention to the internal battle within the American cabinet, with Secretary of War Henry Stimson, who advocated trials, waging a long battle against Secretary of State Hans Morgenthau, who favored summary executions and the blitzing of German industrial power. President Roosevelt shifted to a more temperate position when it became apparent that it was more politically expedient to ensure Germany survived as a viable trading partner. Ibid., 169.

65 Bass layers his depiction of the internal policy battles within the higher echelons of American policymaking with an account of the external battles on the highest echelons of international relations. The US push for trials battled against the British and Soviet preference for the execution option. Eventually Robert Jackson, who later served as America's Chief Prosecutor in Nuremberg, negotiated terms for the London Charter that reflected the American vision for a war crimes tribunal. Finally, Bass notes that the scope of the Nuremberg prosecutions was also one that emerged through fraught negotiations within the USA and amongst allies. In the early stages of negotiation, there was much support for focusing only on acts of German aggression that entailed breaches of international law against other nations. There was doubt about whether there were political and legal grounds to also take on atrocities within Germany. Thus, initially the Holocaust itself was going to be sidestepped and treated as an internal matter. Eventually, however, with lobbying from the American Jewish diaspora and discussions within the American team negotiating the London charter, the US position called for a broader focus on anti-impunity. This expanded prosecution agenda succeeded in winning the day in negotiations with the allies as well. Ibid., 173–180.

66 Bass quotes Robert Jackson's opening statement at the trials to frame his own claims about Nuremberg's significance in the history of war crimes adjudication. Ibid., 147.

67 Ibid., 166, 164.

68 See also Mahmood Mamdani's chapter in this volume.

69 Jackson's opening statement for the Prosecution at Nuremberg gave Bass's book its subtitle and the broader theme that ties the fight against impunity for the wrongs of war to the legalist triumph over the quest for vengeance: "That four great nations, flushed with victory and stung with injury stay the hand of vengeance and voluntarily submit their captive enemies to the judgment of the law is one of the most significant tributes that Power has ever paid to Reason." "Second Day, Wednesday, 11/21/1945, Part 04," in Trial of the Major War Criminals before the International Military Tribunal, Volume II. Proceedings: 11/14/1945-11/30/1945 [Official English text] (Nuremberg: IMT, 1947), 98–102.

70 Obama, for instance, has employed the Nuremberg trials themselves to make the argument about American exceptionalism arguing that "the Nuremberg trials" were "part of what made us different" in ways that "taught the entire world about who we are." Barack Obama quoted in Jack Goldsmith, "The Shadow of Nuremberg," *New York Times, Sunday Book Review*, BR8 (January 22, 2012).

71 For example, in the wake of post 9/11 US strikes on Afghanistan in October 2001, the editors of *Monthly Review* began their November issue noting that "in Britain, empire was justified as a benevolent 'white man's burden.' And in the United States, empire does not even exist; 'we' are merely protecting the causes of freedom, democracy and justice worldwide." "After the Attack … The War on Terrorism," *Monthly Review* 53, no. 6 (2001), Note from the Editors.

72 See Michael Ignatieff, *Empire Lite: Nation Building in Bosnia, Kosovo, Afghanistan* (London: Vintage, 2003).

73 See Antony Anghie, *Imperialism, Sovereignty and the Making of International Law* (Cambridge: Cambridge University Press, 2005).

74 See Martii Koskenniemi, "Between Impunity and Show Trials," *Max Planck Yearbook of United Nations Law* 6 (2002): 1–35.

75 See Costas Douzinas, *Human Rights and Empire: The Political Philosophy of Cosmopolitanism* (Abingdon, Oxford: Routledge-Cavendish, 2007).

76 See Didier Fassin, *Humanitarian Reason: A Moral History of the Present*, trans. Rachel Gomme (Berkeley, CA: University of California Press, 2011).

77 See David Kennedy, *The Dark Sides of Virtue: Reassessing International Humanitarianism* (Princeton, NJ: Princeton University Press, 2004).

78 See Nathaniel Berman, *Passion and Ambivalence: Colonialism, Nationalism and International Law* (Leiden: Martinus Nijhoff, 2012).

79 See Eva Fauen, "Top 10 Allied War Crimes of World War II," December 14, 2012, accessed May 26, 2015, http://listverse.com/2012/12/14/top-10-allied-war-crimes-of-world-war-ii.

80 See Kurt Vonnegut, *Slaughterhouse Five* (New York: Random House, 1991); Richard Overy, "The Post-War Debate," *Firestorm: The Bombing of Dresden, 1945*, eds. Paul Addison and Jeremy Crang (Chicago, IL: Ivan R. Dee, 2006), 123–142.

81 See book by Herbert Marcuse's grandson, Harold Marcuse, *Legacies of Dachau: The Uses and Abuses of a Concentration Camp, 1933–2001* (Cambridge: Cambridge University Press, 2001).

82 Agreement for the Prosecution and Punishment of the Major War Criminals of the European Axis, and Charter of the International Military Tribunal (August 8, 1945), Chapter II, Art. 6.

83 "Trial of the Major War Criminals Before the International Military Tribunal, Nuremburg," Vol. 19 (Day 187), July 26, 1946, accessed May 26, 2015, http://avalon. law.yale.edu/imt/07-26-46.asp.

84 See Goldsmith, "The Shadow of Nuremberg," in conversation with President Obama.

85 For instance, see Auriol Weingold's story on Churchill's use of the war in catalyzing US animus towards the "Quit India" movement. Auriol Weingold, *Churchill, Roosevelt and India: Propaganda during WWII* (New York: Routledge, 2008).

86 More radical proposals, such as Keynes' proposal for an International Clearing Union to help debtor countries, were defeated by the Americans in favor of the IMF. George Monbiot, "Clearing Up This Mess," *The Guardian*, November 18, 2008.

87 Elizabeth Bogwardt, *A New Deal for the World: America's Vision for Human Rights* (Cambridge, MA: Harvard University Press, 2007).

88 The Atlantic Charter, August 14, 1941, accessed May 26, 2015, http://avalon.law.yale.edu/wwii/atlantic.asp.

89 Bass, *Hand of Vengeance*, 283.

90 Ibid.

91 For more on the "tribunalizing of justice," see Kamari Maxine Clarke, *Fictions of Justice: The International Criminal Court and the Challenge of Legal Pluralism in Sub-Saharan Africa* (Cambridge: Cambridge University Press, 2009).

92 Bass recounts the obstacles – political, military, economic, and bureaucratic – that needed to be surmounted. This included struggles to get the Security Council to pass a resolution establishing a tribunal, ensuring it got funded, staffing it with those competent and committed to the criminalization project, devising a legal strategy that reached those most responsible, and cooperation with NATO military forces to ensure that those indicted could be detained and brought to The Hague for trial. Ibid., 215, 219, 262–263.

93 See Slaughter, "International Law in a World of Liberal States."

94 As Clarke's analysis of the pre-ICC debates indicate, the particular content of the ICC mandate was not a foregone conclusion at the beginning of the discussions regarding an international court. It is only through the course of the '90s that this mandate narrowed to its current focus on individual culpability for "extraordinary" crimes such as genocide, crimes against humanity, and war crimes. See Clarke, *Fictions of Justice*.

95 For a critical perspective on the post-Cold War rise of "global civil society," see Neera Chandhoke, "The Limits of Global Civil Society," *Global Civil Society 2002*, eds. Helmut Anheier et al, (Oxford: Oxford University Press, 2002), 35–53. See also Ronaldo Munck, "Global Civil Society: Royal Road or Slipper Path?," *Voluntas: International Journal of Voluntary and Nonprofit Organisations* 17 (2006): 325–332.

96 France, and to some extent the United Kingdom, are more invested in negotiating terms for conflict resolution and safeguarding their troops; if the political climate for peace negotiations and troop safety is inhospitable to accountability processes, they bend towards impunity. In Bass's telling, the United States has a

greater commitment to reaching what he considers higher moral ground but only when US troops are not at risk. Bass, *Hand of Vengeance*, 224–227.

97 Ibid., 277–278.

98 Ibid., 325–326.

99 Ibid., 326.

100 Ibid., 327.

101 Kirsten Ainley, "The International Criminal Court on Trial," *Cambridge Review of International Affairs* 24, no. 3 (2011): 309–333, 309.

102 For instance, Ainley celebrates the ICC as moving "away from politics and towards ethics in international relations," while also saying that the ICC remains a politicized organization where the jockeying between states shape the ambit of the ICC's work. Ibid.

103 Gary Bass, *Freedom's Battle: The Origins of Humanitarian Intervention* (New York: Alfred A. Knopf, 2008), 24.

104 Dipesh Chakrabarty, *Parochializing Europe: Postcolonial Thought and Historical Difference* (Princeton, NJ: Princeton University Press, 2007).

PART II

HOW AND WHERE DOES ANTI-IMPUNITY OPERATE?

4

The South African Truth Commission and the AZAPO Case: A Reflection Almost Two Decades Later

D.M. Davis[*]

The adoption of this Constitution lays the secure foundation for the People of South Africa to transcend the divisions and strife of the past, which generated gross violations of human rights, the transgression of humanitarian principles in violent conflicts and the legacy of hatred, fear, guilt and revenge. These can now be addressed on the basis that there is a need for understanding but not vengeance, a need for reparation but not retaliation, a need for *ubuntu* but not for victimisation.

Constitution of the Republic of South Africa, Act 200 of 1993

In 1996, in *Azanian Peoples Organization (AZAPO) v. South Africa*,[1] the newly formed Constitutional Court of South Africa was confronted with a challenge to a key component of the negotiated settlement which had culminated in an agreement to a democratic constitution. The settlement, embodied in the Constitution,[2] called for the creation of a Truth and Reconciliation Commission (TRC), which was subsequently established in terms of the Promotion of National Unity and Reconciliation Act (Amnesty Act).[3] Of critical importance to the challenge was section 20 of the Act, which contained detailed provisions concerning amnesty for acts "associated with a political objective."[4] In the event that the Committee on Amnesty, established by the same law,[5] found that any act, omission, or offense was associated with a political objective as defined,[6] it had the power to grant amnesty. Once amnesty had been granted, the offender could no longer be held criminally liable for any offense which was related to the act or omission. No prosecution could be instituted against him or her. In addition, the offender could no longer be held civilly liable or personally accountable for the payment for damages sustained by a victim.[7] In short,

---

[*] I wish to acknowledge the insightful ideas which I gleaned from conversations with John and Jean Comaroff and Kate O'Regan.

no legal proceedings could be successfully pursued against any person who had been granted amnesty.

The majestic conception of a new society based upon freedom, equality, and dignity, as proclaimed in the 1996 Constitution, stood in sharp contrast to those paragraphs that guaranteed amnesty and which were reflective of the nature of the problematic compromise that had brought about the agreement and enshrined in the Constitution. Amnesty was initially guaranteed by way of a "postamble" to the interim Constitution:

> In order to advance such reconciliation and reconstruction, amnesty shall be granted in respect of acts, omissions and offences associated with political objectives and committed in the course of the conflicts of the past. To this end, Parliament under this Constitution shall adopt a law determining a firm cut-off date, which shall be a date after 8 October 1990 and before 6 December 1993, and providing for the mechanisms, criteria and procedures, including tribunals, if any, through which such amnesty shall be dealt with at any time after the law has been passed.[8]

The "mechanism" subsequently created by the Amnesty Act represented a bifurcated process: while the TRC was required to grapple with the moral and political questions which flowed from the violent history of apartheid, the members of the Amnesty Committee, who were never part of the TRC and therefore did not share in any of its decision-making, constituted a judicial forum tasked with the determination of whether amnesty should be granted to any applicant, but strictly in terms of the criteria contained in section 20 of the Amnesty Act.

Unsurprisingly, a number of those who had suffered great loss at the behest of the apartheid state – including the family of the late Steven Biko, one of the most important political thinkers and activists in South African history, who was brutally murdered by the Security Police while in detention without trial – sought to attack the constitutionality of this legislation. In essence, their case was based on the argument that agents of the apartheid state had unlawfully murdered, tortured, and maimed leading activists during the conflict. Members of their families or interested parties possessed a clear right to insist that these agents of a repressive regime should be prosecuted and punished. Furthermore, those responsible for this sustained brutality should be required by the ordinary courts to pay adequate civil compensation to the victims or dependents of the victims. Courts should also be required to impose an obligation upon the state to make good to these victims or dependents the serious losses they had suffered in consequence of the criminal and delictual acts of employees of the apartheid state.

The Constitutional Court found itself in the unenviable position of determining the legality and legitimacy of an amnesty process that had been determined by a courageous national leadership but that arguably deprived some of apartheid's survivors of the type of justice to which they saw themselves entitled. The Court's decision to uphold amnesty – controversial at the time and nearly unthinkable today – suggests the need to locate anti-impunity arguments within domestic political landscapes. Pursuing or forgoing prosecutions in the aftermath of atrocity is not only deeply fraught but fundamentally political; a decontextualized application of anti-impunity may itself lead directly back to a state of violence.

While some today might argue that the South Africa case represents the "impunity" approach to transitional justice, in fact it problematizes the binary between "impunity" and "anti-impunity." It does so in two ways. First, institutions and practices that seemingly embody only one approach, in fact often incorporate both. South Africa's institutions were inflected by an anti-impunity approach. For example, the amnesty process was a conditional one, predicated upon prosecutions for those who did not apply for or did not receive amnesty; this deeply imbricated it with retributive justice. The TRC, while embodying a restorative approach in certain ways, was a highly legalistic institution. Its final report included a list of individuals recommended for prosecution. Second, advocates for both impunity and anti-impunity often imply that their particular "side" has few costs. As a result, the debate sometimes obscures the significant consequences of either path for transitional or post-conflict states. The Court in *AZAPO* harbored a realistic fear of the violent consequences of a decision against amnesty and made its decision accordingly. Yet its upholding of a conditional amnesty process had the unintended consequence of creating a near total amnesty for perpetrators, a systemic failure which had its own penalties for the new South Africa, in particular an almost complete disregard for redress by way of social and economic reconstruction.

In Part I of this chapter, I revisit the *AZAPO* decision in terms of both the immediate context and the decisions made by the judges with regard to interpreting international and constitutional law. Part II reflects on the relationship between the case and production of memory, history, and democracy in post-apartheid South Africa. In Part III, I argue that the South African case problematizes the binary between impunity and anti-impunity and explore the political consequences and necessity of the Court's decision in *AZAPO*. I conclude by reflecting on the implications of these aspects of South Africa's transition for the broader debate concerning prosecution as the appropriate remedy for past human rights violations.

I. REREADING *AZAPO*

A. *Justice in Transition: The Case in Context*

The legal challenge brought against the Amnesty Act was a dramatic affair. Many of the judges, all recently appointed to the newly constituted Constitutional Court, had known the victims and the applicants. It was impossible for members of the Bench to divorce themselves from a history which, in the words of Justice Mahomed:

> …was shrouded in secrecy and not easily capable of objective demonstration and proof. Loved ones have disappeared, sometimes mysteriously and most of them no longer survive to tell their tales. Others have had their freedom invaded, their dignity assaulted or their reputations tarnished by grossly unfair imputations hurled in the fire and cross-fire of a deep and wounding conflict.[9]

Manifestly, this was a difficult case for the Court. Early in his judgment, Justice Mahomed revealed the essence of the excruciating problem confronting the members of Court:

> Every decent human being must feel grave discomfort in living with a consequence which might allow the perpetrators of evil acts to walk the streets of this land with impunity, protected in their freedom by an amnesty immune from constitutional attack, but the circumstances in support of this course require carefully to be appreciated. Most of the acts of brutality and torture which have taken place have occurred during an era in which neither the laws which permitted the incarceration of persons or the investigation of crimes, nor the methods and the culture which informed such investigations, were easily open to public investigation, verification and correction.[10]

Having set out the context in which the case had been argued and the manifest discomfort of the Bench in dealing with the passionate pleas of the applicants – who insisted that those members of the "security forces" who had abused their authority and callously murdered, maimed, or tortured loved members of their families, should be subjected to the application of law – Justice Mahomed sought to present the architecture of the amnesty program as representing a better alternative for those desperately seeking the truth about the fate of their loved ones and, in particular, the desire to determine the circumstances in which they perished. He wrote:

> That truth, which the victims of repression seeks so desperately to know is, in the circumstances, much more likely to be forthcoming if those responsible

for such monstrous deeds are encouraged to disclose the whole truth with the incentive that they will not receive the punishment which they undoubtedly deserve if they do. Without that incentive there is nothing to encourage such persons to make the disclosure and to reveal the truth which persons in the position of the applicants so desperately desire.[11]

Realizing the extent to which this argument might have sounded unsatisfactory to the applicants, Justice Mahomed sought to buttress his approach by locating the provision of amnesty within the nature of the negotiated transition itself:

> Even more crucially, but for a mechanism providing for amnesty, the "historic bridge" itself might never have been erected. For a successfully negotiated transition, the terms of the transition required not only the agreement of those victimized by abuse but also those threatened by the transition to a "democratic society based on freedom and equality". If the Constitution kept alive the prospect of continuous retaliation and revenge, the agreement of those threatened by its implementation might never have been forthcoming, and if it had, the bridge itself would have remained wobbly and insecure, threatened by fear from some and anger from others. It was for this reason that those who negotiated the Constitution made a deliberate choice, preferring understanding over vengeance, reparation over retaliation, *ubuntu* over victimisation.[12]

In emphasizing the critical role of amnesty in constructing and maintaining the "historic bridge" between apartheid and democracy, Justice Mahomed laid the ground for a decision that was ultimately conditioned by national political dynamics.

B. *International Law: Its Application by the Court*

The applicants invoked the argument that amnesty was not a legal option available to a democratic South Africa, in that it was in breach of international law. The applicants contended that the state was required by the Geneva Conventions to prosecute perpetrators of gross human rights violations under the terms of the article, which states: "The High Contracting Parties undertake to enact any legislation necessary to provide effective penal sanctions for persons committing, or ordering to be committed, any grave breaches of this Convention."[13] "Grave breaches" were defined to include willful killing, torture, or inhuman treatment as well as willfully causing great suffering or serious injury to body or health.[14] In its response, the Court noted that there was not a single and uniform international practice that had been presented to it, which, in turn, would have clearly revealed that the path chosen by the South African negotiators was incongruent with international law. The Court's response demonstrated its determination to preserve the historic "bridge" that the Constitution represented,[15] and which was designed to convey South African society from a racist past to a democratic future, even if that determination required a somewhat creative interpretation of international law and its relationship to the South African Constitution.

The Court made two main decisions with regard to international law: first, it found for a dualist conception of international law reception in South Africa and second, it concluded that, even if international law applied, the Geneva Conventions were inapplicable to the South African conflict because it was an internal conflict. In the process, it excluded consideration of customary international law, and in particular any discussion of whether actions by the apartheid regime's security forces could be classified as international crimes necessitating prosecution.

1. International Law in the new South Africa

Significantly, the *AZAPO* case was not the first opportunity afforded to the Court to examine the application of international law in the new democracy. A year earlier in *S v. Makwanyane*,[16] a case which dealt with the constitutionality of the death penalty, the Court set out its approach to international law thus:

> International agreements and customary international law … provide a framework within which chapter 3 … can be evaluated and understood, and for that purpose, decisions of tribunals dealing with comparable instruments … may provide guidance as to the correct interpretation of particular provisions of chapter 3.[17]

In his judgment in *Makwanyane*, Justice Chaskalson, the President of the Court, referred to the constitutional obligation contained in section 35(1) of the 1993 Constitution in terms by which a Court, when interpreting the Constitution, shall have regard to public international law applicable to the protection of the rights entrenched in chapter 3 (the Bill of Rights). He found that public international law included non-binding as well as binding law that "may both be used under the section as tools of interpretation."

In justifying this conclusion, Justice Chaskalson relied on the work of John Dugard,[18] in particular where Dugard suggested that section 35 of the interim Constitution requires a court to take into account "all the sources of international law recognized by Article 38(1) of the Statute of the International

Court of Justice."[19] For this reason, Justice Chaskalson was prepared to accept that both international agreements and customary international law provided a framework within which the Bill of Rights could be evaluated and understood. For this purpose, decisions of tribunals dealing with regional and international instruments, including the United Nations Committee on Human Rights, the Inter American Commission on Human Rights, the Inter-American Court of Human Rights, the European Commission on Human Rights, and the European Court of Human Rights, should be analyzed in order to provide guidance to South African courts as to the correct interpretation of the provisions of the Bill of Rights contained in chapter 3 of the Constitution.

Given the holding in *Makwanyane* just a year earlier, lawyers for the applicants might reasonably have expected their claim in *AZAPO* to be upheld. In particular, the creation of the amnesty scheme in terms of section 20 of the Amnesty Act required an analysis through the prism of applicable international law; in particular, the four Geneva Conventions.[20] The applicants' argument for the unconstitutionality of the Amnesty Act was based upon the same principle of monism adopted by the Court in *Makwanyane*. However, in *AZAPO*, Justice Mahomed said:

> International conventions and treaties do not become part of municipal law of our country, enforceable at the instance of private individuals in our courts until and unless they are incorporated into the municipal law by legislative enactment."[21]

Thus, within a year, the Court had switched from an adherence to monism to a preference for dualism as the guiding principle in its approach to international law. Whereas the court in *Makwanyane* appeared to readily accept the inextricable link between international law and domestic constitutional law, the court in *AZAPO* saw constitutional law as the gatekeeper of any application of international law to domestic constitutional adjudication.

2. Reading the Geneva Conventions

To the extent that dualism may not have carried sufficient weight to justify the Court's approach to international law in *AZAPO*, the judgment then dealt with the applicable Geneva Conventions, finding on technical grounds that these Conventions were inapplicable to the South African conflict. It held further that a distinction could be drawn between the positions of perpetrators of acts of violence during the course of war and violent acts perpetrated during other conflicts which took place within the territory of a sovereign state as a consequence of a struggle between the armed forces of that state and other dissident armed forces operating within the state under a responsible command. Focusing attention upon the latter category, Justice Mahomed found that there was no obligation on the part of a contracting state to ensure the prosecution of those who might have performed acts of violence or other acts which would ordinarily be characterized as serious violations of human rights.[22]

Having drawn these distinctions, which severely weakened the persuasive authority of international agreements as laid out a year earlier in *Makwanyane*, the Court was able to conclude that, in contrast to the punishment meted out to representatives of an invading hostile power, the same consequences did not apply where violations of human rights had occurred in consequence of a conflict between "different formations within the same State" and which subsequently impacted "the permissible political direction which that [S]tate should take with regard to the structures of the [S]tate and the parameters of its political policies and where it becomes necessary after the cessation of such conflict for the society traumatized by such conflict to reconstruct itself."[23] In this case, on the court's reading of international law, there was no obligation to institute criminal prosecutions.

C. Deferring to the Transition

The Court then turned to the argument that had been raised against the provision of amnesty in respect of the imposition of civil liability on individual wrongdoers. It conceded that the concept of amnesty as it appeared in the Constitution could be interpreted to cover only amnesty from criminal liability as the word "amnesty" could be construed to hold a limited meaning. However, the justification for the process of amnesty and its necessity to ensure acceptance of those transitional mechanisms designed to produce a democratic South Africa was sufficient to justify the constitutionality not only of criminal amnesty but of prohibiting civil liability as well.

The Court advanced one final and significant argument in support of its finding. It employed the concept of deference toward choices made initially by the negotiators of the Constitution and later by the legislature. The Court acknowledged that the negotiators were "leaders of the nation" who had been "compelled to make hard choices."[24] They could have chosen to direct the state to give priority to the prosecution of "formidable *delictual* claims"[25] of those who suffered from acts of murder, torture, and assault perpetrated by employees of the state. Such a choice, which would affect not only the state's political priorities but also the expenditure of state resources, would necessarily "divert[], to that extent, desperately needed funds from crucial areas of

education, housing, and primary healthcare."[26] The negotiators were entitled
to make a particular choice between competing demands that were inherent
in any attempt to resolve the problems posed by the brutal history of apartheid.
For this reason, the Court was not prepared to second-guess the precise route
that these negotiators carved out in order to ensure the transportation of South
African society from its present location of apartheid to a new road towards
democracy.

II. MEMORY, HISTORY, AND DEMOCRACY AFTER *AZAPO*

In ruling against the applicants, the Court in AZAPO was at the same time taking a position – implicit or sometimes explicit – on the relationship between
anti-impunity and three critical issues: the lasting memory of harm, the writing of apartheid's history and the political construction of a new democracy,
and the political context of transition.

A. *Memory*

As is apparent from the reasoning of the Court, the judgment was predicated
upon a recognition that it was the history of apartheid that had powered the
constitutional project toward the model of an egalitarian society prefigured
in the Constitution. The memory of a sustained history of racial discrimination and the brutal use of power to perpetuate the rule of an illegitimate
regime, including physical, economic, and psychological duress, helped to
shape the nature of the specific provisions in the Bill of Rights contained in
the Constitution. The text was designed to address this violent history by way
of reconciliation, reparation, *ubuntu*,[27] and understanding. In its judgment,
the Court recognized that the applicants did not agree with this particular
solution to redress the past and reconstruct society. Memory of this violent history was the source for the applicants' contention that amnesty should be set
aside as being unconstitutional. But by resisting the construction of a bridge
between a past that continued to exist and a future still to be built, the applicants, in the Court's view, failed to recognize the inevitable which Justice
Mahomed set out thus: "[m]uch of the unjust consequences of the past could
not ever be fully reversed. It might be necessary in crucial areas to close the
book on that past."[28]

The amnesty arrangements sought to "close the book on the past." This
objective lay at the heart of the compromise articulated in the postamble to
the Constitution. The question left unanswered by the choice made by the
constitutional negotiators and which, in turn, was ignored by the Court in the

AZAPO case was whether criminal trials, which generally focus on individual perpetrators, could have afforded a greater understanding of the political context in which these actions had taken place and in terms of which the entire apartheid machinery was required to be located. The Court took the view that a plausible and reasonable choice had been made that it was more likely that the truth would be revealed by wrongdoers if they could apply for amnesty as opposed to being prosecuted for their actions.[29]

B. *The Production of History and the Construction of Democracy*

A second question then arises within the context of the broader impunity/anti-impunity debate with which this volume is concerned: whether the use of criminal trials would have been a preferable option both for the development of a coherent narrative of the history[30] and for the promotion of a deliberative process to democratic transformation of the society.

Not only does a trial represent a restrictive forum for developing this narrative as a result of questions of legal admissibility and relevance of evidence but, as Martti Koskenniemi has observed with regard to the *Milošević* trial:

> Focusing on the individual abstracts the political context, that is to say describes it in terms of the actions and intentions of particular well situated individuals.[31]

Similar criticism is applicable to the work of a truth commission. The problem of the kind of truth that emerges from the work of a truth commission is luminously explicated in George Orwell's novel *1984*:

> the past is whatever the records and the memories agree upon. And since the Party is in full control of all records ... it follows that the past is whatever the Party chooses to make it ... when [the past] has been recreated in whatever shape is needed at the moment, then this new version is the past, and no different past can ever have existed.[32]

By its very nature, a truth commission must reject or exclude a range of competing narratives in order to complete its report, which then constitutes an official account of a collective memory. This account, which is produced by eminent citizens, may prove difficult to alter and politically impervious to contradiction. Thus, the version of history produced by a truth commission may be as limited as that which might be produced at a criminal trial for not dissimilar reasons to those advanced by Koskenniemi: namely, that the account is predicated on a prevailing conception of authority and the dominant political discourse that flows therefrom. As Richard Wilson has noted, the principal failure of the TRC was its failure to engage with the many affected communities who were more concerned with vengeance, accountability, and responsibility than with the notions of reconciliation and forgiveness that lay at the root of the official narrative.[33]

The conception of history produced by a truth commission holds significant further implications as it percolates through the key organs of the newly constructed state. For example, in its interpretation of a constitution, a court will have recourse to this official history in order to understand a particular provision of the constitution and therefore determine a dispute through a particular but contested historical prism.[34] Thus, the grand narrative of South African history developed by the TRC permits the text of the Constitution to be read with the assistance of an account of history that might not be a product of the judge's own personal, political, or philosophical views.

The court in AZAPO emphasized the importance of the "historic bridge" described in the postamble to the Constitution. It saw the Constitution as constructing an historic bridge between the past of a deeply divided South African society characterized by strife, conflict, untold suffering, and injustice and a future founded upon a recognition of human rights, democracy, and peaceful coexistence together with development opportunities for all South Africans, irrespective of color, race, class, belief, or gender. The key premise upon which the Court's reasoning was predicated may be understood in these terms: but for a mechanism providing for amnesty, the bridge may never have been erected. Absent the bridge, the prospect of retaliation and revenge through the institution of criminal trials would have increased or, at the least, "the bridge itself would have remained wobbly and insecure, threatened by fear from some and anger from others."[35]

However, if amnesty helped secure the bridge, it also gave rise to a particular conception of history which would present an ongoing obstacle in the mediation between official, historical, social, and individual accounts, the latter of which could develop counter narratives of the past. In turn, this presents an obstacle to the ambition for a contested conception of transformative constitutionalism to be fought out between different groups holding divergent visions for the future of a non-racial and non-sexist democracy. If the official version of history crowds out any other narrative, transformation is conflated into an authoritarian move rather than a deeply deliberative one.

The history which the TRC ultimately produced was inevitably limited by its investigative mandate. Colin Bundy notes correctly that the TRC reduced "the systematic discrimination and dehumanization of a colonial order which had been centuries in the making to that of a sense of gross human rights violations from 1960–1993."[36]

C. Political Context of Democracy

That the choice to opt for a truth commission together with amnesty held consequences for the future of South African democracy is but one component of the question. A further part concerns the possibility of a viable political context which would have supported criminal trials. Within the South African context the debate between impunity and anti-impunity was sought to be resolved by recourse to the bridge which was required to transport the country to the commencement of the road toward democracy.

Significantly, anti-impunity advocates examining the AZAPO case tend to ignore the political context while focusing on the question of the legality of the amnesty provisions under international law. In particular, some scholars have argued that the AZAPO judgment stood in sharp contrast to the evaluation of human rights law and humanitarian law together with the contents of a number of new treaties that make specific provision for individual accountability, which together are claimed to represent "the necessary conditions for the justice cascade";[37] that is, a move which seeks to hold former leaders of repressive regimes legally accountable and has increasingly become the norm for the treatment of human rights violators.[38]

In her chapter in this volume, Karen Engle examines how the Inter-American Court has struck down amnesty laws in Chile, Uruguay, and Brazil. Even at the time of the decision – prior to the IACtHR's litigation – the South African Court's approach to international law proved to be controversial. Given the unusual nature of the decision, it is perhaps even more important to examine the animating theory upon which the judgment was based. That requires a further examination of the Court's employment of international law, for it is in its employment of the law that its political theory can best be discerned.

The Court eschewed any recourse to customary international law and thus failed to engage in a sustained enquiry as to whether this body of law required South Africa to prosecute members of the previous government for international crimes. There was no determination that an action alleged to have been committed by the apartheid regime's security forces and which fell within the jurisdiction of the Amnesty Committee stood to be classified as an international crime and thus whether there was an obligation to prosecute the perpetrators of these crimes.

This omission was striking, given that apartheid had been labelled a crime against humanity by a 1984 United Nations General Assembly resolution.[39] Similarly, the 1973 International Convention on the Suppression and Punishment of the Crime of Apartheid[40] and the 1968 Convention on the Non-applicability of Statutory Limitations to War Crimes and Crimes against

Humanity[41] lent support to that application and content of international law at the time the case was argued.[42] Furthermore, in its treatment of the Geneva Conventions and in particular Protocol II, which deals with non-international armed conflicts, the Court held that there was no bar to amnesty because Article 6(5) of the Protocol encouraged the granting of the broadest possible amnesty. The judgment made no mention of any possible obligation under customary international law to prosecute security officials and members of the government whose actions constituted crimes against humanity, notwithstanding that customary international law rules occupied a higher status under municipal law than unratified Geneva conventions and the relevant Protocols.

In his judgment, Justice Mohamed refers in passing to an article by Diane Orentlicher,[43] but significantly does not engage with the arguments raised therein. Orentlicher suggests that by requiring prosecutions from national governments, international law helps ensure that these governments do not forego criminal trials simply because it may be politically expedient to do so. For the purposes of her analysis, she draws a critical distinction between military insubordination and a challenge that poses a genuine and serious threat to national life. Governments that emerge from a history of repression should be expected to assume some reasonable level of risk associated with prosecutions, including a significant measure of military discontent. The justification she offers can be expressed thus: when international law requires punishment for atrocious crimes, it provides "a counterweight" to those groups that pressure governments against amnesty.[44] Orentlicher noted the argument that significant punishment could deter abusive regimes from relinquishing power but contended that, on balance, this concern was outweighed by the more harmful effects of a failure to establish a deterrent to systematic violations of fundamental human rights. For Orentlicher, the prospect of criminal prosecution is rarely a decisive factor in the occurrence of transition. Drawing on the transitional experiences of Greece and Argentina, Orentlicher contends that the demands of justice and political stability are best reconciled through a program of prosecutions that has defined limits, in particular by way of "exemplary trials."[45]

The Court's failure to discuss this argument made clear that it was engaged in a strategic political decision; in particular, it decided to limit the scope of international law applicable to the case before it. In its earlier judgment in *Makwanyane*, the Court had employed international law extensively to buttress its ultimate finding about the unconstitutionality of the death penalty; hence the adoption of a monist approach to international law. In its decision in AZAPO, a judgment handed down no more than a year later, it changed tack by adopting a dualist approach to reduce the obstacle that an application of international law might have presented to a decision to uphold the legality of the Act. In so doing, the Court referred to Orentlicher's article but made no attempt to engage with the question of any reasonable risk that ought to have been taken to hold legally responsible those officials who had committed murderous deeds during the apartheid period. By contrast, the Court was overly anxious to emphasize the importance of the maintenance of the bridge to a new democracy. However, it noted that the "amnesty contemplated is not a blanket amnesty against criminal prosecution for all and sundry, granted automatically as a uniform act of compulsory statutory amnesia."[46]

Both the *Makwanyane* and *AZAPO* decisions were profoundly political. In *Makwanyane*, the Court asserted its particular conception of a new constitutional order which compelled it to distance itself from the institution of the brutal punishment of the past and proclaim eloquently the importance of dignity as a central value for the new society. In *AZAPO*, the court was faced with what it clearly perceived as an overwhelming responsibility to pronounce upon the constitutionality of legislation which the negotiators of the Constitution saw as a critical component in guaranteeing a relatively peaceful route toward a new democratic dispensation.

The Court could have struck down the amnesty provision as contained in section 20 of the Act and, with it, the entire truth and reconciliation process which had been central to the negotiated compromise. Instead, it held to the view that the prospects for "facilitating the constitutional journey from the shame of the past to the promise of the future"[47] were best achieved through the prospect of amnesty. In short, the Court saw itself as the guardian of the political compromise which included the creation of the Court itself.

D. Conditional Amnesty – the Implications?

As the Court observed, the South African legislation adopted a form of conditional amnesty that left open the possibility of prosecuting those who refused to apply for amnesty or who failed to receive amnesty. For this reason, Antje du Bois-Pedain has argued that a system of conditional amnesty coupled with a credible and coherent prosecution policy against those who did not seek amnesty or were refused amnesty was ethically justifiable and sustainable in terms of international law.

Significantly, du Bois-Pedain makes the point that the South African conception of conditional amnesty would prove neither to be a trigger nor a block to the prosecutorial competence of the ICC under the Rome Statute. She further contends that, whereas the criminal trial attributes individual criminal responsibility, amnesty as employed in South Africa was designed to emphasize the political dimension of the crime and hence collective responsibility for apartheid.[48] This kind of argument has been heavily criticized by Mahmood Mamdani who has argued that the work of the TRC entailed so narrow a focus on violations of the body that it ignored the wider structural implications of apartheid.[49] In short, "the TRC focused on torture, murder, rape, all outside the law, ignoring everything that was distinctive about apartheid and its machinery of violence."[50]

The Court did not consider the idea that criminal trials would fail to highlight the structural dimensions of apartheid. It also did not address the possibility that the TRC might establish an official history that would create closure but also constrain other narratives – although that may have been expecting too much of a Court that did not have the benefit of hindsight. In summary, the judgment was an exercise in risk management. Faced with an intricately negotiated political settlement, the Court deferred to the contents of that decision, preferring not to play what it perceived to be dice with the future of the country by a more rigorous application of the contours of international law.

III. COSTS AND CONSEQUENCES OF CONDITIONAL IMPUNITY

For many anti-impunity advocates today, the South African case represents either an exception to the rule for prosecutions or a past case demonstrating the progressive evolution of international law against impunity. The many costs and consequences of the South African transition's dependence on amnesty and the TRC highlight the political as well as legal reasons to reconsider amnesty. Yet given the prevailing forces at the time and the extraordinary risk of violence, the Court had little choice in its decision.

The *AZAPO* decision did not arrive without cost. First, the promised prosecutions, which would have legitimized those amnesties that were granted, largely failed to take place. Second, significant reparations which would arguably have powered a thick societal reconciliation did not materialize. Finally, the history produced by the TRC failed to account for politics, race, and structure in significant ways.[51] Some of these failures were built into the system while others were contingent upon events as they unfolded. Together, they highlight the consequences of *AZAPO* for the society as a whole.

Despite arguments portraying it as the exemplar of "impunity," South Africa's amnesty system was in fact of a conditional nature, predicated on the idea that those who did not apply for amnesty would face the rigors of the criminal justice process. Yet very few criminal trials actually took place.[52] Arguably the most compelling indication of the failure of the conditional

amnesty process was the acquittal in 2002 of military officer and heart sur-
geon, Dr. Wouter Basson. Basson was one of the leading figures in South
Africa's chemicals and biological warfare program. The charges brought
against him were based upon his participation with the South African
Defence Force against organized groups in Namibia and Angola and conduct related to his team-leading position in South Africa's bacterial and
chemical warfare program.[53]

In 2002, Basson was acquitted on all charges. The state appealed the decision. Although the Constitutional Court declared that South African courts
had jurisdiction over charges brought against Basson that had been committed outside of South Africa, it found that since the trial court had assessed and
rejected the evidence relevant to these charges, a fresh prosecution could not
be instituted. The state's only chance of success on appeal was thus rejected
and Basson became a cardiologist in private practice.

If the *Basson* case did not cast a serious adverse assessment on the system
of conditional amnesty, the flaws in the system were further exposed after a
systemic review of material handed over by the TRC with a view to further
investigation by a team of experienced prosecutors, who concluded that reasonable prospects of prosecution existed in only 16 of the 459 cases originally
identified for possible criminal prosecution.[54]

The only cases in which criminal law was employed against those who were
responsible for apartheid crimes involved former Minister of Law and Order
Adriaan Vlok and head of the South African Security Police General Johan
van der Merwe. Apart from Basson, they were the only high-ranking apartheid
agents ever charged. Both trials ended with plea bargains, which were hardly
satisfactory outcomes given the opaque nature of the plea bargaining procedures employed. By 2005, the state gave up. Prosecutorial guidelines were
issued that empowered prosecutors to close all cases in which a crime could
have qualified for amnesty under the Act. The conditional amnesty had thus
proved to be far more unconditional than the designers had intended when
the legislation was crafted.

The fund created for reparations as a result of the TRC was initially in
the amount of 1 billion Rand. Approximately 17,000 people benefitted from
these funds. In 2013, the Department of Justice published a notice inviting
comments relating to draft regulation relating to community reparations. No
further action appears to have been taken.[55] Little more has been done to
implement the TRC's recommendation, which should have provided reparations for at least 110,000 victims and made payments that were five times more
than the amounts received for the state.[56]

Far less accountability for the brutal conduct of apartheid security forces was produced than had been promised when the Amnesty Act was introduced. In addition, as already noted, the official narrative developed by the TRC did not provide a nuanced narrative which could have helped to constitute a solid foundation for a politics with which to power a truly transformed society: the deliberative democracy that had been prefigured in the Constitution. In his chapter in this volume, Mamdani offers the pointed criticism that, as the TRC process solely identified criminal violence that exceeded the existing political order, it ended up either excusing political violence or failing to provide a coherent critique thereof. Further, the TRC offered little by way of a "forward-looking" analysis that could provide a direction for substantive political reform.[57]

IV. AZAPO RECONSIDERED

South Africa's history problematizes the binary of impunity/anti-impunity that both international lawyers and human rights advocates, as well as critics, seem increasingly to support. The South African case suggests that framing amnesties as inherently illegal obscures the possibility that post-conflict contexts might require tempering legal judgment with political considerations. At the same time, the TRC's formal reliance on *both* conditional amnesty and criminal procedure and prosecutions – as well as its problematic use of both, as described in the prior Part – offer cautionary examples for future transition processes. The implications of this argument can be illustrated by considering a court adjudicating today on the facts raised by the AZAPO case.

As Karen Engle points out in her chapter, Juan Méndez has written that the South-African-style "conditional amnesty" may have been compliant with international law in 1994, but not today.[58] He suggests that:

> It may be for this reason that despite the important precedent set by the South African TRC experience, its example has been followed by other states with respect to truth telling, but not with respect to limited or conditional amnesty.[59]

Méndez does not rule out the possibility of amnesties today, but he suggests that they would have to be limited in scope in a way that the South African process was not:

> Though international law provides clear boundaries prohibiting broad amnesties, this does not foreclose the possibility of using limited amnesties as a mechanism for resolving international and internal conflicts. Limited amnesties are not only consistent with international law; they are also an important tool in the conflict resolution process. It is for this reason that the

international community should not only accept them but actively promote them, so long as these amnesties do not serve as a disguise for impunity for international crimes.[60]

The South African amnesty extended far beyond those "clear boundaries," and arguably became a "disguise for impunity for international crimes." It certainly did not constitute the kind of limited amnesty of a kind referred to by Méndez. Further, it failed to develop an effective system of penalties for those who refused to participate in the process, many of whom were doubtlessly guilty of war crimes, crimes against humanity, and sustained practices of torture. The entire process failed in its promise to institute a system of comprehensive reparations for victims. Given the vast problems with the amnesty system as it eventually played out, one can imagine an argument against South-Africa-style amnesties not only on doctrinal grounds but also on political ones. Yet the Court at the time had little choice. For the justices, the costs of destroying the "historic bridge" the amnesty system supported far outweighed the possible consequences of upholding it.

In this sense, the argument that the Amnesty Act would now be illegal under international law does not answer a key question: whatever its reading of international law, could and would a national Court, such as the Constitutional Court, now find differently from the holding in AZAPO? As the case demonstrates, the answer would depend on the balance of political forces confronting the Court at the relevant time. In 1988, Harold Wolpe captured the then-prevailing conjuncture in South Africa with great clarity when he wrote that South Africa was in an unstable equilibrium:

in which the white bloc while holding state power and having at its disposal the armed and security forces was unable to suppress the mass opposition which in turn, did not have the immediate capacity to overthrow the regime and the system. In this situation a space was opened up for initiatives for a reformist solution to the country's crisis on the basis of a negotiated settlement.[61]

This counter-factual of the AZAPO case in the present legal context gives rise to a series of conclusions. First, the distinction between a TRC process and criminal law is not a clear one. While the TRC was not strictly a court of law, its procedures mimicked the law. The TRC thus represented a form of "juridification of the past" so that the rights and wrongs of the conduct of the parties during the long struggle for democracy were the subject of a determination by procedures which were simulacra of legal procedures. It was this fetishization of "the judicial" that prompted Mamdani to criticize the excessive legalism of the TRC and its consequent inability to distinguish law from justice.[62] In turn, this observation served to soften the distinction between the obligation to prosecute the perpetrators of sustained practices of institutional torture, crimes against humanity, and war crimes, on one hand, and an "amnesty cum-TRC type" process, on the other. As the Comaroffs observe, all of these processes, whether conditional amnesty or recourse to criminal law, are caught up in the cultural habitus of new liberalism, all the various incantations of which are predicated on the argot of rights.[63] The South African experience thus serves to mandate a move beyond the restrictive binary of amnesty/criminal justice.

In addition, the South African case suggests that the choices among different configurations along the spectrum from total amnesty to complete prosecution (two impossible extremes) come with critical and often painful costs for transitional societies that cannot be determined by recourse to legal doctrine. South Africa emerged from its transition as a society with surprisingly little political violence. While crime rates soared, in particular rates of murder and rape, which have continued to increase exponentially,[64] the political violence that could have engulfed the society had the AZAPO decision taken a different turn, abated with surprising speed after the first democratic election in 1994. The role of conditional impunity coupled to a truth commission constituted important building blocks for the bridge which transported the country away from the brutal civil war of the early 1990s. Whatever the implications of international law, the South African Constitutional Court was faced with little alternative other than to support the edifice that made its own existence possible. The balance of political forces rather than purity of international legal doctrine was critical to the resolution of the route to be followed in the immediate period after the apartheid government embarked on a meaningful process of negotiations.

Yet conditional impunity did come with significant costs. In short, the South African model of conditional amnesty illustrates the difficulty of crafting an amnesty arrangement into a viable process of accountability in which the objectives of truth, justice, and significant restitution might be achieved.[65] But it also warns against an uncritical application of anti-impunity, no matter the political context. Faced with the same balance of forces described by Wolpe[66] shortly before the negotiated settlement became a reality, it is doubtful that a turn to anti-impunity would be seen — even in 2015 – as a viable option for a transition to democracy.

That conclusion, however, does not remove the possibility of a different application of the amnesty model. It could be argued that the primary problems described in this chapter lay with the design and conduct of the TRC and its link to conditional amnesty. The TRC was predicated on a particular religious conception of forgiveness by victims and repentance on the part of perpetrators of apartheid crimes. This approach may have prevented a genuine move toward reconciliation powered by a reconstruction of a society committed to a process of substantive restorative justice, the objective of which was the transformation of the social and economic landscape that had been so racially skewed by apartheid.

V. CONCLUSION

Both conditional amnesty and the TRC were products of a political compromise hammered out by negotiators who were representing opposing parties, neither of which had achieved a knockout blow to its opponent during the intense and violent struggles which preceded the negotiated settlement. The failure to achieve the kind of restorative justice which would have materially altered the lives of millions of black South Africans must be viewed within the context of this political compromise of which the TRC and conditional amnesty formed only a small part. And this view should give pause to those who view the problem as being caused by noncompliance with an obligation to prosecute.

The democratic South Africa was born of a "messy" compromise. The judgment in *AZAPO* bears testimony to the ambiguity of this process. But without this process, a sustained period of political violence rather than the possibility of a journey toward a substantive democracy might have been the narrative that this chapter would then have been compelled to describe.

The lesson for the broader impunity/anti-impunity debate with which this volume is concerned is that there is a danger of an uncritical and apolitical transposition of international or regional law into the national arena. In particular, the politics in which the debate takes place must be within the context of the national that is more immediate than the international and fraught with complex and intricate contest. Even in the more fulsome expansion of the scope of international law almost twenty years after the *AZAPO* case and the precedent of the Inter-American Court of Human Rights in cases such as *Gomes Lund*,[67] it is doubtful whether a national court in the position of the South African Constitutional Court in *AZAPO*, faced with a deliberative and open process of negotiations which concluded transitional arrangements, would opt to side with the advocates of anti-impunity.

NOTES

1 *Azanian Peoples Organisation (AZAPO) and Others* v. *President of Republic of South Africa*, 4 SA 672 (South Africa Constitutional Court, 1996) ("AZAPO").

2 South African Constitution of 1996, Act 108 of 1996. This was preceded by the so-called "Interim Constitution," Interim South African Constitution of 1993, Act 200 of 1993.

3 Act 34 (South Africa 1995).
4 Ibid., § 20(1)(b).
5 Ibid., § 23.
6 Ibid., § 20(2)-(3).
7 Ibid., § 23(7).
8 Interim South African Constitution of 1993, Chapter 16.
9 AZAPO at para. 17.
10 Ibid.
11 Ibid.
12 Ibid. at para. 19.
13 International Committee of the Red Cross, *Geneva Convention (IV) Relative to the Protection of Civilian Persons in Time of War*, art. 149 (75 U.N.T.S. 287, 1949) ("Geneva Convention IV").
14 Ibid., art. 147.
15 AZAPO at para. 19
16 S v. *Makwanyane & Another*, 3 SA 391 (South African Constitutional Court, 1995).
17 Ibid. at para. 35.
18 John Dugard, "International Human Rights," *Rights and Constitution: The New South Africa Legal Order*, eds. David van Wyk et al. (Oxford: Oxford University Press, 1994), 192–195.
19 Ibid., 193.
20 International Committee of the Red Cross, *Geneva Convention (I) for the Amelioration of the Condition of the Wounded, Sick in Armed forces in the Field*, art. 50 (75 U.N.T.S. 31, 1949) ("Geneva Convention I"); International Committee of the Red Cross, *Geneva Convention (II) for the Amelioration of the Condition of Wounded, Sick and Shipwrecked Members of Armed Forces at Sea*, art. 51 (75 U.N.T.S. 85, 1949) ("Geneva Convention II"); International Committee of the Red Cross, *Geneva Convention (III) Relative to the Treatment of Prisoners of War*, art. 130 (75 U.N.T.S. 135, 1949) ("Geneva Convention III"); Geneva Convention IV, art. 147.
21 AZAPO at para. 26.
22 Ibid. at paras. 30–31.
23 Ibid. at para. 31.
24 Ibid. at para. 44.
25 Ibid. (emphasis added).
26 Ibid.
27 *Ubuntu* is a Nguni word, meaning "a person is a person through other people." Accordingly, one's humanity is affirmed through the recognition of the "other."
28 AZAPO at para. 2.
29 See, in particular, remarks in *AZAPO* at para. 36.
30 See the criticism of an approach in which a criminal trial is expressly employed to justify a pre-determined political project by Hannah Arendt in *Eichmann in Jerusalem: A Report on the Banality of Evil* (New York: Penguin Books, 1992). Arendt argued that the essence of the trial should have focused upon Eichmann being part of the Nazi crime against humanity in which the crime was perpetrated upon the Jewish people, but it was only the choice of victim and not the nature of the crime that could be sourced in the long history of anti-Semitism. See Arendt, *Eichmann*

in Jerusalem, 269. By contrast, in her view, the chief prosecutor Gideon Hausner and the Prime Minister of Israel, David Ben-Gurion, saw the trial as one in which the crime was a specific one against Jews and hence the trial became an assertion of Israel as a state which would ensure that it would never happen to Jews again.

31 Martii Koskenniemi, *The Politics of International Law* (Oxford: Hart Publishing, 2011), 180.

32 Cited by Michael Bishop, "Transforming memory transforming," *Law, Memory and the Legacy of Apartheid: Ten years after AZAPO v President of South Africa*, eds. Karen van Marle and Wessel Le Roux (Pretoria: Pretoria University Law Press, 2007), 44.

33 Richard Wilson, *The Politics of Truth and Reconciliation: Legitimising the Post Apartheid State* (Cambridge: Cambridge University Press, 2001), 164–174.

34 Pierre de Vos, "A Bridge Too Far? History as Context in the Interpretation of the South African Constitution," *South African Journal of Human Rights* 17, no. 1 (2001): 1–33; Ruti Teitel "Transitional Jurisprudence: the Rule of Law and Political Transformation," *Yale Law Journal* 106, no. 7 (2009): 2009–2080.

35 *AZAPO* at para. 19.

36 Colin Bundy, "Truth … or Reconciliation," *Southern Africa Report* 14, no. 4 (1999): 8–12, 10.

37 Kathryn Sikkink, "The Age of Accountability: the Global Rise of Individual Criminal Accountability," *Amnesty in the Age of Human Rights Accountability: Comparative and International Perspectives*, eds. Francesca Lessa and Leigh A. Payne (Cambridge: Cambridge University Press, 2012), 40. See also Mark Freeman and Max Pesky, "The Amnesty Controversy in International Law" in ibid., 45.

38 As an example of an argument published shortly after delivery of the judgment, that the Court had not taken adequate account of international humanitarian law, see John Dugard, "Is the Truth and Reconciliation Process Compatible with International Law?," *South African Journal of Human Rights* 3 (1997): 258–268. See, in particular, 262–263.

39 See, in general, M. Cherif Bassiouni, *Crimes Against Humanity in International Criminal Law* (Dordrecht: Martinus Nijhoft Publishers, 1992).

40 *International Legal Materials* 13 (1974), 50–58.

41 *International Legal Materials* 8 (1969), 68–73.

42 In particular see John Dugard, "The Truth and Reconciliation Process," 263 fn. 23.

43 Diane Orentlicher, "Settling Accounts: The Duty to Prosecute Human Rights Violations of a Prior Regime," *Yale Law Journal* 100, no. 8 (1991): 2537–2615.

44 Ibid., 2548–2549.

45 Ibid., 2599.

46 *AZAPO* at para. 32.

47 *AZAPO* at para. 50.

48 Antje du Bois-Pedain, "Accountability Through Conditional Amnesty: The Case of South Africa," *Amnesty in the Age of Human Rights Accountability*, eds. Francesca Lessa and Leigh A. Payne (Cambridge: Cambridge University Press, 2012), 238–262, 257–260.

49 Mahmood Mamdani, "The Truth According to the TRC," *The Politics of Memory: Truth, Healing and Social Justice*, eds. Ifi Amadiume and Abdullahi An-Na'im (London: Zed Books, 2000), 176–183.

50 Ibid., 181.
51 See the criticism by Mamdani, "The Truth According to the TRC," and Wilson, *The Politics of Truth.*
52 Ole Bubenzer, *Post TRC Prosecutions in South Africa: Accountability for Political Crimes After the Truth and Reconciliation Commission's Amnesty Process* (Leiden: Martinus Nijhoff Publishers, 2009).
53 These facts are to be found in *The State v. Wouter Basson*, 1 SA 171 (South African Constitutional Court, 2005).
54 Antje du Bois-Pedain, "Post Conflict Accountability and the Demands of Justice: Can Conditional Amnesties take the Place of Criminal Prosecutions," *Critical Perspectives in Transitional Justice*, eds. Nicola Palmer et al. (Portland, OR: Intersentia, 2012), 472.
55 Khulumani Support Group, "Article on the 'Unfinished business of reparations in South Africa,'" *Truth and Memory*, July 8, 2014, accessed July 3, 2015, www. khulumani.net/truth-memory/item/979-article-on-the-unfinished-business-of-repa- rations-in-south-africa in the pan-african-reparation-perspectives-bulletin.html.
56 Howard Varney, "South Africa: 20 years on: ANC Rules but the Legacy of Apartheid Still Lingers," *International Center for Transitional Justice*, May 28, 2014, accessed December 18, 2015, www.ictj.org/news/20-years-anc-rules- legacy-apartheid-still-lingers.
57 See Mahmood Mamdani's chapter in this volume.
58 Juan E. Méndez, "Foreword" in Lessa and Payne, *Amnesty.*
59 Ibid., xxiii.
60 Ibid., xvi. As an example, Méndez cites the case of Northern Uganda, which enacted the Uganda Amnesty Act. The Act applied to those who voluntarily left the Lord's Resistance Army. This, in his view, was a justifiable amnesty, in that LRA soldiers were often forcibly recruited as children, which made these soldiers victims as well as perpetrators.
61 Harold Wolpe, *Race, Class and the Apartheid State* (London: James Currey, 1988), 103.
62 Mamdani, "The Truth According to the TRC," 182–183.
63 Jean Comaroff and John L. Comaroff, *Theory from the South: Or, How Euro- America is Evolving Toward Africa* (Boulder, CO: Paradigm Publishers, 2011), Chapter 1.
64 According to the South African Police Service Report for April 2012–March 2013, murder rates increased from 15,609 in 2011–2012 to 16,259 in 2012–2013. Sexual offenses increased over the same period from 64,514 to 66,837. South African Police Service, *South African Police Service Annual Report 2012/13* 114, August 31, 2013, accessed July 3, 2015, www.gov.za/sites/www.gov.za/files/SAPS_Annual_ Report_2012-2013_FullDoc_a.pdf.

South Africa's murder rate is about four and a half times higher than the global average of 6.9 per 100,000. Of course, it is often difficult to distinguish between political and other forms of violence, particularly when the grinding levels of poverty, stark inequality, and the slow process of socio-economic transformation impacts significantly upon levels of criminal violence.

65 du Bois-Pedain, "Accountability," 262 fn. 32.

66 Wolpe, *Race, Class*, 101–103 fn. 38.
67 *Gomes Lund et al.* v. *Brazil* (Inter-American Court of Human Rights, 2010). For further discussion of this case see Karen Engle's chapter and Fabia Veçoso's chapter in this volume.

5

Anti-Impunity Politics in Post-Genocide Rwanda

Zinaida Miller*

...[T]he trying of those suspected of having been responsible for genocide is inescapable for the Government and the people of Rwanda. It is, in effect, a preliminary to national reconciliation ...

–Government of Rwanda[1]

The 1994 Rwandan genocide has become the most heavily adjudicated conflict in recent world history.

–Timothy Longman[2]

Even before Rwanda's devastating 1994 genocide had ended, international human rights groups were calling for criminal prosecutions.[3] Once the Rwandan Patriotic Front (RPF) had taken over from its genocidal predecessor in a military victory, such calls increased. International and domestic leaders alike wanted to fight impunity in Rwanda – and to do so through criminal law. Although aspects of this consensus eventually disintegrated in the face of disagreements over the practice and institutionalization of justice, the parties remained committed to trials as a primary response to genocide. Faced with the recent examples of South Africa's amnesties and Truth and Reconciliation Commission on one side, and the UN Security Council-established International Criminal Tribunal for the Former Yugoslavia on the other, the new Rwandan government stood firm in its priorities in the

* For extremely helpful comments and consultation at a variety of stages of the writing process, my thanks to Robert Blecher, D.M. Davis, Ian Johnstone, Lisa Kelly, David Kennedy, Helen Kerwin, Fionnuala Ní Aoláin, Kyle Shen, and Peter Uvin. I am also grateful to participants in the Institute for Global Law & Policy Proseminar on Anti-Impunity and the Rapoport Center conference, "Impunity, Justice and the Human Rights Agenda." I am particularly indebted to Karen Engle for her insightful editing and discussion as well as for her inspiration for this volume.

immediate aftermath of the genocide: retribution before reconciliation, justice over truth, prosecution before restoration.[4]

Eventually, the fight against impunity took place at three levels: through an international tribunal established by the Security Council to try the worst offenders, national trials, and an ostensibly local and traditional process called gacaca, which was in fact state-run and more reinvented than revisited. Although the three sets of institutions pursued the suspects under their mandates in different ways, they operated together under the umbrella of fighting Rwanda's culture of impunity. While complementary in some ways, they were also embedded in a hierarchical system of justice: the most serious suspects were tried by the international tribunal, which held primacy over the national courts that were initially tasked with trying all other perpetrators, and the gacaca tribunals subsequently tried all those who could not be addressed through the national legal system. The relationship between national trials and gacaca was in many ways a pragmatic one born of the impossibility of trying all alleged perpetrators, while the relationship between the ICTR and Rwandan justice institutions was one of specified differentiation.

Post-genocide Rwanda formed itself in part around the mythos, practice, and institutions of fighting impunity. The Rwandan government understood a postcolonial culture of impunity to be one of the central causal factors of the genocide: because violence against Tutsi Rwandans had remained unpunished for decades, genocide had become plausible and possible. As the Rwandan Ambassador to the US stated in 1998, even four years after the end of the genocide, "[t]he basic goal of the government is to deal with the culture of impunity that has characterized post-independence Rwanda."[5] The discourse and narrative of correcting a longtime culture of impunity resonated with, even helped catalyze, the mid-1990s international human rights, transitional justice, and legal communities, which were then actively debating the relationships among criminal law, reconciliation, and justice.[6]

In this chapter, I argue that post-genocide impunity and anti-impunity discourse and practice in Rwanda reveal two critical tensions. First, the multiple levels of justice and ways of fighting impunity in Rwanda reveal a marked ambivalence between an international legal and policy rhetoric of criminal law as impartial and apolitical and a political understanding of anti-impunity as a force for social and political transformation. On the one hand, criminal law – particularly international criminal law – was intended as a neutral instrument deploying a universal set of rules and procedures. On the other, trials and courts were envisioned in the Rwandan context as a method for dramatically changing society, placing criminal law and the (punitive) state at the center of a broad transformative project. In this latter guise, anti-impunity played a significant role in the effort to consolidate the new government's legitimacy and authority.

Second, the Rwandan case reveals the tensions among the different objectives housed within the fight against impunity: between individual guilt and structural causes of conflict, between restorative and retributive approaches, and among the goals of reconciliation, history, truth, and justice. Rwanda's complex history of justice and impunity exemplifies Bronwyn Leebaw's caution: "It is possible for transitional justice institutions to establish accountability, promote remembrance, and challenge denial, yet at the same time advance political myths that obfuscate responsibility, distort the legacy of political violence, and encourage people to forget potentially volatile issues."[7] Because Rwanda's justice scheme played a pivotal role in transitional justice and in the international fight against impunity, it remains an important exemplar of the limitations and conflicts endemic to anti-impunity.

In this chapter, I seek to illuminate how local and international elites used their shared discourse of anti-impunity, particularly in the first decade following the genocide, to develop distinct projects and practices. Where international groups emphasized the apolitical and impartial nature of anti-impunity work, exemplified by international justice, national elites mobilized the discourse not only to pursue genocide justice but also to consolidate power, assert authority, and establish legitimacy.

Part I provides a brief background to anti-impunity in Rwanda, highlighting the nature of the Rwandan transition, the ascension of the post-genocide government, and the three levels of adjudication of the genocide. Part II then delves into the meaning of impunity and anti-impunity in the Rwandan context. It argues that the fight against impunity stood for two different objectives that sometimes conflicted: on one hand, impartial justice achieved through an apolitical international criminal law and on the other, deep social transformation created through both law and politics. The first relied in part upon the depiction of the genocide as a crime against all humanity while the second located the fight against impunity in a distinctly national project of Rwandan political and social change.

Part III uses the Rwandan case to advance four critiques of the anti-impunity project within transitional justice. First, the fight against impunity often brings with it a high degree of impunity for particular actors and acts. Second, emphasizing criminal law narrows the meaning of both violence and justice, focusing on physical harms rather than inequality or economic injustice. Third, imagining clear distinctions between impunity and anti-impunity approaches underestimates the degree to which retributive methods can crowd out or influence non-retributive practices. Finally, the turn to anti-impunity in transitional justice in particular has meant elevating lawyers as the midwives of transition and, in the process, downplaying or distorting historical production and memorialization.

These critiques are not unrelated. At least in Rwanda, persistent perceptions of trials as one-sided victors' justice at times undermined their capacity to produce reconciliation. The funneling of resources to retributive justice institutions foregrounds criminal law not only over other types of law but also over other political, social, or economic responses to violence. When coupled with the broader transformative agenda lodged within anti-impunity discourse and practice, these preoccupations contribute to an implicit blueprint for a new state and society. Looking more closely at that blueprint reveals the politics, inequalities, and power dynamics that persist after transition.

I. THE ROAD TO ANTI-IMPUNITY

One of the signal claims of anti-impunity discourse has been its broad applicability and universal relevance. Specific harms, no matter where they take place or in what political or historical context, require criminal prosecution. As I discuss in Part II, that claim was made repeatedly after the Rwandan genocide. To better understand the second meaning of anti-impunity – its political, embedded, and locally contingent character as a basis for the post-genocide government's authority – we need to begin with the history of violence in Rwanda itself. This part briefly recounts the history of violence that underpinned both the ascension of the current government to power and its claims to fight impunity. It then turns specifically to the three levels of genocide trials, placing them in the context of the relationship between international and national norms and practices.

A. *Ethnicity and Violence in Rwanda*

Although accounts differ as to the status of Hutu and Tutsi in the precolonial era, all agree that the Belgian colonial administration rigidified ethnic categories and created administrative, educational, and employment preferences for Tutsi Rwandans. Using racist "Hamitic" theories of the natural superiority of Tutsi (whom they identified as closer to Europeans and thus to "civilization"), the Belgian rulers created ethnic identity cards that marked Hutu and Tutsi (and Twa) as rigid, internally homogeneous categories.[8] As a result, "[b]y the end of the colonial period in Rwanda, though not all Tutsi were wealthy and powerful, most of those who were wealthy and powerful were Tutsi."[9] The production of inflexible categories around ethnicity and class laid the ground-work for both physical and structural violence in the postcolonial era.

The period from the end of Belgian rule to the 1994 genocide was character-ized by a series of critical moments of violence. In particular, two major inter-nal conflicts affected the historical narrative and political context (as well as the discursive background) for the genocide and its aftermath: the 1959–62 vio-lence and "Hutu Revolution" and the 1990–94 civil war. In addition to several other violent periods, these events set the stage for not only the genocide but also the post-genocide order. Ethnic rhetoric, including about which groups were insiders and outsiders, played an important role in fomenting conflict. It also consolidated the identities of perpetrator and victim, leading to the post-genocide government's efforts to "erase ethnicity" and replace it with "rwan-dicity." Violence committed between 1959 and 1994 also became central to the government's official narrative, which placed the blame for the genocide in part on the prior decades of unpunished and unaddressed anti-Tutsi violence.

In the 1950s, after decades of institutional preferences for Tutsi Rwandans, a Hutu counter-elite began agitating for political change and was eventually sup-ported by the Belgian rulers – despite Belgium's previous decades of support for Tutsi control.[10] The events between 1959 and 1962 are generally characterized as the "Hutu Revolution" or the "Social Revolution," a combination of events that included not only the overthrow of the Tutsi monarchy but "the instal-lation of a Hutu president and Hutu-dominated government, the purging of Tutsis from positions of local authority, and widespread anti-Tutsi violence."[11]

Over the decades of Hutu rule following the revolution, there were multiple incidents of ethnic violence and massacres, as well as a continuous dynamic (both local and regional) of refugee flight, incursion, and violent response.[12] A 1973 coup led by Juvénal Habyarimana brought him to power, leading to increased regional tensions in addition to the existing Hutu/Tutsi divisions. The coup leaders claimed they wished to "end ethnic division and regional favoritism and to restore national unity" but in practice did little to live up to their own rhetoric.[13] In her groundbreaking account of the genocide, Alison Des Forges argues that incursions by Tutsi refugees and the violence commit-ted against Tutsis in Rwanda "in response" were utilized by Hutu leaders over the decades to "bolster the sense of Hutu solidarity ... From these attacks, they crafted the myth of the Hutu revolution as a long and courageous strug-gle against ruthless forces of repression."[14] Tutsi refugees in Uganda eventu-ally formed the Rwandan Patriotic Front (RPF), an organization dedicated to armed struggle in order to achieve a return to Rwanda and the end of the Habyarimana government.[15]

On October 1, 1990, the military wing of the RPF launched an initial attack from its training grounds in Uganda into Rwandan territory. The Habyarimana government responded with a brutal internal crackdown, which it justified by falsely claiming that the RPF had reached Kigali.[16] The next three years were characterized by territorial gains by the RPF; refugee flight from RPF-controlled areas, where violence and insecurity were later reported; arrests and violence against Tutsi civilians; several failed attempts at negotiations and ceasefires; and growing regional tensions and internal opposition to the Habyarimana government.[17]

In a bid to quiet internal dissent in the face of poverty, inequality, and dissatisfaction with the regime's regional favoritism, the Habyarimana government instituted a strategy to marginalize and exclude Rwandan Tutsi as "outsiders," tarring them as connected with the RPF and inciting fear among the Hutu population that they would be subordinated to the Tutsi minority in the event of an RPF victory. Over the course of the early 1990s, Habyarimana and his close colleagues "worked to redefine the population of Rwanda into 'Rwandans,' meaning those who backed the president, and the 'ibyitso' or 'accomplices of the enemy,' meaning the Tutsi minority and Hutu opposed to him."[18] They utilized both physical violence and propaganda to fulfill their objectives.[19]

In early 1993, a combination of internal and international pressure led Habyarimana to negotiate the Arusha Accords with the RPF, which included power-sharing provisions and plans for a transitional government, elections, and respect for human rights.[20] Uvin argues that the international push for democratization and the pressure to negotiate at Arusha took little account of Rwanda's economic situation or political complexity.[21] The fears engendered by the Accords contributed to the strength of a growing "Hutu Power" group "which cut across party lines and embodied the ethnic solidarity that Habyarimana had championed for several years."[22]

Over the course of 1993 and the beginning of 1994, preparations for major attacks against the Tutsi minority expanded, including the mass circulation of firearms to militias and machetes to Hutu men. By March 1994, the Hutu Power leaders "were determined to slaughter massive numbers of Tutsi and Hutu opposed to Habyarimana, both to rid themselves of these 'accomplices' and to shatter the peace agreement."[23] On April 6, 1994, a plane carrying Rwandan President Juvénal Habyarimana and Burundian President Cyprien Ntaryamira was shot down over Rwanda, sparking mass slaughter of Rwandan Tutsi as well as of Hutu who opposed the Habyarimana government. Over the next hundred days, at least 500,000 and up to a million Rwandans were killed, including perhaps 75 percent of the country's Tutsi population.[24] At the same time, fighting between the Rwandan army and the RPF resumed. On July 18, 1994, the RPF declared the war to be over and formed a new government.[25]

The new government claimed legitimacy on three bases. In addition to having saved the country from the scourge of genocide and being the representative of the long-oppressed Tutsi, the government claimed to fulfill the requirements of the internationally sanctioned Arusha Accords. Although the government ostensibly assumed the mantle of pluralism, the modified version of the Arusha Accords that it followed, as well as a series of more direct actions over the following years, contributed to consolidating RPF control.[26] Modifications included amendments to the Fundamental Law that strengthened the power of the executive and placed the RPF in a dominant position.[27] Habyarimana's former party, along with any other parties or individuals involved with the genocide, were banned; the RPF was awarded the presidency (Pasteur Bizimungu) and the newly created post of Vice President (Paul Kagame).[28] Faustin Twagiramungu, of the formerly internal Hutu opposition party Mouvement Démocratique Républicain (MDR), became Prime Minister, as had been agreed in the Arusha Accords (he resigned approximately a year later and went into exile).[29] On April 22, 2000, the Transitional National Assembly elected Paul Kagame President of the Republic.[30] Kagame has remained in his position since that day.

B Institutions to Fight Impunity

The post-genocide needs of the Rwandan state were extensive. The country was emerging from a four-year civil war and a recent genocide. In addition to preexisting issues, including high population growth and limited resources and land, the post-conflict state needed to help survivors physically, financially, and psychologically, resettle refugees and internally displaced people, and rebuild and restructure an economy that had lost much of its infrastructure and human resources. At the same time, both the national government and the "international community" were preoccupied with the arrest and prosecution of *génocidaires*.

Transitional justice eventually took place at three levels, prompting its embrace by international actors as a pluralist and holistic mode of transitional justice. Directly after the genocide, Rwandan officials and international actors called for a war crimes tribunal to try the top perpetrators of the genocide. The calls for international justice reflected in part the anger of Rwandan officials over the failure of the international community to prevent or halt the genocide. In September 1994, the Rwandan government accused the international community of "evident reluctance ... to set up an international tribunal to expose and punish the criminals who are still at large. This is tantamount to diluting the question of genocide that was committed in Rwanda."[31] The accusation reflected an ongoing dynamic of international guilt and national accusation. Two months later, the Security Council established the International Criminal Tribunal for Rwanda (ICTR) under Chapter VII of the UN Charter on November 8, 1994.[32]

The ICTR was given temporal jurisdiction over crimes committed between January 1 and December 31, 1994 and subject matter jurisdiction over genocide; crimes against humanity; and violations of Common Article 3 of the Geneva Conventions and Additional Protocol II. The Tribunal was granted primacy over national prosecutions, meaning it could take up any case and, in doing so, defer national prosecution.[33] Unlike the complementarity scheme implemented later by the International Criminal Court, the primacy clause of the ICTR's rules reinforced the existing hierarchy between international and domestic justice: the "worst" offenders would be tried at the international level. That dynamic revealed a deeper tension between the rhetoric of cooperation and the enforcement of hierarchy between international and national.

Despite its initial calls for an international tribunal, the Rwandan government eventually voted against its establishment, citing disagreements over its location outside Rwanda (in Arusha, Tanzania); its exclusion of the death penalty (on the ground that the planners of the genocide could escape execution while those they commanded would be subject to it in Rwandan national courts); its temporal jurisdiction (which the Rwandan government argued should begin on October 1, 1990 to include a "long period of planning during which pilot projects for extermination were successfully tested"); and the inclusion of crimes other than genocide in the Statute.[34] The government did not, however, reject the projects of criminalization – or even international criminal justice – as a whole, continuing to embrace the retributive approach.

Parallel to the ICTR, the government proceeded with trials at the national level. In 1996, a Genocide Law criminalized genocide and crimes against humanity as defined under international law.[35] Despite the commitment to prosecutions, practical considerations quickly overwhelmed the new government. By June 1995, 46,000 individuals had been charged with genocide-related crimes and detained in overcrowded prison facilities.[36] Soon, the numbers grew to 120,000 people, held in prisons built to hold no more than 18,000.[37] Many of these individuals had no criminal file opened on them.[38] The devastated Rwandan justice system had few resources to address the problem of criminal trials on such an immense scale. More than half the judges in the country had fled or been killed; there were few lawyers left in the country; those who entered from Uganda were often unfamiliar with the Rwandan legal system and with French, its lingua franca; and the numbers of people who had participated in the genocide rendered the pursuit of justice a daunting task.[39] In addition, the justice system that predated the genocide had itself suffered from both the tolerance of the Habyarimana regime of ongoing human rights abuses and the general difficulties of a justice system in an underdeveloped country.[40]

Key to the 1996 law was a system of confessions and plea bargains intended to mitigate the logistical difficulties of prosecutions on such a grand scale and based upon the hierarchy of crimes established under the law. Under the 1996 law, individuals who made an "admissible confession" (comprised of a detailed description of the acts, names of any accomplices or other perpetrators, an offer to plea guilty, and an apology) were eligible for radically reduced sentences depending upon which category of offenses characterized their actions.[41] National genocide trials began in 1996, trying many alleged perpetrators over the course of the next years, but a relatively small number in relation to the thousands who had been detained.[42] Filip Reyntjens points out that relatively few of those held took advantage of the plea-bargaining option.[43] As a result, by 1998, the number of those imprisoned had increased rather than diminished. Human rights organizations reported on due process concerns, the failure to respect defendants' rights, and the treatment of suspects and witnesses.[44]

Several years after the genocide, the Rwandan prisons remained full far beyond their capacity with accused *génocidaires*, and many estimated that, at the current rate of trial (about a thousand persons a year), it would take nearly a century to try every prisoner.[45] In addition, there were ongoing concerns about the violation of basic human rights. According to leading Rwandan human rights organizations, "detention bec[a]me a principle and liberty the exception and ... presumptions of guilt prevail[ed] over the presumption of innocence."[46] In response to the seeming impossibility of pursuing the necessary prosecutions, Rwanda created what Lars Waldorf calls "the most ambitious experiment in transitional justice ever attempted: mass justice for mass atrocity."[47] Because the government was committed to prosecuting not only the leaders but every individual who had participated in the genocide, it required a new system that could pursue trials at a level commensurate with not only the number of victims but the enormous number of perpetrators.

In 2001, after several years of contemplation and consultation, the Rwandan government passed the first Gacaca Law (subsequently amended a number of times), creating a new system for dealing with accused perpetrators based on a traditional Rwandan dispute resolution practice.[48] That practice used community elders to deal with issues of "property, inheritance, personal injury, and marital relations."[49] The original practice was based on social harmony rather than punishment and guilt, although some measure of sanction (often restitution) was imposed on whoever was found to be at fault.[50] As conceptualized for the *génocidaires*, the gacaca courts addressed "murder, manslaughter, assault, and property offenses committed during the genocide."[51] They differed from the traditional version in the seriousness of the crimes they investigated, the judges, who were elected community members (including women) rather than elders, and the link to the state prosecutorial system.[52] Using the categories of offense created by the 1996 Genocide Law, the gacaca system incorporated the trade of reduced sentences for confessions.[53] At the earliest stage of considering gacaca as a necessary third level of genocide adjudication, "despite reference to the historically conciliatory processes of earlier iterations …, the objectives of the new post-genocide gacaca courts were oriented toward punitive sanctions."[54] Over time, the mandate was broadened to include objectives such as reconciliation and truth-telling, but – as discussed further in Part III – gacaca courts continued to emphasize individual accountability and retributive justice.[55]

If the ICTR's primacy rule revealed a particular justice hierarchy between international and national, gacaca appeared to represent the re-insertion of the local into the project of justice. Yet, from its inception, gacaca occupied a complex place in the relationship between international and domestic. Donors responded enthusiastically to the gacaca proposal. Human rights advocates raised concerns from the beginning with regard to due process and fair trial guarantees, but the overall attitude was one of general support – even if tempered with a sense of necessary compromise.[56] Gacaca was a process defined as local, designed by the national, and produced by the international. Its legitimacy drew on international interest both in "local" and "traditional" mechanisms (of which gacaca quickly became the exemplary figurehead) and in domestically-driven justice processes.[57] In addition to answering the logistical conundrum of trying thousands of perpetrators, gacaca also responded to the repetitive critiques of the ICTR as physically distant from the victims, unresponsive to their needs, directed at external consumers, and uninterested in outreach. The gacaca system was offered as a compromise approach to several interwoven challenges faced by both Rwanda's overstretched justice system and a growing transitional justice industry: it would be both restorative and retributive; it would be monitored internationally and regulated nationally while operating locally; and it would relieve the regular justice system of its impossible burden. As time went on, it seemed that the relationships among these competing ideas represented less a harmonious conjunction than an unstable and conceivably untenable compromise. Nonetheless, the courts completed their tenure, to a chorus of congratulation and criticism. Some scholars argue that the gacaca system successfully produced greater social reconciliation while others suggest that it operated in part as a political tool of a government bent upon promoting a particular agenda and consolidating central power, sometimes through the suppression of dissent and the institutionalization of what many perceived as victor's justice.[58] As the gacaca system shut down in 2012, approximately two million cases had been heard.[59]

II. THE MEANINGS OF ANTI-IMPUNITY

We can see two primary meanings of anti-impunity in the Rwandan context. Sometimes the fight against impunity operates as a defense against politics itself: law, particularly international criminal law, was invoked by both international lawyers and policymakers and by Rwandan officials as a barricade against a violent and chaotic domestic politics that might infect the international rule of law. From this perspective, anti-impunity depended upon impartial international judgment, a universalist commitment, and a linkage between crimes committed in Rwanda and those that had been or could be committed elsewhere. At other times, however, the pursuit of justice after genocide was couched in terms of Rwandan social and political transformation. Rwandan government accounts placed the fight against impunity in a deeply local story about precolonial harmony, colonial domination, and decades of unpunished violence against the Tutsi. Fighting impunity in this regard meant not only mass prosecutions but the elimination of ethnic categories altogether. In this sense, the fight against impunity was a central aspect of the new government's consolidation of power and its struggle for stability. One of the ways in which these differing meanings were maintained, even when they seemed to clash, was by locating each idea in a different institution. Thus, the ICTR was often justified as an escape from domestic politics while the gacaca courts were designed to engage with justice at a local and inescapably political level.[60] At the same time, support of the gacaca courts by international human rights organizations often came with the caveat that the process required due process, impartiality, and fair trial guarantees that would reduce the possibility of political influence.

A. Anti-Impunity as Anti-Politics[61]

International criminal justice relied for its legitimacy on operating above – or outside – domestic Rwandan politics. The UN Commission of Experts justified international prosecutions on the basis of their "independence, impartiality, and objectivity."[62] An international court would avoid "the possibility of any prosecution that is undertaken against suspects being in any way tinged by suspicion of vengeance or subjectivity."[63] The Tribunal would contribute to reconciliation by demonstrating "that justice exists and, on the other hand, that justice will be applied with impartiality."[64] The implicit assumption in these assertions was that the international community itself had no political interest in the outcome of trials in Rwanda or, indeed, in the justice process as a whole. Rather, as impartial observers interested only in the protection of international peace and security, human rights, and humanity as a whole, international judges could make decisions based purely on the facts presented, thus protecting the vitality of the international rule of law as well as avoiding accusations of victor's justice. At the same time, the Court would contribute to the development of international law and would offer necessary legal expertise to the Rwandan situation.[65] Just as the crimes were perpetrated against all humanity, so too the law itself was the preserve of the international community.[66] The ICTR, along with the ICTY, was also understood as a useful precursor for a permanent International Criminal Court that would embody the impartiality of the ad hoc tribunals and cement the resurrection of international criminal justice.[67] Anti-impunity discourse at and around Rwanda after the genocide, particularly at the ICTR, previewed what Nouwen and Werner found among International Criminal Court officials years later: "the Court's fight against impunity is also a struggle with, or even against, politics."[68]

The first manifestation of the assertion of criminal law over politics occurred before the genocide or civil war had even ended. Human rights organizations took an early position that criminal justice must take precedence over any political bargains in peace agreements. Human Rights Watch (HRW) directed the international community to ensure that "no form of impunity be offered to those responsible for genocide and other crimes against humanity." HRW suggested that a UNHCR representative attend any negotiations among the parties to the conflict specifically to:

> insist that impunity not be granted as part of a peace settlement. No participant in the negotiations should be permitted to trade cooperation with international efforts to arrange the crisis, by arranging a ceasefire or in making peace, for protection for himself or any other person accused of genocide or crimes against humanity.[69]

Although the transitional justice field as a whole was still engaged in debates at the time over the relative importance of truth, justice, peace, and reconciliation[70] – debates that continued in the South African context for several years – Rwanda prompted a striking response: justice over peace. The RPF's victory shortly thereafter – and thus the obviation of any further peace negotiations – reinforced international calls for ensuring the permanent end of impunity in Rwanda.

Soon after the genocide, calls for trials became part of the rhetoric of protecting international law and international harms from politics and violence. International sources began depicting the atrocities in Rwanda as crimes against an amorphous international community. The Commission of Experts established directly after the genocide declared in its preliminary report that "the gravity of human rights violations committed in Rwanda ... extends far beyond Rwanda."[71] Numerous delegates at the Security Council meeting to pass a resolution establishing the ICTR invoked the injury done to the international community, as well as the international responsibility to respond to the acts in question. The Spanish representative declared that "[t]he international community could not remain indifferent in the face of those deeds. It is not only the Rwandan people that is affected by such grave violations of human rights and the fundamental values of mankind, but the entire international community."[72] Creating an international tribunal would not only mark violations against humanity as a whole but demonstrate the political will and capacity of the international community to fulfill expectations of justice: "The establishment of a tribunal in these exceptional circumstances ... is a signal of the international community's determination that offenders must be brought to justice."[73] The Rwandan government agreed that "the international community ... was also harmed by the genocide and by the grave and massive violations of international humanitarian law."[74]

In the international context, these statements provided necessary justification for Security Council involvement and international jurisdiction over the genocide in Rwandan territory. For expert international observers, the ICTR was "carrying the fight against impunity beyond the country's borders" and thus confirming that "the international community accepts the universal dimension of the issues here, which might otherwise remain narrowly confined within this small landlocked country."[75] According to the ICTR itself, it would make a "fundamental contribution to international peace and security in the twenty-first century."[76]

In the resolution establishing the Court, the Security Council claimed that the ICTR would "contribute to ensuring that such violations are halted and effectively redressed."[77] Establishing the ICTR would send a "message that the international community is not prepared to leave unpunished the grave crimes committed in Rwanda."[78] According to the UN's post-genocide investigatory commission, the advancement of international criminal law would itself create deterrence: "The coherent development of international criminal law better to deter such crimes from being perpetrated in future not only in Rwanda but anywhere, would best be fostered by international prosecution rather than by domestic courts."[79] International actors used anti-impunity discourse to signal the importance of an international criminal response to the Rwandan genocide. Not only was prosecution imperative, but at least some perpetrators had to be prosecuted in international fora that would signal global condemnation and deterrence. After the sentencing of Jean Kambanda and Jean Paul Akayesu, ICTR Prosecutor Louise Arbour stated that the sentences represented "the most significant steps to date in the eradication of the culture of impunity in Rwanda and elsewhere in the world."[80] These statements served simultaneously to contextualize the violence as particular to Rwanda and extrapolate it to a widespread phenomenon.

B. Anti-Impunity as Transformation and Legitimation

If one meaning of the fight against impunity lay in the capacity of criminal law, particularly international criminal law, to address violence that had been committed against the international community as a whole, the other meaning located the fight in a distinctly national project: political and social transformation. Each level of genocide adjudication promised transformation through trials.

From the beginning, international reports lauded the ICTR as a reconstructive force for a divided Rwanda.[81] This sense of an external court with independent powers and separate jurisdiction which could in turn assist in Rwanda's progress toward a reconciled, liberal democratic state based on the rule of law depicted not only a largely anti-political international sphere, but one that had the capacity to lead Rwanda forward – out of its violent past and toward its peaceful future. Correcting the culture of impunity would promote reconciliation, since internal division rested on the absence of visible justice. The Court would promote justice and reconciliation in order to avoid the descent into "the memory of madness and barbarism" that would otherwise overtake the Rwandan citizenry.[82]

International policy reports suggested the need for a "new political culture in Rwanda"[83] and argued for the importance of visible, performative justice to achieve it. Impunity was not only the absence of the rule of law but the inability to see justice being done. As a US Institute of Peace Report contended, the ICTR must "provide Rwandans with a message and a visible image that justice is being done ... This very public display through the trials is vital in order to exorcise the long-entrenched culture of impunity."[84] Prosecuting the perpetrators of the genocide would not only be justice but would perform law, thus fulfilling both a functional and transformative purpose.

Transformation required a vision not only of the past from which the society had emerged but also the particular future into which it would transform. The Rwandan government offered a distinct image of each. The past was marked by ethnic division, violence, and impunity; the future would be characterized by national identity, peace, and retributive justice. In this guise, the fight against impunity had an underlying purpose: to solidify the authority and legitimacy of the government as not only a voice for victims but a protector of the rule of law. As Rachel Ibreck argues, the official discourse "emphasizes the construction of the state as representative of a new moral order ... It presents ... justice and an opposition to genocide as the founding ideals of a new nation."[85]

For the Rwandan government, fighting impunity was not only about performing justice or enacting the rule of law, although these remained critical. The government's understanding of impunity was long term, historically rooted, and included not only the need for punishment for violent acts but for promoting societal division itself. Prosecutions would not only be for those who committed genocidal acts but for those who denied them. Moreover, the multi-level nature of post-genocide justice would ensure a comprehensive approach to overcoming impunity. The legislation establishing the gacaca tribunals emphasized the need for "prosecutions and trials of perpetrators and accomplices without only aiming for simple punishment, but also for the reconstitution of the Rwandese society."[86]

The governmental historical narrative offered details for the more general notion of reconstitution, reconstruction, and transformation found in both international and domestic rhetoric. Upon its twentieth anniversary, the ICTR produced a film entitled *20 Years Challenging Impunity*. The film claims that the tribunal was founded based on a request by "Rwandan survivors" to create a court that would, "through justice ... put the country they remembered back together."[87] When placed in the context of the government's ideas about justice and impunity, the "country they remembered" seems to be not the recent past but a more distant one. The Rwandan government considered the fight against impunity as a way to return Rwanda to an imagined precolonial era of harmony that had been interrupted, distorted, and destroyed by the imposition of colonial ethnic categories. Having constructed ethnic groups, according to this narrative, the colonial rulers proceeded to manipulate the relationship between them, leading to a postcolonial era of frequent and heinous unpunished violence against Tutsi Rwandans and culminating in genocide.[88] The RPF narrative in this regard was also about the rejection of a more recent past: the post-genocide government, it contended, offers a radical change from the prior era of impunity and a return to the precolonial harmony that predated ethnic division.[89]

Scholars have questioned the history and theory advanced by the regime, suggesting that the precolonial era was far more conflictual and that the undeniable years of violence did not necessarily link causally to the genocide.[90] The narrative serves a particular purpose, however. The government's depiction of precolonial harmony produced the Rwandan people as historically unified, which suggested that the exceptional brutality of the genocide – or the massacres that preceded it – could be overcome by retraining and cultural transformation, particularly through justice efforts.[91]

In December 2001, the Rwandan Assembly passed a law against "discrimination and sectarianism."[92] The law revisits the linkages among impunity, (dis)unity, and genocide in the explanation for the necessity of anti-divisionism legislation, which included the fact that "no one has ever been prosecuted and punished for sowing divisions and discrimination among citizens, but this practice was instead encouraged until it was abused by those who prepared and perpetrated the genocide and massacres, which befell the country in 1994."[93] The law criminalizes "the use of any speech, written statement or action that divides people, that is likely to spark conflicts among people, or that causes an uprising which might degenerate into strife."[94] The law has been widely used as a political tool against opponents of the sitting government.[95] The 2003 Constitution states: "propagation of ethnic, regional, racial, or discrimination or any other form of division is punishable by law."[96] The Constitution similarly criminalizes the "revisionism, negationism, or trivialisation of genocide," an article that has, according to some, similarly become part of a broader campaign to suppress dissent.[97]

Waldorf and Straus suggest that these practices can be seen as part of a project of "ambitious social engineering" intended to "change how Rwandans understand themselves and the social categories around them."[98] Practices of reeducation, including through trials, were intended to transform Rwanda from a country of Hutu, Tutsi, and Twa to one of Rwandans. Since ethnic division was an invention of the colonial era, according to the RPF narrative, it could be undone. In this sense, to be against impunity in the Rwandan context is not merely to be for trials and against amnesty. It is also to be for "rwandicity" and against ethnicity; to be for the current government and against its predecessors and opponents; to be for unity and against dissent.

III. THE TRIALS AND TRIBULATIONS OF FIGHTING IMPUNITY

The debates over the meaning and practice of fighting impunity in Rwanda took place during a period of ferment within the broader transitional justice field. Although the mid-1990s transitional justice field was still rife with general debates over the utility of criminal trials,[99] most actors unquestioningly embraced such trials for Rwanda. That certainty sprang from the calls by the Rwandan leadership for prosecutions but also from the newfound confidence of international lawyers in the post-Cold War era and from the seemingly undeniable truth that Rwanda's violence, like Yugoslavia's, was of a type and severity that could not countenance alternative measures.

The ostensibly indisputable need for trials in the Rwandan case suggests the power of anti-impunity arguments. They create implicit hierarchies of law and justice and they make plausible the trading off of other norms or practices against the unquestionable good of fighting impunity. In the Rwandan case, the post-transition government's very public embrace of a criminal law approach helped it to maintain a privileged position among international donors and policymakers even as it committed human rights violations at home and abroad and violently limited both democracy and dissent. In the early years of the transitional justice field, the scholarship focused on the bargains struck between outgoing military regimes and their democratic successors or between economic and political elites. Rwanda's story exemplifies the need to attend to another set of bargains: those struck between new governments and international actors.

In this part, I use the Rwandan case to question the broader turn toward anti-impunity in transitional justice that it arguably helped solidify. Rwanda raises significant questions about the primacy of prosecution and the attendant assumptions of legal and international impartiality in post-conflict settings. With specific attention to Rwanda, I offer four critiques of the embrace of anti-impunity in transitional justice: (1) the failure to attend to the interwoven nature of impunity and anti-impunity; (2) the preservation of economic injustice; (3) the limiting nature of imagining retributive and non-retributive measures as clearly defined and oppositional categories; and (4) the production and distortion of history.

A. *The Impunity of Anti-Impunity*

Anti-impunity all too often brings with it a high degree of impunity, even for serious war crimes. Sometimes that impunity stems from the impossibility of prosecuting all perpetrators; at others it is the result of an explicit political choice to prosecute only one side in a conflict. In Rwanda, we see the latter, most evident in the ruling party's evasion of prosecution at both the international and national levels. Such one-sided prosecutions have the effect not only of undermining the justice project itself but of highlighting the complicity of law in post-conflict politics.[100]

Both an early UNHCR mission and the 1994 UN Commission of Experts found evidence of violence committed by the RPF both prior to and after the genocide. Reports differ, but the UNHCR mission, whose report was suppressed by the UN, reportedly found that the RPF killed anywhere from 25,000 to 45,000 people between April and August 1994.[101] The UN Commission of Experts recommended in its final report that "investigation of violations of international humanitarian law and of human rights law attributed to the Rwandese Patriotic Front be continued by the Prosecutor for the International Tribunal for Rwanda."[102] Despite these early findings of possibly widespread violence committed by the RPF, its leadership remained largely immunized from prosecution due to the ICTR's failure to prosecute and the Rwandan judiciary's unwillingness to do so.

Efforts by each prosecutor at the ICTR to pursue indictments against RPF commanders resulted in such high-level resistance by the Rwandan government as to make it virtually impossible to complete any investigations.[103] When Carla del Ponte, the ICTR Prosecutor, made a concerted effort to pursue RPF indictments, the Rwandan government retaliated by refusing to issue visas for any ICTR witnesses, effectively halting the Tribunal's operations.[104] The relationship soured to such a degree that del Ponte eventually left the Tribunal, in part due to governmental pressure.[105] The result of the ICTR's failure in this regard has been what Waldorf and Haskell dub an "impunity gap."[106] As a result, the ICTR became part of a system accused often of performing a "victor's justice" that diminishes possibilities for sustainable peace.[107] The gacaca courts too have been subject to critiques of one-sided justice. As Palmer points out, "The failure to include war crimes [in the legal mandate of the gacaca courts] meant that any allegations of crimes committed by RPF soldiers during the civil war and the genocide were excluded from gacaca's jurisdiction."[108]

As Alison Des Forges put it in 1999, "[d]espite talk of the need for accountability, the international community … has been satisfied with a mere pretense of justice for the 1994 abuses."[109] Concerns about this possibility had been voiced even earlier:

> To permit impunity for the current abuses [by the RPF and sympathizers] would … undercut the legitimacy of the new government in the eyes of many Rwandans and the international community, undermine any efforts at national reconciliation, and likely contribute to a new escalation in the cycle of violence.[110]

In fact, of course, the RPF's skillful deployment of anti-impunity discourse, including at the national level, allowed it to win and retain that very legitimacy.

Yet the civil war's victors have not been the sole escapees from the anti-impunity agenda. When the UN Security Council established the ICTR, it did so in part to atone for its recent failure to act to prevent the genocide. Ironically for the Rwandan government, the focus on individual justice that it has endorsed may have contributed in some ways to mitigating the possibilities for emphasizing external responsibility for the genocide it claims, which dates back much earlier than the Security Council acknowledged. That is, the official historical account by the Rwandan government of the factors leading to the genocide emphasizes the failures of international actors to intervene for decades preceding the genocide as multiple massacres took place. As the Rwandan representative stated in the discussion over the establishment of the ICTR:

> Since 1959, Rwanda has repeatedly experienced collective massacres ... But whenever such tragedies occurred the world kept silent and acted as though it did not understand that there was a grave problem of the violation of human rights. Unfortunately, the perpetrators of these crimes were never brought to justice for their acts. The recent genocide in Rwanda, which awaked, shocked, and saddened the international conscience, is the direct result of this culture of impunity.[111]

Others have noted the use of "genocide guilt" or credit by the Rwandan government to secure international support for its policy agenda.[112] Within the specific discussion of transitional justice, however, this account reads the culture of impunity as not only domestic but international. Justice – specifically criminal justice – was the responsibility not only of the national government but of a seemingly indifferent world.

The government's account also places the blame for originating violent ethnic tensions – and thus for beginning a long process that culminated in genocide – squarely on Belgian colonialism.[113] According to the narrative, Rwandans lived harmoniously and peacefully prior to external intervention that reshaped their society and produced ongoing violence. Because that violence remained unpunished by an uncaring international community, it laid the ground for the genocide. In this sense, international responsibility appears twofold, first through the active intervention of colonialism and second by the passive failure to halt the violent legacy of colonial rule.

That responsibility has remained largely unaddressed. As the Rwandan representative noted with regard to the ICTR: "... certain countries, which need not be named here, took a very active part in the civil war in Rwanda. My Government hopes that everyone will understand its concern at seeing those countries propose candidates for judges and participate in their election."[114] In

1995, an international conference in Rwanda recommended that "Belgium, the former colonial power ... acknowledge its historic responsibility in the genesis of ethnistic ideology."[115] Yet none of the transitional justice institutions dedicated to accountability for the genocide has opened the possibility for holding international actors to account for the effects of colonialism or the failures to intervene prior to and during the 1994 genocide and the structural violence that flowed from the history of colonialism. This is not a surprising outcome; certainly, experiences in other countries suggest that the transitional justice field as a whole has a poor track record in this regard.[116] However, the emphasis on a retributivist model that focuses on individual prosecution makes it all the more difficult to conceptualize responsibility by external or international actors, whether recently or in the more distant past.

B. *Economic Injustice*

Domestic and international criminal law responses to impunity, as we saw above, explicitly sought to transform Rwandan political culture. Their attention – or inattention – to economic transformation is significant as well. On one hand, trials made little effort to link impunity to economic factors such as land distribution, scarce resources, and inequality, as well as to the causes and effects of violence, war, and genocide. As a result, the institutions tasked with fighting impunity and building justice were less attendant to the structural factors underpinning the injustice itself. At the same time, the Rwandan government's embrace of transitional justice institutions, particularly criminal prosecutions, solidified its favorable position with the international donor and policy communities. The convergence of international and domestic anti-impunity agendas facilitated a set of ongoing economic relationships between Rwanda and international organizations and powerful states. As Engle discusses, support for criminal law and thus for the central state more generally constitutes an important aspect of neoliberalism.[117] In the Rwandan context, this meant strengthening the post-genocide government's political position and its economic agenda.[118]

The three levels of trials had relatively little to say about political economy or structural causes of conflict. From a legal perspective in a criminal trial, questions of structure and inequality are largely irrelevant. They appear occasionally as contextual factors but have no central place in the decision-making process. Leaving these questions to an accompanying truth commission might appear to resolve this problem (although in the Rwandan case, no truth commission exists[119]) but the primacy of criminal law makes it likely that such questions will remain as background and context rather than understood as key factors. When addressed in the mode of reparations or compensation – even assuming that promised sums are paid out – an individualized approach tends to predominate, leaving structural concerns once more to the side.[120]

It is worth noting that this is not a problem for criminal law alone – but the growing primacy of retributive approaches in transitional justice both contributes to, and helps to signal, the preoccupations of the field.[121] To date, many scholars have argued that the transitional justice field as a whole has been spectacularly poor at addressing issues of structural violence, inequality, and economic rights.[122] Just as minimizing or excluding RPF prosecutions changes the historical record, so too does the marginalization of economic factors from prosecutions.[123] The role of international financial institutions in structuring unequal economies or the effects of brutal austerity measures on conflict have been radically under-discussed within the transitional justice field and its institutions. As Anne Orford points out, the invisibility of the international economic order or of international organizations in structuring conflict and crisis occurs not only through transitional justice but as part of the broader post-conflict reconstruction project.[124] Issues of inequality or distribution are frequently outsourced to reparations policy or compartmentalized into land commissions. In Rwanda, as in many other countries emerging from conflict, the redistribution of land and other resources has been pursued on a parallel track to transitional justice efforts.[125]

Greater emphasis on criminal law and retributive justice reinforces these endemic limitations. Criminal courts try individuals, not structures. They pursue particular violations, not a situation of structural violence. The pursuit of individual senior perpetrators can fail to account for "the complex collective factors that contribute to violence."[126] Yet the inextricable nature of inequality, structural violence, and distribution from the causes and effects of violence, war, and human rights violations suggests that the former cannot be easily separated from institutions examining the latter.[127] When economic issues make their way into transitional justice institutions, they are often either limited to contextual inquiry or to economic crimes such as corruption that can be more easily individualized and traced. The cumulative effect of ratcheting up attention and funding for high-level prosecutions is to enforce a hierarchy of harms in which the spectacular violence pursued in international courtrooms is dubbed the most serious while the horrific indignities and suffering of daily life in a poor country or conflict zone are naturalized as largely inescapable and unchangeable.[128]

In the Rwandan context, accounting for inequality and scarcity as aspects of the enabling environment for genocide highlights aspects of the violence that might remain otherwise unexplored in a transitional justice context.[129] To recognize the role of land and resource scarcity and inequity in the genocide is not to suggest a direct causal relationship but rather to ask how to rethink justice in a way that might draw attention to – or even aim to mitigate or repair – these factors.

Wealth, land, and labor arguably played a constitutive role not only in Rwandan conflict but in the construction of internal difference. Ethnic classification itself likely developed in relation to a combination of economic factors (such as the means of livelihood), colonial institutions, and internal conflicts.[130] Most accounts suggest that the labels hardened in the nineteenth century under King Rwabugiri, who instituted an unequal forced labor system called *uburetwa* and, as a result, "provoked a new awareness across the whole society that resulted in the emergence of the hierarchized social categories. From this point on, 'Hutu' and 'Tutsi' would no longer designate a relative category with respect to labor dependency or occupation but became an absolute one."[131]

Postcolonial violence revolved around these now rigidified categories, but region, class, and unequal distribution remained significant factors. For example, anthropologist Catherine Newbury argues that despite the chaos, violence, and ethnicized political discourse of 1959–61, "rural dwellers often distinguished powerful and wealthy Tutsi from Tutsi commoners. The primary targets of attack were those who were in a position of power."[132] Understanding the events surrounding independence as largely an "ethnic revolution" obscures the complexities of the Hutu-Tutsi categories as political, historically contingent, and variable; "considerations of class and power" as well as regional and local variation were immensely significant.[133] Similarly, the post-1973 government of Prime Minister Habyarimana was infamous for its favoritism of the northwest, which supplied most of the key posts in his government, the army, and state-run companies.[134] Under the Habyarimana government, divisions increased not only between Tutsi and Hutu but between a small Hutu group experiencing privileged benefits and the wider population, which continued to suffer from massive poverty. Despite the government's claims that it "represented all rural segments in the country," in fact it "was dominated by a wealthy, powerful clique (the 'Akazu')."[135]

Reading in economic injustice also suggests greater attention paid to the role of external factors and actors in structuring the economy. The decade prior to the genocide was economically catastrophic in Rwanda, due to a combination of falling coffee prices (a major export), rising population, eroding land, and environmental factors (such as disease and drought), as well as the civil war that began in 1990.[136] The government took on increasing debt in order to maintain its spending and adopted a set of structural adjustment policies under an agreement with the World Bank and International Monetary Fund.[137] The sense of hopelessness and misery derived from disastrous economic conditions was unequally distributed, contributing to an enabling environment for violence. There was "growing regional polarization in political access, social polarization between rich and poor, and a strong awareness of increasing marginalization among urban poor and the majority of rural dwellers."[138] These divisions, overlaid upon or inflected with, ethnic labels and historical resentments, opened the space for a genocidal response.

While accounts differ with regard to the direct causal impact of international economic policies on the genocide, it would be difficult to dismiss altogether their influence on Rwandan life and politics, whether then or now.[139] A notable international conference held in Kigali in 1995 included in its recommendations a request that "the international community donors and international financial institutions [do] not ... compel Rwanda to adopt economic policies that are likely to accentuate inequalities, sharpen tensions between citizens and weaken institutions" – a recommendation that reflected a belief that international economic policies contributed to an enabling environment for violence.[140] To foreground economic injustice and inequality requires accounting for structural violence and the constitutive nature of land and labor in Rwanda – as well as potentially the role of external actors, as discussed above.

C. False Binaries

In transitional justice and human rights alike, we often see a dichotomy between anti-impunity and impunity, suggesting clear categories and commitments: being for anti-impunity requires being against amnesties. Prosecutions require punishment. Criminal law eschews political goals while political agendas muddy retributive approaches. Yet the reality – as all involved actors know – is more complicated. First, even amnesties may be premised on the possibility of prosecution. The South African system, often noted for granting amnesties, was in fact initially premised on prosecutions. Perpetrators who did not apply for or did not receive amnesty at the Truth Commission were, in principle, to be prosecuted through the regular justice system.[141]

More centrally, however, the practices themselves can bleed into each other – but in a tilted manner. We often see retribution opposed to restoration in the transitional justice field. Yet the primacy of the first has affected the implementation of the second. This was true in South Africa, where the TRC's Amnesty Committee operated in ways reminiscent of a courtroom, with committee members holding powers similar to those of judges. In Rwanda, the evolution of the gacaca hearings also illustrates the metastasizing nature of criminal law approaches.

Although derived in part to solve the logistical problem of trying daunting numbers of alleged perpetrators, gacaca was at the same time welcomed by international donors and transnational scholars and practitioners for its reconciliatory aims, participatory and local nature, and precedent in a historically rooted Rwandan institution. The emphasis on confession, forgiveness, guilty pleas, and community participation suggested that societal restoration might take priority – although individual accountability remained significant throughout.[142] Over time, however, gacaca took on increasingly retributive aspects. By 2005, Penal Reform International, based on extensive fieldwork, noted that gacaca tribunals had become "veritable criminal courts, endowed with ample jurisdictional competences." They had the legal authorization to investigate, "to issue summonses, to order preventive detentions, but also to impose sentences."[143]

Their dual status as retributive and restorative mechanisms left the gacaca courts open to a host of human rights criticisms. From the beginning, discussion of the gacaca system vacillated between international pressure from human rights groups to increase its impartiality and fairness and encouragement of its locally embedded character to facilitate social reconciliation. Despite efforts to reconcile the two agendas, the tension between them built over time. International organizations, particularly human rights groups, paid less attention to the intrusive role of the national government in local communities or the possibility that local disputes were being adjudicated through the lens of genocide, focusing instead on arguments over due process.[144] Penal Reform International pointed out the conflict between different priorities, arguing that "the Gacaca process will clearly have to leave behind the purely retributive realm in order to enter another which should be that of social restoration ..."[145] These criticisms located gacaca as part of a massive experiment in transitional justice "blending local conflict-resolution traditions with a modern punitive legal system," and yet responsible for living up to international standards of fair trial and good governance.[146] Over time, the balance seemed to shift toward increasingly quasi-criminal institutions, meant to live up to the protections and standardization ostensibly offered by retributive processes.

D. *Legalizing and Solidifying Contested Histories*

The focus on fighting impunity, particularly in the narrow way in which that fight has been construed, can lead to an impoverished historical and political analysis of conflict. In part this narrow focus is due to transitional justice having largely become a legal project – moreover, an international legal project. Lawyers have become the preeminent experts in and of transition, more so than historians, political scientists, economists, or anthropologists. Relatedly, human rights has become in some ways the preserve of international experts, potentially making it less an emancipatory language for social justice and more a legal, expert project restricted to an elite set of speakers.[47]

The predominance of trials, which tend to decontextualize and individualize violence, is one effect of the legalistic gaze on the processes of conflict and transition. There is a long-running debate about whether trials should be responsible for telling the history of a conflict.[48] Regardless of one's position on the topic, in practice international tribunals in particular have frequently been tasked – whether by their statutes or the victim communities they claim to serve – with writing history and producing reconciliation. One of the stated reasons for the Rwandan government's vote against the establishment of the ICTR was its temporal jurisdiction, which the government interpreted as unduly limiting. Without a longer timeline in its mandate, the government argued, the Court could not take account of the planning stages of the genocide or of the repetitive violence against the Tutsi. The ICTR could not do justice to individual cases or to the larger historical account it would produce, explicitly or not, without the proper timeframe.

Anthropologists Nigel Eltringham and Richard Wilson have drawn attention to the distortions in definition and history produced by the ICTR, which relied on conceptions of race and ethnicity as "durable and objective facts, as factual as the dead bodies in the ground. If a group's existence was not a hard fact but a soft fact dependent on a subjective state of mind (as most social facts are), then judges behaved as if this destabilized the entire edifice of the Tribunal's mandate to prosecute the crime of genocide."[49] As the Rwandan experience confirms, it is not in post-conflict courtrooms alone that history, sociology, and law clash.[50] Yet the stakes for judicially written history are particularly high in transitional contexts, when history and memory often play central roles in the consolidation and stabilization of new regimes.[51]

IV. CONCLUSION

Although often framed as an eternal struggle against universal wrongs, the fight against impunity changes meanings depending on the battlefield on which it takes place. In Rwanda, to be against impunity was not merely to be for impartial trials or against amnesty. It was to be for political and social transformation. Rwandan officials deployed anti-impunity rhetoric and institutions to elevate national identity over ethnicity, unity over dissent, and the government's historical narrative over other interpretations. To be against impunity was understandably to be for a future of law and justice and against a past of violence, division, and conflict. At the same time, there were other, less visible, ways in which the Rwandan fight against impunity drew conceptual and political lines, including by failing to challenge the roles of the ruling party, external actors, or structural factors in the production of violence and genocide.

Institutions of transitional justice operate in the space between transformation and continuity, speaking and practicing fundamental change in some realms while preserving and protecting privilege in others. Those dueling projects of conservation and renovation are produced by a combination of international and domestic law, funds, ideas, agendas, and politics. The story of anti-impunity in Rwanda suggests a dynamic but ambivalent relationship between international and national ideas and practices about recovery from atrocity. Neither national narratives nor international expertise triumphed; rather, a specific marriage of the international anti-impunity framework and national politics resulted over years of interaction. In the process, notions of international criminal law operating as a bulwark against violence and as a force for stability co-existed with a national agenda of political and social transformation. The anti-impunity agenda both vindicated the increasingly criminal preoccupations of parts of the international legal community and served a crucial legitimating function for a new government that claimed the mantle of representing victims.

There can be little argument about the legacy of grievous violence, abuse, and atrocity in Rwanda. Reckoning with that past and fostering a future of both peace and justice remain crucial. As with most other transitional contexts, however, questions persist about the nature of that violence, the appropriate manner of justice, and the certainty of resolution. Of the brutal conflict that took place in the former Yugoslavia, Dubravka Ugrešić writes:

> In the name of the present, a war was waged for the past; in the name of the future, a war against the present. In the name of a new future, the war devoured the future. Warriors, the masters of oblivion, the destroyers of the old state and builders of new ones, used every possible strategic method to impose a collective amnesia. The self-proclaimed masters of life and death set up the coordinates of right and wrong, black and white, true and false.[152]

Transitional justice has always sought to fight oblivion and amnesia, sometimes by punishing those self-proclaimed masters of life and death, sometimes by giving victims a new future, sometimes by retelling the history of what went before. The more that battle comes to rely on a specific fight against a particular type of impunity, the more tempting it becomes for those who wage peace to set up new coordinates of truth and falsehood or right and wrong. To reconsider the process of transition and the project of justice, we need to rethink how those coordinates come about, who pays for their institutionalization, what effects they have, and whom and what in the end they address or neglect.

NOTES

1 Government of Rwanda, Programme of National Reconciliation and Socio-Economic Rehabilitation and Recovery (1995).
2 Timothy Longman, "Trying Times in Rwanda: Reevaluating Gacaca Courts in Post-Genocide Reconciliation," *Harvard International Review* 32, no. 2 (Summer 2010): 48–52.
3 See, e.g., Human Rights Watch, "Genocide in Rwanda: April-May 1994," (May 1, 1994); Amnesty International, "A Call for UN Human Rights Action on Rwanda and Burundi" (April 30, 1994).
4 Over time, the Rwandan government did develop institutions to address the legacy of the genocide through reconciliation and re-education, including the National Unity and Reconciliation Commission. I focus here specifically on the justice mechanisms, which were organized around criminal law and played the most central role for both the government and international donors.
5 Neil J. Kritz et al., "The Rwanda Tribunal and Its Relationship to National Trials in Rwanda," *American University International Law Review* 13, no. 6 (1998): 1470–1493, 1487.
6 See Karen Engle's chapter in this volume.
7 Bronwyn Leebaw, "The Irreconcilable Goals of Transitional Justice," *Human Rights Quarterly* 30, no. 1 (2008): 95–118, 118.
8 Catharine Newbury, "Ethnicity and the Politics of History in Rwanda," *Africa Today* 45, no. 1 (1998): 7–24, 11. For a detailed discussion of the "Hamitic hypothesis," see Mahmood Mamdani, *When Victims Become Killers: Colonialism, Nativism, and the Genocide in Rwanda* (Princeton, NJ: Princeton University Press, 2002): 79–87.
9 Catharine Newbury, "Background to Genocide: Rwanda," *Issue: A Journal of Opinion* 23, no. 2 (1995): 12–17, 12.
10 Mamdani, *When Victims Become Killers* 106–114; Catharine Newbury, *The Cohesion of Oppression: Citizenship and Ethnicity in Rwanda, 1860–1960* (New York: Columbia University Press, 1989), 183; Scott Straus, *The Order of Genocide: Race, Power, and War in Rwanda* (Ithaca, NY: Cornell University Press, 2008), 21. Rwanda was declared a republic in 1961 and independent in 1962.
11 Straus, *The Order of Genocide*, 21.
12 Thousands of Tutsi civilians were killed between 1962 and 1964 and Tutsis were purged from schools and businesses and then forced out of the country in droves in 1973. Many of the 1973 refugees helped to form the RPF. Straus, *The Order of Genocide*, 184–191.
13 Straus, *The Order of Genocide*, 188–191. See also, Alison Des Forges, "*Leave None to Tell the Story*": *Genocide in Rwanda* (New York: Human Rights Watch, 1999): 42

(discussing the increasing tensions between Hutu from the north and the south, despite Hutu solidarity rhetoric).

14 Des Forges, *Leave None to Tell the Story*, 40. Broader regional dynamics, which I neglect here, also played a significant role. Mamdani, *When Victims Become Killers*, 157.

15 Mamdani, *When Victims Become Killers*, 175; Des Forges, *Leave None to Tell the Story*, 54.

16 Des Forges, *Leave None to Tell the Story*, 54–55.

17 Des Forges, *Leave None to Tell the Story*, 58–63; Mamdani, *When Victims Become Killers*, 186; Peter Uvin, *Aiding Violence: The Development Enterprise in Rwanda* (Westford, CT: Kumarian Press, 1998), 60–61.

18 Des Forges, *Leave None to Tell the Story*, 8.

19 "They directed massacres of hundreds of Tutsi in mid-October 1990 and in five other episodes before the 1994 genocide. In some incidents, Habyarimana's supporters killed Hutu opponents – their principal political challengers – as well as Tutsi, their declared ideological target." Des Forges, *Leave None to Tell the Story*, 8.

20 Protocol of Agreement on Power-Sharing within the Framework of a Broad-Based Transitional Government between the Government of the Republic of Rwanda and the Rwandese Patriotic Front (Jan. 9, 1993).

21 Uvin, *Aiding Violence*, 63.

22 Des Forges, *Leave None to Tell the Story*, 9.

23 Jean-Paul Kimonyo, Noel Twagiramungu, and Christopher Kayumba, *Supporting the Post-Genocide Transition in Rwanda: The Role of the International Community* (The Hague: Netherlands Institute of International Relations, December, 2004).

24 Des Forges, *Leave None to Tell the Story*.

25 Tor Sellström and Lennart Wohlgemuth, The International Response to Conflict and Genocide: Lessons from the Rwanda Experience: Study 1 (Historical Perspective: Some Explanatory Factors), 53.

26 Amnesty International, "Rwanda: Violence and Intimidation Threaten First Post-genocide Elections," www.amnesty.org.uk/press-releases/rwanda-violence-and-intimidation-threaten-first-post-genocide-elections.

27 Filip Reyntjens, "Post-1994 Politics in Rwanda: Problematising 'Liberation' and 'Democratisation'," *Third World Quarterly* 27, no. 6 (2006): 1103–1117, 1105.

28 Jean-Paul Kimonyo, Noel Twagiramungu, and Christopher Kayumba. "Supporting the Post-Genocide Transition in Rwanda: The Role of the International Community," Clingendael Conflict Research Unit Working Paper 32, (2004): 6.

29 Ibid., 6; Reyntjens, "Post-1994 Politics in Rwanda," 1105. For the original agreement appointing Twagiramungu, see Peace Agreement between the Government of the Republic of Rwanda and the Rwandese Patriotic Front ("Arusha Accords") (1993), Art. 6.

30 Kimonyo, Twagiramungu, and Kayumba, 15.

31 United Nations Security Council, Resolution 955, Establishing the International Tribunal for Rwanda, Annex (S/1994/1115, U.N. Doc. S/RES/955, 1994).

32 Ibid.

33 Statute of the International Tribunal for Rwanda, Art. 8(2).

34 United Nations Security Council 3453rd Meeting (S/PV.3453, Nov 8, 1994), 15–16. See comments by Rwandan Government.

35 Organic Law No. 08/96 (1996).

36 United Nations Commission on Human Rights, Report on the Situation of Human Rights in Rwanda Submitted by Mr. René Degni-Ségui, Special Rapporteur, para. 70 (E/CN.4/1996/7, 1995).

37 Penal Reform International, Integrated Report on Gacaca Research and Monitoring: Pilot Phase, January 2002–December 2004 (2005).

38 James C. McKinley, Jr., "76,000 Still in Jail in Rwanda Awaiting Trial in '94 Slayings," *New York Times,* June 24, 1996.

39 William Schabas, "Justice, Democracy, and Impunity in Post-Genocide Rwanda: Searching for Solutions to Impossible Problems," *Criminal Law Forum* 7, no. 3 (1996): 523–560, 559; Government of Rwanda, Programme of National Reconciliation and Socio-Economic Rehabilitation and Recovery (1995).

40 International Crisis Group, Five Years After the Genocide in Rwanda: Justice in Question (1999), 3.

41 Organic Law No. 08/96 (1996), arts. 4–17.

42 "By 1998 only 1,292 persons had been judged and relatively few accused persons had confessed, disappointing hopes that plea-bargains would reduce the enormous number of persons to be tried." Human Rights Watch, Law and Reality: Progress in Judicial Reform in Rwanda (2008), 15. See also International Crisis Group, Five Years After the Genocide in Rwanda: Justice in Question (1999), 12.

43 Filip Reyntjens, *Political Governance in Post-Genocide Rwanda* (Cambridge: Cambridge University Press, 2013), 217.

44 For example, Amnesty International, Rwanda – Unfair Trials: Justice Denied (Apr. 8, 1997).

45 Penal Reform International, Integrated Report on Gacaca Research and Monitoring. Pilot Phase, January 2002–December 2004 (2005); Peter Uvin and Charles Mironko, "Western and Local Approaches to Justice in Rwanda," Global Governance 9, no. 2 (2003): 219–231, 223.

46 Kimonyo, Twagiramungu, and Kayumba, 50.

47 Lars Waldorf, "Mass Justice for Mass Atrocity: Rethinking Local Justice as Transitional Justice," *Temple Law Review* 79, no 1 (2006): 1–87, 3.

48 Organic Law No. 40/2000 (2001). The law was amended several times, with the most significant revision passing in 2004. See Organic Law No. 16/2004 (2004).

49 Originally a local dispute resolution mechanism, the term "gacaca" means "small grass" or "lawn" in Kinyarwanda. Waldorf, "Mass Justice for Mass Atrocity," 48.

50 Penal Reform International, "Integrated Report," at 8–9; Waldorf, "Mass Justice for Mass Atrocity," 51.

51 Waldorf, "Mass Justice," 48.

52 Ibid., 52.

53 See Anu Chakravarty, *Investing in Authoritarian Rule: Punishment and Patronage in Rwanda's Gacaca Courts for Genocide Crimes* (Cambridge: Cambridge University Press, 2016): 10–14.

54 Nicola Palmer, *Courts in Conflict: Interpreting the Layers of Justice in Post-Genocide Rwanda* (New York: Oxford University Press, 2015), 118–119.

55 Ibid., 119

56 Peter Uvin, The Introduction of a Modernized Gacaca for Judging Suspects of Participation in the Genocide and the Massacres of 1994 in Rwanda: A Discussion Paper (2000).

57 Barbara Oomen, "Donor-Driven Justice and its Discontents: The Case of Rwanda," *Development and Change* 36, no. 5 (2005): 887–910, 905.

58 See, e.g., Palmer, *Courts in Conflict*; Joanna Pozen, Richard Neugebauer, and Joseph Ntaganira, Assessing the Rwanda Experiment: Popular Perceptions of Gacaca in its Final Phase," *International Journal of Transitional Justice* 8, no. 1 (2014): 31–52; Phil Clark, *The Gacaca Courts, Post-Genocide Justice and Reconciliation in Rwanda: Justice Without Lawyers* (Cambridge: Cambridge University Press, 2011); Waldorf, "Mass Justice for Mass Atrocity"; Susan Thomson and Rosemary Nagy, "Law, Power and Justice: What Legalism Fails to Address in the Functioning of Rwanda's Gacaca Courts," *International Journal of Transitional Justice* 5, no. 1 (2011); Bert Ingelaere, "Do We Understand Life After Genocide? Center and Periphery in the Construction of Knowledge in Post-Genocide Rwanda," *African Studies Review* 53, no. 1 (2010): 41–59.

59 Charkravarty, Investing in Authoritarian Rule, 7 (citing Government of Rwanda figures).

60 For a nuanced examination of the relationship among the different courts, particularly with regard to the meanings generated by those involved with them, see Palmer, *Courts in Conflict*.

61 I borrow this term from James Ferguson. James Ferguson, *The Anti-Politics Machine, Development, Depoliticization, and Bureaucratic Power in Lesotho* (Minneapolis, MN: University of Minnesota Press, 1994), 255–256. In the anti-impunity context, I use the term to signal the ways in which a particular form of legalism can "technocratize," decontextualize, and depoliticize violence and conflict.

62 United Nations Security Council, Preliminary report of the Independent Commission of Experts established in accordance with Security Council resolution 935 (1994), para. 137 (S/1994/1125, Oct. 4, 1999). (Hereinafter Commission of Experts Preliminary Report.)

63 United Nations Security Council 3453rd Meeting (S/PV.3453, Nov 8, 1994). See remarks by representative from France.

64 Ibid. See debate by representative from Argentina.

65 US Institute of Peace, Rwanda: Accountability for War Crimes and Genocide – A Report on a United States Institute of Peace Conference (1995), 8. See also Preliminary report of the Independent Commission of Experts established in accordance with Security Council resolution 935, para. 138: "An international tribunal can more effectively take account of the relevant international legal norms in their specificity because that forms its special field of competence. Domestic courts are not likely to be as familiar with the technique and substance of international law."

66 Jose E. Alvarez, "Crimes of States/Crimes of Hate: Lessons from Rwanda," *Yale Journal of International Law* 24, no. 2 (1999): 365–480, 368.

67 Laïty Kama, "Foreword by the President of the International Criminal Tribunal for Rwanda," *International Review of the Red Cross* 37, no. 321 (1997): 604.

68 Sarah Nouwen and Wouter G Werner. "Doing Justice to the Political: The International Criminal Court in Uganda and Sudan," *European Journal of International Law* 21, no. 4 (2010): 941–965, 942.

69 Human Rights Watch, Genocide in Rwanda, April–May 1994 (1994), 17.

70 See Karen Engle's chapter in this volume. See also Leebaw, "The Irreconcilable Goals of Transitional Justice."
71 Commission of Experts Preliminary Report, para. 138.
72 United Nations Security Council 3453rd Meeting (S/PV.3453, Nov. 8, 1994). See remarks by representative from Spain.
73 Ibid. See remarks by representative from United Kingdom
74 Ibid. See remarks by representative from Rwanda.
75 International Crisis Group, Five Years After the Genocide in Rwanda: Justice in Question (1999), 1.
76 ICTR General Information, available at www.unictr.org/AboutICTR/GeneralInformation/tabid/101/Default.aspx.
77 Resolution 955.
78 United Nations Security Council 3453rd Meeting (S/PV.3453, 1994). See remarks by representative from Argentina.
79 Commission of Experts Preliminary Report, at para 138.
80 "Statement by Louise Arbour, Prosecutor of the International Criminal Tribunal for Rwanda," CC/PIU/342-E, 1998, Sept. 4, 1998, www.icty.org/en/press/statement-justice-louise-arbour-prosecutor-international-criminal-tribunal-rwanda.
81 The ICTR will "serve the purposes of justice and reconciliation between all the Rwandese." United Nations Security Council. 3453rd Meeting (S/PV.3453, 1994). See remarks by representative from Spain.
82 Ibid., at 18. See remarks by representative from the United States.
83 Krishna Kumar and David Tardif-Doughlin, The International Response to Conflict and Genocide: Lessons from Rwanda: Study 4 (Rebuilding Postwar Rwanda: The Role of the International Community) USAID Evaluation Special Study No. /6 (1996), vi.
84 The ICTR must "provide Rwandans with a message and a visible image that justice is being done ... This very public display through the trials is vital in order to exorcise the long-entrenched culture of impunity." US Institute of Peace, Rwanda: Accountability for War Crimes and Genocide (1995), 10.
85 Rachel Ibreck, "A Time of Mourning: The Politics of Commemorating the Tutsi Genocide in Rwanda," *Public Memory, Public Media, and the Politics of Justice*, eds. Philip Lee and Pradip Nina Thomas (New York: Palgrave MacMillan, 2012).
86 Organic Law N° 40/2000 (2001).
87 See "20 Years Challenging Impunity," Legacy website of the International Criminal Tribunal for Rwanda, http://unictr.unmict.org/.
88 See, e.g., Rwanda Ministry of Finance and Economic Planning, Rwanda Vision 2020 (July 2000) ("Since the eleventh century, Rwanda existed as a nation ... [Its] unity ... was also based on the clan groups and common rites with no discrimination based on ethnicity. The colonial power ... exploited the subtle social differences and institutionalized discrimination. These actions distorted the harmonious social structure, creating a false ethnic division with disastrous consequences.") See also, Republic of Rwanda, Office of the President of the Republic, The Unity of Rwandans Before the Colonial Period and Under the Colonial Rule Under the First Republic (1999), 8 ("[Prior to colonization], [a]ll Rwandans liked their country and were feeling that they shared the Rwandan nationality").

89 Ibreck, "A Time of Mourning."

90 "The account of history promulgated by the current regime and its supporters ... differs substantially from the view shared by most historians, suggesting the degree to which current interpretations of the Rwandan past are ... being shaped by ideological considerations, albeit an ideology that may be intended to promote national unity." Timothy Longman and Theoneste Rutagengwa, "Memory, Identity, and Community in Rwanda," My Neighbor, My Enemy: Justice and Community in the Aftermath of Mass Atrocity, eds. Eric Stover and Harvey Weinstein (2004), 168. See also Nigel Eltringham, *Accounting for Horror: Post-Genocide Debates in Rwanda* (London: Pluto Press, 2004); Jan Vansina, *Antecedents to Modern Rwanda: Nyiginya Kingdom* (Madison, WI: University of Wisconsin Press, 2004), 199; Newbury, *The Cohesion of Oppression*. For discussion of the lack of causal link between pre-genocidal violence and the genocide, see Straus, *The Order of Genocide*, 176.

91 As in other transitional contexts, the narrative also serves the function of constructing a new identity "upon a discontinuous historicity, where the past is not a past of pride, but of abuse. The past history of the nation qua nation is a history of a catalog of violations, and pride is only to be found in resistance, by the struggle to recover an 'authentic' ... tradition." Richard A. Wilson, *The Politics of Truth and Reconciliation in South Africa: Legitimizing the Post-Apartheid State* (Cambridge: Cambridge University Press, 2001), 16. In the Rwandan case, both pasts co-exist: a past of pride prior to colonialism and a past of abuse after its inception.

92 Republic of Rwanda. Law no 47–2001 of 18-12-2001 Instituting Punishment for Offenses of Discrimination and Sectarianism (2001).

93 Ibid.

94 Ibid., arts. 1–2.

95 Frontline Rwanda, Disappearances, Arrests, Threats, Intimidation and Co-Option of Human Rights Defenders 2001–2004 (2005) ("Since early 2002, the Government has used the law on divisionism to manipulate issues of ethnicity for political advantage, labeling both Hutu and Tutsi politicians outside the RPF as 'divisionists'.")

96 Republic of Rwanda Constitution (2003), art. 33.

97 Rwandan Constitution, art. 13; Lars Waldorf, "Instrumentalizing Genocide: The RPF's Campaign Against 'Genocide Ideology'," *Remaking Rwanda: State Building and Human Rights after Mass Violence*, eds. Scott Straus and Lars Waldorf (Madison, WI: University of Wisconsin Press, 2011), 52.

98 Lars Waldorf and Scott Straus, "Introduction: Seeing Like a Post-Conflict State," *Remaking Rwanda: State Building and Human Rights After Mass Violence*, eds. Scott Straus and Lars Waldorf (Madison, WI: University of Wisconsin Press, 2011), 8. Clark objects to the use of the "social engineering" terminology in Phil Clark, "Bringing the Peasants Back In, Again: State Power and Local Agency in Rwanda's Gacaca Courts," *Journal of Eastern African Studies* 8, no. 2 (2014): 193–213.

99 The role of prosecutions in general remained contested on several grounds: among others, their destabilizing potential, political impossibility, high cost, and lowered likelihood of generating truth or narrating history.

100 See Vasuki Nesiah's chapter in this volume.

101 The results of the UNHCR mission were leaked to the press and discussed in detail in Des Forges' 1999 report on Rwanda for Human Rights Watch. Des Forges, *Leave None to Tell the Story*, 555. See also Eltringham, *Accounting for Horror*, 105–06.

102 United Nations Security Council, Final report of the Independent Commission of Experts established in accordance with Security Council resolution 935, para. 100 (S/1994/1405, 1994) In her 1999 report for Human Rights Watch, Alison Des Forges concluded that "killings [by RPF soldiers] were … too many and too much alike to have been unconnected crimes executed by individual soldiers or low-ranking officers. Des Forges, *Leave None to Tell the Story*, 558.

103 Leslie Haskell and Lars Waldorf, "The Impunity Gap of the International Criminal Tribunal for Rwanda: Causes and Consequences," *Hastings International & Comparative Law Review* 34, no. 1 (2011): 49–85; Lars Waldorf, "A Mere Pretense of Justice: Complementarity, Sham Trials, and Victor's Justice at the Rwanda Tribunal," *Fordham International Law Journal* 33, no. 4 (2009): 1221–1277.

104 Waldorf, "A Mere Pretense of Justice," 1232.

105 Ibid., 1235–1236.

106 Haskell and Waldorf, "Impunity Gap".

107 Haskell and Waldorf, "Impunity Gap"; Eltringham, *Accounting for Horror*.

108 Palmer, *Courts in Conflict*, 119.

109 Des Forges, *Leave None to Tell the Story*, 559

110 US Institute of Peace, Rwanda: Accountability for War Crimes and Genocide, 18.

111 United Nations Security Council, 3453rd Meeting (S/PV.3453, 1994). (emphasis added)

112 Johan Pottier, *Re-Imagining Rwanda: Conflict, Survival and Disinformation in the Late Twentieth Century* (Cambridge: Cambridge University Press, 2002).

113 The National Unity and Reconciliation Commission, in a representative statement indicates that "[b]efore the colonial period, all Rwandans used to live harmoniously in the same community," cites the Belgian destruction of local traditions, which "impacted on relationships among Rwandans and the way the country was governed; discrimination and genocide ideology spread. As a consequence, Rwandan society was destroyed … The ultimate consequence of all this was the 1994 genocide perpetrated against Tutsis." Republic of Rwanda, National Itorero Commission (Strategy) (2011). The National Land Policy similarly depicts the precolonial economic system as "a factor of national unity and cohesion" which was largely – although not entirely – destroyed by Belgian colonization. Republic of Rwanda, National Land Policy (2006), para 2.2.

114 United Nations Security Council, 3453rd Meeting (S/PV.3453, 1994).

115 Republic of Rwanda, Office of the President, Genocide, Impunity, and Accountability. Dialogue for a National and International Response (1995), para. 15.

116 See, e.g., Jeremy Sarkin, *Colonial Genocide and Reparations Claims in the 21st Century: The Socio-Legal Context of Claims under International Law by the Herero against Germany for Genocide in Namibia, 1904–08* (Westport, CT: Praeger Security International, 2009).

117 See Karen Engle's chapter in this volume, 19.

118 For a more detailed discussion of the politics of donor aid and Rwandan pol-
    icy, see Rachel Hayman, "Funding Fraud? Donors and Democracy in Rwanda,"
    Remaking Rwanda: State Building and Human Rights after Mass Violence, eds.
    Scott Straus and Lars Waldorf (Madison, WI: University of Wisconsin Press, 2011).
119 Jeremy Sarkin, "The Necessity and Challenges of Establishing a Truth and
    Reconciliation Commission in Rwanda," *Human Rights Quarterly* 21, no. 3
    (1999): 767–823.
120 As in other contexts, reparations have largely remained unpaid. Unlike the ICTR,
    the national level chambers could adjudicate reparations claims and survivors
    can bring civil claims against perpetrators and the state. Bornkamm notes that
    "the courts regularly condemned the Rwandan state ... with the perpetrator to
    pay enormous amounts of compensation to the victims. The government, how-
    ever, was reluctant to comply with these judgments." The government did create
    the Fonds national d'assistance aux victimes les plus nécessiteuses du génocide
    et des massacres, later replaced with a new version, to assist the neediest survi-
    vors, which was mandated with a greater social rather than reparative function.
    Concerns about corruption were raised, however, as well as the possibility that
    the fund's allocation process was promoting division rather than reconciliation.
    Paul Christoph Bornkamm, *Rwanda's Gacaca Courts: Between Retribution and
    Reparation* (New York: Oxford University Press, 2012), 132–134.
121 For a detailed discussion of the imbrication of transitional justice with specific
    ideas about political economy, see Hannah Franzki and Maria Carolina Olarte,
    "Understanding the Political Economy of Transitional Justice: A Critical Theory
    Perspective," *Transitional Justice Theories*, eds. Susanne Buckley-Zistel, Teresa
    Koloma Beck, Christian Braun and Friederike Mieth (New York: Routledge, 2014).
122 Rama Mani, "Dilemmas of Expanding Transitional Justice, or Forging the
    Nexus between Transitional Justice and Development," *International Journal of
    Transitional Justice* 2, no. 3 (2008): 253–265; Zinaida Miller, "Effects of Invisibility:
    In Search of the 'Economic' in Transitional Justice," *International Journal of
    Transitional Justice* 2, no. 3 (2008); 266–291; Ismael Muvingi, "Sitting on Powder
    Kegs: Socioeconomic Rights in Transitional Societies," *International Journal
    of Transitional Justice* 3, no. 2 (2009): 163–182. But see Lars Waldorf, "Socio-
    Economic Wrongs."
123 Waldorf and Haskell, "Impunity Gap," 78.
124 Anne Orford, *Reading Humanitarian Intervention: Human Rights and the Use of
    Force in International Law* (Cambridge: Cambridge University Press, 2003), 69.
125 In the aftermath of the genocide, the government embarked on what Waldorf and Straus
    have called a project of "transformative authoritarianism" in which land legislation,
    villagization programs, and agricultural policy have played a major role. Scott Straus
    and Lars Waldorf, "Introduction," 5. For discussion of post-genocide land and agricul-
    tural reforms, see Chris Huggins, "The Presidential Land Commission: Undermining
    Land Law Reform," *Remaking Rwanda: State Building and Human Rights after
    Mass Violence*, eds. Scott Straus and Lars Waldorf (Madison, WI: The University of
    Wisconsin Press, 2011); Catharine Newbury, "High Modernism at the Ground Level"
    The Imidugudu Policy in Rwanda," *Remaking Rwanda*, eds. Scott Straus and Lars
    Waldorf (2011); Chris Huggins, "Agricultural Policies and Local Grievances in Rural
    Rwanda: Growing Conflict?," *Peace Review* 21, no. 3 (2009): 296–303.

126 Kieran McEvoy, "Beyond Legalism, Towards a Thicker Understanding of Transitional Justice," *Journal of Law and Society* 34, no. 4 (2007): 411–440, 438. See also Mamdani, *When Victims Become Killers*.

127 See, e.g., Paul Gready and Simon Robbins, "From Transitional to Transformative Justice: A New Agenda for Practice," *International Journal of Transitional Justice* 8, no. 3 (2014): 339–361.

128 Susan Marks makes a parallel point, suggesting that a focus on "rights to fair pay and decent conditions" carries with it an "implicit message ... that exploitation is work gone wrong" rather than that exploitation is an inherent aspect of the capitalist system. Susan Marks, "Exploitation as an International Legal Concept," *International Law on the Left: Re-Examining Marxist Legacies*, ed. Susan Marks (Cambridge: Cambridge University Press, 2008).

129 The Rwandan government is not unaware of the linkages between violence and inequality, but this has not lent itself to a justice system that incorporates the relationship between the two. In its 2002 Poverty Reduction Strategy Paper, the government writes, "Perceptions of inequality and social exclusion in the broadest sense have been a major feature of Rwanda's history and were the basis for the manipulation of the Rwandese people and ethnicisation of all aspects of life which laid the foundation for the genocide of 1994." The Government of Rwanda, Ministry of Finance and Economic Planning Poverty Reduction Strategy Paper (2002), para 263.

130 Newbury, "Ethnicity and the Politics of History in Rwanda," 10.

131 Vansina, Antecendents to Modern Rwanda, 137. The uburetwa system, to which almost all Hutu and no Tutsi were eventually subject, required one or two days out of five to be given to unremunerated labor for the local chiefs. Vidal characterizes uburetwa as particularly despised as a marker of dependence. Claudine Vidal, "Économie de la Société Féodale Rwandaise," *Cahiers d'Études Africaines* 14, no 53 (1974): 52–74, 54 (trans. mine).

132 Newbury, "Ethnicity and the politics of history in Rwanda."

133 Newbury, *The Cohesion of Oppression*, 182.

134 Straus, *The Order of Genocide*, 23; Pottier, *Re-Imagining Rwanda*, 35.

135 Catharine Newbury, "Ethnicity and the Politics of History in Rwanda." "Akazu" or "little house" is generally used to refer to the small clique within the Habyarimana government that held the wealth and power and became the chief architects of the genocide.

136 Pottier, *Re-Imagining Rwanda*, 16; World Bank 1994, para. 1.3; Uvin, *Aiding Violence*, 62.

137 Uvin, *Aiding Violence*, 55–56.

138 Newbury, "Background to Genocide," 15.

139 For the strongest version of the argument placing responsibility with the IFIs, see Michel Chossudovsky, "Economic Genocide in Rwanda," *Economic and Political Weekly* 31, no. 15 (1996), 938–941.

140 Republic of Rwanda, Office of the President, Genocide, Impunity, and Accountability: Dialogue for a National and International Response, para 17.

141 Almost no prosecutions took place, however, making it a de facto situation of widespread amnesty. See D.M. Davis's chapter in this volume. Davis relies in part on Jean and John Comaroff, *Theory from the South: Or, How*

Euro-America is Evolving Toward Africa (Boulder, CO: Paradigm Publishers, 2011), Chapter 1.

142 Bert Ingelaere, "From Model to Practice: Researching and Representing Rwanda's 'Modernized' Gacaca Courts," *Critique of Anthropology* 32, no. 4 (2012): 388–414, 395.

143 Penal Reform International, Integrated Report on Gacaca Research and Monitoring: Pilot Phase, 10.

144 Jennie Burnet, *Genocide Lives in Us* (Madison, WI: University of Wisconsin Press, 2012), 212.

145 Penal Reform International, Integrated Report on Gacaca Research and Monitoring: Pilot Phase, January 2002–December 2004, 53. Reyntjens includes the retributive side of gacaca in his list of ways in which the practice differed from the "traditional" version on which it is supposedly based: "... the 'new' gacaca was retributive or punitive, not restorative as was the old one." Reyntjens, *Political Governance in Post-Genocide Rwanda*, 224.

146 Human Rights Watch, Justice Compromised: The Legacy of Rwanda's Community Based Gacaca Courts (New York, 2011), 1.

147 David Kennedy, *The Dark Sides of Virtue: Re-Assessing International Humanitarianism* (Princeton, NJ: Princeton University Press, 2004). See also Martti Koskenniemi, "The Politics of International Law – 20 Years Later," *European Journal of International Law* 20, no. 1 (2009): 7–19.

148 See, e.g., Nigel Eltringham, "'We Are Not a Truth Commission': Fragmented Narratives and the Historical Record at the International Criminal Tribunal for Rwanda," *Journal of Genocide Research* 11, no. 1 (2009): 55–79; see also Richard Ashby Wilson, *Writing History in International Criminal Trials* (Cambridge: Cambridge University Press, 2011); McEvoy, "Beyond Legalism" 419; Bronwyn Leebaw, *Judging State-Sponsored Violence, Imagining Political Change* (New York: Cambridge University Press, 2011).

149 Wilson, *Writing History in International Criminal Trials*, 187. See also Eltringham, *Accounting for Horror*.

150 See Natalie Davidson's chapter in this volume.

151 In the Rwandan context, plural or competing narratives appeared too dangerous in a country that had so recently suffered horrific violence produced in part by the ideology of history. "We know that the manipulation of history was one of the tools of extremist propaganda that preceded and accompanied the 1994 disaster." (trans. mine). National Unity and Reconciliation Commission, *Histoire du Rwanda: Des Origines à la Fin du XXe Siècle* (2011), v–vi.

152 Dubravka Ugrešić, *The Culture of Lies: Antipolitical Essays* (University Park, PA: The Pennsylvania State University Press, 1995), 6.

6

Whose Exceptionalism? Debating the Inter-American View on Amnesty and the Brazilian Case

Fabia Fernandes Carvalho Veçoso[*]

The authoritarian past of Brazil continues to be a conspicuous topic of discussion in the country. On March 31, 2014, on the occasion of the 50th anniversary of the military coup in Brazil, President Dilma Rousseff delivered a speech that gained a great deal of attention because of her statements on the 1979 Brazilian amnesty. That law is still in effect despite *Gomes Lund et al. v. Brazil*, a 2010 Inter-American Court of Human Rights (IACtHR or Court) decision ruling that its application violates the American Convention on Human Rights (ACHR or Convention).[1] President Rousseff's statement makes clear that she sees the amnesty as part of a democratically negotiated agreement, "a process that was built step by step in each of the elected governments after dictatorship."[2] As she noted:

> We regained democracy in our own way, through struggles and irreparable human sacrifices, but also through national pacts and agreements. Many of them translated into provisions of the 1988 Constitution. ... I respect and revere those who fought for democracy, facing illegal state brutality, and I will never stop praising them. I also recognize and value the political pacts that led us to democracy.[3]

Rouseff's speech came as a surprise to some. As someone who had been detained and tortured for her membership in the armed opposition to the military regime, many thought she should oppose the amnesty law. In fact, the IACtHR based much of its decision in *Gomes Lund* on the rights of victims of the dictatorship to have access to criminal courts, which it saw as facilitating truth.

* I thank Karen Engle and D.M. Davis for their careful reading of previous versions of this chapter, and Zinaida Miller's thoughtful comments. My gratitude to the participants of the 2013 Institute for Global Law and Policy proseminar on impunity. All English translations by the author.

Gomes Lund integrates the "Inter-American view on amnesty," an expression coined by Judge García-Ramirez, discussed in Part II. In a set of five cases involving Peru, Chile, Brazil, Uruguay, and El Salvador, the IACtHR determined that the amnesty laws adopted by these countries (all states parties to the convention) were incompatible with the ACHR. Human rights violations had not been investigated and their perpetrators had not been prosecuted because of the adoption of these domestic amnesty laws in the context of regime change in the five countries. The IACtHR ordered states parties to investigate, prosecute, and punish violations.

This chapter challenges this line of cases, with a focus on the IACtHR's treatment of Brazil. My main argument is that the Court's articulation of a universalist approach to amnesty, in which nearly all amnesties lack legal effects under the ACHR, refuses to engage with the complex issues related to the implementation of human rights protection in concrete situations of regime change. In other words, this approach de-contextualizes and disconnects the complexity of transitional justice and the protection of human rights during processes of political transformation.

As such, I disagree with much of the criticism of Brazil's insistence on maintaining its amnesty law. Indeed, while some have described Brazil as a "pariah of international law"[4] or considered its response to the IACtHR's judgments as constituting a form of "Brazilian exceptionalism,"[5] I suggest that the IACtHR and its reading of international law should have attended better to the particularities of Brazil's transition to democracy. To this end, this chapter will briefly describe the Inter-American view on amnesty in its first part. A discussion of the Brazilian case will follow, based on a contextual analysis of transitional justice in the country. The third part will challenge the Court's assertion that the Brazilian amnesty law is per se contrary to international law because of a duty to punish human rights violations. The Court did not articulate any comprehensive legal justification that took into account the Brazilian context of regime change in order to invalidate the Brazilian amnesty law. On the contrary, the IACtHR dismissed the local strategy to cope with a violent past, arguing that amnesties are per se contrary to the ACHR provisions.

Although it is not my intention to assert that the local perspective is always the superior one for addressing the legacy of authoritarian regimes, this chapter aims to shed light on Brazilian amnesty from within Brazilian history, law, and politics. The history leading up to the implementation of the amnesty law, the law's subsequent expansions and broadening, and its continued use today, despite the amnesty being struck down by the IACtHR, indicate a significant decision in Brazil to adopt amnesty as part of the work of regime change and justice.[6] With this background in mind, I conclude that both trials and amnesties, among other tools, were legal strategies available to implement human rights in the Brazilian context of regime change. The Brazilian choice for amnesty, I argue, should not be seen as a wrongful act per se, though a deeper investigation of the background and history in the case of Brazil may be warranted in order to evaluate the adequacy of the country's transitional strategies.

I. THE INTER-AMERICAN VIEW ON AMNESTY: FOUR KEY CASES[7]

Discussing the IACtHR's universalist approach to amnesty encompasses the Court's view on the impossibility of eliminating "any record of crimes occurring, by barring criminal prosecutions and/or civil suits."[8] Following the Court's reasoning, human rights violations require the holding of trials, with no room for impunity. In this setting, amnesties are seen as per se contrary to the protection of human rights.

This approach ignores the different scopes amnesty may have, as Mallinder describes by applying a different perspective from the IACtHR and by considering concrete experiences on the use of amnesties. There is "blanket amnesty," which casts the committed crimes into oblivion without any investigation of the facts. In a similar vein, "self-amnesties" relate to laws enacted unilaterally by the government to prevent criminal prosecution of state agents. Limited amnesties also exist, coupled with the investigation of facts, as illustrated by the South African case of granting amnesty in exchange for truth. Moreover, amnesty may be granted to political prisoners. In short, according to Mallinder, concrete cases show that there are different scopes for amnesty, not just impunity.[9] By eliding the distinction among the different scopes of amnesty and impunity, the IACtHR fails to recognize contextually dependent characteristics of amnesty, some of which may respond to the needs of the victims and their families and follow successful precedent in establishing a lasting truth-based peace, instead of obscuring the responsibility and wrongs of the perpetrators of human rights violations.

The Inter-American view on amnesty[10] began taking shape in the Court's evaluation of Peru's amnesty law in *Barrios Altos*. On November 3, 1991, intruders shot at attendees at a party in the neighborhood of Barrios Altos, in Lima. Fifteen people were killed and four survived. Judicial investigations initiated in April 1995 showed that the individuals who broke into the house were members of the Peruvian Army, and part of the Colina Group, which employed a violent anti-subversive program during President Alberto Fujimori's administration.[11]

Closely related to the judicial investigations of the *Barrios Altos* case, as the Court pointed out in its factual account of the case, were two self-amnesty laws enacted in Peru in 1995.[12] The Peruvian self-amnesty laws No. 26.479/95 and No. 26.492/95 were applied to the perpetrators of the Barrios Altos killings, which resulted in the termination of criminal proceedings related to the case. By the time this case made its way to the IACtHR, Peru had seen a transition to democracy. It assumed international responsibility for the human rights violations that took place. At the same time, it claimed difficulties in dealing with domestic legal obstacles posed by the amnesty laws.

The innovative position adopted by the IACtHR in *Barrios Altos* lies in its determination, for the very first time, of the non-applicability of all provisions of amnesty, statutes of limitation, and any others that establish measures designed to eliminate responsibility in cases of serious human rights violations. That is, these provisions cannot be applied to prevent the investigation and punishment of those responsible for such violations, including torture, extrajudicial execution, and enforced disappearance, which are all prohibited and not subject to derogation under international law.[13]

According to the Court, the Peruvian self-amnesty laws constituted violations of articles 1.1 and 2 of the Convention,[14] as well as articles 8 and 25, the latter two relating to the right to a fair trial and the right to judicial protection, respectively. The amnesty laws prevented the identification of human rights perpetrators to the extent that they hindered investigation and access to justice. The victims and their families were not allowed to know the truth about the facts, and therefore were not entitled to reparations under Peruvian law.[15]

In his concurring opinion in *Barrios Altos*, Judge Cançado Trindade developed in more detail the basis for universalist reasoning regarding amnesty and human rights. There was no clear departure from the decision taken by the majority in *Barrios Altos*, but a deeper theoretical explanation of this universalist approach. Cançado Trindade reasoned that self-amnesty laws affect non-derogable rights, such as the rights to life and to personal integrity. To the extent that human rights include values considered by Cançado Trindade as naturally or objectively superior, the role of states should be limited by the provisions of international human rights law, with no possibility of counterclaim. The superior position of these rights is set a priori, and opposing it would be a clear error.[16] Judge Cançado Trindade ended his opinion by asserting that:

> It ought to be stated and restated firmly, whenever necessary: in the domain of the International Law of Human Rights, the so-called "laws" of self-amnesty are not truly laws: they are nothing but an aberration, an inadmissible affront to the juridical conscience of humanity.[17]

Barrios Altos established a strong precedent on domestic amnesties by the Court. Chile was the next country to have its self-amnesty law scrutinized in the *Almonacid-Arellano* case.[18] On September 16, 1973, at the beginning of the military rule in Chile, policemen arrested and shot Mr. Almonacid-Arellano when he was leaving home, and he died the next day. Later, Decree Law No. 2.191/78, initiated by the military regime, provided the benefit of amnesty in Chile.

The primary question at issue in *Almonacid-Arellano* was the *ratione temporis* jurisdiction of the Court, since the murder occurred in 1973 and Chile recognized the jurisdiction of the Court only for facts which occurred later than March 11, 1990. The argumentative strategy adopted by the Court was intended to surpass the *ratione temporis* exception, and the IACtHR analyzed the alleged violations of articles 8 and 25, as well as violations of articles 1.1 and 2, following these steps: (a) asking whether Mr. Almonacid-Arellano's murder was a crime against humanity; (b) if it was, whether the crime could be made subject to amnesty; (c) if the crime could not be amnestied, whether Decree Law No. 2.191/78 provided amnesty for the crime and whether Chile would violate the Convention by keeping the amnesty law, and (d) determining whether the Chilean justice system's application of the amnesty law would violate articles 8 and 25.

The IACtHR evaluated each issue with a universalist, anti-impunity approach, consistent with its previous opinion in *Barrios Altos*. First, the Court concluded, Mr. Almonacid Arellano's murder was a crime against humanity. Next, crimes against humanity are not subject to prescription and therefore fall outside the scope of an amnesty law. Further, the Court ruled that Decree Law No. 2.191/78 did in fact provide for amnesty for the crime, and Chile had violated the Convention by keeping the amnesty law in force upon ratification of the Convention. Finally, the Court held that the amnesty law had been applied during the domestic investigation of the murder of Mr. Almonacid-Arellano, and this application violated the rights set forth in articles 8 and 25 of the Convention, along with articles 1.1 and 2, to the extent that the investigation of facts is hindered upon the application of a self-amnesty law, restricting access to justice and truth to the victims and their families, as well as preventing appropriate reparations for the violations.[19]

The Court included a new argument in its reasoning on amnesty in *Almonacid*. The crime against humanity claim was added to shape the violations as infringements of *jus cogens*; this bolstered the argument that amnesty laws are per se contrary to the ACHR. The IACtHR's reasoning could therefore be deemed stronger and the role of the Court against domestic laws firmer.

Barrios Altos and *Almonacid* laid the ground for determination of *Gomes Lund,* and this Inter-American view on amnesty was applied to the latter. The case of *Gomes Lund* dealt with the enforced disappearance of 62 people between 1972 and 1974, perpetrated by state agents of the Brazilian military regime against the Guerrilla of Araguaia. Members of the Brazilian Communist Party and peasants of the Araguaia region[20] articulated a movement of armed resistance against the regime, whose reaction was focused toward the extermination of the guerrilla.[21] The violations related to enforced disappearances were not investigated and their perpetrators were not prosecuted in Brazil because of Brazilian Amnesty Law No. 6.683/79, passed by the Parliament and enacted on August 28, 1979.

The *ratione temporis* jurisdiction of the Court was discussed in the *Gomes Lund* case too, as Brazil recognized the jurisdiction of the Court only for facts which occurred later than December 10, 1998. The IACtHR asserted its jurisdiction in this case because of the permanent character of enforced disappearances, a violation that continues producing legal effects "until the whereabouts of the disappeared person are made known and the facts are ascertained."[22] Moreover, the Court affirmed its jurisdiction for violations "which are founded in facts that occurred or persisted as of December 10, 1998."[23]

Brazil was held responsible by the Court; it found that, because enforced disappearances entail violations of *jus cogens,*[24] only criminal prosecutions shall be deemed effective as a legal response.[25] Once more, the international law vocabulary of *jus cogens* played a prominent role in the Court's reasoning.[26] The country has still not fully complied with the IACtHR decision,[27] as the 1979 amnesty is still in force in Brazil, preventing criminal prosecutions from taking place.

Though the Court made efforts to assess the Brazilian transitional process in some detail (referring to the dictatorship in historical context,[28] explaining the contours of the Guerrilla of Araguaia,[29] noting the Brazilian public policy on political deaths and disappearances of persons since the 1990s,[30] and the operation of such public policy with respect to the enforced disappearance victims in the case of *Gomes Lund*[31]), the particularities of the Brazilian context did not change the IACtHR's general understanding of domestic amnesty.

As will be examined in detail in the next part, Brazil experienced a different context of state violence than Peru and Chile. Moreover, the claim for amnesty has changed over time; where as it began as a demand by social movements to release political prisoners, it transformed into a political agreement aimed at regime change. Accordingly, reference to the 1979 law as a self-amnesty tells only one part of the story of transition in Brazil.

In *Gomes Lund*, the Court applied the Inter-American view on amnesty in order to highlight the inadequacy of the transitional strategy adopted by Brazil:

> This Court has previously ruled on the matter and has not found legal basis to part from its constant jurisprudence that, moreover, coincides with that which is unanimously established in international law and the precedent of the organs of the universal and regional systems of protection of human rights. In this sense, regarding the present case, the Court reiterates that "amnesty provisions, the statute of limitation provisions, and the establishment of exclusions of responsibility that are intended to prevent the investigation and punishment of those responsible for serious violations to human rights such as torture, summary, extrajudicial, or arbitrary executions, and enforced disappearance are not admissible, all of which are prohibited for contravening irrevocable rights recognized by International Law of Human Rights."[32]

The Court emphasized that this was an inadequate strategy because it did not include criminal prosecution of violators of human rights:

> The Court positively values the numerous measures of reparation and non-repetition adopted by Brazil, which will be discussed in the chapter on reparations in the present Judgment. While these measures are important, they are not sufficient given that they have failed in providing access to justice for the next of kin of the victims.[33]

The fourth IACtHR case regarding a domestic amnesty law was the Uruguayan case of *Gelman*.[34] The case involved the forced disappearance of Maria Gelman in 1976, perpetrated by state agents of Argentina and Uruguay as part of the so-called "Operation Condor."[35] The Uruguayan amnesty law (*Ley de Caducidad*), enacted in 1986 by the democratic government of Uruguay, hindered investigation of Gelman's disappearance and prevented punishment of those responsible for the alleged violation.

In *Gelman*, the Court expressed the view equating amnesty and self-amnesty. Accordingly, regardless of how an amnesty law is adopted, and independent of the authority that enacts the law, the important question for the Court is the so-called *ratio legis*: whether these domestic laws leave serious human rights violations unpunished. If the laws do provide amnesty to perpetrators of serious human rights violations, then the laws are per se invalid under the ACHR.[36]

In addition to the argument of the amnesties' *ratio legis*, in *Gelman* the IACtHR dealt with the relationship between democracy and human rights. The Court's argument related to two referenda held in Uruguay in 1989 and

2009. On both occasions, the population voted in favor of the validity of the *Ley de Caducidad*. The IACtHR responded to the referendum results by stating that international human rights law constitutes a relentless limit on democratic majority rule. In setting aside the amnesty law, the Court again confirmed the full entrenchment and applicability of the Inter-American view on amnesty. The IACtHR did not discuss the concrete details of the two referenda in Uruguay; it did not ask whether the referenda on amnesty were truly free and democratic, or whether the voting process was somehow manipulated by the government. The Court solely affirmed that majority rule is not good enough to guarantee human rights protection.[37]

This point is important for the present argument because it highlights the universalist approach of the Court when assessing amnesties in contexts of regime change. No deeper contextual analysis is included in the Inter-American view on amnesty. Moreover, the Court does not differentiate the contexts of transition in Peru, Chile, Brazil, and Uruguay. The cases related to these contexts must be addressed equally merely because amnesties were adopted in the four countries. The assertion of a unique *ratio legis* for amnesties is the hallmark of the Court's approach.

The four cases together show that the IACtHR considers amnesty laws invalid per se and thus lacking legal effects, without any deeper contextual consideration. Contextual consideration may include a broad range of questions, such as: How was the amnesty law at issue in the case enacted in that country? Who participated in the drafting of the law? Was the process of adopting the amnesty law democratic? If not, why? What were the political conditions at the time? How was the amnesty law structured? What were the crimes covered by the amnesty law? Who were the beneficiaries of the law, and who were excluded from its protection? What were the legal effects of the amnesty?[38] As noted by Louise Mallinder, "the scope and legal effects of amnesty laws around the world can look very different."[39]

As will be seen in the next section, this decontextualized approach taken by the Court when evaluating domestic amnesty laws failed to properly assess the complexity of the Brazilian transition in *Gomes Lund*. The IACtHR maintained its legal reasoning based on a *jus cogens* vocabulary, with no deeper analysis of the Brazilian process of regime change.

II. THE BRAZILIAN TRANSITIONAL EXPERIENCE

This section of the chapter departs from the Court's universalist approach to amnesties. By adding contextual analysis on the Brazilian process of regime change, my objective is to underline the complexity not considered by the

Court when addressing *Gomes Lund*. Stressing this fault of the Inter-American view on amnesty is the core of my critique of the Court's role in addressing cases of transitional justice and human rights. Similar analyses could be made of the Peruvian, Chilean, and Uruguayan contexts. Here, I focus on the Brazilian transitional experience.

Brazil's dictatorship lasted twenty-one years, from 1964 to 1985, and had at least three different stages. The first stage lasted from the military coup on April 1964 to the consolidation of the regime; the second started in December 1968, when the repression reached its peak with the issuance of Institutional Act No. 5, which allowed the government to terminate elective mandates, to suspend political rights of citizens, to resign or to retire judges and other public officials, to ban political demonstrations, and to suspend the writ of habeas corpus in crimes against national security;[40] the third stage, called *distensão* (distention), started under the mandate of President Ernesto Geisel (1974–1979), and was characterized by a slow political opening that would last until the end of the regime in 1985.[41] This last stage included the abolition of Institutional Act No. 5, the press slowly starting to regain freedom, and amnesty proposals being openly debated among civil society.[42]

According to its 2014 report, the Brazilian National Truth Commission (NTC) investigated serious human rights violations (torture, killings, enforced disappearance, and concealing dead bodies) and confirmed 434 killings and enforced disappearances related to the Brazilian dictatorship.[43] Specifically, it found that 191 persons were killed, 210 disappeared, and the remains of 33 missing people were located.[44] The NTC recognized that these numbers are lower than the total number of victims of the regime, but it could not fully access the Armed Forces' archives. In the area of political persecution, the NTC found that between 1964 and 1973, 4,841 individuals had their political rights suspended; 513 senators, congresspeople and city councilors had their mandate revoked; 35 union leaders lost their political rights; 3,783 public officials lost their positions; and 1,313 military officials were expelled from the Armed Forces.[45]

One of the most important issues to be considered when evaluating the Brazilian amnesty case – though it went ignored by the IACtHR – is that amnesty was not a unilateral demand of the military regime. Rather, various social groups, such as the Female Movements for Amnesty, the Brazilian Committee for Amnesty, and the Societies for the Protection of Human Rights, were demanding amnesty well before 1979.[46] By the 1960s, shortly after the military coup, demonstrations favoring the granting of amnesty for political opponents of the regime were produced in light of the state repression.[47] However, it was from the 1970s onwards that the popular movement for amnesty for political prisoners gained strength in Brazil,[48] including demonstrations of women, students, lawyers, organizations related to the more progressive wing of the Catholic Church, metallurgists, and others.[49] At first, the military regime ignored these claims, but by the end of the 1970s, considering the broad reach of popular demonstrations, the regime was forced to tackle the topic,[50] as the country transitioned into the context of *distensão*, encompassing a slow and gradual political opening.

The popular demonstrations favoring adoption of amnesty in Brazil stemmed from a discourse of restoration of democracy, with an emphasis on reorganization of the rule of law and the respect for the rights of political prisoners[51] in a context of intense political persecution waged by the military regime, including imprisonment, the loss of political rights, and widespread torture. Notably, the popular demands for amnesty did not include as beneficiaries state agents who perpetrated human rights violations – though military personnel suspended and/or banned from the regime were included in these popular campaigns.

The creation of the Brazilian Committee for Amnesty in February 1978, in Rio de Janeiro, was an important step in Brazil's transitional justice strategy that encompassed this discourse of rights coupled with the demand for amnesty. The committee incorporated various social movements that favored granting amnesty to political prisoners and to those who had left the country in exile, and adopted a discourse defending their human rights, affirming the necessary release of all political prisoners (including those who undertook armed opposition against the regime – that is, those considered to be terrorists according to the dictatorship), and the extensive restoration of political rights.[52]

Illustrative of the coupling of amnesty to human rights in the Brazilian context in the 1970s is the "Letter of Salvador," written during the National Meeting for Amnesty, held in September 9, 1978, in the city of Salvador. This document is divided in three main parts: "the amnesty we fight for," "amnesty and democratic freedoms," and "amnesty and political reforms." The second part stated:

> The struggle for amnesty is necessary and essential for obtaining a greater achievement: democratic freedoms. We are convinced that all basic elements that attribute fairness to the struggle for amnesty are given in the current political moment, and integrate the democratic conscience of our people. The struggle for amnesty is connected with the struggles of all Brazilian people for better life and work conditions, for better salaries, against the high cost of living, for better feeding, housing, transportation, education, and health conditions, and for the ownership of the land where people work.[53]

The following passage clearly articulated the human rights claims:

> These are the reasons why we are struggling for AMNESTY. IMMEDIATELY. And we affirm the urgent need of broad freedom of expression, freedom of speech, freedom of press, freedom of cultural and artistic expression, and freedom of thought. These are the reasons why we are struggling for AMNESTY. IMMEDIATELY. And we affirm everyone's rights to association and assembly, the free organization of workers in their unions, working places and homes. And we declare the fairness of the right to strike. These are the reasons why we are struggling for AMNESTY. IMMEDIATELY. And we declare as fair and legitimate all political activity through which all groups of people may express their interests, present their projects to the whole society, and, therefore, participate in the political processes of the Brazilian nation. In this setting, we defend the broad freedom of organization of all political parties [54]

In general terms, amnesty was characterized by these social movements as being broad (for all acts against the regime), general (for all victims of state repression), and unrestricted (without discrimination between the potential beneficiaries).[55] The popular demands for amnesty helped power an influential discourse that spread throughout Brazilian society and appeared at diverse events, such as football games, student gatherings, and national anniversary celebrations, among others.[56]

As a result, legislative debates were held regarding the adoption of amnesty in 1979, reflecting the context of the end of the 1970s, which was strongly marked by the social campaigns advocating for the adoption of the benefit. Notwithstanding, Brazilian people differed in their view on the scope, degree, and content of an amnesty benefit. Different claims were made as to who amnesty would apply to and for which kinds of offenses: would it apply to all crimes, only to criminal convictions, or only to political crimes? Would the perpetrators of political persecution along with the politically persecuted themselves be considered beneficiaries of the amnesty, or would only one of these groups receive such a benefit?[57]

The legislative discussion about amnesty began with a draft legislation prepared by the executive branch and sent to the National Congress for deliberation on June 27, 1979. The following day, a presidential message about the amnesty was read in the legislature. President Figueiredo (1979–1985) asserted that it was the right time for national pacification and the establishment of democratic coexistence, but he stressed that those people convicted of common crimes would not benefit from the right to amnesty – this would mean that those convicted of terrorism would not be included in the amnesty.[58] Under the military rule, terrorism, assault, kidnapping, and personal attacks were all considered common crimes as set forth in the National Security Law, the legal framework for state repression during Brazilian dictatorship.

A Joint Committee was in charge of analyzing the government's proposed draft legislation. It was formed by members of the ruling party, Alliance for National Renovation (ARENA), and the opposition party, Brazilian Democratic Movement (MDB).[59] At the beginning of August 1979, Teotônio Vilela (MDB) assumed the presidency of the Joint Committee. In his inauguration speech, problems with the government's amnesty project were brought to light:

> The proposal does not exclude those that the regime sees as responsible for terror. It benefited some people, leaving out those judicially convicted. Two accused by the same fact will have completely opposed treatment. The convicted people will stay in prison. Those not convicted will recover their rights, and will not be held accountable for the committed acts. There is no logical argument, nor ethical principle, that justifies such odious inequality.[60]

During the legislative debates, the government's amnesty draft received 305 amendments prepared by 134 parliamentarians, including 49 parliamentarians from the ruling party ARENA. The main cause for such a high number of amendments was the restricted and discriminatory character of the government's proposed amnesty project. For example, one proposed draft dealt with torture, and excluded torture from the amnesty benefit, but on the other hand extended the benefit to those people convicted of terrorism, assault, kidnapping, and personal attacks, all common crimes under the National Security Law.[61] The debates concerning the amnesty legislation reflected different positions, making clear it was not simply a shield to avoid prosecution by state agents.

The government's draft was criticized by political prisoners and by those supporting political opposition to the regime. Those critics voiced concerns that the project excluded individuals convicted of those common crime offenses set forth in the National Security Law, conditioned the return of civil servants to their respective positions only upon meeting certain requirements, and did not provide for the immediate release of political prisoners. In this sense, the amnesty proposed by the executive was more restrictive than the one advocated by various social movements in the 1970s.[62] The vote was held in two sessions on August 21 and 22, 1979, and the main contours of the executive's amnesty proposal remained unaltered.[63]

A. *The Amnesty Law*

The Amnesty Law No. 6.683/79 was enacted and promulgated by President Figueiredo on August 28, 1979. In accordance with Article 1 of the Amnesty Law,[64] the benefit was granted for the period from September 2, 1961 to August 15, 1979, to those who committed political or "related crimes," as well as electoral crimes; in other words, to state agents. Accordingly, the paragraph added to Article 1, which had been so contested in the debates leading up to the law's adoption, determined the scope of the Amnesty Law. The first paragraph defined "related crimes" as offenses of any nature related to political crimes, while the second paragraph laid out the exclusion of individuals convicted of terrorism, assault, kidnapping, and personal attack from the amnesty benefit.[65] The first paragraph prevented prosecutions of human rights violations perpetrated by state agents, one of the main topics of contestation between the regime and its opponents.

Amnesty was also granted to those individuals who had political rights suspended, to public officials (including members of the military punished by the regime), and union representatives. However, the return of public officials to their previous positions was not automatic. The law established that it depended on availability, and on the interests of public administration, as set out in Article 3; this illustrates the limited contours of the 1979 Amnesty Law.

The debate over the content and dimension of the Brazilian amnesty did not stop with enactment of the law. New and different amnesty proposals were sent to the National Congress after that, including the case of those representing the interests of military agents that were punished during the military rule.[66] Constitutional Amendment No. 26, adopted on November 27, 1985 by the National Congress, called for a new constitutional assembly in Brazil. Among its provisions, Article 4 of the amendment renewed the granting of amnesty, without changing the main scope of the 1979 law, though it did provide for the restitution of labor rights.[67] On October 5, 1988, Brazil enacted a new democratic constitution. It not only granted amnesty, but also broadened its scope. Article 8 of the "Transitional Constitutional Act" extended the time period for which amnesty applied, encompassing September 18, 1946 to October 5, 1988, and expanded who received the amnesty benefit to include those affected by acts of exception because of political motivation.[68] In *Gomes Lund*, the IACtHR did not take into account all these transformations.

Thus, while the Amnesty Law in Brazil had its starting point in 1979, the amnesty law has subsequently been amended[69] and expanded constitutionally in a context that is still evolving in the country.[70] The 1979 Amnesty Law consolidated an initial effort toward regime change in Brazil, and successfully provided for the beginning of overcoming dictatorship through the release of political prisoners.[71] As the process of political transformation continued, other measures were adopted after the 1979 amnesty, adding new dimensions to this process. Under the government of Fernando Henrique Cardoso (1995–2002),[72] Law No. 9.140/95 recognized the death of 136 missing people. Through this law, Brazil acknowledged its responsibility for acts committed during dictatorship, but there was no initiation of criminal prosecutions. Instead, as expressly stated in Article 2 of Law No. 9.140/95, its effects would be guided by the principles of national reconciliation and peace contained in the law of 1979.[73]

Brazil's recognition of responsibility came about as a result of activities by the victims' families, especially the work of the Commission of Family Members of Political Prisoners, Killed and Disappeared, and the group "Torture: Never Again."[74] The government started negotiations between victims' families and government representatives, aimed at enacting a law on the matter of killings and disappearances.[75] Law No. 9.140/95 created a Special Commission for Political Deaths and Disappearances responsible for expanding the original list of 136 victims.

On November 13, 2002, toward the end of Cardoso's second term, Law No. 10.559/02 created a new legal regime for amnestied people, including a program of reparations and financial compensation for those individuals who had been politically persecuted under dictatorship in Brazil. In other words, the new law would finally include both sides of the conflict. According to Article 1 of this law, the legal regime for amnestied people encompasses the following rights: declaration of political amnesty ("a sort of official state apology"[76]), economic reparations, the right to consider time spent in exile and in prison for retirement purposes, the students' right to conclude courses that were interrupted by the military regime, and the public officials' right to be reintegrated into their original jobs. Moreover, Law No. 10.559/02 expressly repealed certain provisions of the Amnesty Law of 1979, such as Article 2 on the reintegration of public officials.[77]

Under Luiz Inácio Lula da Silva's presidency (2003–2010), Brazilian reparations policy was expanded by way of new symbolic mechanisms: the project "Right to Memory and Truth" created a government record of killings and disappearances; "Amnesty Caravans" called for public declarations of amnesty to the victims at the locations where violations took place; and the project "Revealed Memories" made available to the public archives from the dictatorship period.[78] Furthermore, under Lula's government, the Brazilian National Truth Commission was created,[79] and a law concerning access to public documents was issued,[80] both in November 2011.

The creation of the NTC has been perceived by Brazilian legal scholars as related to IACtHR's holding in *Gomes Lund*.[81] The law expressly creating the NTC was passed in 2011 – after *Gomes Lund* was handed down in 2010 – but the 2009 Third National Program on Human Rights under Lula's government had actually called for the creation of a truth commission in the country.[82] Therefore, the holding in *Gomes Lund* alone does not adequately account for the existence of the NTC. Nevertheless, the concrete establishment of the NTC in 2012 seems to be closely connected to the international context of the IACtHR decision.

The NTC issued its final report on December 10, 2014. The three-volume report amounts to around 3,500 pages, and contains detailed descriptions of individual cases of violations. The establishment of the NTC was accompanied by the creation of other truth commissions in the country, based on cities, universities, unions, and local branches of the Brazilian Bar Association. The NTC worked in dialogue with these smaller truth commissions, without any relation of hierarchy between them;[83] thus, the recent years in Brazil may be characterized as an intense period of truth-seeking.

The scope of the chapter does not allow for a deeper analysis of the NTC report – an enterprise that requires a specific study.[84] I will briefly mention a few aspects of the report, with special attention to one of its recommendations. The 2011 law that created the NTC determined its scope: it has competence to investigate, but not prosecute, serious human rights violations committed from September 18, 1946 to October 5, 1988. The mandate of the NTC included four serious violations: torture, extrajudicial executions, enforced disappearances, and concealing of dead bodies. The NTC decided to complement its statutory mandate with two other serious human rights violations: arbitrary detentions and sexual violence as a specific form of torture.[85]

Here it becomes clear that the NTC's work is focused on the violations perpetrated by state agents during dictatorship in Brazil. Accordingly, at the outset of Volume I, the NTC states its commitment to the claims of the political prisoners and the claims of those who were persecuted during the military regime.[86] The report does not assess the acts of the regime's political opponents, who also used violence to resist state violence, such as kidnapping foreign ambassadors. This explanation is not explored by the NTC's report, but it is possible to understand the choices of the NTC because political opponents in Brazil were already persecuted by Military Justice during dictatorship. In other words, the facts related to the role of the political opposition in the country had already been investigated, which is not the case for state violence.

The final report reached four main conclusions: serious human rights violations were committed during the investigated period (especially during dictatorship), these violations had a systematic character, they constitute crimes against humanity, and they persist in the current Brazilian context. Seventeen institutional measures and eight normative proposals composed the NTC's recommendations.

International law plays an important role in the NTC's report, especially the use of the same rationale of the Inter-American view on amnesty. Recommendation 2 established the duty to punish the serious human rights violations investigated by the NTC. The report does not call for revision of the Brazilian Amnesty Law, but it states that amnesty shall not be applied in the cases of serious human rights violations described in the NTC's report. The text of recommendation 2 closes with a brief description of the IACtHR's case law on amnesty, quoting the same cases used in this chapter. And it is stated that:

> The rationale of the Inter-American Court is clear: self-amnesty laws are prohibited under international law; they perpetuate impunity and promote injustice, hindering access to justice for the victims and their families, a direct violation of the state duty to investigate, sanction, prosecute, and make reparation for serious human rights violations.[87]

The NTC is a political organ and it is competent to establish recommendations. A different issue is the implementation of the report's recommendations by the Brazilian state. This story has not ended in Brazil, as another important dimension regarding the Brazilian process of political transformation was opened with the work of the NTC.[88]

B. *The constitutional challenge*

In 2008, the Brazilian Bar Association (OAB) filed a complaint before the Brazilian Federal Supreme Court (STF) claiming that the 1979 Amnesty Law violated constitutional provisions. The claim of breach of fundamental precept (ADPF n. 153) had as its main object Article n. 1, paragraph 1 of the 1979 Amnesty Law, which provided the legal foundation for not prosecuting military personnel who have committed human rights violations.

The OAB asked the Supreme Court for a clearer interpretation of this provision, in order to declare that amnesty could not be extended to the violations perpetrated by state agents of the military regime. The OAB also claimed that Article 1, paragraph 1 from the Amnesty Law was not incorporated into the 1988 constitution,[89] because Article 5 prohibited amnesty being granted to perpetrators of torture.

In an April 2010 decision, in which the Supreme Court was divided seven to two, the petition of OAB was rejected. Briefly, the Brazilian Court asserted that the 1979 Amnesty Law conveyed a political decision related to a historical moment, as a reconciled strategy of transitional justice. STF affirmed the bilateral, broad, and general aspects of the Amnesty Law. Moreover, the Court explained that human rights treaties that forbid the practice of torture, including the ACHR and other instruments, entered into force after the amnesty law was enacted, and the constitutional provision on torture was adopted after the 1979 Amnesty Law. The constitution, according to the Supreme Court, does not reach amnesty laws enacted prior to its validity.

Finally, a majority of the Supreme Court held that the constitutional order established in 1988 reaffirmed the provisions of the 1979 Amnesty Law as an act of constituent power, in a decision handed down only seven months before the IACtHR's decision on *Gomes Lund*. Thus, amnesty was integrated into the new democratic order and should be considered as its founding act. Its review should therefore be undertaken by the legislature and not by the constitutional court.[90] However, the Supreme Court asserted that all remaining obstacles related to the full disclosure of activities of the Brazilian dictatorship should be overcome, as a clear consequence of the right to truth.[91] The Amnesty Law is, therefore, in full force in Brazil at this time.[92]

The decision of the Supreme Court has been widely criticized, especially by Brazilian international law scholars, who use the IACtHR case law as an objective yardstick to assess the country's transitional process. According to one scholar, the constitutional court decision confirmed the "volatile Brazilian understanding regarding the international obligation to prosecute major violators of human rights, and the Brazilian indifference to the principle of *aut dedere aut iudicare* ..."[93]

The Brazilian experience of democratic transition highlights diverse features concerning the enactment and provisions of amnesty. There is no doubt that human rights violations have been perpetrated, both by state agents and political opponents. Violations committed by state agents were not investigated, nor prosecuted, because of the Amnesty Law. However, political acts committed by the regime's opponents, such as "terrorism," were considered common crimes under the military legal framework, and were prosecuted by the dictatorship itself, as the report *Brazil: Never Again* demonstrated. Amnesty was granted by the regime within a context of popular demands for the benefit, and these popular demands focused on the restitution of rights of those who opposed military rule. Even if the 1979 Amnesty Law originally excluded some of those who had been politically persecuted, the regime's opponents regained their voice within the Brazilian context, which included the restoration of political rights, the release of political prisoners, and the return of politically exiled individuals.

Therefore, rather than ignore the crimes of a repressive military regime, calls for amnesty enabled debates among civil society to establish new agreements and a transition strategy between the political forces of the country. Indeed, the scope of the 1979 Amnesty Law was transformed with the new constitutional order, as well as under Cardoso's and Lula's governments, by way of an inclusive trend aimed at broadening the political declaration of amnesty to all individuals who suffered under the Brazilian dictatorship.

Today, the Amnesty Law still stands. Despite the legislative proposals to repeal the 1979 law[94] and the activism of the victims' families for criminal prosecutions, the Brazilian amnesty remains in force. Paulo Abrão and Marcelo D. Torelly argue that there is "social resistance to changing the scope of the amnesty law."[95] To support this claim, they quote the result of a public opinion poll, according to which 40 percent of the respondents would support holding trials for human rights violations committed by state agents during the Brazilian dictatorship, while 45 percent would oppose it.[96]

It is worth noting that the Brazilian transition and the 1979 Amnesty Law were the result of a political pact.[97] When approached with this perspective, the persistent character of the Amnesty Law calls into question the concrete possibilities for changing the political pact founded on amnesty. In my opinion, our elites still seem committed to the political bargains related to amnesty, partial as it was, leaving no room for criminal prosecutions of state agents. The speech by president Dilma Rousseff on the 50th anniversary of the 1964 military coup, cited at the beginning of this chapter, seems to disclose the continuing power of the political pact sealed in 1979.

In sum, the IACtHR approach eschewed evaluating the Brazilian transitional experience. Focusing on human rights violations and impunity reduces the complexity of this context, obscuring the positive aspects of granting amnesty in Brazil. This argument will be discussed in the last part of this chapter.

III. THE VIRTUES OF THE BRAZILIAN AMNESTY

Positive aspects of granting amnesty can certainly be highlighted, notwithstanding the IACtHR's universalist approach that amnesty is per se unlawful. The main objective here is not to analyze successful implementation of amnesty laws, but to assert that, when assessing a concrete case, important aspects related to amnesty and the reasons for its adoption in a certain societal and political context may remain submerged under the claim of an absolute duty to punish human rights violations. In addition, this analysis highlights that amnesty and impunity for human rights violations are not in binary opposition; indeed, Brazil has made significant strides in truth-seeking and reparation of victims even while the Amnesty Law remains in force.

The close relationship between amnesty and the domestic context of political transition is one of these positive aspects, since the process of granting amnesty encompasses the limitations related to political struggles in a country and pragmatic considerations about what to do (or not to do) for regime change.[98] Contrary to trials, which focus on individual accountability, amnesty takes into account and is sensitive to the political nuances of internal processes of political transformation. Without suggesting that human rights claims and obligations operate beyond politics, as if it were possible to end the "inconvenience" of politics,[99] amnesty may create an opening to take up other political issues as a key element in dealing with situations of regime change.

Brazil provides a case study for these political and societal undertakings. Without a strict duty to punish individual perpetrators, Brazil had more space to shape its process of political change; the 1979 Amnesty Law was a starting point for this transformation, not its end. As I indicated previously, all political prisoners had been released in Brazil by 1980, and political opponents regained a voice in the Brazilian political arena, permitting a nascent context of regime change. Amnesty also enabled the restitution of revoked rights, the return of the exiled, and the review of administrative and judicial convictions and investigations.

This understanding may disregard the victims of human rights violations perpetrated during dictatorship in Brazil,[100] as the reasoning of the IACtHR underscores. Nonetheless, this claim has to be assessed considering the details of the Brazilian transitional experience. Accordingly, the Court's main argument is that only criminal proceedings assure the victims' right to access to justice, the right to know the truth about the facts, and the right to reparations. To the extent that amnesties prevent criminal prosecutions, those victims' rights would be impossible to vindicate. However, if we consider the policies undertaken by the Brazilian government in the post-amnesty context – policies which include the Amnesty Law's transformation into a law of broad reach backed by constitutional guarantee – most of Cardoso's and Lula's innovations were articulated in legal terms aimed at giving the law substance and concrete influence, notably for victims and their families. First, the recognition of Brazilian responsibility for forced disappearances enabled a program of reparations for the victims of the regime. Second, the special legal regime for amnestied people encompassed an extensive program of reparations, including not just financial compensations, but also the state declaration of political amnesty, and the reintegration of students' and employees' rights. Third, the National Truth Commission and the 2011 law concerning access to public documents directly relate to the right to know the truth about the past.

Thus, by and large, when the context of Brazilian amnesty is taken into account, it becomes clear that almost all elements that seek to protect the victims' rights are present. The absence of trials in Brazil did not imply the total disregard of the victims' rights, nor the absence of strategies to deal with the violence of the military rule. On the contrary, it is possible to assert that amnesty in Brazil promoted the realization of human rights in a long-term perspective.

The right that remains the subject of further discussion is the right to access to justice. For the IACtHR, access to justice is conceived solely in terms of individual criminal prosecutions, a very restricted understanding of justice. It is uncertain whether individual criminal responsibility will be sufficient to cope with complex conflicts related to structural causes.[101] For instance, holding trials may entail strategic choices by accused individuals regarding the disclosure of facts and production of evidence for the purpose of receiving a not guilty verdict or a reduced conviction. Accordingly, justice for the victims of violations is never a certain outcome when considering individual criminal prosecutions.

Related to the victims' rights is the question of the victims' perspective. The argument that countries have a duty to prosecute seemingly views victims as a single unit, with fixed interests in time and space. This view places victims within a homogeneous group of people who always think of justice in terms of criminal prosecutions, regardless of the particularities of the concrete situation. But victims' perspectives change over time and are affected by several factors. A continued risk of physical violence, economic welfare, the cultural traditions of a community, and its political views,[102] are all factors which exist outside of the framework of a formal choice between trials or amnesty. Amnesty can be a useful tool to account for this variability of interests, assuming that decisions are not unchangeable. In a recent study, Louise Mallinder discusses the alternation related to the adoption of mechanisms of transitional justice in concrete situations in Argentina, Bosnia-Herzegovina, South Africa, Uganda, and Uruguay. Considering the continually renegotiated character of transitional justice, she says:

> transitional states rarely face a binary choice between amnesty and justice, but rather may undergo a continual process of re-negotiation of the balance between impunity and accountability as the transition evolves. Indeed, during political transitions countries rarely follow a linear path towards justice.[103]

In the Brazilian case, the issue of the victims' perspective is especially interesting as the claim for amnesty was articulated not just by the regime itself, as a shield to avoid prosecution, but also by its opponents, in the name of the rights of the victims of the dictatorship.

Amnesty may allow a different discussion about human rights, as a discourse that may open space for political struggles.[104] Amnesty sheds light on different understandings about the protection of human rights, as a discourse that permits the establishment of new political consensus. These rights can be articulated in a responsible way, considering a variety of possible outcomes in the world rather than an inflexible, one-size-fits-all approach. In other words, tangible improvements in reality are also related to concrete political action, which may relate to the affirmation of human rights in legal texts, but are not restricted to such strategy. The protection of human rights and strategies of transitional justice are necessarily varied and complex.

The debate about the virtues of the Brazilian amnesty makes it possible to articulate an argument about the indeterminacy of human rights discourse. As Martti Koskenniemi explains, for every understanding of a legal rule, there is a contrary view or an exception. For each principle, there is a counter-principle, and for each institutional policy, a policy in the opposite direction.[105] In light of the position of the IACtHR favoring trials and invalidating amnesty, which is justified by plausible legal arguments, it is possible to articulate a discourse about the virtues of the Brazilian amnesty also based on plausible legal arguments.

The human rights discourse allows for argumentative diversity. The meaning of human rights, their scope, and their limits are not established unequivocally, but depend on how they are interpreted. Thus, rights receive meaning to the extent that they are related to some context or purpose.[106] Affirming the indeterminacy of human rights discourse is not to say that any solution can be accepted. Rather, the appropriateness of legal alternatives to enable peaceful processes of regime change cannot be thought of by means of objective criteria or external patterns of practice – as done by the IACtHR when articulating the *jus cogens* vocabulary. The usefulness of legal alternatives has to be discussed in order to take into account the political and moral choices undertaken in each specific situation of transitional justice.

The key point is that these decisions about human rights and what strategies to take in the process of transitional justice are motivated by political choices and cannot be reduced to neutral outcomes. Decisions are derived from real people and real institutions. Assuming that there are competing legal alternatives and that the choice among them is available to everyone involved in the argumentative practice of international law brings a dimension of responsibility to the people involved in this practice.[107]

IV. CONCLUDING REMARKS

This chapter explored how anti-impunity discourse operates in the practice of the Inter-American Court of Human Rights, with a focus on its treatment of Brazil. My objective was to discuss the Inter-American Court of Human Rights' arguments about criminal prosecutions as a necessary way to deal with human rights violations in the context of regime change, underscoring that there are no neutral or objective legal decisions to be taken.

It seems inevitable to recognize that the Court develops such a position for its own ends. To ensure a decisive influence in Latin America, there was a need to diminish the local context's importance. Thus, without further analysis of the political contingencies of the Brazilian case, the Court referenced the incompatibility between domestic amnesty and the American Convention, highlighting the inadequacy of the Brazilian transition.

The Court, in determining the legal necessity of holding trials in Brazil, imposes legal solutions without considering what has been discussed at the local level. There are no reasons under the argumentative practice of international law that justify accepting a natural superiority of the IACtHR in light of contextual experiences.[108]

The main objective of this chapter is not to offer practical guidelines for the performance of the IACtHR, but to suggest that, by and large, the Inter-American Court could have decided the *Gomes Lund* case, as well as other amnesty cases, using an approach that seeks dialogue with the local dimension and with the particularities of the context, assuming explicitly its own political and legal choices. The main argument is not to defend amnesty laws or to argue against trials, but to highlight the superficial legal justification the Court presents to invalidate the Brazilian amnesty as something against peremptory rules of international law.

Without intending to represent the final word in regard to the Brazilian transition, the Court could have contributed to the local public debate by offering different perspectives and assessing the Brazilian case on its own merits. Here, the questions presented earlier would guide such an assessment: How was the Amnesty Law enacted? Who participated in the drafting of the law? Was the process democratic? If not, why? What were the political conditions at the time? How was the Amnesty Law structured? What were the crimes covered? Who were the beneficiaries, and who were excluded? What were the legal effects of the amnesty? Answering these questions would enrich the Court's arguments, offering robust reasons to eventually invalidate the Brazilian amnesty.

All things considered, it may be said that amnesty was needed for the democratic transition in Brazil. This statement does not mean that this past political choice is unchangeable. Brazilian people may change it (and maybe it is time to start this process in Brazil), but people should consider whether to do so under a responsible public debate concerning our violent past, while taking into account the consequences of shedding light on complex schemes of political power and violent repression.

NOTES

1 *Gomes Lund et al.* v. *Brazil* (Inter-American Court of Human Rights, 2010).
2 Julliana Braga, "Dilma Talks about 1964, and Points to the Country's Debt to Dead and Missing People," Globo, March 31, 2014, accessed March 3, 2015, http://g1.globo. com/politica/50-anos-do-golpe-militar/noticia/2014/03/para-dilma-lembrar-do-golpe-faz-parte-da-consolidacao-da-democracia.html (translation by author).
3 Ibid. (emphasis added).
4 Title of a talk held on September 2011 at the State University of São Paulo, "How Much Truth May Brazil Bear?," accessed March 3, 2015, http://comunicacao.fflch. usp.br/sites/comunicacao.fflch.usp.br/files/Filosofo.pdf.
5 James Cavallaro, "Human Rights Exceptionalism in Brazil," CDDRL, PHR News, February 3, 2011, accessed March 3, 2015, http://fsi.stanford.edu/news/cavallaro_on_human_rights_exceptionalism_in_brazil_20110203/.
6 Glenda Mezarobba, *Um Acerto de Contas com o Futuro: a Anistia e suas Consequências, um Estudo do Caso Brasileiro* (São Paulo: Associação Editorial Humanitas; FAPESP, 2006), 18.
7 The recent decision in the case of *El Mozote* will not be included in the present analysis. *El Mozote* discusses the compatibility between the Salvadoran "Law of General Amnesty for the Consolidation of Peace," enacted by the Salvadoran Legislative Assembly in 1993, and the ACHR. The analysis of the IACtHR is focused on international humanitarian law, and even if this ruling constitutes a remarkable step in its case law, its discussion surpasses the scope of this chapter. According to the Court:

> However, contrary to the cases examined previously by this Court, the instant case deals with a general amnesty law that relates to acts committed in the context of an internal armed conflict. Therefore, the Court finds it pertinent, when analyzing the compatibility of the Law of General Amnesty for the Consolidation of Peace with the international obligations arising from the American Convention and its application to the case of the Massacres of El Mozote and Nearby Places, to do so also in light of the provisions of Protocol II Additional to the 1949 Geneva Conventions, as well as of the specific terms in which it was agreed to end hostilities, which put an end to the conflict in El Salvador and, in particular, of Chapter I ("Armed Forces"), section 5 ("End to Impunity"), of the Peace Accord of January 16, 1992.

Massacres of El Mozote and Nearby Places v. *El Salvador*, at para. 284 (Inter-American Court of Human Rights, 2012).

8 Louise Mallinder, *Amnesty, Human Rights and Political Transitions* (Oxford: Hart Publishing, 2008), 5. According to this legal definition of amnesty provided by Mallinder, "In extinguishing liability for a crime, amnesty assumes that a crime has been committed. In this way, amnesties are retroactive, applying only to acts committed before the laws were passed." Ibid.

9 Mallinder, *Amnesty*, 6–7.

10 The expression "The Inter-American view on amnesty" was coined by Judge Sergio García-Ramírez in his separate opinion in the case of *La Cantuta* v. *Peru*:

> To sum up, the Inter-American Court's position on this issue [amnesty] upholds: (a) the full force and effect of the obligations to respect rights and ensure their exercise, under Article 1 of the American Convention on Human Rights (ACHR), notwithstanding any domestic-law obstacles that might hinder due compliance with such obligations that the State has undertaken, acting in its sovereign capacity, upon becoming a party to the Convention; (b) the resulting eradication of the impunity that such obstacles might allow in connection with particularly egregious crimes; and (c) the State's duty to adopt, at the domestic law level, such measures as may be required to enforce said duties and root out impunity, pursuant to the provisions of Article 2 of the ACHR.

La Cantuta v. *Peru*, Separate Opinion of Judge García-Ramírez, at para. 3 (Inter-American Court of Human Rights, 2006).

11 *Barrios Altos* v. *Peru*, at para. 2 (Inter-American Court of Human Rights, 2001).

12 Ibid. at para. 2.

13 Ibid. at para. 41.

14 Laurence Burgorgue-Larsen and Amaya Úbeda de Torres. *The Inter-American Court of Human Rights. Case Law and Commentary* (Oxford: Oxford University, 2011), 724. Organization of American States, American Convention on Human Rights, arts. 1, 2 (1144 U.N.T.S. 144, Nov. 22, 1969). Art. 1 concerns the obligation to respect rights, and Art. 2 the obligation of state parties to adopt legislative or other measures to protect the rights and freedoms contained in the Convention.

15 *Barrios Altos* at para. 44 (emphasis added).

16 Ibid. at paras. 10–11 (Cançado Trindade, J., concurring). Accordingly:

> (...) the laws of self-amnesty, besides being manifestly incompatible with the American Convention, and devoid, in consequence, of legal effects, have no legal validity at all in the light of the norms of the International Law of Human Rights. They are rather the source (*fons et origo*) of an international illicit act: as from their own adoption (*tempus commisi delicti*), and irrespectively of their subsequent application, they engage the international responsibility of the State. Their being in force creates per se a situation which affects in a continuing way non-derogable rights, which, as I have already indicated, belong to the domain of *jus cogens*.

17 Ibid. at para. 26.

18 *Almonacid-Arellano et al.* v. *Chile* (Inter-American Court of Human Rights, 2006).

19 Ibid. at para. 93–129. "Insofar as it was intended to grant amnesty to those responsible for crimes against humanity, Decree Law No. 2.191 is incompatible with the American Convention and, therefore, it has no legal effects." Ibid. at para. 171 (operative part of the award).

20 "The region where the events took place was located at the borders of the states of Maranhão, Pará and the actual Tocantins, where the river Araguaia passes through." *Gomes Lund* at para. 88, footnote 79.

21 See also the report "Right to Memory and Truth," available in Portuguese, accessed March 3, 2015, http://portal.mj.gov.br/sedh/biblioteca/livro_direito_memoria_verdade/livro_direito_memoria_verdade_sem_a_marca.pdf.

22 *Gomes Lund* at para. 17.

23 Ibid. at para. 18.

24 Ibid. at para. 105.

25 Ibid. at para. 109.

26 The broad use of *jus cogens* vocabulary by the IACtHR has already been noted by some scholars. Illustratively, see Catherine Maia, "Le Jus Cogens dans la Jurisprudence de la Cour Interamericaine des Droits de L'Homme," *Le Particularisme Interaméricain des Droits de l'Homme*, eds. Ludovic Hennebel and Hélène Tigroudja (Paris: Pedone, 2009), 271–312, 276–277; Gerald L. Neuman, "Import, Export, and Regional Consent in the Inter-American Court of Human Rights," *European Journal of International Law* 19 (2008): 101–123.

27 As of March 2015.

28 Ibid. at paras. 85–87.

29 Ibid. at paras. 88–90.

30 Ibid. at paras. 91–93.

31 Ibid. at paras. 112–125. According to the Court, the members of the Guerrilla of Araguaia, "represent half of those politically disappeared in Brazil." Ibid. at para. 124.

32 Ibid. at para. 171.

33 Ibid. at para. 178.

34 *Gelman v. Uruguay* (Inter-American Court of Human Rights, 2011).

35 Ibid. at para. 44.

> This was the context of the so-called "Operation Condor," a code name given to the alliance of the security forces and intelligence services of the Southern Cone dictatorships in their repression of and fight against individuals designated "subversive elements." The activities deployed as part of this Operation were coordinated basically by the military personnel of the countries involved. The Operation systematized and improved clandestine coordination between the "security forces and military personnel and intelligence services" of the region. The system of codes and communications had to be efficient for "Operation Condor" to function, and so that the lists of "'most wanted subversives" could be managed easily by the different States.

36 Ibid. at para. 229.

37 Ibid. at paras. 238–239.

38 I thank Natalie Davidson for putting part of these questions in this way.

39 Louise Mallinder, "Amnesties' Challenge to the Global Accountability Norm? Interpreting Regional and International Trends in Amnesty Enactment," *Amnesty in the Age of Human Rights Accountability: Comparative and International Perspective*, eds. Francesca Lessa and Leigh A. Payne (Cambridge: Cambridge University Press, 2012), 69–96, 75.

40 Right to Memory and Truth, 21–27.

41 Ibid., 21.

42 Ibid., 27.

43 Report available only in Portuguese, accessed March 3, 2015, www.cnv.gov.br/.

44 Ibid., Ch. 18 "Conclusions and recommendations," at para. 5.

45 Ibid., Ch. 3 "Historical context of the serious human rights violations between 1946 and 1988," at para. 89.

46 These groups were officially labelled as "movements for amnesty" during the Second Congress for Amnesty, which took place in Salvador in November 1979. Fabíola Brigante Del Porto, "The Fight for Amnesty in the Brazilian Military Regime: the Constitution of the Civil Society and the Construction of Citizenship," accessed March 10, 2015, www.fpabramo.org.br/sites/default/files/2-FabiolaP3-1.pdf. See also Paulo Abrão and Marcelo D. Torelly, "Resistance to Change: Brazil's Persistent Amnesty and its Alternatives for Truth and Justice," *Amnesty in the Age of Human Rights Accountability*, eds. Francesca Lessa and Leigh A. Payne (Cambridge: Cambridge University Press, 2012), 152–181, 153–154.

> It is important to emphasize that the Amnesty Law in Brazil was the result of popular demand, unlike the passage of other amnesty laws in the region. For example, the Argentinian amnesty was imposed by the authoritarian regime and was an explicit self-amnesty designed to maintain impunity for the crimes perpetrated by the state. In Brazil, the amnesty was supported by civil society because it was originally intended to pardon crimes of resistance committed by the politically persecuted who had been banished, exiled, and imprisoned, thus promoting amnesty "as freedom and reparation."

47 Mezarobba, *Um Acerto de Contas*, 23; Danyelle Nilin Gonçalves, "Os Múltiplos Sentidos da Anistia," *Revista Anistia, Política e Justiça de Transição* 1 (2009): 272–295, 273.

48 Gonçalves, "Os Múltiplos Sentidos da Anistia," 274.

49 Mezarobba, *Um Acerto de Contas*, 27–28.

50 Ibid., 33.

51 Ibid., 27.

52 Gonçalves, "Os Múltiplos Sentidos da Anistia," 275.

53 Letter of Salvador, September 9, 1978, accessed March 3, 2015, http://novo.fpabramo.org.br/content/carta-de-salvador (Translation by the author).

54 Ibid. (Translation by the author).

55 Mezarobba, *Um Acerto de Contas*, 31.

56 Gonçalves, "Os Múltiplos Sentidos da Anistia," 276.

57 Ibid., 277.

58 Mezarobba, *Um Acerto de Contas*, 37–39.

59 Abbreviations in Portuguese.

60 Mezarobba, *Um Acerto de Contas*, 40–41.

61 Ibid., 43.

62 Mezarobba, *Um Acerto de Contas*, 43–45.

63 Ibid., 48–50.

64 Law No. 6.683/79 (Brazil 1979).

65 Ibid.

66 Mezarobba, *Um Acerto de Contas*, 55–57.

67 Constitutional Amendment No. 26 (Brazil 1985).

68 Transitional Constitutional Act (Brazil 1988).

69 Mezarobba, *Um Acerto de Contas*, 18.

70 Ibid., 148–149.

71 After the 1979 law, the Brazilian Superior Military Court assessed its ongoing proceedings aiming at releasing those prisoners accused of offenses set forth in the National Security Law – as the people already convicted for such offenses were not included among the amnesty beneficiaries. On November 20, 1979, President Figueiredo signed a decree pardoning twenty-five political prisoners who were serving sentences in the country. In the same year, the Christmas pardon benefited those convicted to serve prison sentences of no more than four years, provided that part of the sentence had already been served. Those individuals convicted for prison sentences of more than four years, included those convicted for offenses set forth in the National Security Law, had their sentences reduced. In many cases, this reduction implied immediate release. In 1980, the last Brazilian political prisoner was released. Ibid., 52.

72 João Baptista de Oliveira Figueiredo was the last military ruler in Brazil. His mandate lasted from March 15, 1979 to March 15, 1985. He was followed by José Sarney (1985–1990), a civilian indirectly elected for the presidency. The first direct and free elections after dictatorship were subsequently held in Brazil, and Fernando Afonso Collor de Mello was elected. Because of corruption practices, Collor was impeached by the National Congress, and his mandate lasted from March 15, 1990 to October 2, 1992. The vice president Itamar Augusto Cautiero Franco assumed, and finished the mandate on January 1, 1995. Fernando Henrique Cardoso was elected in the second Brazilian presidential election after military rule, held at the end of 1994.

73 Law No. 9.140/95 (Brazil 1995).

74 To shed light on the political and military schemes of repression in Brazil, a group of researchers worked in secrecy for more than five years, from 1979 to 1985, collecting and copying all documents from 707 cases related to military justice proceedings. The cases were all from the Brazilian Superior Military Court, decided between April 1964 and March 1979, and were related to those individuals accused of political activity against the regime (but considered common crimes under the military legal framework). Lawyers who used to work defending political prisoners collaborated on this project, obtaining access to the proceedings and copying them as a whole, using as an excuse the Amnesty Law recently approved in 1979 and the need to clarify the status of their clients with the new benefit. More than one million pages were collected and analyzed. A short version of the whole project was published as a book, under the name *Brazil:*

Never Again (In Portuguese, *Brasil: Nunca Mais*), on July 15, 1985, and quickly became a best seller in Brazil. Arquidiocese de São Paulo, *Brasil: Nunca Mais* (Petrópolis: Vozes, 1985), 21–27, www.docvirt.com/docreader.net/DocReader. aspx?bib=BibliotBNM&PagFis=520&Pesq=.

75 Right to Memory and Truth, 33–34.

76 Ibid.

77 Law No. 10.559/02 (Brazil 2002).

78 Abrão and Torelly, "Resistance to Change," 156.

79 Law No. 12.528/11 (Brazil 2011).

80 Law No. 12.527/11 (Brazil 2011).

81 Flavia Piovesan, "Lei de Anistia, Direito à Verdade e à Justiça: o Caso Brasileiro," *Interesse Nacional* 17 (2012): 9, accessed March 10, 2015, http://interessenacional. uol.com.br/index.php/edicoes-revista/lei-de-anistia-direito-a-verdade-e-a-justica-o-caso-brasileiro/9/.

82 Secretaria de Direitos Humanos da Presidência da República, Programa Nacional de Direitos Humanos (2010), accessed March 10, 2015, http://portal.mj.gov.br/sedh/pndh3/pndh3.pdf.

83 Report, Ch. 1 The Creation of the National Truth Commission, at paras. 19–26.

84 For an account in English, see Kai Ambos and Eneas Romero, The Report of the Brazilian Truth Commission: Late Truth Without Justice?, accessed March 10, 2015, www.ejiltalk.org/12892/.

85 Report, Ch. 7 Conceptual framework of grave violations, at paras. 2–3.

86 Ibid., Historical antecedents, at para. 12.

87 Ibid., Recommendation, at para. 18. (Translation by the author.)

88 It is not easy to foresee how the Brazilian state will act from now on. In any case, I do not agree with Kathryn Sikkink and Bridget Marchesi, who published a recent article in *Foreign Affairs* commenting on the Brazilian NTC: "The key test of the truth commission's impact, then, is whether it can provide not only public acknowledgement to victims and a record for collective memory, but also spur the Brazilian state to hold offenders accountable. Yet virtually every other country in the region has either overturned or circumvented its amnesty laws in order for prosecutions to proceed – making it hard to believe that Brazil won't ultimately follow suit." Kathryn Sikkink and Bridget Marchesi, "Nothing but the Truth: Brazil's Truth Commission Looks Back," *Foreign Affairs*, February 26, 2015, accessed March 15, 2015, www.foreignaffairs.com/articles/143180/kathryn-sikkink-and-bridget-marchesi/nothing-but-the-truth. This position shares the same faith in criminal prosecutions as does the Inter-American view on amnesty. The Brazilian context is not trivial. There are important obstacles to be overcome with respect to the holding of trials in the country, as this part of the chapter aims at exploring.

89 Brazilian Constitution of 1988 (revised 2005).

90 According to Article 60(I) of the Brazilian Constitution, constitutional amendments may be proposed by at least one-third of the members of the Chamber of Deputies or the Federal Senate. Ibid.

91 Federal Supreme Court of Brazil, "Allegation of Breach of Fundamental Precept No. 153," (ADPF 153), April 29, 2010.

92 The 2010 STF decision is not definitive and it may be changed, especially considering the recent new composition of the Supreme Court. Currently, there are

three concrete legal possibilities for changing the validity of the 1979 Amnesty Law: OAB has one application pending judgment in ADPF 153, in which it asked the opinion of the Supreme Court on the IAClHR's decision on *Gomes Lund*; in May 2014, the left-wing party Socialism and Liberty filed a new complaint before the STF (ADPF 320), asking STF to recognize the binding effects of *Gomes Lund*; and claim (*Reclamação*) 18.686 deals with criminal responsibility of those involved in the disappearance of Rubens Paiva, a congressman; this procedure is suspended at this time because of the 2010 decision. Report, Ch. 1 The creation of the NTC, at para. 33.

93 Deisy Ventura. "A interpretação judicial da Lei de Anistia brasileira e o direito internacional," A *Anistia na Era da Responsabilização: o Brasil em Perspectiva Internacional e Comparada*, eds. Leigh A. Payne, Paulo Abrão, and Marcelo D. Torelly (Brasília: Ministério da Justiça, Comissão de Anistia and Oxford: Oxford University Press, Latin American Centre, 2011), 308–343, 313.

94 A recent attempt is Senator Randolfe Rodrigues's proposal of a bill to review the 1979 amnesty (draft legislation no. 237/2013). The Senate Commission on Human Rights approved it on April 2014, but other Senate commissions have to approve it before having a vote. Ricardo Setti, "Review of the Amnesty goes Forward in the Senate," Veja, April 10, 2014, accessed June 27, 2014, http://veja.abril.com.br/blog/ricardo-setti/tag/lei-de-anistia/.

95 Abrão and Torelly, "Resistance to Change," 168.

96 Ibid., 233.

97 "In sum, throughout the process, the steps that Brazil would follow towards democratization were being designed in a context mentored by the military and negotiated among the elites, but, at the same time, various questions consolidated in the process of the fight for amnesty needed to be considered." (Translation by the author). Jessie J.V. de Sousa, "Anistia no Brasil: um Processo Político em Disputa," A *Anistia na Era da Responsabilização: o Brasil em Perspectiva Internacional e Comparada*, eds. Leigh A. Payne, Paulo Abrão and Marcelo D. Torelly (Oxford: Oxford University, Latin American Centre, 2011), 188–211, 208.

98 Approaches that assert the value of amnesty highlight "amnesty as essential to striking the political bargains that facilitate institution building and strengthen the rule of law." Tricia D. Olsen, Leigh A. Payne, and Andrew G. Reiter, "Conclusion: Amnesty in the Age of Accountability," *Amnesty in the Age of Human Rights Accountability: Comparative and International Perspective*, eds. Francesca Lessa and Leigh A. Payne (Cambridge: Cambridge University Press, 2012), 336–357, 340.

99 Jan Klabbers. "Redemption Song? Human Rights versus Community-Building in East Timor," *Leiden Journal of International Law* 16 (2003): 367–376, 374.

100 Olsen, Payne, and Reiter also highlight this question when talking about the positive aspects of amnesties: "Though many may consider amnesties unjust for victims of human rights violations, they may justify their use in terms of their long-term capacity to reduce future injustices or deflect other grave social harms." Olsen, Payne, and Reiter, "Conclusion," 340.

101 Martti Koskenniemi, "Between Impunity and Show Trials," *Max Planck Yearbook of United Nations Law* 6 (2002): 1 ("In the temples of justice, legal rituals seems victorious over the chaos of war Complex conflicts with intractable structural causes

are distilled to individual agency"); Sarah M.H. Nouwen, "Justifying Justice," *The Cambridge Companion to International Law*, eds. James Crawford and Martti Koskenniemi (Cambridge: Cambridge University Press, 2012), 327–351, 343.

102 Mallinder, *Amnesty, Human Rights and Political Transitions: Bridging the Peace and Justice Divide* (Oxford: Hart, 2008), 11.

103 Louise Mallinder, "Beyond the Courts? The Complex Relationship of Trials and Amnesties," *International Criminal Law*, ed. William A. Schabas (Cheltenham: Edward Elgar, 2011), 758–775, 758–759.

104 When debating human rights violations in contexts of regime change, the legal instruments available to cope with a violent past, such as amnesties, shall not be considered in a vacuum, but with respect to the political struggles that are present in such contexts. The position related to the resumption of the political dimension by the human rights discourse is articulated by David Kennedy, for whom human rights neutrality would be a dark side of humanitarianism:

> Neutral intervention. The human rights vocabulary promises Western constituencies a neutral and universalist mode of emancipatory intervention. This leads these constituencies to unwarranted innocence about the range of their other ongoing interventions and unwarranted faith in the benign natures of a human rights presence. Thinking their interventions being benign or neutral, they intervene more often than they otherwise might. Their interventions are less effective than they would be if pursued in other vocabularies.

David Kennedy, *The Dark Sides of Virtue: Reassessing International Humanitarianism* (Princeton, NJ: Princeton University, 2004), 23. In turn, Martti Koskenniemi asserts that the absolutist character of human rights would be part of the liberal project related to this discourse:

> The absoluteness of rights discourse is not, however, an accidental property in it, but follows from its justifications within liberal theory, its purpose to create a set of unpolitical normative demands intended to "trump" legislative policies or administrative discretion. The very point of rights as a special type of normative entitlements lies in their absoluteness, their uncontextual validity, and immediate applicability.

Martti Koskenniemi, "The Effect of Rights on Political Culture," *The Politics of International Law*, ed. Martti Koskenniemi (Oxford: Hart, 2011), 133–152, 149.

105 Martti Koskenniemi, "International Law and Hegemony: A Reconfiguration," *The Politics of International Law*, ed. Martti Koskenniemi (Oxford: Hart, 2011), 223.

106 Martti Koskenniemi, "Human Rights, Politics and Love," *The Politics of International Law*, ed. Martti Koskenniemi (Oxford: Hart, 2011), 153–168, 158.

107 David Kennedy, *The Dark Sides of Virtue*, xxiv–xxvi.

108 Roberto Gargarella debates the complex relations between rights, democracy, and punishment with respect to the *Gelman* case. In a recent essay, he stated the importance of the decision's legal and political implications, which relate to "fundamental issues in contemporary constitutional theory." His discussion of the

problem of rights is closely connected to my argument that the IACtHR lacks deep contextual knowledge:

> The second problem is related to rights, and the simple term I will use to identify it is (ii) the problem of disagreement. This problem involves the understandable differences of opinion that we encounter in every democratic society, not only in terms of which rights deserve protection, but also, and here [] is where I am particularly interested, disagreement over the meaning, content, and scope of the rights that we offer protection and, by extension, the question of what means should [be] employed to protect them. My overall intuition in this respect is that the deep and sensible disagreements about rights and their protection require a more dialogical (and therefore less authoritarian) approach to the question, especially when attempting to resolve "hard cases."

Roberto Gargarella, "No Place for Popular Sovereignty? Democracy, Rights and Punishment in *Gelman* v. *Uruguay*," presented at annual SELA conference at Yale University, June 7, 2013, accessed February 11, 2014, www.law.yale.edu/documents/pdf/sela/SELA13_Gargarella_CV_Eng_20121130.pdf

7

The Distributive Politics of Impunity and Anti-Impunity: Lessons from Four Decades of Colombian Peace Negotiations

Helena Alviar García and Karen Engle*

In 2005, the *New York Times* published an editorial criticizing the then newly passed Colombian transitional justice law, entitled the Justice and Peace Law.[1] The law had resulted from negotiations between right-wing paramilitary groups and the Colombian government. It offered reduced sentences for paramilitary members who would participate in the Justice and Peace process, with the claimed goal of guaranteeing the rights of victims to truth, justice, and reparation.[2]

Many critics of the government opposed the law on the ground that it would lead to impunity for members of the paramilitaries. As the *Times* editorial put it:

> Colombia has just passed a law to demobilize paramilitary fighters, which the government calls the "Justice and Peace Law." It should be called the "Impunity for Mass Murderers, Terrorists and Major Cocaine Traffickers Law" … The current law will bring neither justice nor peace. No confession is required to get the shortened sentences offered by the law. Paramilitary leaders are supposed to disclose their illegal assets and describe their criminal organizations. But there is no credible penalty for lying or hiding their wealth.[3]

In a battle often framed as between peace and justice, human rights and victims' organizations, both national and international, largely agreed. In contrast, then-President Álvaro Uribe defended the law against these accusations, primarily in the name of peace: "When there is a peace process, there cannot be

* We would like to thank Zinaida Miller for her excellent comments on an early draft of the chapter and Farid Benavides for his guidance on Colombian criminal law issues. We are also grateful to a number of research assistants in both Bogotá and Austin, including David Gómez, Cianan Good, Emilio Lehoucq, Tania Luna. We are especially thankful to Helen Kerwin, who assisted substantially with research, analysis, and editing.

full criminalization in the name of justice."Perhaps aiming to strike a balance between peace and justice with reduced sentences (as opposed to amnesties), he further noted: "Nor can there be total impunity in the name of peace."[4]

Seven years later, however, Uribe's successor (and former defense minister), President Juan Manuel Santos, announced that he would negotiate with the left-wing Revolutionary Armed Forces of Colombia (FARC). He proposed a Legal Framework for Peace, eventually adopted as a constitutional amendment by Congress, which allowed for the possibility that alternative or suspended sentences might be offered to FARC members. In response, Uribe took a different tack, opposing any peace that would come with "impunity." Not only did he deny that any "lasting peace" could result from a process that permitted the political participation (and economic model) of the FARC,[5] he also invoked the International Criminal Court (ICC) to claim that amnesties or pardons would violate international law.[6] In December 2014, he even organized nationwide protests under the banner of "Peace without Impunity" that attracted, by the estimates of the organizers, 40,000 participants across fifteen Colombian cities.[7]

As the Santos administration began to engage in peace negotiations with the FARC, it defended the possibility that negotiations might lead to an agreement in which traditional forms of criminal punishment might not be applied to the FARC. It did so in part by attempting to expand the notion of justice beyond criminal justice. The nation's General Prosecutor, Eduardo Montealegre, for example, called for a "modern" understanding of justice, contending that it is impossible to prosecute all crimes in a longstanding conflict such as the Colombian one.[8] Montealegre also contended that international standards are not as rigid as others had described them.[9] Similarly, President Santos himself asserted that "those who want justice are disposed towards being very flexible" with regard to the possible punishments that will ultimately be decided upon by the peace process.[10] He also called upon the international community to show understanding: "All of this [international support] will assist us in finding the balance between allowing the maximum amount of justice while, at the same time, ensuring peace … we have asked of the international community that it be flexible so that this harmony might be achieved."[11]

As these examples help demonstrate, in twenty first-century Colombian politics, all political sides have deployed at different times the language of justice and impunity to defend their particular approaches to peacemaking. In this chapter, we consider these various deployments in further detail, in part by harkening back to an earlier era – the last two decades of the twentieth century – when the amnesties and pardons that were regularly offered to left-wing guerrilla members were not particularly controversial. We are interested in how and why they became controversial in the ensuing years. Relatedly, we consider how both twentieth-century amnesties, on one hand, and the twenty-first-century discourse of impunity, on the other, have often been used to sideline broader conversations about the inequality of land and resources that have long contributed to armed conflict in Colombia.

With regard to contemporary negotiations between the government and the FARC, we contend that too much of the discussion, including by human rights organizations, has centered on transitional justice and impunity. At the same time, insufficient attention has been paid to another part of the agreement, that involving agricultural and land reform. While the government and the FARC began with significantly opposing views on rural development (classical liberal versus dependency theory), the FARC eventually agreed to a draft that veers little from existing law and policy, much of which has been in place for decades.

In exploring these themes and ideas, the chapter proceeds as follows: Part I provides a brief history of Colombia's internal conflict. Part II begins to sketch ideological shifts in the use of the term "impunity," by summarizing some of the peace processes that took place during the last two decades of the twentieth century. In these earlier negotiations, amnesties and pardons were little contested, at least for what were considered political and related crimes (though what did or should fit into those categories was disputed). Impunity was not mentioned in these negotiations or their aftermath; rather, the debate centered on the economic and political distribution of power. Part III continues to explore the shift, by analyzing the rise of anti-impunity discourse in the late twentieth and early twenty-first century, beginning with the legal frameworks that have undergirded it. It then considers the role that anti-impunity played in debates about and legal responses to, first, then-president Uribe's negotiations with the paramilitaries and, second, negotiations between the Santos government and the FARC. Part IV argues that while the government, the FARC, and domestic and international human rights and media organizations have focused extensively on the draft provisions of amnesties and alternative sentencing, they have failed to consider seriously how the agricultural and land reform draft leaves unaddressed many of the issues that have long prevented sustainable peace. In the Conclusion, we offer some final reflections on Colombia's twentieth- and twenty-first-century peace processes.

I. BRIEF HISTORY OF THE COLOMBIAN CONFLICT

For over half a century, Colombia has been embroiled in armed violence among the national army, leftist guerrilla groups, right-wing paramilitary organizations, and drug traffickers.[12] The left-wing guerrilla groups – including the FARC, ELN (National Liberation Army), and M-19 (Movement of April 19th) – emerged from the 1950s through the 1970s.[13] The FARC is the oldest and largest of the guerrilla groups and is heavily influenced by Marxist, dependency theories that promote land and resource redistribution as well as the nationalization of natural resources.

In 1990, the M-19 reached a peace agreement with the government. The following year, President César Gaviria set up a Constitutional Assembly to overhaul the conservative 1886 Constitution. He extended an offer to all existing guerrilla groups to be a part of the assembly, but made it clear that he would continue to oppose militarily those who were unwilling to participate in the design of the new Constitution. The FARC and the ELN were among the guerrilla groups that declined to participate.

During this same time, Colombia saw a surge in guerrilla activity and organized crime.[14] For example, while in 1985 the guerrillas were operating in approximately 175 municipalities,[15] in 1992, they were acting in 437 municipalities – 43 percent of the national territory. They were also increasing their income through, among other things, drug trafficking and kidnapping.[16] In addition, Pablo Escobar was waging his "war against the state," in which he used many terrorist tactics, particularly car bombs in Bogotá.[17] Between 1982 and 1992, the homicide rate in Colombia doubled,[18] and kidnappings went from almost none in 1980 to about 1,500 in 1992.[19]

In response to increasing violence by guerrilla groups, right-wing paramilitary groups, often in coordination with large landholding drug traffickers, had begun to form in the 1980s. Claiming that there was little or no state presence to protect their property, they operated as local self-defense entities. Once the peace agreement was reached with the M-19 and other minor groups in the early 1990s, paramilitary activity turned primarily toward the FARC and its perceived sympathizers.

The United Self-Defense Forces of Colombia (AUC), founded in 1997, was the umbrella organization for the paramilitary forces. It unified a disparate array of organizations that opposed the FARC; in practice, it aimed to purge leftist support from wealthy territories by causing the forced displacement or execution of many civic leaders in those regions.[20] It is widely accepted that the paramilitaries acted in some cases in cooperation with the military, and were financed by powerful political and economic elites.[21] The violent action of these groups made many communities fear them more than they already feared the FARC. According to the Historical Memory Group,[22] the paramilitaries carried out a wave of indiscriminate violence that included mutilations, torture, and the displacement of millions through violent appropriation of land and resources as well as illicit and violent activities leading to the murder of thousands of civilians.[23]

Over the years, the government and these various non-state military groups have made numerous attempts to reach peace agreements. Many of the efforts have included amnesties or pardons for some of those engaged in conflict. As part of the negotiations, left-wing guerrilla groups have nearly always called for economic redistribution and agrarian reform.

By 2006, the AUC was formally demobilized. In 2012, negotiations between the government and the FARC began in earnest and, as of mid-2016, the bulk of an agreement was in place. In 2014, the government began preliminary peace talks with the ELN but, as of March 2016, formal negotiations had not yet begun.

The remainder of this chapter considers the various attempts, successful and otherwise, at brokering peace agreements since the late 1970s. It does so with an eye toward the legal and political structures and debates surrounding them, particularly with regard to economic redistribution and amnesties.

II. LATE TWENTIETH-CENTURY PEACE NEGOTIATIONS: AMNESTIES AND ECONOMIC DISTRIBUTION

Beginning in the early 1980s, presidents from both the Conservative and Liberal parties attempted to negotiate peace with left-wing guerrilla groups. Such attempts generally included the grant of amnesties or pardons for political crimes, which were, according to the 1980 Penal Code, rebellion, sedition, and riot.[24] This Part considers these grants of amnesties and pardons. What is perhaps most remarkable about them from today's vantage point is that they were relatively unremarkable at the time and were generally readily accepted by Congress.

Not coincidentally, we believe, at the same time that Congress accepted broad amnesties and pardons, it often rejected or at least deferred the demands for economic and social redistribution made by guerrilla groups. For the most part, the passage of the laws seemed to function as a way for the political elite to attempt to end the violence without having to attend to the substantive positions of the armed opposition on matters of economic inequality and distribution. That is, Congress demonstrated flexibility with regard to the treatment of political crimes but rigidity with regard to economic reform in an approach that, as we will see, is mirrored in the Santos administration's negotiations with the FARC. From the late 1970s through the end of the century, the period we consider in this section, Congress and in a few cases the President – invested with temporary, extraordinary powers – passed a number of different laws granting amnesty or pardons.[25] (See Table.)

To provide a sense of the ways in which these laws emerged, we concentrate here on two grants of amnesties or pardons offered to left-wing guerrillas in the late 1970s and early 1980s.[26] We also use these laws and discussions around them to illuminate the initial stages of debate surrounding the exclusion of certain crimes from amnesties and pardons, as well as the treatment of social, economic, and political reform. The first we analyze was proposed to Congress by a Liberal party president and the second by a Conservative party president.

Liberal party member and President Julio César Turbay Ayala (1978–1982) successfully proposed a law to grant limited amnesty to the M-19 movement. Turbay had been highly criticized because he had issued Decree 1923 of 1978, called the Security Statute, which provided the military with criminal jurisdiction to detain, hold, search, and expedite processes against suspects. The enforcement of that statute led to massive human rights violations according to both local and international organizations.[27] Partly because of the pressure regarding the application of the statute, Turbay abolished the decree in 1981 and entered into peace talks with guerrilla groups, among them the M-19.

At Turbay's urging, Congress enacted Law 37 of 1981. Although Turbay's principal concern was the demobilization of the M-19, the law was general; it granted amnesty to any Colombian citizen and pardon to any political prisoner for acts of rebellion, insurrection, or riot, and "related crimes." The law marked the beginning of a new wave of amnesties in Colombia by explicitly excluding certain crimes from their purview.[28] Specifically, the statute excluded "cases in which the crimes of rebellion, sedition or riot were related to kidnapping, extortion, homicide committed outside combat, arson, poisoning of water sources or water deposits, and in general, acts of ferocity or barbarity."[29] The law also established a long and burdensome procedure to determine eligibility for the benefit.[30]

In the end, the M-19 did not take advantage of the amnesty law. Some argue that the M-19 viewed it as requiring an unconditional surrender, given the uncertainty of the protracted process.[31] The peace commissioner in charge of advancing the talks, former Liberal president Carlos Lleras Restrepo, later claimed that the peace initiative failed because the government's sole aim was to provide a limited amnesty, linked to a complete rendition on the part of armed groups without offering any of the economic, social, or political

TABLE *Amnesties and Pardons Granted between 1981 and 1997*[46]

Demobilized Group	President and Presidential Term	Amnesty or Pardon Law	Crimes Excluded from the Benefit	Crimes Included in the Benefit
(unsuccessfully aimed at M-19)	Julio César Turbay Ayala (1978–1982)	Law 37 of 1981	Kidnapping, extortion, homicide committed outside combat, arson, poisoning of water sources or water deposits, and in general, acts of ferocity or barbarity.	Acts of rebellion, insurrection, or riot, and all "related crimes."
(unsuccessfully aimed at M-19, FARC–EP, ADO y EPL)	Belisario Betancur Cuartas (1982–1986)	Law 35 of 1982	Cruel homicide committed outside combat or placing the victim in a condition of defenselessness or inferiority.	Rebellion and sedition and related offenses
M-19	Virgilio Barco Vargas (1986–1990)	Law 77 of 1989	Cruel homicide committed outside combat or placing the victim in a condition of defenselessness; acts of ferocity or barbarism; members of terrorist organizations.	Rebellion and sedition and related offenses.
The Workers Revolutionary Party (PRT); The Popular Liberation Army (EPL); The Quintin Lame Armed Movement (MAQL)	César Gaviria (1990–1994)	Decree 213 of 1991	Genocide; cruel homicide committed outside combat or placing the victim in a condition of defenselessness or inferiority; acts of ferocity or barbarism.	Rebellion and sedition and related offenses.

Ernesto Rojas Armed Command (CER)	César Gaviria (1990–1994)	Decree 1943 of 1991	Atrocious crimes; homicide committed outside combat or placing the victim in a condition of defenselessness or inferiority.	Rebellion and sedition, conspiracy and related offenses.
The Socialist Renovation Stream (CSR); Urban Militias of Medellín; The Francisco Garnica Front	César Gaviria (1990–1994)	Law 104 of 1993	Atrocious crimes; genocide; cruel homicide committed outside combat or placing the victim in a condition of defenselessness or inferiority; kidnapping, acts of ferocity or barbarism, crimes with mandatory minimum prison sentence of 8 years.	Rebellion and sedition, conspiracy and related offenses.
The Revolutionary Independent Armed Command Movement	Ernesto Samper (1994–1998)	Law 418 of 1997	Atrocious, ferocious or barbaric acts; terrorism; kidnapping; genocide; homicide committed outside combat or placing the victim in a condition of defenselessness.	Rebellion and sedition, conspiracy and related offenses.

transformation the groups demanded.[32] President Turbay contended, however, that the amnesty failed because of the exclusions it included.[33]

In 1982, Belisario Betancur, a member of the Conservative party, won the presidential election. President Betancur supported a broader amnesty than that offered by Congress under Turbay's government, promoting Law 35 of 1982 for political prisoners and all rebels who were willing to lay down their arms.[34] Aimed at M-19 and FARC members, it granted amnesty or pardon for political and related crimes committed before the law came into force.[35] Its only exclusions were of killings that took place outside of combat if they were executed with cruelty or placed the victim in a position of helplessness or inferiority.[36] This law provided a simpler procedure than the earlier legislation, and did not even require a petition from interested parties.[37]

Although morally conservative, President Betancur was socially progressive. According to historians, he was the first president to recognize the social causes of the conflict.[38] At least initially, he linked the peace process to economic, political, and social structural reform to eradicate what he identified as the causes of violence: hunger, unemployment, and illiteracy.[39] He acknowledged that economic underdevelopment, weak state presence in some areas, lack of public investment, and poverty were the causes of guerrilla violence.[40] He was aware that there would need to be significant changes in terms of wealth distribution to attain lasting peace.[41] He promoted both political and economic reforms that he considered essential to the achievement of peace, and proposed strengthening the state and increasing social investment in economically and socially affected zones.[42]

President Betancur was prepared to grant amnesty in order to promote his social agenda for peace. Yet, while Congress readily approved his proposed amnesty laws and appeared to lack any qualms about them, it rejected the president's efforts at major structural reforms.[43] For the M-19 and FARC, amnesty was insufficient. Rather, both insisted that the amnesty law would have to be accompanied by significant political, economic, and social reforms.[44] In general terms, they called for the modernization of public institutions, the broadening of democracy, guarantees for political opposition, social justice, and economic redistribution. Throughout these years, FARC's position on redistribution remained consistent. In a memorandum to the Peace Commission in 1983, for example, it demanded:

> a democratic peace in Colombia, that is, peace with democracy, peace with broad political and civil liberties for the people, peace without hunger and government retaliation ... peace with the army, peace without torture, peace with equal opportunities, peace with social justice, peace with salaries

according to living costs, peace with participation in the design and development of public policies, peace without unemployment, peace with housing, peace with land for the landless masses, peace without monopolistic control of national economic life, peace with equitable distribution of resources and national goods, peace without the interference of North American financial capital.[45]

Even today the FARC's language is strikingly similar although, as we will see, this perspective is not necessarily represented in its recent draft agreement with the government on agrarian reform.[46]

While Betancur managed a ceasefire agreement with the M-19 and the FARC to facilitate negotiations, the negotiations ultimately failed. Believing that neither the Executive nor Congress would comply with the administration's promise to resolve the issues of resource distribution that underpinned their violent struggle, both groups returned to armed resistance in 1985.[47] On November 6, 1985, the M-19 took over the Colombian Palace of Justice and held members of the Supreme Court hostage in a siege that led to a military raid and the death of nearly one half of the Court's members. M-19 members claimed that their purpose was to put Betancur on trial "for not complying with the peace agreements."[48]

Subsequent administrations – under the presidencies of Virgilio Barco (1986–90), César Gaviria (1990–94), and Ernesto Samper (1994–98), all of the Liberal party – continued to negotiate, with mixed success, with guerrilla groups. Two presidential decrees in 1991 and one law in 1993 provided for amnesties and pardons, but – as with those under previous administrations – excluded a large number of offenses. They nevertheless resulted in the demobilization of the M-19 and other guerrilla groups, though not the FARC or the ELN. (See Table.)

The 1991 decrees facilitated the participation of the M-19 and other demobilized groups in the historic Constitutional Assembly that took place that same year. Indeed, a party composed of former members of the M-19 was one of the major political forces in the Constitutional Assembly. And one of the three presidents of the Assembly, Antonio Navarro, was a former member of the M-19. For this reason, many scholars see the 1991 Constitution as the first one in Colombian history that was not imposed by the winners, but was an agreement reached by all the political forces represented in the Assembly at the time.[49]

The parties at the Constitutional Assembly understood that the armed conflict was not only about national security, crime, or violence, but also about economic, social, and political exclusion. As such, the assembly offers a striking exception to one of the main arguments of this chapter: that economic and social causes of conflict have been consistently sidelined. The acknowledgment, however, was short-lived, as resistance to debating and transforming social and economic conditions continued well into the twenty-first century. Guerrilla warfare also continued, as the FARC and the ELN refused to demobilize and participate in the Constitutional Assembly. Though President Ernesto Samper and his Conservative party successor, President Andrés Pastrana, engaged at some level in peace talks with the remaining guerrilla groups, they were ultimately unsuccessful.

III. TWENTY-FIRST CENTURY: THE RISE OF ANTI-IMPUNITY

During the twenty-first century, in line with the general trends outlined in this volume by Karen Engle and Fabia Veçoso, offers of amnesties, pardons, and even reduced sentences became contested in Colombia. Anti-impunity became the cry of both the left and the right, albeit not always at the same time. The seeds of this trend can be found in constitutional, legislative, and judicial transformations beginning in the early 1990s. In this Part, we first consider some of the legal background supporting the shift before returning to contemporary debates around negotiations with the paramilitaries and the FARC.

A. *Legal background: 1991–2003*

In 1991, after the Constitutional Assembly, Colombia passed a new Constitution to replace the one that had been in existence for just over a century. Like its predecessor, the new Constitution specifically authorized Congress to grant amnesties and pardons, and allowed the President to grant pardons under certain circumstances.[50] It also established a Constitutional Court, which was soon asked to begin to consider the constitutionality of some aspects of the Penal Code and other laws that would grant or lead to amnesties, pardons, reduced sentences, or alternative sentencing.

In a high-profile case in 1997, the Constitutional Court demonstrated a wariness of amnesties and pardons, and sought to restrict significantly the category of crimes that could be considered "related to" political crimes.[51] The case was brought by a group of army officers led by General Harold Bedoya Pizarro, Commander of the Colombian National Army at the time, challenging the Constitutionality of Article 127 of the Penal Code. The provision, dating from 1980, stated that "rebels or seditious individuals will not be subject to punishment for punishable acts committed in combat, so long as they are not acts of ferocity, barbarity, or terrorism." The complaint was filed in February

1997, immediately following a press conference at which the heads of the Colombian Army, Navy, Air Force, and Police came together to present an eleven-page letter in support of the challenge to the President of the Court.[52]

The complaint was largely sparked by a 1993 Supreme Court decision ratifying pardons granted to seven members of the Popular Liberation Army (EPL) who had killed two Colombian soldiers. Their Article 127 pardons occurred under President Gaviria's Decree 213 of 1991, which precluded the prosecution of members of those demobilized guerrilla groups that had agreed to participate in the Constitutional Assembly. The Supreme Court had found the pardons properly granted because the crimes had been committed in combat and thus covered under the decree.[53] Although many members of the military and Colombian elite had been outraged by the Supreme Court ruling at the time,[54] Bedoya and his colleagues waited four years to present the case to the Constitutional Court. They did so only a few months before Bedoya announced his intention to run for president, and just before he was forced into retirement, in part because he refused to negotiate with the FARC.

In their complaint, Bedoya and other military officers argued that Article 127 was being used to discriminate against the military and police since only guerrilla members were being pardoned. Moreover, they contended that by permitting such pardons, Article 127 violated the right to life of the police and military, as protected by the Colombian Constitution and the international human rights treaties included in the constitutional framework.[55] Although the case arose in the context of growing skepticism among international and regional human rights advocates over amnesties and impunity, the only involvement of human rights groups was to oppose Bedoya's interpretation of international law. Specifically, several Colombian human rights and civil society groups intervened to urge the Court to uphold the provision on the ground that it was in line with international humanitarian law because it did not "authorize acts of barbarity or the assassination of combatants outside of armed conflict."[56]

The Court struck down Article 127, although it did so in a way that avoided the rights claims, finding instead that the provision in effect created "a general, anticipated, and timeless amnesty" that only Congress is authorized to grant under the Constitution. The Court went further, though, to suggest that, as a general rule (and in line with the "observed trend in the world"),[57] political crimes should not be defined to include crimes of violence, whether they occur inside or outside combat: "[T]he fact that it is difficult to eradicate violence cannot lead criminal law to cave in and eliminate punishment ....

[T]hat the State has not been able to control violence is no reason for criminal law to legitimize it under the pretext that it is of a political nature."[58]

Importantly, the Court was divided in its ruling, along lines commonly seen with regard to the legality and practicality of amnesties and pardons. In a dissenting opinion, Justice Carlos Gaviria Díaz and Justice Alejandro Martínez Caballero harshly criticized the majority opinion on two grounds. First, they contended that the Court was changing a long-standing legal tradition of allowing reduced sentencing or eliminating punishment in the cases of offenses related to political crimes. Secondly, they were concerned that the ruling could potentially hinder future peace negotiations with remaining guerrilla groups.[59]

In 2002, in line with the solidifying anti-impunity trend at the time in Colombia and elsewhere, and alongside the Court's reluctance to uphold laws that provide amnesties and pardons for certain crimes, even when linked to the exercise of political ones, Congress passed Law 733 of 2002. The law increased punishment for crimes such as kidnapping, extortion, and terrorism. More importantly, for our purposes, it stated that no perpetrator of kidnapping, extortion, or terrorism could benefit from an amnesty or pardon. Given their atrocious nature, it explained, such crimes could never be considered to be related to political crimes.[60]

When Congress passed a framework law for President Uribe's negotiations with the paramilitaries in 2002 (which are the subject of the next section), it modified and extended previous laws to empower the government to take certain steps to create conditions to advance peace talks.[61] It reiterated that a pardon can never be granted for acts of extreme ferocity or barbarity, terrorism, kidnapping, genocide, killing outside combat, or placing the victim in a defenseless state.[62] It also removed a requirement that the group with which the government is negotiating be recognized as a political group, providing a way to bring in the paramilitaries without having to make an argument that they were acting politically.[63]

B. Anti-Impunity Ascends: Negotiating with the Paramilitaries

When President Uribe came to power in 2002, he began conversations with the right-wing paramilitary groups organized under the AUC. In 2003, the government and the AUC signed the Santa Fe de Ralito Agreement, which set out preliminary terms for a peace process. Those terms included a ceasefire, demobilization of AUC members, concentration of demobilized paramilitaries in safe zones protected by the armed forces, the achievement of peace through the strengthening of state presence and law enforcement throughout the Colombian territory, and an end to drug trafficking.[64]

Although there was nothing in the agreement itself about amnesties or pardons,[65] the issue soon emerged. In August 2003, after the agreement was signed, the government proposed a draft law to Congress that included the regulatory background for the accord. A chapter of the draft law provided for alternatives to prison for paramilitaries who were judged and convicted, even of crimes that would not normally be eligible for amnesty under Colombian law, such as crimes against humanity.[66]

In their first broad-based opposition to a law or proposed law granting leniency as part of a peace agreement, human rights organizations – both local and international – and victims' organizations criticized the draft law.[67] In general, they argued that it failed to respect the rights to truth, justice, and reparation for victims that are guaranteed by international human rights and humanitarian law as well as the Colombian Constitution.[68] For Catalina Botero and some of those she consulted for a report on the draft law, crimes against humanity – regardless of which side committed them – simply should not be treated in the way that ordinary crimes might be treated in a restorative justice scheme.[69] Thus, her report concluded "that people, from whichever group or movement, who are responsible for the most grave violations of international humanitarian law and crimes against humanity should be condemned to a reasonable and proportionate period of effective imprisonment."[70]

Although critics generally agreed with Botero that crimes against humanity could not be included in amnesties, they disagreed on the extent to which the aim of peace might otherwise serve as a counterweight to an emphasis on criminal justice. Botero, for example, recognized that "in the context of a peace process, there are no universally satisfactory formulas to resolve the tensions – juridical, ethical, political – that are produced in the attempt to reconcile the objective of peace with the obligation to investigate, sanction, and make reparation for human rights violations and violations of international humanitarian law."[71] In contrast, the Colombian Commission of Jurists (CCJ), one of the most significant human rights NGOs in Colombia, rejected the idea that peace could justify foregoing criminal prosecutions. It did so in part by denying the very distinction between peace and justice. It explained: "The temptation to sacrifice the former on the altar of achieving the latter tends to be a constant. Thus, there are those who believe that it does not matter that there is no justice for what happened in the past, so long as there is peace in the future."[72] Contending that such "pragmatic" thought "fails to see the teachings of reality regarding the negative consequences of sacrificing the essential values of a society," the CCJ concluded that "peace without justice is a false peace, whose fragility will be revealed sooner or later."[73]

Regardless of their position on whether, in principle, some justice might be sacrificed for peace, virtually all human rights advocates agreed that alternative sentences favored the integration of paramilitary members into mainstream social and political life without either appropriately attending to questions of justice and criminal proportionality or adequately providing reparation to victims.[74] Some cautioned that enacting the alternative sentencing without substantial debate and agreement from the Colombian population would merely delay a necessary dialogue about justice and punishment for past crimes.[75]

Eventually, the pressure from both local and international critics became unbearable. In June 2004, the draft was finally withdrawn.[76] In 2005, Congress passed the Justice and Peace Law to provide the legal architecture for the demobilization of paramilitary forces (and, nominally, of guerrilla forces). Although the law included the term "alternative sentencing," unlike the draft law, such sentences still required prison terms – of five to eight years.[77] The law differed from the earlier draft law as well, by justifying alternative (reduced) sentences on the need for truth in addition to peace. That is, the law emphasized that its implementation "should promote the investigation of what happened to victims."[78]

Even with these changes, the Justice and Peace Law was heavily criticized from inside and outside the country as a "law of impunity."[79] The CCJ was particularly critical, decrying the process as "a peace we can't believe in at an impossible price."[80] Amnesty International decried the law, saying, "by failing to guarantee that those accused of human rights violations are subjected to exhaustive and impartial investigations through processes conforming to international norms regarding truth, justice, and reparation, the [law], in practice, will promote impunity" and deny the rights of victims.[81] A large number of national and international NGOs voiced their opposition to the law before the Inter-American Commission on Human Rights.[82]

In 2006, the CCJ challenged the constitutionality of the law, contending before the Constitutional Court that the law constituted a "system of impunity that allows the granting of the benefit of alternative punishment … based on a procedure that guarantees neither truth, nor justice, nor reparation." Additionally it argued that Article 71, making the establishment of or membership in a paramilitary group a political crime (sedition), was unconstitutional.[83] Several other human rights organizations filed amicus briefs in the case, pointing to numerous sources of international and national law indicating that the types of crimes committed by these groups could not be excluded from ordinary criminal punishment.[84] In its brief, the International Commission of Jurists argued that the modification of the crime of sedition proposed by the law would lead to impunity and noted that "the imposition of derisory sanctions, in contempt of the principle of proportionate punishment, constitutes a recognition of impunity under international law."[85]

The Constitutional Court upheld most of the law against these challenges, but without denying the need to fight impunity. Citing its own previous jurisprudence, the Court situated its decision in its recognition of the "central importance of the fight against impunity and of the rights to truth, justice, and reparation in relation to serious human rights abuses."[86] It held as a preliminary matter that the law did not provide for either an amnesty or a pardon because it neither extinguished the crime nor declined to impose punishment once a final judgment was rendered. It was emphatic that, although individuals would be sentenced to substantially less time than they might be in a normal judicial process, "even so, the punishment does not disappear."[87] It nevertheless recognized that even reduced sentencing "undoubtedly affects constitutional rights and principles such as the right to justice for victims."[88]

The Court framed much of its decision as an issue of balancing, in the context of transitional justice, not only the rights of justice and truth, but also of peace and reparation. The contents of these rights, it insisted, are established in international law and in the Colombian Constitution (including in the Constitution's incorporation of international law).[89] In considering what is necessary to achieve "justice in transition," the Court noted that "it is impossible to restore justice, peace and victims' rights at the same time."[90] It rejected the argument that peace might justify sacrificing justice, stating that "[p]eace does not justify everything. The value of peace cannot be absolute in scope, since it is also necessary to ensure fairness, and the victims' right to justice."[91] At the same time, it insisted that "the Constitutional right to justice may take a wide range of forms," and "this substantial reduction of punishment is constitutionally necessary in the pursuit of peace."[92]

Concluding, then, that reduced sentences still constitute a form of punishment and that they might be required to facilitate peace, the Constitutional Court upheld the substantive provisions of the Justice and Peace Law. With the law upheld, demobilization of the AUC and other paramilitaries was carried out from 2006 to 2008 though, as the war has continued, new paramilitary forces have arisen.

C. Anti-impunity: Negotiating with the FARC

While Uribe focused on the demobilization of paramilitaries through a negotiated compromise, he had a very different attitude toward the FARC. For him, the FARC should be treated – and defeated – militarily.

When Juan Manuel Santos, who had been Uribe's Minister of Defense, was elected president in June 2010, most assumed that he would continue Uribe's policies with regard to the FARC. President Santos therefore surprised many when he began to explore a political settlement with the FARC. Following a secret exploratory phase and initial conversations in Oslo, Norway, formal negotiations began in Havana, Cuba on November 15, 2012. Since then, the parties have engaged in secret negotiations on six issues: political participation; illegal drugs; agrarian development; victims' rights; the end of the conflict; and the implementation, verification, and signature of the agreements.[93]

Although both sides maintained that there is no final agreement until there is agreement on all issues, the basic content of the settlements on each issue was released along the way. The first area of negotiation involved political participation, and agreement was reached in November 2013, just shy of one year after the start of the negotiations. In May 2014, a deal was reached with regard to illegal drugs. In June 2014, agrarian reform was agreed upon, although the contents of the agreement were not made publicly available until September 2014. In September 2015, the parties announced, with regard to victims' rights, a reparations scheme that includes some pardons, amnesties, and alternative sentencing including for security forces. In January 2016, the parties agreed to a deal on ending the conflict.

Any final agreement will need to be approved by the legislature and withstand any constitutional challenges that might be brought against it, meaning that public opinion about and reaction to the agreement (whether through a referendum or otherwise) will play an important role in whether it is ratified. Although journalists, academics, civil society groups, and international governmental and non-governmental organizations responded to parts of the agreement as they were announced, by far the area that has generated the most controversy is that on victims' rights. The FARC put alternative sentencing on the table from the beginning, so that even the establishment of the Legal Framework for Peace, the framework legislation passed in 2012 to enable the peace negotiations, depended upon its inclusion.

In this section we consider the roles that anti-impunity discourse and advocacy – especially by Colombian human rights organizations, international and regional human rights governmental and non-governmental organizations, and even prosecutors of the ICC – have played in the negotiations between the Colombian government and the FARC with regard to pardons, amnesties, and alternative sentencing. In the next part, we contrast this focus with the virtual absence of attention to agrarian reform proposals by these same actors, suggesting that the campaign against impunity might have displaced concern for the structural causes of violence and the need to address them deliberately and explicitly.

Much of the discussion around anti-impunity began with the Legal Framework for Peace. FARC members had insisted that they would not spend even one day in prison, and the framework added two transitory articles to the Constitution that would permit the use of prosecutorial discretion as well as suspended or alternative sentencing as tools of transitional justice. We opened the chapter with some of the criticisms launched by Uribe against this framework. He was joined by others, such as Francisco Santos, a right-wing politician who intended to (although ultimately did not) run for president. Santos placed billboards in the main Colombian cities comparing Pablo Escobar with Iván Márquez, the head negotiator of FARC. The caption between the pictures states: "Guess who has killed more policemen. We want peace without impunity."[94]

Criticism on the issue of impunity was not limited to the right, however. In fact, many local and international human rights groups, like Human Rights Watch,[95] Fundación País Libre,[96] and the Colombian Commission of Jurists[97] also condemned the framework as violating international law by permitting impunity for human rights violations.[98] In July 2012, the CCJ presented a constitutional challenge to the law,[99] demanding the removal of key phrases that would limit criminal liability for ex-combatants. Between then and the Constitutional Court's decision in August 2013, international institutional actors began promoting certain interpretations of international law that would prohibit most amnesties. The 2013 Annual Report of the UN High Commissioner for Human Rights, for example, stated, much as the Constitutional Court had done with regard to the Justice and Peace Law, that the peace process would require "profound consideration of what is understood by 'peace'" by all involved.[100] While admitting that "many possible solutions" and a "holistic approach" should be favored, the report made clear that it saw amnesties as illegal: "As opposed to avoiding past violations through amnesties and other forms of impunity, which simply violate human rights obligations, the past should be used to transform Colombia."[101] Fabrizio Hochschild, head of the UN office in Colombia, reiterated the opposition to at least some amnesties, stating that "amnesties for crimes against humanity cannot be supported by the UN."[102]

One of the most significant international interventions in the case came from ICC Prosecutor Fatou Bensouda, who sent a letter to the Constitutional Court indicating that suspending sentences for those most

responsible for serious crimes falling within the jurisdiction of the ICC
(war crimes, crimes against humanity, and genocide) would be a violation
of Colombia's international legal obligations.[103] This same correspondence also suggested, however, that suspended sentences for those not most
responsible, and reduced sentences of the sort used in the Justice and Peace
Process for those with primary responsibility, would not necessarily infringe
international legal obligations.[104]

The Constitutional Court basically took for granted the position of the
ICC and others with regard to amnesties for the crimes under the ICC's
jurisdiction (that they were off the table), but kept in mind as well that not
everyone could be prosecuted. It posed the question as follows: "The legal
issue raised is whether the possibility of using the criteria of selection and
prioritization for the prosecution, judgment, and punishment of the most
severe human rights and international humanitarian law violations committed by the most responsible and pardoning the rest is permissible under the
Constitution."[105] The Court ultimately found that, although "the employment of mechanisms of transitional justice generate constant collisions
among state obligations," competing state obligations could be balanced
by prioritizing the investigation and sanction of the most serious violations
of international human rights and humanitarian law and the punishment
of those most responsible for those violations.[106] The Court's reasons were
largely pragmatic:

> [T]he case-by-case investigation of human rights violations may end with
> a generalized situation of impunity … [A] maximalist vision [of human
> rights enforcement] constitutes an impenetrable obstacle to the adjudica-
> tion of human rights violations, as these crimes are characterized by the
> fact that they are committed by many hands, and the political realities and
> practical difficulties in carrying out universal trials generates an extended
> impunity: everyone should be punished, and so no one is. In this way, the
> possibility of centering the investigation on a series of crimes committed by
> those most responsible and the application of special measures to those less
> responsible comes from the factual impossibility of having an investigative
> strategy that proceeds legally against all suspects in a process of transitional
> justice.[107]

The Court continued by insisting that moving away from a "case-by-case"
investigative strategy would in fact combat impunity, by creating "macropro-
cesses" of investigation of massive human rights violations that all victims can
participate in, "which are not structured by chance, but by contextualized
investigations and analysis of structures of organized criminality."[108]

As negotiations between the Colombian government and the FARC continued, the Court's decision helped shape what would be considered permissible for the parties to agree to. The ICC also continued to attempt to shape those parameters. In a visit to Bogotá in May 2015, the Deputy Prosecutor of the ICC delivered a speech entitled "Transitional Justice in Colombia and the Role of the International Criminal Court." He made clear that the ICC had little to say about amnesties for those crimes that do not involve genocide, crimes against humanity, or war crimes.[109] Further, even for those crimes that would fall under the ICC's jurisdiction, he noted that "effective penal sanctions may ... take many different forms." What is important is that they "serve appropriate sentencing goals, such as public condemnation of the criminal conduct, recognition of victims' suffering, and deterrence of further criminal conduct."[110] He also indicated that since the ICC only has the capacity to prosecute those "most responsible," its focus on Colombia would be on whether in fact the country was prosecuting that group.[111]

On September 23, 2015, the Colombian government and the FARC announced that they had reached an agreement to create a "Special Jurisdiction for Peace," comprising Justice Chambers and a Peace Tribunal, to try individuals responsible for crimes during the armed conflict. The agreement promises that "the broadest possible amnesty for political crimes and related crimes" will be granted. Following international legal trends and both avoiding and mimicking the previously troubled language of political crimes, the parties agreed that amnesty will not extend to crimes against humanity, genocide, or other grave human rights violations. The Special Jurisdiction for Peace, which is intended to "end impunity, obtain truth, contribute to the reparation of victims, and judge and sanction those responsible for grave violations committed during the armed conflict, particularly the most grave and representative crimes, guaranteeing non-repetition," will have the power to give sentences of varying lengths (generally between five and eight years) for individuals convicted of crimes. The length and type of sentences will depend on the gravity of the crimes and whether the individual took responsibility for the crime from the start. To receive reduced sentences in cases within the Special Jurisdiction for Peace, the accused must "contribute full truth, provide reparations to victims, and guarantee non-repetition" of the acts. Those who confess their crimes and contribute to the construction of both collective and individual truth may benefit by having their liberty restricted outside of the regular prison system.[112]

Human rights advocates have been mixed in their responses to the agreement. Human Rights Watch has been most vocal in its opposition, claiming the agreement violates international law. José Miguel Vivanco, director of the organization's Americas Division, responded to the September announcement of the agreement almost immediately, stating that the Special Jurisdiction "would ... allow those most responsible for mass atrocities to completely avoid prison."[113] To suggest additional support for his view, he added: "It is difficult to imagine how an arrangement in which those most responsible for mass atrocities avoid any prison time could survive a careful review by the ICC prosecutor."[114] When the draft of the agreement was released in December, Vivanco declared it to be a "piñata of impunity."[115] Amnesty International also expressed concern, less about jail time, and more about who would be considered "most responsible," since everyone else would essentially be granted amnesty. It called for independent criminal investigations to be carried out to make sure such individuals were not implicated in human rights violations.[116]

Other human rights actors have been more hopeful. Even the director of the CCJ, the organization that led the challenge to the Legal Framework for Peace, has heralded the agreement as an important step forward in the fight against impunity – for all parties to the conflict. Responding to critics of the agreement from the right, he has suggested that the Special Jurisdiction will have teeth: "Precisely because it is an agreement designed to guarantee justice and confront impunity, it has been repudiated by those who have something to fear."[117] Further, Rodrigo Uprimny, legal scholar and director of the Colombian human rights NGO Dejusticia (Center for Law, Justice and Society), has publicly contested Vivanco's description of the accord as a "piñata of impunity." "An impunity agreement," he notes, "would have been if the FARC and the government had agreed to a general and unconditional amnesty, including for war crimes and crimes against humanity." While accepting that some of Vivanco's criticisms of the accord may be valid, he puts stock in the fact that alternative sentences will still include restrictions of liberty and will only be granted in exchange for reparations for victims. It is an imperfect justice, he concedes, but "imperfect justice is not the same as impunity."[118]

Two institutions that have loomed in the background of the accord have been the ICC and the Inter-American Court of Human Rights. While the ICC Office of the Prosecutor, as we have seen, has been fairly direct about what it would consider impermissible, the IACtHR has also offered guidance, albeit a bit more subtly. As Engle discusses in her chapter in this volume, in a

2012 decision striking down an amnesty that precluded prosecution of members of the army of El Salvador for the El Mozote massacre, a majority of the judges signed a concurring opinion suggesting that certain amnesties made in the context of a peace agreement (which it claimed the Salvadoran amnesties were not) might be permissible.[119] The author of that opinion was Judge Diego García-Sayán, who was then President of the Court. In his last few months on the Court when the draft agreement between the FARC and the Colombian government was first announced, Judge García-Sayán commented publicly on it, saying:

> The central elements of the accord are in concordance with international law. Those responsible for grave crimes – which are excluded from amnesty – will be subjected to criminal proceedings before the special jurisdiction [for peace] and to diverse levels of punishment. To stipulate serving punishments through restriction of liberty in special conditions does not contradict international law.[120]

While an endorsement of the accord by a sitting judge on the Inter-American Court might at one level seem surprising, at another it is not, given that the agreement seems to have been carefully drafted to make an arguable claim that it satisfies the demands of the Court's jurisprudence. Of course, even if the "Inter-American view of amnesty," as Veçoso puts it in her chapter in this volume, is shifting, that the agreement seems to have been entered into with it in mind demonstrates the power that it and its general opposition to amnesty have in the region.

Notwithstanding Vivanco's suggestion to the contrary, the ICC has also refrained, at least as of March 2016, from criticizing the draft accord. The ICC published a press release the day after the draft agreement was released "welcom[ing]" the news of the agreement and noting "with optimism" that the agreement "is designed … to end impunity for the most serious crimes."[121] It did promise to review carefully the draft agreement as part of the ongoing ICC preliminary investigation in Colombia.

These responses, alongside the absence of significant criticism by many human rights actors, suggest that there might well be some turn away from the equation of traditional forms of criminal justice and anti-impunity that others in this volume have documented. At a minimum, we see here what Engle suggested with regard to Colombia and Northern Ireland: When actual peace agreements are at stake, there might continue to be more flexibility than many advocates have assumed. Uprimny's response to the accord provides an example of such reasoning. If properly implemented, he wrote, it "could get us out of the inferno of a bloody, fifty-year war with dignity and significant levels of justice."[122]

IV. WHAT IS MISSED IN THE FOCUS ON IMPUNITY
AS CRIMINAL JUSTICE?

As we saw in the previous part, in the context of the peace agreements with
both the paramilitaries and the FARC, debates among politicians, scholars,
and human rights advocates in the twenty-first century have primarily centered on impunity. To be against impunity for the paramilitaries was not only
to oppose amnesties and pardons, but even reduced sentences. But when
FARC leaders conditioned peace on their demand that they should not spend
one day in prison, the FARC and the government spent an inordinate amount
of time and energy – in the midst of criticisms and pressure from many different perspectives – to reach an agreement on victims' rights that is arguably in
accord with international law.

Less attention has been paid to another compromise the FARC and the
government have reached in the recent negotiations. That compromise suggests that even if the tide has turned slightly with regard to impunity, it has
changed little in terms of economic distribution. As strongly as FARC leaders
insisted they would not spend one day in prison, the government has maintained that private property and the existing development model would not
be subjects of negotiation. Indeed, when the initial conversations of the peace
began in Oslo, the head of the government committee declared: "neither
the economic development model, nor military doctrine, nor international
investment are a part of this discussion."[123] He was undoubtedly responding in part to opposition to the peace process by landowners, ranchers, and
businessmen. Fedegán, the Colombian Federation of Cattle Ranchers, for
example, had complained about the expropriation it believed that the FARC
would attempt under the guise of "agrarian reform."[124] The head of the guerrilla negotiation group responded to the government by saying "peace does
not mean the silence of the rifles. It means transforming the political, military and economic structure of the state."[125] It appears that the government's
position has prevailed, as important discussions about resource distribution
have largely been muted throughout the peace process. Consequently, the
long-standing conflicts over land and resource distribution that have lain at
the heart of Colombia's armed conflict and – we believe – are central to
resolving it, are likely to continue.

The distribution of wealth is extremely unequal in Colombia. According to
the World Bank, based on 2013 data, Colombia's GINI index is 53.5, making it
one of the world's most unequal countries in terms of distribution of income.[126]
Further, as of 2009, 28.5 percent of the country's most productive land was
held by just 1.6 percent of the population.[127] According to the Colombian

Agriculture Ministry, around 6.5 million hectares of land, "including some of the most fertile, was stolen, abandoned or forcibly changed hands in other ways between 1985 and 2008 as a result of the conflict."[128]

In 2011, Congress passed a land restitution law. Yet, the law, in large part because it is not being used, has failed to affect the high concentration of land ownership. While nearly six million people have been displaced by the conflict, Amnesty International has reported that, as of August 2014, only about 64,000 claims had been lodged for land restitution under the law. Of these, only about 650 had been ruled on (with restitution judges and magistrates finding in favor of the land claimants in 96 percent of cases). Through those cases, only 30,000 hectares (or about .005 percent of all the land that has "forcibly changed hands" during the conflict) have been restored.[129]

This issue might have been ripe for peace talks, particularly given the stark theoretical differences between the FARC and the government on economic distribution. Yet, the draft agreement suggests that the FARC made significant compromises, which has been missed by the many journalists who have read the agreement as evidence that there is little difference between the government and the FARC on most issues related to agricultural development.[130] Compromise or not, the draft agreement has largely gone unnoticed (or at least undiscussed) by human rights and civil society NGOs, despite the centrality of land concentration to the conflict and its impact on the human rights of a large portion of the population. In these final few pages, we aim to address that gap in attention by bringing some consideration to the substance and significance of the compromises reached on agricultural reform.

The draft agreement is divided into three broad topics: access to land and formalization of property rights, development programs designed for regional differences, and the incorporation of agrarian reform in national plans.[131] Although it is promoted by the parties as an important new agreement, unlike the part of the accord on victims' rights, most of its provisions simply reiterate policies that are already in existence.

The part of the agreement on access to land, for example, creates a land trust, the Fondo de Tierras.[132] The trust will include: public land that is not being used (a trend in Colombian rural policy since the 1930s) or that has been illegally appropriated and retaken by the government (as provided for in previous land restitution law[133]); land recovered under strengthened land restitution programs (which have been in place since 2011 with, as indicated above, mixed results[134]); land that is the product of a reconfiguration of environmental boundaries (which have been in place since the early 1950s[135]); private land that has not been used according to its social and ecological function (in place since the late 1930s for the case of the social function[136] and since 1991 for the ecological function[137]); and land expropriated for social and public purposes once the owners have been compensated (in place since 1991[138]). The only lands this trust would add that are not already in principle available for redistribution are "donated lands." As of now, there is little reason to think the provision would affect land concentration in any significant way, and its voluntary nature cuts against the aims and philosophy behind most land reform. Another section on land includes access to special credit and subsidy programs for poor peasants to acquire land (which has been provided for since 1994),[139] property formalization (which has been the banner of the rural neoliberal agenda for the last ten years, and was codified in Colombian law more recently[140]), the protection of rural family-owned plots through Unidad Agrícola Familiar (set in place in 1994[141]), and the protection of peasant reserve zones (which began in the 1990s[142]).

The two other parts of the agreement, development programs with a territorial focus and national planning for agrarian reform, include the formalization of rural employment, the improvement of health and education in the countryside, and the strengthening of women's access to land. Again, none of these provisions or emphases is new. Indeed, they all have been included in public policies since the early 1970s.[143]

In sum, what the parties eventually agreed upon is not nearly as radical as the FARC's positions over the years would have suggested or what the Colombian elite feared. The agreement seems to have allowed the government to hold to its early position that the current Colombian economic model would not be up for negotiation while allowing the FARC to suggest, intentionally or not, that it would move the government toward decreasing land concentration.

V. CONCLUSION

The Colombian case offers a demonstration of the complex ways in which anti-impunity discourse and the formalistic legal interpretation that supports it have been used by both the right and the left in the twenty-first century. Even as the 2015 peace negotiations took an unexpected turn with regard to provision for noncarceral punishment for some FARC members,[144] the issue of impunity dominated and, at several points, almost brought to an end the negotiations between the parties. Although human rights criticism of the draft agreement has been less harsh than what might have been expected, nearly everyone concedes that how it is interpreted and enacted will be key, as any final peace agreement will need to be ratified by the electorate and upheld by the judiciary.[145] Thus, the aspects of any final accord on victims will likely continue to receive the bulk of the attention of both domestic and international human rights organizations. What will undoubtedly continue to receive less attention are the aspects of the accord on land distribution and development.

If in the twentieth century a permissive approach to amnesties and pardons was often used as a means to avoid consideration of the wider political and reform agenda, a very different approach in the twenty-first century has led to many of the same results. By making the discussion mostly about impunity, interlocutors succeed in marginalizing broader debates around issues that are arguably causative of the conflict and certainly germane to the peace process as a whole. Issues such as economic inequality and the roles of land concentration, development policy, and even the war in such inequality are obscured, as an insistence on individual criminal (if not carceral) accountability dominates.

NOTES

1 "Colombia's Capitulation," *New York Times*, July 6, 2005, accessed October 3, 2015, www.nytimes.com/2005/07/04/opinion/colombias-capitulation.html?_r=0.

2 Law No. 975 (Colombia 2005), arts. 1, 3.

3 "Colombia's Capitulation."

4 "Justicia y Paz es Equilibrada y Universal, Dice el Gobierno," *El Colombiano*, July 6, 2005, accessed October 3, 2013, www.elcolombiano.com/BancoConocimiento/J/justicia_y_paz_es_equilibrada_y_universal_dice_el_gobierno/justicia_y_paz_es_equilibrada_y_universal_dice_el_gobierno.asp.

5 As he put it in 2012: "When you think of new generations, then it would be great to have a lasting peace, but it must be with social justice, and without impunity. A peace achieved as a consequence of the vanity of power, providing political power to criminals and giving the country away to the Chavista economic model, is a false peace, ephemeral, that simply creates incentives for the reproduction of violence. It is a bad legacy for Colombia." "La Paz Tiene que Ser con Justicia Social y sin Impunidad: Álvaro Uribe," *El Universal*, October 19, 2012, accessed October 6, 2013, www.eluniversal.com.co/cartagena/nacional/la-paz-tiene-que-ser-con-justicia-social-y-sin-impunidad-alvaro-uribe-95211.

6 Juan Pablo Toro, "Santos ha Ofrecido Impunidad a las FARC: Álvaro Uribe Vélez," *El Universal*, April 21, 2013, accessed November 22, 2015, http://archivo.eluniversal.com.mx/internacional/82317.html ("[O]ffering 'impunity' today through amnesties or pardons clashes with the duties imposed by the International Criminal Court [...]").

7 "Concluyó Marcha Liderada por el Uribismo en Distintos Lugares del País," *El Tiempo*, December 13, 2014, accessed October 3, 2015, www.eltiempo.com/politica/proceso-de-paz/marcha-paz-sin-impunidad/14970455.

8 "Cara a Cara Entre el Fiscal y el Procurador," *El Espectador*, May 9, 2013, accessed October 3, 2015, www.elespectador.com/noticias/paz/cara-cara-entre-el-fiscal-y-el-procurador-articulo-421248.

9 "¿Admitirá el País Amnistías o Indultos para las FARC y el ELN?," *Semana*, May 10, 2012, accessed October 3, 2015, www.semana.com/politica/articulo/admitira-pais-amnistias-indultos-para-farc-eln/257745-3.

10 "No Autorizaría Ataque contra 'Timochenko' Si lo Ubican: Santos," *El Espectador*, August 13, 2015, accessed October 3, 2015, www.elespectador.com/noticias/paz/no-autorizaria-ataque-contra-timochenko-si-ubican-santo-articulo-578923.

11 "Santos Pide a Comunidad Internacional Apoyo a Justicia Transicional," *El Tiempo*, June 26, 2015, accessed October 3, 2015, www.eltiempo.com/politica/proceso-de-paz/santos-pide-a-comunidad-internacional-apoyo-a-justicia-transicional/16006705.

12 See generally Marco Palacios Rozo, *Violencia Pública en Colombia: 1958–2010* (Bogotá: Fondo de Cultura Económica, 2012).

13 FARC's origins can be traced from a series of peasant self-defense movements founded in 1949. It was originally formed in order to protect peasants from state violence and to articulate claims for access to land and resources. See Eduardo Pizarro, *Las FARC: De la Autodefensa a la Combinación de Todas las Formas de Lucha* (Bogotá: Tercer Mundo Editores, 1992). The ELN was founded in 1964. It became publicly known in January 7, 1965 when its members carried out an attack on the village of Simacota, located in Santander, a northern region of Colombia. See Roberto Sancho, *Guerrilla y Terrorismo en Colombia y España: ELN y ETA* (Bucaramanga: Editorial UNAB, 2003), 33. Finally, the M-19, primarily an urban guerrilla organization, formally began in 1974, but it started to emerge in 1970, after the elections of April 19, marked by electoral fraud against Gustavo Rojas Pinilla, the candidate of the ANAPO. See Darío Villamizar, *Aquel 19 Será: Una Historia del M-19, de sus Hombres y sus Gestas: Un Relato entre la Guerra, la Negociación y la Paz* (Bogotá: Planeta Colombiana Editorial, 1995), 38–52.

14 Eduardo Cifuentes Muñóz, "Los Estados de Excepción Constitucional en Colombia," *Ius et Praxis* 8, no. 1 (2002): 117–146.

15 Fredy Preciado, "Restricciones a la Democracia Local en Municipios con Presencia de Grupos Alzados en Armasen Colombia," *Revista IIDH*, 34–35 (1995): 279–328, 280.

16 See, e.g., *Sentencia C-031/93* (Colombian Constitutional Court, 1993), section III, 1.2.1.

17 Gustavo Duncan, *Más que Plata o Plomo: El Poder Politico del Narcotráfico en Colombia y México* (Bogotá: Planeta, 2014), 265.

18 Jorge Giraldo Ramírez, "Política y Guerra sin Compasión," *Centro de Memoria Histórica*, 2015, 4, accessed January 20, 2016, www.centrodememoriahistorica.gov.co/descargas/comisionPaz2015/GiraldoJorge.pdf.

19 Mauricio García Durán, "El Conflicto Armado Colombiano: ¿el Fin del Fin?," *CINEP*, 2008, 15, accessed January 20, 2016, www.alboan.org/docs/articulos/canales/alboan/InformeCINEPsitu.pdf.

20 See Mauricio Romero, *Paramilitares y Autodefensas, 1982–2003* (Bogotá: Instituto de Estudios Políticos y Relaciones Internacionales, 2003). According to Romero, "[b]y using violence against unarmed civilians accused of being sympathizers of the guerrilla, the paramilitaries recovered control over areas in which there were not only security problems for local proprietaries and external investors, but also

sharp political conflicts and an intense social mobilization towards rights and recognition." Ibid., 15.

21 See Claudia N. López Hernández et al., *Y Refundaron la Patria: de Cómo Mafiosos y Políticos Reconfiguraron el Estado Colombiano* (Bogotá: Debate, 2010), 119 ("From Court records and testimonies of demobilized paramilitaries we know that they (paramilitary groups) frequently coordinated violent actions with Government Security Agencies, allowing both of them to solve their problems."). See also 19 *Tradesmen v. Colombia*, para. 85(b) (Inter-American Court of Human Rights, 2004) (military "acquiesced" to a meeting between paramilitaries where killing of tradesmen was planned); *"Mapiripán Massacre" v. Colombia*, para. 96.1 (Inter-American Court of Human Rights, 2005) (military provided uniforms, equipment, arms to paramilitaries for massacre and declined to intervene during five-day operation); *Ituango Massacres v. Colombia*, para. 125.56 (Inter-American Court of Human Rights, 2006) (military, stationed in town, declined to intervene during successive massacres despite expressed concerns by civilian population); *Operación Génesis v. Colombia*, para. 250 (Inter-American Court of Human Rights, 2013) (military and paramilitary collaborated to displace afrodescendant families in Chocó).

22 The Historical Memory Group is a public entity that aims to collect and recover all the documentary material – oral testimonies and other evidence – relevant to the Victims and Land Restitution Law. It was created by the National Reconciliation Commission in accordance with Law No. 975, art. 50 (Colombia 2005), which tasked the commission with writing a public report about the evolution of illegal armed groups in Colombia. The Victims' and Land Restitution Law, Law No. 1448, art. 54 (Colombia 2011), transformed this commission into a public entity with administrative and financial autonomy, now known as the Historical Memory Center.

23 Centro de Memoria Histórica, *An International Economic Development Program 2012 Report*, 2012, accessed January 26, 2014, www.centrodememoriahistorica. gov.co/descargas/IEDP_2012_COLOMBIA_Human_Rights_Report_GMH.pdf. Paramilitaries were responsible for 41 percent of the displacement that occurred in the country. Other causes of displacement the Group found are guerrilla groups (24 percent), violent conflict between government forces and guerrillas (32 percent), and the alliance between guerrillas and paramilitaries (3 percent). Camilo Gonzalez Posso, "La Verdad en el Abandono Forzado y el Despojo de Tierras," *Centro de Memoria Histórica*, 11, accessed January 26, 2014, http://centromemoria. gov.co/wp-content/uploads/2013/11/15.04.13-LA-VERDAD-DEL-ABANDONO-FORZADO-Y-EL-DESPOJO-DE-TIERRAS-1.pdf.

24 Penal Code (Colombia 1980). Rebellion is defined as "the use of arms, intended to overturn the national government, or to suppress or modify the valid Constitutional or existing legal regime" (Art. 125); sedition constitutes "the use of arms, intended to temporarily prevent the peaceful development of the existing Constitutional or legal regime" (Art. 126); riot is "the tumultuous and violent demand from the authorities of the implementation or omission of certain act" (Art. 128).

25 The Colombian Supreme Court of Justice has usefully differentiated amnesties from pardons as follows: "Amnesty means that the State waives its sovereign authority to prosecute and punish crimes. This is a general and impersonal measure and it can only be proposed by Congress. A pardon is particular because it refers to an

individual or group of people. It is granted by the President of the Republic by means of an administrative act or authorized by Congress." *Ruling 94 of July 12, 1990* (Colombia Supreme Court of Justice, 1990).

26 Under the 1886 Constitution, art. 76.21, Congress was empowered, with a showing of necessity, to grant amnesties for political crimes through the enactment of a law by two-thirds of each of its Chambers (Senate and House of Representatives). The law could be proposed by a member of Congress or by the Executive.

27 Farid Benavides, *El Largo Camino Hacia la Paz* (Bogotá: Editorial Ibáñez, 2013), 26.

28 Political crimes have been exempted in penal codes dating back at least to 1890. Indeed, the 1890 Penal Code was applied in two civil wars in the country: the 1895 civil war and the Guerra de los Mil Días (the Thousand-Day War) from 1892–1902. Debates about what crimes should be excluded from amnesties and pardons have been present since at least the 1950s. While past laws simply excluded "atrocious crimes," Turbay was the first to include a specific list of what such crimes would be.

29 Law No. 37, art. 1 (Colombia 1981).

30 Ana María Bejarano et al., *Discusiones sobre la Reforma del Estado en Colombia: la Fragmentación del Estado y el Funcionamiento del Congreso* (Bogotá: Ediciones Uniandes, Facultad de Derecho, 2001), 28. Available at: https://did.uniandes.edu. co/images/documents/publicaciones/estudios-ocasionales/10.%20discusionesso-brelareforma.pdf. Anyone applying for the benefit was required to do so within four months of the law's enactment, and turn in his or her weapons at the time of application. Law No. 37, art. 3 (Colombia 1981). The public official who received the application was then required to write a report on the applicant's background and claims. Ibid., art. 5. Within five or ten days of the signature of the document, the report would then be sent to a judge, who would rule on the granting of the amnesty. Ibid. arts. 8–10.

31 Fernando Brito Ruíz, "Aspectos Legales de los Procesos de Paz y de Reinserción," *De las Armas a la Democracia*, ed. Carlos Eduardo Jaramillo Castillo (Bogotá: Instituto Luis Carlos Galán, 2000), 166.

32 See "Nosotros si Hubiéramos Hecho el Diálogo con el M-19," *Semana*, Jun. 14, 1982, accessed January 22, 2015, www.semana.com/nacion/articulo/nosotros-si-hubieramos-hecho-el-dialogo-con-el-19/598-3

33 Iván Arias Gerson, "Una Mirada Atrás: Procesos de Paz y Dispositivos de Negociación del Gobierno Colombiano," FIP Working Paper Series No. 4, *Fundación Ideas para la Paz*, 2008, accessed September 16, 2013, www.ideaspaz.org/index.php/pub-licaciones/series/working-papers/item/45-una-mirada-atr%C3%A1s-procesos-de-paz-y-dispositivos-de-negociaci%C3%B3n-con-el-gobierno-colombiano.

34 Palacios Rozo, *Violencia Pública en Colombia: 1958–2010*, 142–143.

35 Law No. 35 (Colombia 1982). According to Article 5, the beneficiaries of the law – all those who committed political crimes prior to the enactment of the law – would not be processed by any authority. The cases of those beneficiaries who had already been convicted or were standing trial should be transferred to a higher court in order to end the trial or extinguish the punishment. Ibid., art. 4.

36 Law No. 35, art. 3 (Colombia 1982). In subsequent regulations, amnesty or pardon were excluded for all non-combat killings. Luz María Sánchez, *Perspectivas Jurídicas Frente a un Eventual Proceso de Paz con los Grupos Guerrilleros* (Bogotá:

Corporación Derechos para la Paz Proyecto Planeta Paz, 2011), 36, https://alfresco. uclouvain.be/alfresco/d/d/workspace/SpacesStore/c57ccoe4-df59-4076-8fb5 af4fcd8fc232/ CARTILLA_PERSPECTIVAS-JURIDICAS.pdf.

37 Law No. 35, arts. 4, 5 (Colombia 1982). See Bejarano et al., *Discusiones sobre la Reforma del Estado en Colombia*, 27.

38 See Ricardo Arias, *IIistoria de Colombia Contemporánea (1920-2010)* (Bogotá: Ediciones Uniandes, 2011), 148-149.

39 Iván Arias Gerson, "Una Mirada Atrás: Procesos de Paz y Dispositivos de Negociación del Gobierno Colombiano."

40 Bejarano et al., *Discusiones sobre la Reforma del Estado en Colombia*, 25.

41 Mauricio Romero, "Nuevas Guerras, Paramilitares e Ilegalidad: Una Trampa Difícil de Superar," *Parapolítica: La ruta de la Expansión Paramilitar y los Acuerdos Políticos*, ed. Mauricio Romero (Bogotá: Nuevo Arco Iris, 2007), 363-394, 364; Bejarano et al., *Discusiones sobre la Reforma del Estado en Colombia*, 23.

42 Bejarano et al., *Discusiones sobre la Reforma del Estado en Colombia*, 24-25. Among the political reforms were. (1) institutionalization and financing of political parties and protection to the opposition, (2) modernization of the electoral system, (3) creation of an administrative career for public functionaries, and (4) opening of the spaces for citizen participation and popular election of mayors with decentralization. Farid Benavides, *El Largo Camino Hacia la Paz* (Bogotá: Editorial Ibáñez, 2013), 102-103.

43 Bejarano et al., *Discusiones sobre la Reforma del Estado en Colombia*, 26.

44 Ibid., 31, 34.

45 FARC Governing Body, "Memorandum to the Peace Commission, January 30, 1983," quoted in *Biblioteca de la Paz: Tregua y Cese al Fuego Bilateral FARC, EPL, M-19 y ADO*, ed. Álvaro Villaraga (Bogotá: Fundación Cultura Democrática, 2008), 146-147.

46 As FARC leader Iván Márquez put it on May Day 2015 on his Twitter account: "Health and education are rights of the Colombian people that cannot be turned into business. #1st of May for Peace with Social Justice (...) The struggle to achieve fundamental rights is legitimate; we must assume it as a necessary duty." See "Farc Reitera Llamado por la Paz con Justicia Social," *El País*, May 1, 2015, accessed March 5, 2016, www.elpais.com.co/elpais/colombia/noticias/ farc-reitera-llamado-llamado-por-paz-con-justicia-social.

47 According to Ana María Bejarano, "[w]ith respect to reforms, considered as a necessary complement to negotiation, it is necessary to point out the fact that Betancur's government directed its priority attention to promoting reforms to the political regime and disregarded economic and social reforms. Agrarian and urban reforms did not receive any attention from the Executive or the Congress." Ana María Bejarano, "Crisis Política, Conflicto Armado y Proceso de Paz," Universidad de los Andes, Facultad de Administración. *Documentos Básicos*, 11 Betancur ultimately had to moderate his political ambitions after facing enormous resistance in Congress. In fact, one of the problems of Betancur's peace process was that it was not even shared by his own political party. As a consequence, he was left alone trying to promote politically difficult reforms. See Farid Benavides, *El Largo Camino hacia la Paz*, 111.

48 Farid Benavides, *El Largo Camino hacia la Paz*, 110.
49 Julieta Lemaitre, *El Derecho como Conjuro* (Bogotá: Siglo del Hombre Editores and Ediciones Uniandes, 2009), 124.
50 Colombian Constitution of 1991, arts. 150, 201.
51 *Sentencia C-456/97* (Colombian Constitutional Court, 1997).
52 See "Asesinatos no son Actos de Combate," *El Tiempo*, February 25, 1997, accessed February 8, 2016, www.eltiempo.com/archivo/documento/MAM-568399.
53 *Radicación 8691-Amnistía* (Colombian Supreme Court of Justice, Sala de Casación Penal, 1993). For the coverage of the decree, see Table.
54 See "Crudo Fallo sobre Tomas Guerrilleras," *El Tiempo*, October 30, 1993, accessed February 1, 2016, www.eltiempo.com/archivo/documento/MAM-251720.
55 *Sentencia C-456/97*, section I.B.
56 *Sentencia C-456/97* (Colombian Constitutional Court, 1997), I.C.2.e. The following human rights groups intervened: Colectivo de Abogados "José Alvear Restrepo;" Centro de Investigación y Educación Popular CINEP; Asociación para la Promoción Social Alternativa MINGA; Corporación de Servicios Profesionales Comunitarios SEMBRAR; Comité Regional para los Derechos Humanos CREDHOS; Corporación Jurídica HUMANIDAD VIGENTE; Corporación Juan Bosco; Corporación Jurídica PROCURAR; Fundación Manuel Cepeda; Corporación Jurídica LIBERTAD; Programa por la Paz; and Fundación para la Defensa y Promoción de los Derechos Humanos REINICIAR. *Sentencia C-456/97* (Colombian Constitutional Court, 1997), section I.C.2.e.
57 Ibid., Consideration 14.
58 Ibid., Consideration 13.
59 See *Sentencia C-456/97* (Colombian Constitutional Court, 1997), Salvamento de Voto.
60 Law No. 733, art. 13 (Colombia 2002).
61 Law No. 782 (Colombia 2002).
62 Ibid., art. 19.
63 Specifically, the new law deleted language requiring that the "armed group at the margin of the law" with which the government was pursuing peace talks be recognized as political in nature. See Law No. 418, art. 50 (Colombia 1997). It was replaced with more neutral language referring to "armed groups at the margin of the law with whom the government is carrying out a peace process." Law No. 782, art. 19 (Colombia 2002).
64 "Colombia: Acuerdo de Santa Fe de Ralito para Contribuir a la Paz de Colombia," *ReliefWeb*, July 15, 2003, accessed May 9, 2013, http://reliefweb.int/report/colombia/colombia-acuerdo-de-santa-fe-de-ralito-para-contribuir-la-paz-de-colombia.
65 The agreement was confidential, but the text was revealed in 2007. "Texto del 'Acuerdo de Ralito'," *Semana*, January 19, 2007, accessed December 12, 2015, www.semana.com/on-line/articulo/texto-del-acuerdo-ralito/83002-3
66 Proposed Law 85 (Colombia 2003), Chapter III, available at: http://portal.uasb.edu.ec/UserFiles/369/File/PDF/CentrodeReferencia/Temasdeanalisis2/globalizacionmigracionyderechoshumanos/actualidad/colombia/Proyecto%20de%20Ley%20Estatutaria%2085%20de%202003%20Senado.pdf ("By which there were enacted certain provisions in pursuit of the reinstatement of members of armed groups that contribute effectively to the achievement of national peace").

67 Groups that were particularly vocal in their opposition included the Fundación Social, the International Center for Transitional Justice (ICTJ), the Asociación de Familiares de Desaparecidos (ASFADDES), and the Colombian Commission of Jurists. In addition, the Office of the High Commissioner of Human Rights in Colombia, as well as many academics and even major political parties and movements that supported Uribe, spoke out against the law. One of the most important Liberal party senators who supported the government at the time, for example, criticized the bill on the grounds that it violated constitutional provisions related to punishment for crimes as well as separation of powers (as the amnesty was led by the Executive), and that it would not guarantee peace. Rafael Pardo Rueda, Remarks, *Seminario Internacional de Alternatividad Penal en Procesos de Paz* (Paper Presentation, Barcelona, February 27–28, 2004), accessed May 19, 2013, http://escolapau.uab.cat/img/programas/procesos/seminario/semio18.pdf.

68 See, e.g., Gustavo Gallón Girado and Catalina Díaz Gómez, "Justicia Simulada: Una Propuesta Indecente," *Colombian Commission of Jurists*, 9, 12, 15, January 22, 2004, accessed December 5, 2015, http://escolapau.uab.cat/img/programas/procesos/seminario/semio03.pdf.

69 Catalina Botero Marino, *Documento de Recomendaciones sobre el Proyecto de Ley Estatutaria No. 85 de 2003-Senado, denominado "de Alternatividad Penal,"* 28–29 (2004), accessed December 5, 2015, http://e-archivo.uc3m.es/bitstream/handle/10016/19155/FCI-2004-6-botero.pdf?sequence=1 (citing Rodrigo Uprimny and Luis Manuel Lasso, Verdad, Reparación y Justicia para Colombia: Algunas Reflexiones y Recomendaciones, *Fundación Social*, January 2004).

70 Ibid., 29.

71 Ibid., 2.

72 Gallon and Díaz, "Justicia Simulada," 6.

73 Ibid.

74 See, e.g., UN High Commissioner for Human Rights, *Report on the Human Rights Situation in Colombia*, February 17, 2004, accessed December 5, 2015, www.hchr.org.co/documentoseinformes/informes/altocomisionado/Informe2003_esp.pdf.

75 See, e.g., Botero, *Recomendaciones*, 27–28.

76 "Congresistas Aceptan Aplazar Proyecto de Alternatividad Penal," *El Tiempo*, December 15, 2004, accessed October 7, 2015, www.eltiempo.com/archivo/documento/MAM-1540672.

77 Law No. 975 (Colombia 2005), arts. 3, 29. Article 3 defined alternativity as "a benefit that suspends the execution of a ruling, replacing it with an alternative sentence in order for the beneficiary to contribute to achieve peace, effective cooperation with justice, the reparation of victims, and the beneficiary's rehabilitation." Article 29 established that a Tribunal had the authority to dictate a prison sentence, which had to be between five and eight years, depending on the gravity of the crimes and the degree of cooperation. In order to grant this benefit, the law established several requirements. See, for example, arts. 10 & 11.

78 Ibid., art. 7.

79 See, e.g., "Sin Paz y Sin Justicia: Aprobada Ley de Impunidad en Colombia," *Comisión Colombiana de Juristas*, June 29, 2005, accessed November 24, 2015, www.coljuristas.org/documentos/boletines/bol_n6_jyp.pdf; "ONGs: Con Ley de Justicia y Paz han sido 5 Años de Impunidad," *Colectivo de Abogados "José*

Alvear Restrepo," August 3, 2010, accessed November 24, 2015, www.colectivode-abogados.org/?Con-la-ley-de-justicia-y-paz-han.

80 "Una Metafórica Justicia y Paz. El Proceso con los Paramilitares se Dirige hacia una Paz Increíble a un Precio Imposible," *Colombian Commission of Jurists*, June 21, 2005, accessed December 5, 2015, www.coljuristas.org/documentos/documento.php?id_doc=70&idioma=es&grupo=.

81 "La Ley de Justicia y Paz Garantizará Impunidad para Autores de Abusos contra los Derechos Humanos," *Amnesty International*, April 26, 2006, accessed November 24, 2015, www.es.amnesty.org/paises/colombia/noticias-relacionadas/articulo/la-ley-de-justicia-y-paz-garantizara-la-impunidad-para-los-autores-de-abusos-contra-los-derechos-hum/. A number of US Senators and the UN High Commissioner for Human Rights in Colombia also expressed disapproval of the law. See Juan Forero, "New Colombia Law Grants Concessions to Paramilitaries," *New York Times*, June 23, 2005, accessed November 16, 2015, www.nytimes.com/2005/06/23/world/americas/new-colombia-law-grants-concessions-to-paramilitaries.html.

82 In the context of a hearing of the Inter-American Commission that culminated in an official statement critical of the Justice and Peace Law, an enormous number of national and international NGOs opposed the law. See *Pronunciamiento de la Comisión Interamericana de Derechos Humanos sobre la Aplicación y el Alcance de la Ley de Justicia y Paz en la República de Colombia*, (OEA/Ser/L/V/II.125, 2006), 3 fn. 9, available at: www.mapp-oea.net/ftp/leyjusticiaypaz.pdf. Colombian NGOs opposing the law included: Comisión Colombiana de Juristas (CCJ), Asociación Campesina de Antioquia (ACA), Asociación de Afrocolombianos Desplazados (AFRODES), Asociación de trabajo Interdisciplinario (ATI), Asociación Líderes en Acción, Asociación Nacional de Mujeres Campesinas, Negras e Indígenas de Colombia (ANMUCIC), Asociación para la Promoción Social Alternativa MINGA, Consultoría para los Derechos Humanos y el Desplazamiento (CODHES), Confederación de Trabajadores de Colombia (CTC), Corporación Apoyo a Víctimas de Violencia Socio Política Prorecuperación Emocional (AVRE), Corporación Cactus, Corporación Casa de la Mujer, Corporación de Servicio a Proyectos de Desarrollo (PODION), Corporación Jurídica Libertad, Corporación para el Desarrollo del Oriente COMPROMISO), Corporación para la Defensa y Promoción de los Derechos Humanos (REINICIAR), Corporación Región para el Desarrollo y la Democracia, Corporación SISMA Mujer, Corporación Vamos Mujer, Escuela Nacional Sindical, Fundación para la Educación y el Desarrollo (FEDES), Humanidad Vigente Corporación Jurídica, Instituto Popular de Capacitación (IPC) de la Corporación de Promoción Popular (CPP), Organización Indígena de Antioquia (OIA), and Movimiento de Víctimas de Crímenes de Estado. Non-Colombian organizations offering amicus opinions on the law included: International Center for Transitional Justice, International Commission of Jurists, the Center for Justice and International Law (CEJIL), Yale Law School's Human Rights Clinic, the Bar Human Rights Committee of England and Wales, and the International Confederation of Free Trade Unions (since merged into the International Trade Union Confederation).

83 The CCJ's argument was basically that the crimes committed by the paramilitaries were not political and therefore could not be given the flexible treatment that

political crimes had been given in the Colombian legal tradition. See *Sentencia C-370/06* (Colombian Constitutional Court, 2006), section III, 1.2.2.

84 See, for example, International Commission of Jurists, *Memorial en Derecho Amicus Curiae presentado por la Comisión Internacional de Juristas ante la Corte Constitucional de la Republica de Colombia sobre la Ley 975 de 2005, llamada Ley de Justicia y Paz,* accessed February 5, 2016, www.acnur.org/t3/uploads/media/COI_1427.pdf?view=1. Summaries of the other amicus filings can be found in *Sentencia C-370/06,* section IV.

85 Ibid.

86 See, e.g., *Sentencia C-370/06* (Colombian Constitutional Court, 2006), section VI, 4.9.6 (discussing the relationship between the fight against impunity and human rights in the context of Colombia's membership of the ICC).

87 Ibid., section VI, 3.3.3.

88 Ibid., section VI, 6.2.2.1.7.1.

89 Establishing the existence of the right to peace in Colombian law, the Court cites, among others, the Preamble to the United Nations Charter, the United Nations Charter, the Preamble to the Universal Declaration of Human Rights, the Charter of the Organization of American States, the International Covenant on Civil and Political Rights (ICCPR), and the International Covenant on Economic, Social and Cultural Rights (ICESCR). On the rights to truth, justice, and reparation, the Court cites the jurisprudence of the Inter-American Court of Human Rights, the Set of Principles for the Protection and Promotion of Human Rights through Action to Combat Impunity (the "Joinet Principles"), the Convention Against Torture, the Inter-American Convention to Prevent and Punish Torture, the Inter-American Convention on Forced Disappearance of Persons, and the Genocide Convention.

90 *Sentencia C-370/06* (Colombian Constitutional Court, 2006), section 5.5

91 Ibid., section 5.5

92 Ibid., section 6.2.2.1.7.2.

93 Available at: http://equipopazgobierno.presidencia.gov.co/especiales/abc-del-proceso-de-paz/acuerdo-general-proceso-paz.html.

94 "Vallas de Francisco Santos no son Propaganda Electoral: CNE," *El Universal,* May 1, 2013, accessed October 7, 2015, www.eluniversal.com.co/cartagena/politica/vallas-de-francisco-santos-no-son-propaganda-electoral-cne-117945.

95 "Human Rights Watch Critica la Impunidad que Generaría el Marco Jurídico para la Paz," *Caracol Radio,* May 2, 2012, accessed October 11, 2015, http://caracol.com.co/radio/2012/05/02/nacional/1335925080_680477.html.

96 "Críticos del Proceso de Paz... No Solo es Uribe," *Semana,* September 15, 2012, accessed December 12, 2015, www.semana.com/nacion/articulo/criticos-del-proceso-paz-no-solo-uribe/26479/-3.

97 "ABC de la Demanda Contra el Marco Jurídico para la Paz," *Caracol Radio,* August 24, 2013, accessed October 11, 2015, http://caracol.com.co/radio/2013/07/24/judicial/1374679080_938785.html.

98 See generally Juan Carlos Monroy, "Marco para la Paz Divide al País y Une a Antagonistas," *El Colombiano,* July 31, 2013, accessed October 11, 2015, www.elcolombiano.com/historico/marco_para_la_paz_divide_al_pais_y_une_a_antagonistas-ECEC_253575.

99 See *Sentencia C-579/13* (Colombian Constitutional Court, 2013). See also
   Sentencia C-577/14 (Colombian Constitutional Court, 2014), upholding another
   part of the Legal Framework for Peace against a constitutional challenge the
   following year.
100 United Nations General Assembly, *Annual Report of the United Nations High
   Commissioner for Human Rights: Report of the United Nations High Commissioner
   for Human Rights on the Situation of Human Rights in Colombia* (A/HRC/22/17/
   Add.3, 2013), para. 9.
101 Ibid., para. 10.
102 "ONU no 'Apoya' Amnistías a Delitos de Lesa Humanidad," *El Tiempo*, May 6, 2013,
   accessed October 6, 2015, www.eltiempo.com/archivo/documento/CMS-12782545.
103 Bensouda sent this letter to the President of the Constitutional Court, Jorge Iván
   Palacio, during the time when the constitutionality of the Legal Framework for
   Peace was being evaluated by the Court. "Una 'Carta Bomba'," *Semana*, August 17,
   2013, accessed October 6, 2015, www.semana.com/nacion/articulo/una-carta-bomba/
   354430–3. According to the Court's judgment, the letter said in part that "[t]he deferral
   of punishment means that the accused will not spend time in jail. I wish to advise you
   that this would be clearly inadequate for those who were the highest ranking members
   responsible for committing war crimes and crimes against humanity." *Sentencia C-
   579/13* (Colombian Constitutional Court, 2013), section I, 3.16 (quoting the letter).
104 *Sentencia C-579/13* (Colombian Constitutional Court, 2013), section I, 3.16.
   Bensouda's exclusive reference to the impermissibility of allowing those most
   responsible for war crimes and crimes against humanity to avoid a prison sentence
   suggests that the ICC was not pronouncing on the permissibility of such arrangements for those not most responsible. And indeed, a second letter from Bensouda
   clarified that "it is the duty of every state to exercise its penal jurisdiction against those
   responsible for international crimes," but that the ICC's own processes "should not
   be considered an authority, precedent, or directive for interpreting the parameters of
   the obligations that national jurisdictions have with respect to the investigation and
   adjudication of international crimes." Ibid. at section I, 3.16.2. The ICC's persistent
   focus on "international crimes" suggests that it was not interested in pronouncing on
   the adjudication of crimes that do not fall within its jurisdiction.
105 *Sentencia C-579/13* (Colombian Constitutional Court, 2013), Consideration 3.
106 *Sentencia C-579/13*, section V, 8.3.1.
107 Ibid.
108 Ibid., section V, 8.3.2.
109 James Stewart, "Transitional Justice in Colombia and the Role of the International
   Criminal Court," 15, May 13, 2015, www.icc-cpi.int/iccdocs/otp/otp-stat-13-05-2015-
   ENG.pdf.
110 Ibid., 10.
111 Ibid., 13–15.
112 "Comunicado Conjunto No. 60 sobre el Acuerdo de Creación de una
   Jurisdicción Especial para la Paz," *Presidencia de la República*, September
   23, 2015, accessed February 5, 2016, http://wp.presidencia.gov.co/Noticias/
   2015/Septiembre/Paginas/20150923_03-Comunicado-conjunto-N-60-sobre-
   el-Acuerdo-de-creacion-de-una-Jurisdiccion-Especial-para-la-Paz.aspx.
   For the text of the full draft agreement released in December 2015, see

Delegados del Gobierno de la República de Colombia (Gobierno Nacional) y las Fuerzas Armadas Revolucionarias de Colombia (FARC-EP), *Borrador Conjunto – Acuerdo sobre las Víctimas del Conflicto*, December 15, 2015, www.mesadeconversaciones.com.co/comunicados/borrador-conjunto-acuerdo-sobre-las-v%C3%ADctimas-del-conflicto.

113 "Colombia: Dealing Away Justice," *Human Rights Watch*, September 28, 2015, accessed October 11, 2015, www.hrw.org/news/2015/09/28/colombia-dealing-away-justice. ("The September 23, 2015 agreement between the Colombian government and Revolutionary Armed Forces of Colombia (FARC-EP) guerrillas would deny justice to thousands of victims of grave violations of human rights and humanitarian law by allowing their abusers to escape meaningful punishment. While the 'Special Jurisdiction for Peace' would create important incentives for violators to confess their crimes, it would also allow those responsible for mass atrocities to avoid spending any time in prison.")

114 Ibid.

115 "Pacto de Justicia en Colombia es una 'Piñata de Impunidad,' Denuncia HRW," *El Espectador*, December 22, 2015, accessed February 17, 2016, www.elespectador.com/noticias/paz/pacto-de-justicia-colombia-una-pinata-de-impunidad-denu-articulo-607243.

116 "Colombia: Agreement Must Guarantee Justice for the Millions of Victims of the Armed Conflict," *Amnesty International*, September 24, 2015, accessed February 14, 2016, www.amnesty.org/en/latest/news/2015/09/colombia-agreement-must-guarantee-justice-for-the-millions-of-victims-of-the-armed-conflict/.

117 Gustavo Gallón Giraldo, "Un Valioso Acuerdo Contra la Impunidad," *El Espectador*, October 1, 2015, accessed October 11, 2015, www.elespectador.com/opinion/un-valioso-acuerdo-contra-impunidad.

118 Rodrigo Uprimny, "¿Piñata de Impunidad?," *El Espectador*, December 26, 2015, accessed February 17, 2016, www.elespectador.com/opinion/pinata-de-impunidad.

119 Karen Engle's chapter in this volume, 33–34

120 Diego García-Sayán, "Colombia: La Paz, Derecho Humano," *El País*, October 8, 2015, accessed November 10, 2015, http://internacional.elpais.com/internacional/2015/10/08/actualidad/1444332924_911716.html. Note, however, that García-Sayán stepped down from the Court in January 2016, and so will not be deciding any challenge to the agreement that eventually arrives at the Inter-American Court.

121 "Statement of the Prosecutor on the Agreement on the Creation of a Special Jurisdiction for Peace in Colombia," International Criminal Court, September 24, 2015, accessed February 17, 2016, www.icc-cpi.int/en_menus/icc/press%20and%20media/press%20releases/Pages/otp_stat_24-09-2015.aspx.

122 Uprimny, "¿Piñata de Impunidad?"

123 Marisol Gómez Giraldo, "'Ni Modelo Económico ni Doctrina Militares tán en Discusión': Gobierno," *El Tiempo*, October 18, 2012, accessed October 7, 2015, www.eltiempo.com/archivo/documento/CMS-12314542.

124 "Críticos del Proceso de Paz ... No Solo es Uribe." In addition, the negotiations were loudly opposed by many ex-military members, including Harold Bedoya, who argued that engaging in negotiations negatively affected the morale "not just of the Army, but of all Colombians." Ibid.

125 "'Nos Queda Difícil que Congreso nos Elabore un Marco Jurídico': FARC," *El Tiempo*, October 18, 2012, accessed May 19, 2013, www.eltiempo.com/politica/proceso-de-paz-las-farc-critican-la-ley-de-restitucion-de-tierras_12314590-4.

126 See http://data.worldbank.org/indicator/SI.POV.GINI/countries/1W?display=default, accessed March 8, 2016. According to the Bank, "Gini index measures the extent to which the distribution of income (or, in some cases, consumption expenditure) among individuals or households within an economy deviates from a perfectly equal distribution. ...[A] Gini index of 0 represents perfect equality, while an index of 100 implies perfect inequality." Ibid.

127 United Nations Development Program, *Colombia Rural: Razones para la Esperanza* (National Human Development Report) (New York: UNDP, 2011), 204, http://hdr.undp.org/sites/default/files/nhdr_colombia_2011_es_low.pdf.

128 "Peace, Land, and Bread," *The Economist*, November 24, 2012, accessed October 7, 2015, www.economist.com/news/americas/21567087-hard-bargaining-starts-peace-land-and-bread.

129 The report continues: "It is of concern that the restitution process is advancing so slowly despite the fact that almost 80% of cases do not have an opponent and so should, in theory at least, be relatively straightforward to resolve. Some 96% of all cases heard so far have been decided by the restitution judges and magistrates in favour of the land claimant. Most of the land restitution cases that have thus far been settled involve families who had already returned to their land prior to the restitution process and are simply seeking formalization of their ownership over the land, rather than restitution per se ... the URT has calculated that by 1 August 2014, 303 families who were not on the land at the time the judicial sentence was issued in their favour now have 'effective enjoyment of the property.' But this does not necessarily mean that they have returned ... UARIV could only confirm that as few as thirty-three families had returned to their farmstead following the issuing of the restitution sentence. The main reasons why land claimants have not been able to return include fear about security in the area where their lands are located; delays by INCODER to issue the claimants with their land titles; and the failure of the URT to implement the agricultural project that land claimants need in order to sustain themselves economically on their land." "A Land Title is not Enough: Ensuring Sustainable Land Restitution in Colombia," *Amnesty International*, November 27, 2014, 29–30, www.amnesty.org/en/documents/AMR23/031/2014/en/.

130 See, for example, "Empezó Debate por la Reforma Agraria que Proponen las FARC," *El Tiempo*, January 15, 2013, accessed October 7, 2015, www.eltiempo.com/archivo/documento/CMS-12514342; "Las Promesas de Santos son el Discurso Agrario de las FARC," *La Silla Vacía*, accessed May 19, 2013, www.lasillavacia.com/historia/las-promesas-de-santos-son-el-discurso-agrario-de-las-farc-40957; "De Riochiquito a Cuba, los Cambios en la Propuesta Agraria de las Farc," *Verdad Abierta*, January 21, 2013, accessed May 19, 2013, http://verdadabierta.com/component/content/article/52-farc/4411-de-riochiquito-a-la-habana-los-cambios-en-la-propuesta-agraria-de-las-farc.

131 Delegados del Gobierno de la República de Colombia (Gobierno Nacional) y las Fuerzas Armadas Revolucionarias de Colombia (FARC-EP), *Borrador Conjunto-Hacia un Nuevo Campo Colombiano: Reforma Rural Integral*, June 6, 2014, www.mesadeconversaciones.com.co/sites/default/files/Borrador%20Conjunto%20-%20%20Pol_tica%20de%20desarrollo%20agrario%20integral.pdf.

132 Ibid., 4.
133 Law No. 160, arts. 48 et seq. (Colombia 1994) and Decree No. 1465, art. 36 (Colombia 2013) represent the most recent legislation and regulation on this issue. These norms establish a specific procedure in order to retake and restitute the land.
134 Land restitution programs were driven through Law No. 1448 (Colombia 2011), which created the Unidad Administrativa Especial de Gestión de Restitución de Tierras Despojadas, an institution in charge of restitution and registration of dispossessed land. Since the entry into force of Law No. 1448 of 2011, other norms have regulated the restitution of land in Colombia, such as Decree No. 4800 (Colombia 2011) and Decree No. 4829 (Colombia 2011), which were enacted in order to materialize the rights of victims of the armed conflict.
135 Law No. 2 (Colombia 1959) declared some public land as Forest Reserve. This law also established the possibility for the Colombian Agriculture Ministry to take out some land from the Forest Reserve to use for agricultural activities. Today, in accordance with Law No. 160 (Colombia 1994) and Law No. 1448 (Colombia 2011), Resolution No. 629, art. 1 (Colombia 2012) of the Colombian Ministry of Environment and Sustainable Development establishes that the environmental boundaries may be reconfigured to advance rural development programs.
136 In relation to the social function, the parameters for the proper use of land are established in Law No. 200, art. 1 (Colombia 1936). This same law (art. 6) states that a breach of Article 1 may lead to an extinction of ownership.
137 Following the Constitution of 1991, art. 58, Law No. 160, art. 52 (Colombia 1994) established that the extinction of ownership is also possible in case of a violation of the rules on conservation, improvement and rational use of renewable natural resources, or of the rules on preservation and restoration of the environment.
138 Expropriation, for social and public purposes, is established in the Constitution of 1991, art. 58. The procedure for this expropriation is set forth in Law No. 160, arts. 31 et seq. (Colombia 1994).
139 In accordance with the Constitution of 1991, art. 64, Law No. 160, art. 1 (Colombia 1994) established the possibility of making access to credit and subsidy programs available to poor peasants. Chapter IV of this law created the Integral Subsidy for Land Acquisition. Additionally, following Law No. 160, art. 20 (Colombia 1994) (modified by Law No. 1450, art. 63 (Colombia 2011)), INCODER's Agreements No. 310 and 324 of 2013 regulated and added new subsidies. Law No. 160, art. 23 (Colombia 1994) also creates the possibility of granting credits to small peasants.
140 For example, Resolution No. 452, art. 1 (Colombia 2010) (modified by Resolution No. 181, art. 1 (Colombia 2013)) creates the Formalization Program of Rural Property, in charge of promoting the formalization of title in part to increase access to credit. In order to support this formalization, several laws have been enacted: Decree No. 4145 (Colombia 2011), Law No. 1561 (Colombia 2012) and Law No. 1579 (Colombia 2012).
141 Law No. 160, Chapter IX (Colombia 1994) regulates the Unidad Agrícola Familiar and establishes several mechanisms for its protection.
142 Peasant reserve zones are regulated through Law No. 160, arts. 79 et seq. (Colombia 1994). The procedure directed to the selection and definition of these zones is

established in Decree No. 1777 (Colombia 1996) and in INCORA's Agreement 24 of 1997.

143 For further discussion of these policies, see Helena Alviar García, "La Discusión en Torno a la Política de Desarrollo Agrario: ¿Perspectivas Encontradas?¿Nuevas Soluciones?,"*Perspectivas Jurídicas para la Paz*, eds. Helena Alviar García and Isabel Cristina Jaramillo Sierra, (Bogotá: Ediciones Uniandes, 2016): 11–39.

144 "Las Cinco Claves del Acuerdo sobre Justicia con las FARC," *El Tiempo*, September 24, 2015, accessed October 7, 2015, www.eltiempo.com/politica/proceso-de-paz/acuerdo-de-justicia-de-santos-y-farc-penas-8-anos-para-autores-de-delitos-graves/16385339.

145 Juan Sebastián Jiménez Herrera, "Una Corte Constitucional para la Paz," *El Espectador*, October 7, 2015, accessed October 11, 2015, www.elespectador.com/noticias/judicial/una-corte-constit.

146 Table based on 1981 and 1982 laws, and on table compiling laws and decrees in successful demobilizations between 1989 and 1998 in Luz María Sánchez, *Perspectivas Jurídicas Frente a un Eventual Proceso de Paz con los Grupos Guerrilleros*, 33–34.

8

From Political Repression to Torturer Impunity: The Narrowing of *Filártiga* v. *Peña-Irala*

Natalie R. Davidson[*]

This chapter explores the roots of anti-impunity discourse in one field: human rights litigation brought before US courts. It revisits the landmark 1980 decision in *Filártiga* v. *Peña-Irala*,[1] the first case in which a US court ruled that international human rights claims could be brought in federal courts under the Alien Tort Statute (ATS). The ATS provides that federal courts have "jurisdiction of any civil action by an alien for a tort only, committed in violation of the law of nations or a treaty of the United States."[2] The statute had been rarely invoked since its enactment in 1789, until the Court of Appeals for the Second Circuit held in *Filártiga* that the statute granted federal courts jurisdiction over a tort claim brought by the family of a young Paraguayan man against a former Paraguayan police officer for torturing the young man to death in Paraguay. For the next three decades, US courts generally followed in the footsteps of *Filártiga*, and opened their doors to damage lawsuits by foreign victims of gross human rights violations occurring abroad. The case has been called the *Brown* v. *Board of Education* of international human rights litigation,[3] and applauded for promoting human rights accountability.[4] It has also been hailed as a model that should inspire other countries to recognize universal civil jurisdiction – that is, jurisdiction in civil litigation grounded not on a link between the case and the forum, but on the universality of the norm invoked, the paradigmatic norm being the prohibition of torture.[5] *Filártiga's* landmark quality has only increased since the US Supreme Court restrictively

[*] For very helpful comments on this and earlier versions of this chapter, I thank Eyal Benvenisti, Leora Bilsky, Avihay Dorfman, and in particular the editors of this book. I also sincerely thank Joel, Nidia and Analy Filártiga, Peter Weiss, Richard Alan White, Martín Almada, Alfredo Boccia Paz, Alberto Candia, Carlos Fontclara, and Raul Gonzalez Allen for sharing their experiences and analyses of the case and of the Stroessner regime with me. Research for this chapter was supported by the David Berg Center for Law and History and the Minerva Center for Human Rights, both at Tel Aviv University.

interpreted the ATS in 2013, holding in *Kiobel* v. *Royal Dutch Petroleum* that
the statute does not generally apply to violations of international law occurring
outside US territory.[6] In the wake of *Kiobel*, *Filártiga* has come to be invoked
as the symbol of a gilded and perhaps lost age.[7] This chapter offers a more
critical reading of the court rulings in *Filártiga* that exposes some limitations
of universal civil jurisdiction. In doing so, it also reveals the need for a theoretical paradigm of universal jurisdiction that could encompass larger structures
of injustice rather than remaining tied to individualized guilt and physical
violence.

This chapter argues that, although the plaintiffs' submissions in *Filártiga*
exposed the Paraguayan state as a systematic violator of human rights, both
the district and appellate courts primarily treated the case as one about individual violence, in particular by drawing an analogy between the torturer
and the pirate. *Filártiga*'s legacy, I suggest, was not only the ability to pursue
human rights claims in US courts. The court pronouncements in the case
bequeathed to successive ATS cases an interpretation of torture that focused
on the individual rather than the state, on the exceptional rather than the
systemic, and on physical cruelty rather than economic injustice.[8] This legacy
persisted even after ATS lawsuits began to target multinational corporations
for involvement in violence in the Global South.

Some have argued that ATS litigation represents a peculiarly American
version of international criminal justice that may be explained by a US tradition of public interest civil litigation,[9] and which produces an individualizing
narrative similar to criminal law. This chapter points to other explanations for
individualization – as well as to some of its regrettable effects. *Filártiga* takes
us back to a time when international criminal prosecutions were not a realistic
option: in the midst of Cold War détente, prior to the rebirth of international
criminal law, and predating the birth of "transitional justice." The case therefore provides an opportunity to examine the origins of anti-impunity discourse
at a time when the human rights field was largely insulated from any discourse
of criminalization.

Through a detailed analysis of the case, this chapter argues that the courts'
individualization of torture in *Filártiga* derived from the legal and political
constraints the courts experienced in their exercise of universal jurisdiction.
Simultaneously constrained by legal doctrine and concerned about their own
legitimacy in challenging the central paradigm of state sovereignty, the courts
resorted to a narrative of individual violence. In the political context of the
late 1970s and early 1980s, individualized accounts of political violence were
particularly apt for providing US courts with legitimacy: they dovetailed with
an emerging discourse about human rights, which was understood as a means

of "doing good" absent the charge of US interventionism in other countries' affairs. This chapter thus offers a combined political and legal explanation that reflects an understanding of law as a process that is neither fully autonomous from politics nor simply reducible to political forces.[10]

In fact, the judges in *Filártiga* were hardly the first to experience these constraints or to respond by producing distorted representations of political violence: the decisions at Nuremberg and against Adolf Eichmann suffered from similarly impoverished visions of state-sponsored violence due to a combination of legal and political constraints. This chapter offers a new perspective on *Filártiga* by situating it in a line of groundbreaking atrocity trials. As in those cases, the result in *Filártiga* was an incomplete narrative that not only masked the economic and US-related aspects of the case but obscured the systemic nature of torture by the Paraguayan government.

Part I presents literature on the representation of history in Nazi trials and in particular on the insight that judicial representations of political violence in atrocity cases have been inadequate due to both legal constraints and judges' exacerbated need for legitimacy when breaking new legal ground. Part II retells the events leading to the *Filártiga* case as symptomatic of structural and economic injustice under Paraguay's Stroessner regime. It then describes a first stage of narrowing: before the case was filed in 1979, it was part of an international human rights campaign against state repression in Paraguay. Although the campaign emphasized the Paraguayan state's systematic use of torture, it ignored some of the structural causes of torture in Paraguay, such as economic injustice and US support for the regime. Part III describes a second stage of narrowing, one that occurred in US courts. While the plaintiff submissions presented the case as implicating the institutionalized practices of the Paraguayan state, and even managed to reintroduce some of the case's links to economic injustice, this story of political repression, resistance, and complicity was lost in the simplified narrative produced both in the Second Circuit's appellate opinion and in the subsequent District Court decision awarding damages on remand. The conclusion elaborates on the costs of the individualized conception of political violence present in the ATS field, and suggests that because this conception poorly reflects the reality of political violence, it leads to inadequate legal analysis.

I. THE CRITIQUE OF LAW'S HISTORICAL NARRATIVES IN NAZI TRIALS

Since Nuremberg, criminal trials of atrocity have been criticized for producing impoverished historical narratives.[11] Notably, many Holocaust scholars have deplored the failure of the International Military Tribunal at Nuremberg to address the mass extermination of European Jews, due to the prosecutors' legally cautious focus on war crimes and crimes against peace – crimes then known to international law – at the expense of the unprecedented category of crimes against humanity.[12] Moreover, as Lawrence Douglas notes, in order to ground the new doctrine of crimes against humanity in the absence of positive sources of law, the prosecution at Nuremberg insisted that the concept reflected principles "derived from the customs and practices of civilized nations."[13] The prosecution's insistence on "civilization" as an antidote to Nazism resulted in a portrait of Nazism as primitive, the result of civilization's failure to contain savage impulses, in sharp contrast with historical scholarship's understanding of the Holocaust as a product of modern civilization.[14]

The historical representation of Nazism at Nuremberg was shaped not only by technical legal constraints, but also by the Tribunal's need for legitimacy. While Douglas generally views the Nuremberg trial as a successful attempt to adapt the law creatively to the novelty of the Holocaust, he shows that the heightened legitimacy concerns in this trial, which relied on the jurisdiction of an ad hoc, victor's international tribunal, led to "tortured history."[15] The Tribunal's emphasis on militarism and the protection of national sovereignty (as opposed to the protection of civilians) was a way to reassure the critics that despite the Tribunal's legal innovations, it would not undermine established legal principles.[16]

Similarly, commenting on the trial in Jerusalem of Adolf Eichmann, the Nazi officer who coordinated the deportation of Jews to extermination camps during World War II, Hannah Arendt objected to the court's analogy of genocide and crimes against humanity with piracy. That analogy was legally useful to the court and helped to bolster its legitimacy[17] since piracy provided a precedent in international law for the court to apply universal jurisdiction and judge acts committed on a foreign territory that concerned neither an Israeli defendant nor victims.[18] In Arendt's view, however, the analogy poorly reflected the state-sponsored nature of Eichmann's crimes:

> The pirate's exception to the territorial principle ... is made not because he is the enemy of all, and hence can be judged by all, but because this crime is committed on the high seas, and the high seas are no man's land. The pirate, moreover,... is, by definition, in business entirely for himself .... Surely, no one will maintain that Eichmann was in business for himself or that he acknowledged obedience to no flag whatsoever. In this respect, the piracy theory served only to dodge one of the fundamental problems posed by crimes of this kind, namely, that they were, and could only be, committed under a criminal *law* and by a criminal *state*.[19]

Some historians have urged distinguishing clearly between legal judgment and the production of a historical account of the events underpinning the litigation.[20] Others have expressed concern that legal justice will be impaired if the trial sets itself objectives other than the determination of individual guilt.[21] Yet as Lawrence Douglas has argued, "[c]ases involving crimes of atrocity inevitably and necessarily usher complex histories into courtrooms. ... The question then is not whether to deal with history, but how to deal with it responsibly."[22]

"Dealing responsibly" with history depends in part on locating the appropriate jurisdiction. The international character of jurisdiction in many atrocity trials may have contradictory effects on the historical narrative. On the one hand, removing the trial from the nation-state might avoid "the compulsion to engage in nation-building rhetoric or in nationalist mythmaking"[23] that takes place in national settings, opening the door to critical histories. On the other hand, the resort to extraordinary forms of jurisdiction exacerbates the prosecutors' and judges' need to legitimate their intervention, producing, in the case of the Nazi trials, tortured history. Moreover, the cultural distance from the society in which the crimes were committed leads to situations in which prosecutors and judges have difficulty understanding the historical context.[24]

With international jurisdiction also comes the use of international norms that contribute to the representation of violence. The alleged supra-national nature of international crimes has led to conceptualizing these events as affronts to all humanity. That notion threatens to impoverish law's historical representation by implying that these crimes are committed by individual monsters – an understanding of the perpetrators which I will hereafter refer to as "demonization."[25] Such an understanding of state-sponsored violence is undermined by Arendt's concept of the "banality of evil,"[26] which emphasizes the bureaucratic, routine setting in which the Nazi crimes were committed.[27] While scholars contest the notion of an amoral, unthinking bureaucrat as an historical and psychological phenomenon,[28] Arendt used her famous phrase to point to the fact that the danger of the totalitarian state lay in the fact that it need not rely on inherently "evil" individuals, but rather on the motivations of ordinary people.[29] The "banality of evil" therefore forms the basis for the now common understanding that ordinary people, and not only dysfunctional sadists, can commit atrocities.[30]

The remainder of this chapter demonstrates that in the *Filártiga* case, as in these Nazi trials, a combination of legal constraints and the courts' need for legitimation in their exercise of an extraordinary form of jurisdiction led the courts to produce an impoverished historical account – in this case by adopting a demonizing discourse that focused on the individual torturer and obscured the institutionalized and banal character of political violence.

II. *FILÁRTIGA* AND THE CAMPAIGN AGAINST TORTURE
IN PARAGUAY

This part begins by retelling the *Filártiga* case as a story of structural injustice, based on historical scholarship and memoirs by persons close to the plaintiffs.[31] It then argues that international human rights advocates narrowed the case to a story of Paraguayan authoritarianism, without linking political repression to structural injustice. Part III contrasts the story of political repression and resistance with the even narrower narrative produced by the Second Circuit in its landmark decision on the case, as well as in the subsequent court decision awarding damages.

A. *A Rebel Doctor in a Sultanist State*

Joelito Filártiga was the son of Joel Filártiga, a doctor and artist from Asunción. Though Joel Filártiga's own father was a friend of Alfredo Stroessner, the general who took power in Paraguay in 1954 and ruled in an authoritarian manner until deposed in 1989,[32] Joel Filártiga was highly critical of socio-economic inequalities in the country.[33] He ran a clinic in the impoverished countryside, where he and his family members provided medical services to peasants.[34] His devotion to the health of peasants and constant criticism of the regime through exhibits of his artwork abroad earned him the ire of the government.[35]

Stroessner remained in power for over thirty-four years through violent repression and alliances with the country's military, political, and economic power blocs.[36] The regime has been described as fitting the regime type known as sultanism,[37] characterized by "a personalistic and centralized government in which functionaries are recruited on the basis of personal loyalty to the ruler .... [and] the incentive to that loyalty lies not in the ruler's personal charisma, but in his ability to dispense and suspend material rewards and privileges."[38] In this "sophisticated system of rewards or punishment,"[39] the economy was manipulated for personal benefit.[40]

Until the end of the 1970s – by which time his regime was well consolidated – Stroessner was able to provide the material incentives to cultivate loyalty by using to his advantage substantial economic, military, and political support provided by the United States in its efforts to counter the spread of communism.[41] The United States did not only contribute to the Stroessner regime's economic and political foundations; it also encouraged the repression in Paraguay of what it perceived to be immediate leftist threats by training Paraguayan officers, soldiers, and police officers in counterinsurgency at US military academies.[42]

As part of the Western bloc, Stroessner's regime was required to adopt the language of democracy.[43] Yet it invoked democracy to justify repression against those accused of Communist (and thus non-democratic) sympathies,[44] and repression was otherwise enabled by ambiguously worded exceptions to formally proclaimed legal rights.[45] Through these exceptions, the regime's actions were characterized by absolute arbitrariness, popularly referred to as the law of *mbarete*, after the term in Guaraní, the indigenous language widely spoken in Paraguay along with Spanish, for the arbitrariness of those who enjoy the protection of the powerful.[46] Repression took many forms, most notably torture, incarceration, and forced exile.

The countryside at times wavered in its support for the ruling party. The Church established Christian Agrarian Leagues, community organizations encouraging peasants to work together and share proceeds, which also provided literacy and *"conscientización"* ("consciousness-producing") programs. Viewing the Leagues' work as a challenge to the patronage system that extended all the way down to the poorest villages, the regime brutally repressed them, claiming they were communist organizations linked to guerrilla movements.[47] In the context of such peasant repression, the Filártigas' free clinic in the countryside constituted an open act of resistance. More profoundly, Joel Filártiga's outspoken criticism of the exploitation and harm of peasants at the hands of agricultural business challenged the system of patronage. The Filártigas were also involved in more direct resistance through their close relationship with the *Organización Político Militar* (OPM), a guerrilla group,[48] though it is doubtful that the police were aware of this.[49] Filártiga and Miranda further claim that Joel's son, Joelito, was a member of the OPM; whether or not that is true, these authors believe that Joelito was tortured to intimidate his father.[50]

In the midst of a wave of heightened repression of peasants, on the night of March 30, 1976, seventeen-year-old Joelito was taken to the police station in the neighborhood of Sajonia, where the family's Asunción residence was located. There, he was interrogated by a number of policemen, including Americo Peña, a police inspector who appears to have borne a personal grudge against the Filártigas. Peña's personal motives appear to have been two-fold: first, Peña probably thought that obtaining information about Joel Filártiga would help him advance his career.[51] Second, Miranda and Filártiga suggest that Peña was jealous of Joelito's friendship with María del Rosario Villalba de Duarte, known as Charro, the daughter of Peña's companion.[52]

Coupled with the regime's ongoing worries about Joel Filártiga's activities in the countryside, Peña's banal personal motivations were given deadly force. After approximately two hours of torture, Joelito died from cardiac arrest.[53] At four a.m., the police woke Dolly Filártiga, Joelito's sister, and asked that she retrieve her brother's body from Peña's home. The police claimed that Joelito had been stabbed by Hugo Duarte, Charro's husband, in a crime of passion after he found Joelito in bed with Charro. The next morning, the press announced the commission of a crime of passion.

From the outset, Joel Filártiga strove to repudiate the official version.[54] As part of the official "crime of passion" story, the state initiated criminal proceedings against Duarte for the murder of Joelito. As is common in civil law jurisdictions, Paraguayan law grants victims of crime the right to join criminal cases as adjuncts to the state attorney.[55] The Filártigas therefore filed a number of motions seeking to broaden the scope of the trial to include "the organizers, accomplices, and anyone else involved in covering up the murder,"[56] as well as Peña and the members of his family.[57] These proceedings proved futile, never serving to hold the police responsible nor to reveal the truth. Moreover, the family and their lawyers were constantly harassed.[58] Peña, for his part, enjoyed the legal services of Emilio Gorostiaga, a member of Stroessner's inner circle.[59] Duarte was eventually found by a Paraguayan court to have killed Joelito, but was exonerated from legal responsibility thanks to a defense available to husbands who find their wives in *"flagrante delicto."*[60] Just like the "democratic" governmental system of which the courts formed a part, the trial was a façade.

B. An American Lawsuit

At the end of 1978, the Filártigas discovered by chance that Peña was living in Brooklyn.[61] After the Filártigas' American friend Richard White brought the issue to the attention of the federal police, Peña and his companion were arrested on April 4, 1979, on the charge of overstaying their tourist visas.[62] On April 5, the Center for Constitutional Rights (CCR), brought into the case by Amnesty International (to which White had previously appealed), held an emergency meeting to debate bringing the Filártigas' claim against Peña under the Alien Tort Statute (ATS). CCR attorney Peter Weiss had long contemplated using the ATS in a way that would give teeth to international law. However, Weiss' colleagues discouraged him from using the ATS, insisting that any such suit would be laughed out of court.[63] This time, Weiss convinced his CCR colleagues that the only chance to keep Peña in the US, notwithstanding the government's intention to deport him, was to invoke the ATS.[64]

On April 6, 1979, Peña was served with a civil complaint on behalf of Joel and Dolly Filártiga, alleging that Peña's acts constituted violations of US treaties and the law of nations under the ATS, as well as of wrongful death statutes.

Convinced by the CCR's arguments that it would not be possible to depose Peña and his companion once they returned home because of the Paraguayan judiciary's lack of independence, the judge in charge of the case, Eugene H. Nickerson, issued temporary restraining orders preventing their deportation.[65] However, on May 15, 1979, Judge Nickerson and the District Court dismissed the lawsuit. As will be recalled, the ATS grants federal courts "jurisdiction of any civil action by an alien for a tort only, committed in violation of the law of nations or a treaty of the United States." The District Court agreed with Peña's argument that, for the purposes of the ATS, the prohibition of torture did not form part of "the law of nations," as that body of law was limited to those "standards, rules or customs affecting the relationship between states and between an individual and a foreign state, and used by those states for their common good and/or in dealings *inter se*."[66] This reasoning followed dicta in *ITT* v. *Vencap*, a lawsuit for fraud brought under the ATS by a foreign investment trust against a venture capital fund, where the court had held that it could not "subscribe to the plaintiffs' view that the Eighth Commandment 'Thou shalt not steal' is part of the law of nations."[67] The CCR appealed, but Peña was nevertheless deported on May 25, 1979.[68]

The plaintiffs argued in their appeal that even if the District Court had been right to adopt *Vencap*'s narrow definition of the law of nations, the prohibition on torture should fall within that definition, as it necessarily concerned relations among states. This was evident, in their view, in the deteriorating relations between Paraguay and the US as a result of what they described as the US government's foreign policy to eradicate torture. The plaintiffs' primary argument, however, was that the *Vencap* test should not be followed. First, the plaintiffs argued that the drafters of the ATS understood the law of nations to apply not only to relations among states, but also to the conduct of individuals, as evidenced by the doctrine of *hostis humani generis* (enemies of mankind), "which holds that certain tortious acts are so reprehensible and universally condemned that universal jurisdiction is accorded to insure that the perpetrators are brought to justice."[69] This doctrine, they further argued, was not understood to be restricted to pirates, but applied to all conduct condemned internationally as heinous.[70] Second, the plaintiffs argued that contemporary international law prohibited torture, and therefore that the *Vencap* test, if it was ever correct in the past, was simply erroneous in the present.[71] Two amicus briefs filed by human rights organizations in support of the plaintiffs also argued that torture by a state official is a violation of the law of nations under the ATS, whether under the *Vencap* test or under contemporary international law.[72]

The CCR was originally apprehensive that the appeal had been assigned to Judge Kaufman, who had served as trial judge in the case against Ethel and Julius Rosenberg, the two Americans executed for espionage in 1953 for passing information about the atomic bomb to the Soviet Union, and had a reputation as a "government man."[73] Within this context, the amicus brief filed on behalf of the United States by lawyers from the State Department and Department of Justice, which was supportive of exercising jurisdiction through the ATS, seems to have been key. Both White[74] and Weiss[75] have suggested that Kaufman seized the case as an opportunity to redeem himself from his association with McCarthyism, a particularly appealing option given that he was not required to oppose the US government's position. The US amicus brief in fact was more innovative than the plaintiffs' argument. In their attempt to cover alternative arguments, the plaintiffs had remained attached to a form of originalist statutory interpretation, arguing that individual wrongdoing was covered by the law of nations because such had been the intent of the framers of the ATS. In contrast, the US government argued that "official torture" violated international law and that international law should be interpreted as it evolves, not as it was in the eighteenth century.[76]

The Circuit Court issued its ruling on June 30, 1980. To determine whether federal courts have subject-matter jurisdiction under the ATS, the Court adopted the reasoning of the US amicus brief, and reviewed contemporary international law to "conclude that official torture is now prohibited by the law of nations."[77] The Court further followed the argument of the US amicus brief[78] in stating that the norms giving rise to jurisdiction under the ATS must "command the general assent of civilized nations,"[79] to avoid one nation imposing its norms in the name of international law.[80] The Court also held that since the law of nations formed an integral part of the common law, the grant of jurisdiction under the ATS was constitutional.

In this, the Court's reasoning addressed and rejected defendant Peña's principal arguments. It also dismissed Peña's other arguments, including his view that the claim was barred by the act of state doctrine, a defense that prevents courts from judging the public acts of another sovereign state committed within that sovereign's territory.[81] It held that the act of state doctrine could not be applicable to an act of torture committed in violation of Paraguayan law and unratified by the Paraguay government.[82] Judge Nickerson delivered a default judgment in June 1981, holding Peña liable, and in 1984 awarded punitive damages in the amount of US$10 million "to reflect adherence to the world community's proscription of torture and to attempt to deter its practice."[83] The Filártigas' efforts to collect judgment have been unsuccessful.[84]

C. *An International Campaign against the Paraguayan State*

The ATS lawsuit was the last stage of an international campaign led by Richard White to support the Filártigas. Crucially, most participants in the campaign understood it to be directed against the Paraguayan government, seen as responsible for the torture and murder of Joelito.

The campaign began with pressure against the Paraguayan government from human rights groups – notably a 1977 booklet by Amnesty International on political repression in Paraguay, which featured Joelito among dozens of cases of "political prisoners."[85] Then, following White's lobbying of US Congressmen, Senator Frank Church asked the US Ambassador to Paraguay to inform him periodically of developments in the case, and further sponsored a letter to Stroessner, co-signed by twenty-one US senators, to express concern about human rights in Paraguay.[86]

White also lodged a complaint with the Inter-American Commission on Human Rights (IACHR) of the Organization of American States (OAS).[87] At the OAS eighth general assembly in 1978, the IACHR presented a special country report on Paraguay, featuring the *Filártiga* case. The report clearly assigned responsibility to the Paraguayan state for allowing human rights violations to occur and go unpunished, and presented human rights violations as government policy.[88] Not one country voted in support of Paraguay, delivering the country a serious diplomatic blow.[89]

The conception of the case as implicating the systematic use of torture by the Paraguayan state – without tying torture to economic injustice – persisted outside the courts once the lawsuit was filed, well into the 1980s. Internal police memoranda I found in Paraguay's national police archive reveal that the government of Paraguay understood the case to implicate its own responsibility.[90] In 1983, an internal police memorandum even referred to Filártiga's lawsuit as "the lawsuit he has filed against the Paraguayan State."[91] The Paraguayan government attempted to settle the issue through diplomacy, to no avail.[92]

By emphasizing the Paraguayan state's systematic use of torture, the international campaign ignored the links between Joelito's torture and Joel Filártiga's criticism of economic injustice and the support for the regime provided by Paraguayan elites as well as by the United States. In this sense, the international campaign's focus on the Paraguayan state narrowed the case, removing from purview important structural conditions enabling repression in Paraguay. Yet even this narrowed version of the facts was richer than the individualized one that would eventually be adopted by the US courts.

III. *FILÁRTIGA* AND THE STRUGGLE AGAINST TORTURER IMPUNITY

The courts in *Filártiga* were presented with briefs that generally portrayed torture as both heinous and political. Not only the plaintiffs' submissions, but even the defendant's arguments reflected a conception of the case as one implicating the Stroessner regime. In contrast, the District and Circuit courts emphasized Peña's individual maliciousness in their holdings, choosing the path of individualization and demonization. This section traces this second stage of narrowing of the *Filártiga* case, and suggests that the courts shifted attention away from the state to the individual torturer for doctrinal reasons as well as to legitimate their jurisdiction in the case.

A. *The First Stage of Litigation: From Filing to the Default Judgment*

Ironically, it was the plaintiffs who originally introduced the doctrine of *hostis humanis generis* and the figure of the pirate, to counter the District Court's narrow interpretation of the law of nations as restricted to the relationship among states.[93] However, the plaintiffs' briefs offered the doctrine of *hostis humani generis* and the analogy to piracy within a broader set of arguments regarding the regime's responsibility for Pena's actions. Many of the plaintiff submissions referred to the responsibility of the regime alongside Peña's, in statements such as "[t]he defendant Peña-Irala disappeared from Paraguay at a time when *his involvement and that of the Stroessner regime* in the torture-murder of Joelito Filártiga and the effort to cover up this deliberate wrongdoing was becoming increasingly notorious and *embarrassing to the regime.*"[94] Peña's acts were also placed in the context of the widespread use of torture by the regime, beyond its persecution of the Filártiga family:

> The torture-murder of Joelito Filártiga is not an isolated incident in Paraguay
> …. It has been argued that torture is applied primarily as a punishment for
> and deterrent to opposition activities.[95]

And indeed, the defendant's arguments reflected the understanding that it was the regime itself that was under attack. The defendant's submissions attempted to deny the political nature of the murder; they consistently referred to an "alleged wrongful killing" or "alleged homicide" and reminded the court that Duarte had confessed to the murder. Yet the same submissions portrayed the lawsuit as political, dismissing the proceedings as a "show-trial" which sought to transform the US court into "a theater for the display of political propaganda."[96]

Voices other than the parties entered the litigation, and overwhelmingly presented the case as one implicating the Paraguayan state. Many of the documents forming part of the international campaign around the case were presented by the plaintiffs to the courts, in order to describe the situation in Paraguay. For instance, attached as an exhibit to the complaint was a copy of the complaint filed with the IACtHR, which does not mention Peña, referring instead to the Government of Paraguay as answerable party.[97] Moreover, the plaintiffs referred to the reports of international organizations and articles in the *New York Times* describing the case in the context of authoritarianism in Paraguay.

Similarly, the State Department amicus brief consistently presented the prohibition of torture as a norm imposing an obligation on states.[98] An amicus brief filed at the beginning of the litigation by human rights organizations on behalf of the plaintiffs contains extensive discussions of the political situation in Paraguay, including the roles of the army, police, and judiciary in what is described as a police state.[99] Two briefs filed in the Second Circuit by international human rights organizations pending appeal adopted a much more individualizing discourse about torture; though they framed the acts as state action where it suited their argument,[100] they denied it elsewhere in order to ward off accusations of a "show trial."[101] In this sense, they foreshadowed the courts' move of demonizing the torturer in order to provide the lawsuit both legal and political legitimacy.

The description of the systematic use of torture in Paraguay was relevant to the plaintiffs' legal arguments in a number of ways. First, implicating the police colored the torture-murder as a violation of international law. The plaintiffs argued that torture constituted a violation of international law either under the *Vencap* test, or because individuals are subjects of international law. Under both of these approaches, the state-sponsored nature of torture was relevant to the plaintiffs' argumentation. To support their argument that torture affects relations among nations under the *Vencap* test, the plaintiffs discussed the deterioration of US–Paraguayan relations due to "the practice of torture by the police in Paraguay."[102] And while arguing that the individual is a subject of international law, the plaintiffs explained that individual responsibility is necessary precisely because the state is involved, in order to remove the shield of state sovereignty which would otherwise protect individuals.[103]

Second, describing the regime's widespread use of torture as well as Filártiga's political dissidence likely made the plaintiffs' claims more credible, by providing a probable motive for the acts. Third, the government sponsorship of the torture-murder further strengthened the plaintiffs' argument about the inability of Paraguay's judiciary to provide legal redress, thereby justifying the turn to US courts. Though exhaustion of remedies was not formally required, the fact that justice was not available in Paraguay was constantly invoked by the plaintiffs to argue that the court should not decline jurisdiction under the doctrine of *forum non conveniens:*

> In light of [the] authoritative findings as to complete subservience of the Paraguayan judiciary to the military dictatorship ruling the country, and the highly political nature of this case, defendant's statements ... that plaintiffs' "right to pursue their remedy for wrongful death exists in Paraguay" and "has been in no way infringed by Paraguayan courts," can only be described as an excursion into the wild blue yonder of free-wheeling fantasy .... In sum, if the allegedly more convenient forum were Canada, Japan or England, as in the ... cases cited by defendant ..., plaintiffs would not be in this Court today. Had they lived in any of these countries, their son and brother would not have died as he did, and they would have no reason to seek the aid of the courts in this country.[104]

Until Peña was deported from the US on May 25, 1979, the failures of the Paraguayan justice system were also invoked to convince the courts that his deportation should be stayed, as the legal system in Paraguay could not be relied upon to cooperate in providing evidence.[105] This led to descriptions of the regime's use of a perpetual state of siege and the lack of independence of the Paraguayan judiciary.[106] The motions also described the harassment suffered by the Filártiga family and their lawyers, including arrests approved by Paraguayan courts, and when doing so presented the Paraguayan government as the principle culprit: "Plaintiffs have invoked the jurisdiction of this Court at great risk to their lives and safety, given the previous retaliation against them and their Paraguayan attorney by the Stroessner regime and its courts."[107]

Thus, the plaintiffs' submissions convey the state's responsibility for Joelito's torture and death and for the judicial system's cooperation. As with the international human rights campaign around the case, this narrative has its limitations. Absent is the crucial part played by the US in training the military and providing Stroessner the means of cultivating domestic legitimacy. To the contrary, the plaintiffs insisted on their lawsuit's compatibility with US foreign policy – both under President Carter and before him.[108]

The courts' holdings narrowed the narrative further. The District Court initially rejected the claim and on remand, issued a brief default judgment. The District Court therefore had no opportunity to make a detailed finding of responsibility, though it later returned to the facts of the case in a damages proceeding. Thus, most important for defining the narrative was the Second Circuit's landmark decision. Others have noted that this decision was "clearly influenced by the Filártiga submissions and the accompanying amicus briefs."[109] The Court – like the District Court's brief dismissal of the claim[110] – hinted at some of the political context within which Joelito's torture and murder occurred. The brief description of the facts of the case at the beginning of the appellate decision refers twice to the fact that Joel Filártiga was a political dissident, and repeats the Filártigas' claim "that Joelito was tortured and killed in retaliation for his father's political activities and beliefs."[111] Through the mention of "the government of President Alfredo Stroessner, which has held power in Paraguay since 1954"[112] and of the fact that Peña was Inspector General of Police in Asunción at the time of the murder, the text suggests that responsibility for the torture lies beyond the defendant and with the Paraguayan government. Furthermore, in its discussion of the prohibition of torture under international law, the Court repeatedly refers to the fact that it is the official torture of persons held in custody that is prohibited. In the description of facts, the Court also mentions the cover-up story, pointing to the fact that Duarte, though he has confessed, "has never been convicted or sentenced in connection with the crime"[113] and that the Filártigas' attorney in Paraguay was persecuted for representing his client.

However, contrary to the plaintiffs' submissions, the Court does not mention the routine use of torture by the regime. Moreover, two significant and often-cited statements by the Court construct the paradoxical image of the torturer as a state official acting alone, without institutional support. First, as we saw above, to dismiss Peña's argument that the lawsuit was barred by the act of state doctrine, the Court noted that it was doubtful "whether action by a state official in violation of the Constitution and laws of the Republic of Paraguay, and wholly unratified by that nation's government, could properly be characterized as an act of state."[114] While the Court could be seen here as making a more normative than descriptive statement (i.e., torture, though it is done by state officials, should not be recognized as an act of state for purposes of the legal doctrine),[115] the statement actually relies exclusively on the fact that Paraguay officially prohibited torture and did not ratify Peña's acts. As a result, this statement made the torture appear more as an individual abuse of that official's position than an institutionalized practice. This statement is significant because it is the Court's only direct reference to the Paraguayan executive other than the mention of "the Government of President Alfredo Stroessner" in the statement of facts.

The understanding of torture as the abusive act of a lone official emerges even more clearly from the oft-cited concluding paragraph:

> Among the rights universally proclaimed by all nations, as we have noted, is the right to be free of physical torture. Indeed, for purposes of civil liability, the torturer has become like the pirate and slave trader before him *hostis humani generis*, an enemy of all mankind. Our holding today, giving effect to a jurisdictional provision enacted by our First Congress, is a small but important step in the fulfillment of the ageless dream to free all people from brutal violence.[116]

By invoking the figure of the pirate, the Court produced a powerful image and appealed to precedent. However, as pointed out by Arendt, the image of the pirate tends to be that of an individual operating on his own – an individualization reinforced here by the constant use of the singular ("the torturer," "the pirate," "the slave trader before him"). Moreover, by using the expression "enemy of all mankind," the Court demonized the torturer, obscuring the institutionalized nature of the practice and the broad networks of support required to maintain it.

B. *The Damage Award and the Political Narrative*

As the damages hearing transcript and plaintiffs' memoranda concerning damages indicate, the damages assessment phase produced even more contextualized narratives than those found in earlier plaintiff submissions. Here, Peña almost disappears from the plaintiffs' texts, and attention shifts to the political situation in Paraguay. This is due in part to the fact that the defendant was absent as a party and a default judgment had been issued. As explained by Jacob Timmerman, an Argentinian journalist who had been subjected to torture in Argentina and who testified at the damages hearing, "[t]orture was condemned as a crime. It was never judged as a problem of our civilization, and this is quite different …. this is the first time in which there is nobody to be accused except for torture itself."[117] The focus at the damage stage also shifted to the victims and their suffering, giving them a platform from which to tell their story – and to choose the framing of the story in both personal and political dimensions. Moreover, the arguments concerning punitive damages provided an opportunity to consider the broader social repercussions of the lawsuit.

During the damages hearing, Dolly and Joel Filártiga described their physical, psychological, and emotional suffering as a result of the murder of Joelito. Joel Filártiga's testimony also described in detail his own experience of being tortured, of witnessing torture, of caring for torture victims, as well as the wide-spread nature of torture in Paraguay.[118] This testimony was used by his lawyers to establish his expertise on torture, laying the ground for his assessment of the length and details of Joelito's ordeal. This narration allowed Joel Filártiga to place his personal tragedy in a broader national story. He testified to having told his son: "I was living under a state of permanent depression and of permanent fear for myself and for my family. I think that's the way 80 percent of the population of Paraguay lives permanently."[119] He also described the special atmosphere of fear around the time of Joelito's murder, with the arrest, torture, and confinement of thousands of peasants. He showed the Court some of his drawings and described what he was trying to convey in each. Through these, he described the exploitation and suffering of peasants, and how Joelito's torture was related to his activism for peasants:

Q: Joel Filártiga, this drawing is dated 1979. Would you describe it for us, please?

A: That's the documentation of what a peasant told me, a peasant by the name Barbosa told me. You may not understand, Doctor, what is happening to you, but because you are too close to it, but we do understand. Your son was killed not because he was the son of Filártiga, but because he was the son of serving us, poor people. The punishment is not just for you, but for us, the poor.[120]

In addition to the Filártigas and Timmerman, Robert White, former US Ambassador to Paraguay, testified. He described in detail the permanent state of siege, repression of opposition, lack of independence of judiciary, and endemic corruption, and also highlighted the use of torture as a tool for economic benefit: "One of the reasons for torture," White testified, "one of the reasons for arbitrary behavior is so [the country's elites] could maintain themselves in power and continue the immense profits." Moreover, he insisted on the institutionalized and banal nature of torture. Asked whether he had a view regarding the extent to which torture is calculated to keep people in line and the extent to which it is an expression of sheer viciousness, he answered:

...there is [sic] certainly certain people in power in Paraguay who are vicious. But I think that really it's something – it's routine. I mean, perfectly normal people who appear normal get up and go to work and their work is torture, and then they come home after work and do whatever normal people do. It's institutionalized in Paraguay.[121]

The plaintiffs' subsequent Post-Trial Memorandum of Fact and Law used these testimonies to argue for the amount of compensatory damages to be awarded, as well as for a high amount of punitive damages (for a total of 10 million dollars). In that document, as in their previous submissions, the plaintiffs combined universalist discourse – the punitive damages, they argued, were "to vindicate the interest of the world of nations in accomplishing the elimination of torture through assuring appropriate sanctions, and to express the moral outrage which the status of torture as a violation of the customary international law demands"[122] – with an understanding of torture as an institutionalized practice. The Memorandum recounted the acts of torture experienced by Joel Filártiga, and the psychological torture he experienced by being forced in prison to watch the torture of another 300 individuals. According to this memorandum, seeing Joelito's body made him remember the torture he had experienced and witnessed, adding to his suffering. Thus, it is as if Joelito's tortured body introduced into the litigation hundreds of other acts of torture in Paraguay.

In addition, the Memorandum contains a section dedicated entirely to "The Role of Torture in Paraguay," and clarifies that the Filártiga tragedy "was no isolated incident in Paraguay but part of a system of lawlessness and cruelty which destroys humanity and sustains Latin America's most brutal dictatorship."[123] The section builds on the testimony of Ambassador White to describe in detail the way torture is used to intimidate "[a]nyone who has the capacity to play a leadership role, or anyone who challenges the system in any way."[124] It discusses the way the official legal norms of the Paraguayan Constitution and written laws mask the absolute arbitrariness of the system under the law of *mbarete*. This discussion of the political uses of law in Paraguay helped the plaintiffs explain why the government presented Joelito's murder as a crime of passion, for in a regime formally committed to individual legal rights, torture could hardly be acknowledged officially. It also depicted the case as a direct challenge to *mbarete*, arguing for a high amount of damages for better symbolic effect.[125] The Memorandum also describes the political climate at the time of the murder, referring expressly to the leftist guerrilla group OPM and to the repression of peasants. It states that "[t]he award will not be for the personal benefit of the plaintiffs, but will be put in a Foundation … devoted to protecting and advancing the health and welfare of the poor people of Paraguay and a symbol that Joelito lives and is helping them."[126]

Through oral testimonies, the CCR had attempted to convey to the magistrate charged with assessing damages that the damages ultimately awarded would form a substantial part of the message sent to Paraguay and human rights violators worldwide.[127] The magistrate, however, did not take on the political role he was offered. The transcript of the damages hearing suggests that he was uncomfortable with the emotions displayed by the Filártigas and by the detailed descriptions of torture.[128] In his recommendation to the court, he portrayed the case as an ordinary wrongful death lawsuit, and recommended awarding a total amount of US$375,000 based on Paraguayan law only, dismissing the plaintiffs' claim that the international proscription of torture should be taken into account for the purposes of determining damages, and therefore declining to award punitive damages, which were not recognized by Paraguayan law.[129]

Following the plaintiffs' objections to the magistrate's recommendations, the District Court sided with the plaintiffs' approach and issued a total judgment of US$10,385,364.[130] However, in doing so, the Court adopted the universalist language of the Second Circuit, which the plaintiffs had also used,[131] but without any accompanying references to the political situation in Paraguay:

> In order to take the international condemnation of torture seriously this court must adopt a remedy appropriate to the ends and reflective of the nature of the condemnation .... If the courts of the United States are to adhere to the consensus of the community of humankind, any remedy they fashion must recognize that this case concerns an act so monstrous as to make its perpetrator an outlaw around the globe.[132]

Thus, in the decision, the award served to demonize the defendant rather than portray his acts as part of a larger system of repression. The torture is described as the malicious act of a lone individual without mention of its systematic nature:

> The court need not comment upon the malice that prompts one man to torture another in reprisal for the deeds of his father or to say to the dead man's sister as she left the corpse "shut up. Here you have what you have been looking for and deserved" .... Nor would any purpose be served by detailing Peña's conduct. Spread upon the records of this court is the evidence of wounds and of fractures, of burning and beating and of electric shock, of stabbing and whipping and of mutilation, and finally, perhaps mercifully, of death, in short, of the ultimate in human cruelty and brutality.[133]

Moreover, the District Court – perhaps inadvertently – suggested that the Paraguayan government and civil society played no part in the case. Indeed, when awarding punitive damages in order "to take the international condemnation of torture seriously,"[134] the Court had to address the seemingly contradictory fact that "damages designated punitive have rarely been awarded by international tribunals."[135] The Court's solution was to point out that the international law precedents regarding damage awards had "developed chiefly in the resolution of claims by one State on behalf of its nationals against the other State, and the failure to assess exemplary damages as such against a respondent government may be explained by the absence of malice or *mala mens* on the part of an impersonal government."[136] The plaintiffs themselves had pointed this out, and distinguished the present case as one in which a defendant was being formally sued.[137] Yet the plaintiffs' Memorandum pointed clearly to Paraguay's *de facto*, if not legal, responsibility, both for institutionalizing torture and for immunizing the defendant. The District Court not only failed to mention the systemic nature of the torture in the case, but also added: "Here Peña and not Paraguay is the defendant. There is no question of punishing a sovereign state or of attempting to hold the people of that state liable for a governmental act in which they played no part."[138] It was unnecessary to draw a sharp distinction between Peña, on the one hand, and the Paraguayan state and civil society, on the other. In fact, the Court went on to argue that there was precedent for the award of punitive damages even against a state.[139]

Both the Second Circuit and the District Court heavily borrowed from the plaintiff submissions. Yet they incorporated only one strand of discourse within those submissions – the universalist – and ignored the connection between the universal condemnation of torture and systemic injustice, as the plaintiffs argued. As a result, like the Nazi trials before them, the courts singled out and demonized a defendant at the expense of a richer, contextualized narrative.

C. Why did the Courts Take the Road of Individualization?

The individualization of the case cannot be traced to familiar arguments about the inherent limits of tort litigation or international human rights, or to the precedent of post-World War II trials. First, the use of political context in the plaintiff submissions makes clear that the choice of tort litigation does not necessarily individualize the case. It was precisely the fact that the victim's family was in control of the proceedings – a characteristic of tort litigation – that enabled their voices to be heard and opened the door to descriptions of the institutionalized nature of torture in Paraguay. Furthermore, the need to assess compensatory and punitive damages led to discussions of repression and economic exploitation in Paraguay, as well as of the banal causes of torture.

Neither is the framing of the case as an international human rights case to blame. The international human rights campaign around the case and media coverage thereof clearly targeted the Paraguayan state. Further, there is no indication that the demonization of perpetrators in Nazi trials influenced the courts. Nazi trials are mentioned neither by the courts nor in the US amicus brief. While Nuremberg was certainly in the background, the few references to World War II, Nazism, and Nuremberg in the other briefs were actually used to point to the state-sponsored nature of violations of international law.[140]

The structure of legal argumentation likewise cannot sufficiently account for the courts' individualization of the case. The courts demonized the torturer in ways that were not legally necessary. The Second Circuit's reference to the doctrine of *hostis humani generis* was not indispensable. The US amicus brief did not mention it, since it did not seek to establish the framers' intent with respect to international law, and relied instead on the argument that the ATS should be read to apply international law as it evolves. In fact, the Second Circuit adopted this argument, and did not mention the *hostis humani generis* doctrine until the closing paragraph, which, though often cited, is neither necessary nor central to the court's reasoning.

Why then did the courts mention this particular doctrine and as a result narrow the case to one of individual justice? I suggest that legal and political constraints on exercising universal jurisdiction led the courts to individualize the case. By describing the individual torturer as *hostis humani generis*, the court perhaps attempted to further ground its decision by implicit reference to a precedent (piracy) – as in the Eichmann case – as well as to avoid the critique that it was judging a foreign government.[141] With respect to the latter, the court would have avoided, first, a legal challenge, given that the Paraguayan state was protected from suit by sovereign immunity.[142] Such a move is similar to the way the court had refuted the institutionalized nature of torture in Paraguay in order to dismiss the applicability of the act of state doctrine. Second, by invoking the figure of the "enemy of all mankind," the court would have staved off a broader political challenge, namely criticism that the extension of jurisdiction was a form of US imperialism or, at the very least, intervention into another country's domestic affairs. The Second Circuit's decision, it should be noted, was written in the midst of the Iran hostage crisis, which according to Judge Kaufman's then law-clerk Bruce Krause, loomed large over the court as it pondered its options in the case.[143] The charge of imperialism was apparently troubling enough to Justice Kaufman that he rebutted it in an article he wrote in the *New York Times* in November 1980.[144] Analogously, by insisting that the punitive damages condemned Peña and not the Paraguayan state, the District Court denied that it was judging a foreign regime.

In a recent study of the rise of human rights to dominance in US foreign policy at the end of the 1970s, historian Barbara Keys argues that human rights offered a way for Americans to reclaim the mantle of moral virtue lost during the Vietnam War, all the while disassociating themselves from repressive allies as well as the appearance of interventionism. Because human rights were to fulfill a limited program of virtuous action, human rights abuses came to be conceptualized as a problem that "lay in individual evil perpetrated by small numbers of wrongdoers, rather than fundamental injustices in which Americans, too, were implicated."[145] The *Filártiga* case appears to have been one of the sites in which such an individualized vision of political violence could be articulated. This happened not because US courts acted as direct conduits for US foreign policy – though the US executive's supportive amicus brief was highly influential on the judges[146] – but because institutional limitations on courts' exercise of universal jurisdiction made the courts particularly sensitive to the political context, in which Americans were called on to proactively "do good" all the while avoiding interference in other nations' affairs.[147] As in criminal Nazi trials, both legal doctrine and the need for legitimacy heavily shaped the narrative, and did so here in the direction of individualization.

IV. CONCLUSION

By tracing the narrowing of *Filártiga* from structural injustice through state-sponsored violence to torturer impunity, I have tried not only to show that the field of ATS litigation was from the outset cast by the courts in terms of individual impunity, but also to remind us of the political complexity that we lose when we focus on the individual. This loss has been enduring. From the mid-1990s, the heated debates concerning ATS litigation shifted away from cases against state officials for torture and centered on claims brought against multi-national corporations for various forms of participation in mass violence in the Global South.[148] Such claims appeared to provide a welcome opportunity for discussions of economic injustice and North-South relations.

Yet despite these developments, judges and academics have continued to theorize ATS litigation and more generally universal jurisdiction through individualized conceptions of violence and the theory of *hostis humani generis*. Judges deciding ATS cases have referred continuously to the Second Circuit's individualizing and demonizing discourse in *Filártiga*.[149] Notably, Justice Breyer's concurring opinion in *Kiobel* relies heavily on the notion of "enemies of mankind." Breyer would justify jurisdiction under the ATS in terms of "an important American national interest, and that includes a distinct interest in preventing the United States from becoming a safe harbor (free of civil as well as criminal liability) for a torturer or other common enemy of mankind."[150] Furthermore, to undermine the majority's reasoning based on the presumption against extraterritoriality in statutory interpretation, Breyer again invokes the figure of the individual pirate:

The majority also writes, "Pirates were fair game wherever found, by any nation, because they generally did not operate within any jurisdiction.". . . I very much agree that pirates were fair game "wherever found." Indeed, that is the point. That is why we asked, in *Sosa*, who are today's pirates? Certainly today's pirates include torturers and perpetrators of genocide. And today, like the pirates of old, they are "fair game" where they are found. Like those pirates, they are "common enemies of all mankind and all nations have an equal interest in their apprehension and punishment.". . . And just as a nation that harbored pirates provoked the concern of other nations in past centuries,. . . so harboring "common enemies of all mankind" provokes similar concerns today.[151]

Because Breyer approaches ATS litigation through the prism of the impunity of new kinds of pirate, he elides the foreign policy concerns raised by the taking of jurisdiction. He states that the risk of international friction should be minimized by restricting jurisdiction to a narrow class of cases, protecting American interests, and "[f]urther limiting principles such as exhaustion, *forum non conveniens*, and comity,"[152] as well as "a practice of courts giving weight to the views of the Executive Branch."[153] But since for him the finding of jurisdiction by definition furthers an American interest, the American interest requirement on its own would not actually limit the number or type of cases that would be accepted in court in any way relevant to the smooth conduct of international relations. Moreover, the limiting principles he mentions have not, in pre-*Kiobel* case law, developed into clear guidelines.[154] This is not to suggest that US courts should never exercise jurisdiction over injustice taking place abroad. Rather, I refer to Breyer's opinion in *Kiobel* to show that an individualized conceptualization of political violence can lead to poor legal arguments.

Academic scholarship has also adopted an individualized understanding of the violence litigated under the ATS. Defenders of extraterritorial jurisdiction under the statute frequently remind us that the ATS is based on the common law doctrine of the "transitory tort" according to which tort obligations follow the tortfeasor across jurisdictional boundaries.[155] This has been used by George Fletcher, for instance, to argue that "[t]he community where the tort (. . .) occurred has no stake in adjudicating the case," an incredible claim.[156] I do not mean to imply that judges, lawyers, and scholars ignore that the human rights violations that have been litigated under the ATS are generally linked to political repression. However, in their discussions of the ATS, many professionals have sought to provide universal civil jurisdiction legal and political legitimacy by individualizing the case and abstracting it from its political context. The need for legitimacy and resulting individualization might be particularly strong when, as in recent years in the build-up to and aftermath of *Kiobel*, the entire field of international human rights litigation in US courts has been under attack. Regrettably, this individualized approach not only impoverishes our understanding of political violence, but also leads to unconvincing arguments about the bases of universal jurisdiction, including those advanced by Fletcher and Breyer. Only by openly and honestly acknowledging that transnational litigation against torturers does not merely concern the "impunity" of the individual torturer (a new kind of pirate), but broader structures of injustice, will we be able to theorize the field in a satisfactory manner and develop convincing justifications, if any, for the exercise of universal jurisdiction.

NOTES

1 630 F.2d 876 (2d Cir. 1980).
2 28 U.S.C. § 1350.
3 Harold Hongju Koh, "Transnational Public Law Litigation," *Yale Law Journal* 100, no. 8 (1991): 2347–2402, 2366.
4 E.g., Beth Stephens, "*Filártiga* v. *Peña-Irala*: From Family Tragedy to Human Rights Accountability," *Rutgers Law Journal* 37, no. 3 (2005–2006): 623–634. Since *Filártiga*, the ATS has been invoked in hundreds of cases. See Kurtis A. Kemper, "Construction and Application of Alien Tort Statute (28 U.S.C.A. § 1350), Tort in Violation of Law of Nations or Treaty of the United States," 64 *A.L.R. Fed. 2d* 417.
5 See e.g. *Torture as Tort: Comparative Perspectives on the Development of Transnational Tort Litigation*, ed. Craig Scott (Portland: Hart, 2001); Beth Stephens, "Translating Filártiga: A Comparative and International Law Analysis of Domestic Remedies for International Human Rights Violations," *Yale Journal of International Law* 27, no. 1 (2002): 1–57; William J. Aceves, "Liberalism and International Legal Scholarship: The Pinochet Case and the Move Toward a Universal System of Transnational Law Litigation," *Harvard International Law Journal* 41, no. 1 (2000): 129–184; George P. Fletcher, *Tort Liability for Human Rights Abuses* (Oxford: Hart, 2008), 8–15.
6 *Kiobel v. Royal Dutch Petroleum Co.*,133 S.Ct. 1659 (2013).
7 E.g. Vivian Grosswald Curran and David Sloss. "Reviving Human Rights Litigation after Kiobel."*American Journal of International Law* 107, no. 4 (2013): 858–863, 858: "The *Filártiga* line of cases supported US human rights policy by sending a clear message that the United States will hold human rights violators accountable and will not allow its territory to be a safe haven for international criminals."
8 This individualizing discourse was particularly striking in Justice Breyer's dissent in *Kiobel v. Royal Dutch Petroleum*. See my discussion in the conclusion.
9 Stephens, "Translating Filártiga," 10–15; Fletcher, *Tort Liability*, 9.
10 In this I follow Robert W. Gordon, for whom "legal forms and practices don't shift with every realignment of the balance of political forces. They tend to become embedded in "relatively autonomous" structures that transcend and, to some extent,

help to shape the content of the immediate self-interest of social groups." Robert W. Gordon, "Critical Legal Histories," *Stanford Law Review* 36 (1984): 57–125, 101.

11 For a review of these critiques, see Richard A. Wilson, *Writing History in International Criminal Trials* (Cambridge: Cambridge University Press, 2011), 1–23.

12 Ibid., 9–10.

13 Lawrence Douglas, *The Memory of Judgment: Making Law and History in the Trials of the Holocaust* (New Haven: Yale University Press, 2001), 83.

14 Ibid., 86–87.

15 Ibid., 65.

16 Ibid., 50–53.

17 For a description of critiques of the Israeli court's assertion of jurisdiction in the Eichmann case, which increased the pressure on the court to legitimate itself, see ibid., 115–117.

18 The court had to justify in particular its assertion of jurisdiction in the Eichmann case since the Genocide Convention did not provide for universal jurisdiction. United Nations General Assembly, *Convention on the Prevention and Punishment of the Crime of Genocide*, art. 2 (1021 U.N.T.S. 277, 1948). For Arendt, the court could have crafted a new conception of territory as a communal space that does not necessarily correspond to geographic territory, and claimed territorial jurisdiction on the basis thereof. In her view, it did not do so due to "the extreme reluctance of all concerned to break fresh ground and act without precedents." Hannah Arendt, *Eichmann in Jerusalem: A Report on the Banality of Evil* (New York: Penguin Books, 1992), 262.

19 Arendt, *Eichmann in Jerusalem*, 261–262. "The new crimes reverse the traditional understanding of the state as the locus of legality, and the analogy to piracy obscures the nature of the problem." Ibid., 208. Using Arendt's work to criticize law's representation of history may strike the reader as odd, given Arendt's insistence on leaving history out of the courtroom (as I discuss below). However, Arendt's writing, though inconsistent in places, contains insights that may be employed without endorsing her work wholesale. Indeed, along with her determination that extra-legal goals be excluded from the trial, Arendt insisted that the trial deliver an accurate representation of Eichmann's criminality as administrative and state-sponsored. Arendt's critique of the pirate analogy can therefore be contrasted with the doctrinal critique offered by Eugene Kontorovich. Eugene Kontorovich, "The Piracy Analogy: Modern Universal Jurisdiction's Hollow Foundation," *Harvard International Law Journal* 451, no. 1 (2004): 183–237. Nonetheless, although she emphasized the "banality of evil" which characterized Eichmann's crimes, she herself demonized him by portraying him as an enemy of humanity. Arendt, *Eichmann in Jerusalem*, 279.

20 E.g. Henry Rousso, *The Haunting Past: History, Memory, and Justice in Contemporary France* (Philadelphia: University of Pennsylvania Press, 2002).

21 "Justice demands that the accused be prosecuted, defended, and judged, and that all the other questions of seemingly greater import – of 'How could it happen?' and 'Why did it happen?,'... – be left in abeyance." Arendt, *Eichmann in Jerusalem*, 5.

22 Lawrence Douglas, "Crimes of Atrocity, the Problem of Punishment and the Situ of Law," *Propaganda, War Crimes Trials and International Law*, ed. Predrag Dojcinovic (Abingdon: Routledge, 2012), 269, 286.

23 Wilson, *Writing History*, 37.

24 See Douglas, "Crimes of Atrocity," 285–286 (discussing examples of ignorance about the former Yugoslavia among judges and prosecutors at the International Criminal Tribunal for the Former Yugoslavia).

25 For a discussion of the "demonization critique" of international criminal law, see David Luban, "A Theory of Crimes against Humanity," *Yale Journal of International Law* 29, no. 1 (2004): 85–167, 120–123.

26 Arendt, *Eichmann in Jerusalem*.

27 For elaboration see Leora Bilsky, "Hannah Arendt's Judgment of Bureaucracy," *Hannah Arendt and the Law*, eds. Marco Goldoni and Christopher McCorkindale (Oxford: Hart, 2012), 271.

28 Devin O. Pendas, *The Frankfurt Auschwitz Trial, 1963–65: Genocide, History and the Limits of the Law* (Cambridge: Cambridge University Press, 2006), 294; Michael Thad Allen, "The Banality of Evil Reconsidered: SS Mid-Level Managers of Extermination through Work," *Central European History* 30, no. 2 (1997): 253–294.

29 Leora Bilsky, *Transformative Justice: Israeli Identity on Trial* (Ann Arbor: University of Michigan Press, 2004), 123, referring to "'Eichmann in Jerusalem': An Exchange of Letters between Gershom Scholem and Hannah Arendt," *Encounter*, January 1964, 51, 56, in which Arendt wrote: "It is my opinion that evil is never 'radical,' that it is only extreme, and that it possesses neither depth nor any demonic dimension. It can overgrow and lay waste the entire world precisely because it spreads like a fungus on the surface."

30 Ron Dudai, "Understanding Perpetrators in Genocides and Mass Atrocities," *British Journal of Sociology* 57, no. 4 (2006): 699–707.

31 The first memoir was written by Analy Filártiga, one of the sisters of young Joelito Filártiga, with a friend of the family, Anibal Miranda. Anibal Miranda and Analy Filártiga, *El Caso Filártiga* (Asunción: Miranda & Asociados, 1992). The second was written by Richard White, an American historian of Paraguay and close friend of the Filártigas. Richard Alan White, *Breaking Silence: The Case That Changed the Face of Human Rights* (Washington, DC: Georgetown University Press, 2004). White lived with the family in the first months following Joelito's death and was a key actor in the family's international campaign.

32 Miranda and Filártiga, *El Caso Filártiga*, 25.

33 Ibid., 26.

34 White, *Breaking Silence*, 6.

35 Miranda and Filártiga, *El Caso Filártiga*, 26.

36 Peter Lambert, "The Regime of Alfredo Stroessner," *The Transition to Democracy in Paraguay*, eds. Peter Lambert and Andrew Nickson (London: Macmillan, 1997), 3.

37 For Marcial Antonio Riquelme, the most accurate term would be "neo-sultanism", "the prefix "neo' serv[ing] to emphasize that this was not a regime headed by a "traditional caudillo" running on the legacy of the Spanish authoritarian political culture but rather a well-articulated regime based on a partisanized army, a party of patronage which fed the loyal bureaucracy, and a modern repressive apparatus systematically used to crush dissent." Marcial Antonio Riquelme, "Toward a Weberian Characterization of the Stroessner Regime in Paraguay (1954–1989)," *European Review of Latin American and Caribbean Studies* 57 (1994): 29–51, 44.

38 Ibid., 42.

39 Ibid., 43.

40 Ibid.

41 Frank O. Mora and Jerry W. Cooney, *Paraguay and the United States: Distant Allies* (Athens: University of Georgia Press, 2007), 161. Foreign aid allowed the regime to construct an overblown public sector, cementing loyalty to the regime and the party (as state employees had to be party members). Lambert, "The Regime of Alfredo 'Stroessner," 10. US economic aid and aid from international institutions provided with the support of the USA allowed the government to expend huge sums in infrastructure and therefore made the regime popular. Mora and Cooney, *Paraguay and the United States*, 168.

42 Mora and Cooney, *Paraguay and the United States*, 163–169. To this was added military aid on site in Paraguay, through sales of military equipment with instruction sessions, and counseling from US military advisors. Fatima Myriam Yore, *La Dominación Stronista: Orígenes y Consolidación, Seguridad Nacional y Represión* (Asunción: BASE, 1992), 171; Mora and Cooney, *Paraguay and the United States*, 175.

43 Fearing that too much pressure to democratize might destabilize the regime, the US administrations of the 1960s pushed only for modest reforms. Under US pressure, Stroessner legalized three opposition parties in the 1960s. Mora and Cooney, *Paraguay and the United States*, 170–171. Far from liberalizing the state, such formal democracy legitimated the regime internally and vis-à-vis the international community. Renée Fregosi, *Le Paraguay au XXe siècle* (Paris: L'Harmattan, 1997), 108.

44 Law 294, titled "In Defense of Democracy" and enacted in 1955, prohibited communism, while Law 209, titled "In Defense of Public Peace and Individual Freedom" and enacted in 1970 criminalized "attacks" on public institutions. Fregosi, *Le Paraguay*, 51.

45 When none of this provided sufficient legal cover for the regime's acts, the constantly-renewed state of siege, in force until 1987, was invoked to justify numerous detentions. Yore, *La Dominación Stronista*, 181–182. Fregosi, *Le Paraguay*, 70.

46 Fregosi, *Le Paraguay*, 57–58.

47 Miranda and Filártiga, *El Caso Filártiga*, 43.

48 According to White, a few weeks after Joelito's murder the couple provided health care to one of the organization's pregnant leaders, living in hiding with her comrades. White, *Breaking Silence*, 70.

49 Ibid., 27.

50 Miranda and Filártiga, *El Caso Filártiga*, 53–54. Due to the compartmentalized structure of the OPM, a former OPM member, Carlos Fontclara, was unable to confirm Joelito's membership or lack of membership in the organization. Interview, *Asunción*, May 3, 2013.

51 White, *Breaking Silence*, 28–30.

52 Miranda and Filártiga, *El Caso Filártiga*, 76.

53 Ibid., 54.

54 Group interview with Joel, Nidia, and Analy Filártiga, *Asuncion*, April 24, 2013.

55 White, *Breaking Silence*, 51.

56 Ibid.

57 Motion cited in White, *Breaking Silence*, 58.

58 Joel Filártiga's wife Nidia and daughter Dolly were arrested on fabricated charges. Ibid., 54. The family also received numerous death threats. Their lawyer was arrested the day after submitting a motion, and later disbarred, sending the message that the case was untouchable. Ibid., 99, 125, 143–44, 243.
59 Ibid., 95.
60 Ibid., 262.
61 Ibid., 187.
62 Ibid., 210.
63 Ibid., 213.
64 Ibid., 214.
65 White, *Breaking Silence*, 221–223.
66 *Filártiga v. Peña-Irala*, No. 79 C 917, Slip. Op (E.D.N.Y. May 15, 1979) (reprinted in Aceves, *The Anatomy of Torture*, 349–51) [hereinafter District Court Dismissal].
67 *ITT v. Vencap*, Ltd., 519 F.2d 1001, 1015 (2d Cir. 1975).
68 Aceves, *The Anatomy of Torture*, 38–39.
69 Appellants' Brief, *Filártiga v. Peña-Irala*, 630. F.2d 876 (2d Cir. 1980) (No. 79 C 917) [hereinafter Appellants' Brief], 28.
70 Ibid., 30–33.
71 Ibid., 35–45.
72 Brief for Amnesty International-USA, the International League for Human Rights, and the Lawyers' Committee for International Human Rights, as Amici Curiae, *Filártiga v. Peña-Irala*, 630. F.2d 876 (2d Cir. 1980) (No. 79 C 917) [hereinafter Amnesty Brief]; and Brief of Amici Curiae the International Human Rights Law Group, the Council on Hemispheric Affairs, and the Washington Office on Latin America, *Filártiga v. Peña-Irala*, 630. F.2d 876 (2d Cir. 1980) (No. 79 C 917) [hereinafter International Human Rights Law Group Brief].
73 White, *Breaking Silence*, 245.
74 Ibid., 257–258.
75 Interview, Tel Aviv, November 1, 2013.
76 Memorandum for the United States as Amicus Curiae, *Filártiga v. Peña-Irala*, 630. F.2d 876 (2d Cir. 1980) [hereinafter US Amicus Brief], 4.
77 *Filártiga*, 630.F.2d at 884.
78 US Amicus Brief, 22.
79 *Filártiga*, 630.F.2d at 881.
80 The US Supreme Court later restricted the applicability of the ATS in *Sosa v. Álvarez-Machaín*, 542 U.S. 692 (2004), where federal courts were instructed to "not recognize private claims under federal common law for violations of any international law norm with less definite content and acceptance among civilized nations than the historical paradigms familiar with which §1350 was enacted." Ibid., 2765.
81 Defendant-Appellee's Brief In Support of Judgment of Dismissal, *Filártiga v. Peña-Irala*, 630 F. 2d 876 (2d Cir. 1980), 34.
82 *Filártiga*, 630.F.2d at 889–890. As to dismissal on grounds of *forum non conveniens*, the court refused to consider it, since it had not been addressed by the lower court. Ibid. 880 fn. 6 and 890.
83 *Filártiga v. Peña-Irala*, 577 F. Supp. 860, 867 (E.D.N.Y. 1984).
84 Aceves, *The Anatomy of Torture*, 76.

85 Amnesty International, *Deaths under Torture and Disappearances of Political Prisoners in Paraguay* (1977). This report led to an avalanche of letters of support to the family from people around the world. White, *Breaking Silence*, 120.

86 Ibid., 163.

87 Ibid., 139.

88 The report refers to "[h]omicides imputed to the authorities". Inter-American Commission on Human Rights, *Report on the Situation of Human Rights in Paraguay*, chapter 2 (OEA/Ser.L/V/II.43doc. 13 corr. 1 1978).

89 White, *Breaking Silence*, 180.

90 In one internal memorandum from 1979, Gorostiaga is reported to have told the police that "the Filartigas' lawyers as well as the international organizations [who filed amici] are promoting a real political trial to the government of Paraguay … If the case is not defended, the judgment will be given in default and if that is the case the Government of Paraguay could be civilly liable for damages." Internal police memorandum signed Eusebio Torres Romero dated August 22, 1979 addressed to Pastor Coronel, the head of the department of "Investigaciones" (my translation).

91 Internal police memorandum signed Alberto Cantero D. dated September 20, 1983 addressed to Pastor Coronel (my translation). Signed by Alberto Cantero D. "Internal Police Memo to Pastor Coronel," September 20, 1983 (author's own translation).

92 White, *Breaking Silence*, 254.

93 The doctrine was first mentioned by the plaintiffs in their May 23, 1979 Application to the Supreme Court for a stay of deportation (reprinted in Aceves, *The Anatomy of Torture*, 379–391). Interestingly, in this application, piracy is mentioned in reference to an interview given by Ambassador White in the Paraguayan press. To counter the notion that the case would do terrible damage to Paraguayan-US relations, "Ambassador White likened the right to sue a torturer to the right, which was originally protected by § 1350, of an alien to sue for piracy irrespective of where the tort occurred or of the nationality of the perpetrator, so long as he is found in this country" (reprinted at 387).

94 Notice of Motion and Motion for Interim Relief Pending Appeal, *Filártiga* v. *Peña-Irala*, 630 F.2d 876 (2d Cir. 1980) (reprinted in Aceves, *The Anatomy of Torture*, 355–366) [hereinafter Notice of Motion], 357 (emphasis added).

95 Appellants' Brief, 6.

96 Defendant Peña-Irala's Memorandum of Law in Support of Motion to Dismiss Complaint and Vacate Stay, *Filártiga* v. *Peña-Irala*, 630. F.2d 876 (2d Cir. 1980) (reprinted in Aceves, *The Anatomy of Torture*, 296 315) [hereinafter Defendant Memorandum] 298.

97 Verified Complaint, *Filártiga* v. *Pena Irala*, 630 F.2d 876 (2d cir. 1980) (reprinted in Aceves, *The Anatomy of Torture*, 215–230).

98 Similarly, in remarks about the process of drafting this brief, Roberts Owen, Legal Adviser of US Department of State, also discussed the case as one "where a foreign government had abused one of its own citizens within its own borders." Address by the Honorable Roberts B. Owen, The Legal Adviser, US Department of State, at the Annual Dinner of the American Branch of the International Law Association, The Princeton Club, New York City (Nov. 14, 1980), reprinted in *Proceedings and*

Committee Reports of the American Branch of the International Law Association, ed. Theodore Giutarri (New York: International Law Association, 1982), 11, 16, reprinted in Aceves, *The Anatomy of Torture,* 46–47.

99 Brief Amicus Curiae in Support of Plaintiff's Motion to Restrain Defendant Immigration and Naturalization Service from Enforcing Defendant Peña-Irala's Departure from the United States, *Filártiga* v. *Peña-Irala,* 630 F.2d 876 (2d Cir. 1980) (reprinted in Aceves, *The Anatomy of Torture,* 267–270) [hereinafter International Human Rights Law Group Brief]. According to Aceves, this brief was submitted by several groups, including the Council on Hemispheric Affairs, the Letelier-Moffitt Human Rights, the Fund of the Institute for Policy Studies, the Clergy and Laity Concerned, and the International Human Rights Law Group. Aceves, *The Anatomy of Torture,* 33.

100 "Torture is a violation of international legal norms, while simple assault is not. The former entails international responsibility precisely because of some measure of State involvement." International Human Rights Law Group Brief, 27.

101 Ibid., 37 (arguing to counter defendant's argument that judicial determination on the merits would be a political show trial: "The Government of Paraguay is not the defendant. This action is a lawsuit alleging that Defendant killed a person brutally and maliciously. It does happen that at the time of the alleged tort, Defendant occupied an official position in Paraguay. But it cannot be inferred from this that any trial of the merits of the case would be so permeated by political concerns as to be unmanageable.").

102 Appellants' Brief, 52.

103 Ibid., 42.

104 Plaintiffs' Memorandum of Law in Opposition to Defendant Peña-Irala's Motion to Dismiss Complaint and Vacate Stay, *Filártiga* v. *Peña-Irala,* 630 F.2d 876 (2d Cir. 1980) (reprinted in Aceves, *The Anatomy of Torture,* 323–42) [hereinafter Plaintiffs' Memorandum], 332.

105 Plaintiffs' Memorandum of Points and Authorities in Support of Order to Show Cause for Stay of Deportation and for Order Permitting Depositions of the Prisoners, *Filártiga* v. *Peña-Irala,* 630 F.2d 876 (2d Cir. 1980) (reprinted in Aceves, *The Anatomy of Torture,* 241–247, 244).

106 Ibid., paras. 13–15.

107 Notice of Motion, 359.

108 The Appellants' Brief stated at 48 that "[h]uman rights which had long played an important role in US foreign policy, were elevated to a preeminent role in President Carter's inaugural address."

109 Aceves, *The Anatomy of Torture,* 52.

110 "The defendant is former Inspector General of Police of Asuncion, Paraguay .... Allegedly the decedent was tortured and murdered in retaliation for the political activities and opinions of his father who is a leading political opponent of General Stroessner, the dictator-president of Paraguay." District Court Dismissal at 349.

111 *Filártiga,* 630.F.2d at 878. This echoes the statements found in the plaintiffs' claim. Verified Complaint, paras. 14–15.

112 *Filártiga,* 630.F.2d, 878.

113 Ibid.

114 Ibid., 890.

115 Indeed, the court immediately clarified that "Paraguay's renunciation of torture as a legitimate instrument of state policy, however, does not strip the tort of its character as an international law violation, if it in fact occurred under color of government authority." Ibid., 890.

116 Ibid, 890

117 Transcript of Hearing on Damages Before the US District Court for the Eastern District of New York, *Filártiga* v. *Peña-Irala*, 630 F.2d 876 (2d Cir. 1980) (reprinted in Aceves, *The Anatomy of Torture*, 613–650) [hereinafter Damage Hearing Transcript], 637.

118 Ibid., 627.

119 Ibid., 628.

120 Ibid., 635.

121 Ibid., 643.

122 Plaintiffs' Post-Trial Memorandum of Facts and Law, *Filártiga* v. *Peña-Irala*, 577 F. Supp. 860 (E.D.N.Y 1984) (reprinted in Aceves, *The Anatomy of Torture*, 655–723) [hereinafter Damage Memorandum], 694.

123 Ibid., 669–674.

124 Ibid., 669.

125 Ibid., 674.

126 Ibid., 675.

127 White, *Breaking Silence*, 267.

128 E.g., Damage Hearing Transcript, 637.

129 US District Court for the Eastern District of New York: Magistrate's Report and Recommendation, *Filártiga* v. *Peña-Irala*, 630 F.2d 876 (2d Cir. 1980) (reprinted in William J. Aceves, *The Anatomy of Torture: A Documentary History of Filartiga* v. *Peña-Irala* (New York: BRILL, 2007), 727–738).

130 *Filártiga*, 577 F. Supp. at 867.

131 For instance, the plaintiffs had cited the closing paragraph of the Second Circuit's decision, Damage Memorandum, 701.

132 *Filártiga*, 577 F. Supp. at 863.

133 Ibid., 866.

134 Ibid., 863.

135 Ibid., 865

136 Ibid.

137 Damages Memorandum, 694–696.

138 *Filártiga*, 577 F. Supp. at 865.

139 Ibid.

140 For example, the Appellants' Brief, 41–42, defines crimes against humanity according to the Nuremberg Charter in order to argue against the view that international law does not address one state's treatment of its citizens.

141 I therefore agree with Kontorovich that "[s]upporters of [modern universal jurisdiction] use the piracy analogy to put themselves on the side of tradition and to suggest that [modern universal jurisdiction] is nothing new, and thus nothing to worry about." Kontorovich, "The Piracy Analogy," 208 (references omitted). Though Kontorovich exaggerates the extent to which universal jurisdiction in ATS case-law relies on the piracy analogy, for as we saw it did not appear in the Second Circuit's decision until the closing paragraph, he is right about its rhetorical use as legitimating device.

142 Under the Foreign Sovereign Immunities Act of 1976 (FSIA), foreign governments are immune from suit in the USA except for categories of claims that reflect liability arising out of private law transactions. 28 U.S.C §§ 1330, 1602–1611. Thus, at the time of the lawsuit, Paraguay was immune from lawsuit, unless it could be proven that the torture fell into one of the FSIA's exceptions. Though the plain language of the FSIA indicates that it is not applicable to individual defendants (immunity it to be granted only to a foreign state, its political subdivisions, or "an agency or instrumentality of a foreign state." 28 U.S.C. § 1603(b)), Peña could have conceivably argued that the action was in effect against Paraguay, triggering sovereign immunity.

143 Bruce R. Krause, "Filártiga Memoir," written to Harold Hongju Koh and cited in Harold Hongju Koh, "*Filártiga* v. *Pena-Irala*: Judicial Internalization into Domestic Law of the Customary International Law Norm against Torture," *International Law Stories*, eds. John E Noyes, Laura Anne Dickinson, Mark W. Janis and David J. Bederman (New York: Foundation Press/Thomson/West, 2007), 45–76.

144 Irving R. Kaufman, "A Legal Remedy for International Torture?," *New York Times*, November 9, 1980, 44 ("The courts will not be transformed into some kind of roaming human-rights commission; the broad response to the phenomenon of torture, of course, is best left to the policy makers in the other branches of government. Nor is the United States, by empowering our courts to hear international claims of torture, engaging in messianic moral imperialism.")

145 Barbara Keys, *Reclaiming American Virtue: The Human Rights Revolution of the 1970s* (Cambridge: Harvard University Press, 2014), 8.

146 Krause writes that the State Department in its brief "came down firmly on the side of the plaintiffs, and this view was, in the end, given dispositive weight by the panel." Cited in Koh, *Filártiga* v. *Pena-Irala*, 52.

147 On courts' practice of taking political conditions into account in order to retain legitimacy, see Amnon Reichman, "The Dimensions of Law: Judicial Craft, Its Public Perception, and the Role of the Scholar," *California Law Review* 96 (2007): 1619–1675, 1643–1648.

148 Beth Stephens, "The Curious History of the Alien Tort Statute," *Notre Dame Law Review* 89, no. 4 (2014): 1467–1543, 1468.

149 See, e.g., *Xuncax* v. *Gramajo*, 886 F. Supp. 162, 185 (D. Mass. 1995) ("As the Second Circuit declared in 1980, 'the torturer has become – like the pirate and slave trader before him – *hostis humani generis*, an enemy of all mankind'"); *Sosa* v. *Álvarez-Machaín*, 542 U.S. 692, 732 (2004) (quoting the Second Circuit's dicta that "[F]or purposes of civil liability, the torturer has become – like the pirate and slave trader before him – *hostis humani generis*, an enemy of all mankind"); *Paul* v. *Avril*, 901 F. Supp. 330, 336 (S.D. Fla. 1994) ("The Court finds that punitive damages are appropriate in this case as the acts committed by the defendant were malicious, wanton, and oppressive. An award of punitive damages must reflect the egregiousness of the defendant's conduct, the central role he played in the abuses, and the international condemnation with which these abuses are viewed. *Filártiga*, 577 F. Supp., 866.").

150 *Kiobel*, 133 S.Ct. 1671. Breyer goes on to reference the Supreme Court decision in *Sosa*, which cited the closing paragraph in *Filártiga*.

151 Ibid., 1672–1673.

152 Ibid., 1674.

153 Ibid.

154 Stephens, "The Curious History of the Alien Tort Statute," 1524–1530.

155 See, e.g., Jeffrey M. Blum and Ralph G. Steinhardt, "Federal Jurisdiction over Inernational Human Rights Claims: The Alien Tort Claims Act after *Filartiga* v. *Peña-Irala*," *Harvard International Law Journal* 22, no. 1 (1981): 53–113, 63.

156 Fletcher, *Tort Liability*, 12.

PART III

ARE THERE ALTERNATIVES TO ANTI-IMPUNITY?

9

Impunity in a Different Register: People's Tribunals and Questions of Judgment, Law, and Responsibility

Dianne Otto[*]

In October 2012 I found myself in a large meeting room in the Phnom Penh Ecumenical Center, where the former high school that served as Pol Pot's notorious Tuol Sleng torture center (S21) was visible from the windows, an ever-present reminder that the quotidian can so easily turn into horror. I was one of four panel members at the Asia-Pacific Regional Women's Hearing on gender-based violence in conflict (Phnom Penh Hearing).[1] The event was organized by the Cambodian Defenders Project, a civil society organization that provides free legal advice and representation to poor and vulnerable people.[2] Together with an audience of over 250 people, which included many victims of Khmer Rouge brutality,[3] I was riveted by the testimonies of survivors of sexual violence that took place during four armed conflicts in the Asia-Pacific region – Bangladesh (1971), Cambodia (1976–79), Timor-Leste (1974–99), and Nepal (1996–2006).[4] As I listened, I agonized, not only about the failures of existing law to punish the perpetrators and provide some form of recognition and justice to the victims, but also about our collective responsibility to "listen with your hearts," as the facilitator had implored us at the start of the hearing, and to find ways to act on these stories and contribute to the realization of justice in the present. What the Phnom Penh Hearing highlighted for me was the potential of such "people's tribunals" to do much more than challenge

[*] Thanks to all those who contributed to the organization of the Asia-Pacific Regional Women's Hearing in Phnom Penh in 2012 and to everyone who participated, especially the women who shared their experiences of strength and survival in the face of great adversity. Thanks also to participants in the Rapoport Center's 2013 Annual Conference, "Impunity, Justice and the Human Rights Agenda," February 7–8, University of Texas at Austin, and to the other contributors to this volume for their helpful feedback and support at the Workshop on Impunity and the Human Rights Agenda, co-organized by Institute for Global Law and Policy and the Rapoport Center, June 3–7, 2013, Harvard Law School. Finally, thanks to my research assistant, Candice Parr, for her superb research support, including her uncanny ability to understand exactly what it is I want her to do.

the inadequacies of the existing law and its institutions by invoking a collective responsibility to see that justice is also done "beyond the law."[5] In this chapter, I reflect on both the challenges presented by people's tribunals to state-authorized practices of legal justice and their summoning of a broader extra-legal responsibility that enjoins us all. I consider how these expressions of popular justice relate to the shift to anti-impunity in human rights discourse and activism, which focuses on individual criminal responsibility, and is the subject of this book.

The Phnom Penh Hearing was located in a rich tradition of people's tribunals. The 1967 International War Crimes Tribunal (Russell Tribunal), convened by philosophers Bertrand Russell and Jean-Paul Sartre in order to establish "beyond doubt" the criminal nature of United States (US) actions in the war in Vietnam,[6] is often cited as the original inspiration for this form of protest, although others recognize earlier precursors.[7] Organized by concerned individuals, non-governmental organizations (NGOs) and/or social movement activists, people's tribunals typically provide a platform for the personal testimonies of victims/survivors, whose experiences of injustice are not recognized as such by formal systems of law. They may also include the expert testimonies of historians, scientists, and lawyers. People's tribunals aim generally to inform public opinion and help build political momentum to pressure states, and often also international institutions, to address the injustices to which they draw attention. Many also have distinctly legal aspirations, which may include law enforcement or reform. While some organizers and commentators refer to them as citizen's (or citizens') tribunals to emphasize their democratic dimensions,[8] I prefer the term "people's tribunals" because it appeals to popular solidarities and notions of justice that extend beyond the limits of state citizenship and authority. I also use the term "peoples' tribunals" where this nomenclature is specifically adopted by tribunal organizers, usually because they wish to indicate that their concern is with collective rights, such as those of colonized and indigenous peoples or minorities,[9] rather than individual justice.

While the laws relating to the use of force (*jus ad bellum*) and the conduct of armed conflict (*jus in bello*) have provided a focus for many people's tribunals, such as the Russell Tribunal and the Phnom Penh Hearing,[10] a vertiginous array of other issues have also been tackled. These include environmental disasters,[11] communal violence,[12] women's everyday experiences of violence and poverty,[13] the mistreatment of refugees and asylum seekers,[14] the rights of indigenous peoples,[15] international economic policies,[16] human rights violations committed by multinational corporations,[17] discrimination against gay men and lesbians,[18] and abuses perpetrated in the name of psychiatry.[19] The reliance on the testimonies of victims and experts is designed to expose what Russell described as "the crime of silence"[20] and rally public opinion to insist on those responsible being held accountable. The accountability envisaged can range from demanding that formal legal proceedings take place, to seeking to (re)imagine state-based law and justice by performing its languages and symbols subversively, hoping to foster a more inclusive people's form of lawfulness.[21] Accountability in this transformative frame is achieved through social and political struggle and through reshaping judgment, law, and responsibility so that the people are served rather than, as perceived, the powerful few.

My discussion journeys through the legal aspirations of people's tribunals in order to examine the extent to which they might be considered a part of the recent enthusiasm for pursuing individual criminal responsibility as a means to end impunity for human rights violations. In examining their legal aspirations, I do not wish to join the debate about the "legitimacy" of people's tribunals.[22] To my mind, they are patently political projects, trying to sway public opinion by filling some of the information gaps and silences in public discourse that serve to deflect disagreement and vilify dissent. Therefore "legitimacy" in the sense of being neutral and objective, and giving an equal hearing to all sides, is not the point. However, the choice of a tribunal format does signify an intention to reflect critically on existing legal rules and practices in order to foster change. I identify three categories of legal aspiration: those tribunals that call on the people to make a critical judgment about the failure of international (sometimes domestic) institutions to enforce the existing law; those that seek to promote new (people's) law that emerges from experiences of marginalization and oppression; and those that seek transformation of the entire system of law, promoting the shared responsibility of the people to struggle against injustice. Clearly, there is no fixed or unified idea of "the people" in these projects, and their appeals to the people are made on a number of different registers. I argue that while people's tribunals have always been critical of impunity for widespread human rights violations (although they may not use this terminology), they offer some salutary reasons for caution about placing too much emphasis on individual criminal responsibility by showing that law, its institutions and practices, may also be part of the problem and that accountability for injustice must be understood in a much broader frame. I conclude by returning to my experience in Phnom Penh and offer some reflections on the more capacious notions of responsibility for justice that people's tribunals promote – responsibility that resides not only with states and their institutions, but also with the people.[23] I make the case that people's tribunals demand a politics of listening that looks to realizing justice both in and beyond the law, based on our common experiences of loss and vulnerability.[24] This transformative vision of justice, which does not rely on state authorization to give it validity – in fact it derives its power and influence from operating without state endorsement – presents a compelling challenge to the tendency toward looking to criminal prosecutions as the main theatre for anti-impunity activism.

I. THE LEGAL ASPIRATIONS OF PEOPLE'S TRIBUNALS

People's tribunals are just one form of civil society activism aimed at highlighting state failures to address injustice. As a form of protest they have proved to be enduring, even when it comes to addressing war crimes, despite the proliferation of state-based transitional justice mechanisms over the last three decades and unprecedented developments in international criminal law, including the establishment of the International Criminal Court (ICC). In 2000, for example, dozens of women's and civil society organizations in the former Yugoslavia launched an effort to organize a Women's Court, with the aim of creating new concepts of justice.[25] The organizers had lost faith in the formal justice institutions, both international and domestic, because of their perceived manipulation by political elites. By utilizing the form of a people's tribunal, they hoped to create a "feminist" justice in response to numerous forms of ethnic, military, gender, economic, political, and personal violence committed during, and as a consequence of, the wars of the 1990s.[26] The "Women's Court – Feminist Approach to Justice" was eventually held in Sarajevo in 2015, where over thirty testimonies of women who had survived the conflict were presented to an attentive audience of several hundred.[27] Nearly all of the testifiers spoke of the empowering and life-sustaining effects of their activist work seeking justice in "solidarity" with other women in the face of the failure of state-based mechanisms of justice.

While disillusionment with formal institutions provides one explanation for the durability of this form of protest, there are at least two others. One of them is that the performance of the juridical power of states presents a particularly potent means to criticize state-sponsored legality. This is evident in President de Gaulle's letter to Jean-Paul Sartre denying his request for the Russell Tribunal to convene in France, despite French opposition to the war in Vietnam. In de Gaulle's view, "justice of any sort, in principle as in execution, emanates from the State" and, therefore, "through its very form, the Tribunal would be acting against the very thing which it is seeking to uphold."[28] While de Gaulle misunderstands the aspirations of people's tribunals which, as Sartre rejoined, set out to inform public opinion rather than replace the existing legal machineries of states,[29] his response is telling in its hyper-sensitivity to the idea that justice may be constituted outside the state. The other reason that people's tribunals have endured is because the language of law has considerable power to legitimate some experiences of reality and dismiss others.[30] Tribunal organizers seek to harness this power to give credibility to dissenting perspectives and recognize subjects whose experience has been rendered unspeakable by law and politics. In this sense, people's tribunals are a symbolic reclaiming of law by those who have been marginalized by mainstream law and politics – euphemistically "the people" – putting the state on notice that it has failed to live up to their expectations of justice.

While not seeking to replace formal law and legal institutions, people's tribunals usually have distinctly legal objectives, setting out to challenge the practices of formal legal institutions and/or promote new developments in the law. By staging a people's performance of law, its languages, and processes, which brings to the fore the perspectives of victims rather than perpetrators, people's tribunals create the platform for a widely accessible critique of state-based law and practices. Judges may be activists or victims or both; testifiers are encouraged to shape and control their own stories; victims are experts; juries are authorized to make decisions of conscience; and members of the audience are implored to take responsibility for what they are hearing. People's tribunals provide an opportunity to critically assess the operation of formal justice mechanisms in light of the testimonies of victims who have no remedy for the injustices they have suffered, which is a compelling way to reveal the failures of law to fulfill its promises of universal application. They expose the precariousness of law's claims to objectivity and truth, and draw attention to the question of judgment and whose interests are served by mainstream legal processes. By their alternative "doing of law," people's tribunals reveal an allegiance between the law and the interests of (powerful) states, and the consequential betrayal of the interests of the people.[31]

In order to explore the challenges that people's tribunals present directly to law, and what this tells us about their relationship to the prioritization of individual criminal justice that this volume of essays examines, I will look at three legal aspirations that are common to people's tribunals: to highlight violations of existing law and the absence or failure of enforcement mechanisms (where the people are the judges); to identify and promote new law (where the people are the sources of law); and to encourage transformative challenges to the existing imaginaries of law (where the people share responsibility for addressing injustice). Many, perhaps most, people's tribunals have elements of all three of these aspirations, juggling critique with hope. Despite their diversity, they all portray legal institutions as a site of struggle over truth and accountability, rather than a place of technical deliberation and neutral judgment. While the goal, broadly stated, is to end the impunity enjoyed by a wide range of actors, in relation to a wide range of offenses, it is my argument that people's tribunals also challenge us to think of responsibility through a much broader lens than that offered by the law in general, and individual criminal responsibility in particular.

A. *People's Judgment Tribunals: Highlighting Violations of Existing Law and the Failures of Enforcement*

In many respects, the Russell Tribunal exemplifies those people's tribunals organized to highlight the failure of existing institutions to apply the law universally and impartially, by bringing the "real" facts to public attention and calling on the people to make a judgment on the basis of those facts. It was organized by private individuals, under the auspices of the Bertrand Russell Peace Foundation,[32] to draw public attention to compelling evidence of illegal use of force and prohibited methods of war in Vietnam by the US and its allies. The aims, agreed at the inaugural session held in London in 1966, were to "arouse the conscience of the world" by making "the truth" about the Vietnam War available to "humanity" so that serious and objective judgment could be made about where responsibility lay for the sufferings of the Vietnamese people.[33] They hoped to build a mass movement that would oppose the war[34] and push for the establishment of a permanent international war crimes tribunal that would substitute "ethical and juridical rules for the law of the jungle."[35] (Perhaps they had something like the ICC in mind, although I suspect they were imagining a court which had the power to indict states as well as individuals.) The Russell Tribunal was a people's tribunal in the sense that it was organized independently of states and appealed to ordinary people to make a judgment on the basis of careful documentation, expert opinion, and personal testimony and, on the basis of that judgment, to take action to see that justice is done. As Russell put it in his Opening Statement to the first session, "We investigate in order to expose. We document in order to indict. We arouse consciousness in order to create mass resistance."[36]

Three substantive sessions of the Russell Tribunal were held in 1967, the larger two in Sweden and Denmark,[37] and a smaller hearing in Japan.[38] The evidence presented was the result of several years of extensive research by teams of volunteer investigators, support committees, and commissions of inquiry,[39] as well as publicly available material painstakingly compiled from media reports and government statements. People from many walks of life were involved: journalists, lawyers, medical experts, authors, playwrights, trade unionists, philosophers, scientists, historians, and, significantly, former American military personnel and Vietnamese victims of US/South Vietnamese atrocities. A vast amount of evidence was presented during the tribunal sessions, debunking US justifications for its involvement in the war (collective self-defense) and attesting to frequent fragmentation bombing raids, widespread use of chemical weapons, poisonous gases, herbicides, and defoliants, destruction of a staggering number of hospitals, schools, irrigation systems, crops, churches, and pagodas, millions of civilians herded into detainment and forced labor camps, and daily torture and mistreatment of prisoners.[40] The evidence also included official US documents and statements, as the US government declined several invitations to send representatives to present its case in person.[41]

Twenty-five prominent intellectuals and activists served as Tribunal Members, whose role was to consider the evidence. In addition to Russell, Sartre, and Vladimir Dedijer (Yugoslavian dissident and international law expert, who served as Chairman and President of Sessions), they included Simone de Beauvoir (French philosopher), James Baldwin (African-American author), Lelio Basso (Italian international lawyer and politician), Mehmet Ali Aybar (Turkish international lawyer and politician), Amado Hernandez (Poet Laureate of the Philippines), Kinju Morikawa (Japan Civil Liberties Union) and Mahmud Ali Kasuri (Senior Advocate, Supreme Court of Pakistan).[42] Their role has been described as akin to that of a Grand Jury, empowered to consider whether the evidence establishes a *prima facie* case with respect to the list of charges read out at the start of each session.[43] The charges related to the crime of aggression (*jus ad bellum*), and a number of crimes relating to the conduct of war (*jus in bello*) including the use of illegal weapons, civilian bombardment, the torture and mutilation of prisoners of war, inhuman treatment of the civilian population, and genocide.[44] Although Samuel Moyn has argued that the Russell Tribunal exemplified the emphasis of the anti-war movement at that time on ending war, which he contrasts with the focus of the contemporary anti-war movement on humanizing the conduct of war,[45] this argument is not borne out by the wide range of charges that were considered. While it is true that the Russell Tribunal found state rather than individual responsibility, concluding that the US had committed the crimes charged and that Australia, New Zealand, South Korea, Japan, Thailand, and the Philippines were accomplices to the crime of aggression,[46] my assessment is that this was driven by the nature of people's tribunals, which are not in a position to assess individual guilt. The *raison d'être* of the Russell Tribunal was to raise awareness, and foster political debate and anti-war activism.

What is striking about the verdict is its meticulous reference to international legal instruments, including the 1907 *Hague Conventions*, the

1928 *Kellogg-Briand Pact*, the *Charter of the United Nations*, the *Statutes of Nuremberg*, the 1948 *Universal Declaration of Human Rights*, the 1949 *Geneva Conventions*, and the 1960 *General Assembly Declaration on Granting Independence to Colonial Countries and Peoples.*[47] It is clear that the Tribunal Members were committed to drawing their conclusions, as best they could, on the basis of international law – indeed the goal was to arouse the conscience of the world by highlighting the *illegality* of the actions of the US and its allies in Vietnam. In taking this approach, the Russell Tribunal was endorsing the law and confining its critique to the failure of states and international institutions to apply it. Yet, despite its faithfulness to existing legal standards and persuasive assemblage of well-researched and amply corroborated evidence, the Russell Tribunal was accused of partisanship[48] and largely dismissed as a kangaroo court by the media and government officials,[49] especially in the US. At the time, Anthony D'Amato argued the unfairness of this response, making the point that "judicial notice" was taken of a large amount of evidence by the Nuremberg and Tokyo war crimes tribunals, which found the massiveness and detail of the evidence of war crimes to be persuasive.[50] The scornful reactions to the Russell Tribunal also militated against the emergence of a mass people's movement opposed to the Vietnam War that organizers hoped to inspire, which took several more years to crystallize. And, as we now know, the establishment of the permanent ICC was to take several more decades.

What the Russell Tribunal did inspire was the proliferation of other people's tribunals. Many of them have also called for the people to make a judgment, according to existing law, on the basis of personal testimonies and expert analyses, where formal political and legal institutions have failed to do so. Two more recent examples are the Women's International War Crimes Tribunal for the Trial of Japan's Military Sexual Slavery held in Tokyo in 2000 (Tokyo Women's Tribunal)[51] and the World Tribunal on Iraq, which comprised a series of hearings around the world between 2003 and 2005, culminating in a final session in Istanbul.[52] These two tribunals also focused on the laws of war, although the Tokyo Women's Tribunal undertook a retrospective analysis of the law that applied during World War II, while the World Tribunal on Iraq, like the Russell Tribunal, was concerned with events as they were taking place. Also like the Russell Tribunal, these tribunals had the support of prominent international lawyers, indicating, for better or worse, the many strong links between activism and lawyering that people's tribunals have drawn upon. The international lawyers involved included Richard Falk, Christine Chinkin and Gabrielle Kirk McDonald. Unlike the Russell Tribunal, which sought to activate a people's movement, these tribunals drew heavily on the energy and resources of already existing global movements – respectively, the women's rights and the antiwar movements.

The Tokyo Women's Tribunal set out to help break the silence about Japan's abduction of thousands of "comfort women,"[53] primarily from Korea, who were forced to provide sexual services to the Japanese military during World War II, and to condemn the failure to hold Japan criminally responsible. Its goals were highly legalistic. Staged as a fictive continuation of the International Military Tribunal for the Far East (IMTFE), which sat in Tokyo from 1946–48, organizers went to great lengths to simulate judicial proceedings.[54] The aim was to correct the historical record and show that, under the international law applicable at the time, Japan and individual Japanese defendants could and should have been charged with crimes against humanity, in relation to the "comfort stations."[55] Unlike the Russell and Iraq Tribunals, the concern was not with the legality of the war itself, but with the mistreatment of civilians by Japan during the war. The Tokyo Women's Tribunal was organized by a group of NGOs in the Asia-Pacific region, together with surviving "comfort women" and supportive individuals,[56] taking inspiration from feminist involvement in the negotiations for the establishment of the ICC during the 1990s and assisted by many in the global women's rights movement.[57] Perhaps this connection to feminist activism associated with establishment of the ICC, which was primarily concerned with *jus in bello*, accounts for the Tokyo Tribunal's lack of concern with *jus ad bellum*. The orientation of the Tokyo Tribunal may also support Moyn's contention that the contemporary anti war movement is preoccupied with punishing atrocity rather than ending war.[58]

Like the Russell Tribunal, groups of volunteers gathered evidence in the eight countries of nationality of the comfort women, utilizing new archival evidence unearthed by researchers in Japan.[59] The case was presented by the "prosecution"[60] to a panel of four "judges" in the form of personal testimonies of about twenty survivors (some by video) and two former Japanese soldiers, who corroborated the women's evidence, as well as reports from several experts.[61] A Japanese law firm was appointed as *amicus curiae* to present a defense on behalf of the Japanese Government, which had not responded to the invitation to participate.[62] Volumes of written evidence were also submitted. There was a daily audience of more than 1,000 people.[63] The judges were leading international jurists and legal scholars,[64] consistent with the ambition to emulate formal legal proceedings as closely as possible. The aim was to strengthen the global movement calling for *legal* responsibility to be acknowledged by Japan and remedial measures granted – namely, a full and frank apology from the Japanese government and the payment of adequate reparations for the past and continuing suffering of survivors.

Unlike the Russell Tribunal, the Tokyo Women's Tribunal indicted individuals (all deceased), in addition to invoking Japan's responsibility as a state, which is not possible in the jurisdiction of the ICC. The accused included Emperor Hirohito and nine others who had served as wartime government officials and field commanders. With the exception of Hirohito, who was granted amnesty from prosecution by the US at the time, the defendants had been convicted of war crimes by the IMTFE. The Tokyo Women's Tribunal judges presented their preliminary judgment on the last day of the hearing, declaring that their authority to do so came from the peoples of the Asia-Pacific region and, indeed, of the world.[65] They found Hirohito guilty, on the basis of command responsibility, for rape and sexual slavery as a crime against humanity,[66] and the Japanese government to be in violation of its treaty and customary obligations relating to slavery, trafficking, forced labor, and rape amounting to crimes against humanity.[67] It called upon Japan to make reparations for the harms inflicted on the comfort women, including a full and meaningful apology and the payment of adequate compensation.[68] The judges also found that initial responsibility for the failure to prosecute these crimes at the time lay with the World War II Allies, particularly the US, despite being in possession of evidence of the comfort system.[69] The final judgment, delivered in The Hague a year later, provided detailed legal analysis and set out all the findings of the judges, including the guilt of the other indictees.[70]

The World Tribunal on Iraq was even more ambitious than the Russell and Tokyo Women's Tribunals in its geographical spread and engagement with a global (antiwar) people's movement. It grew from the massive protests that took place on February 15, 2003, before the US- and United Kingdom (UK)-led military intervention in Iraq, when some 11 million people took part in street demonstrations in eighty countries.[71] After the military intervention took place despite the protests, the idea of holding a people's tribunal was raised at anti-war meetings in several cities, including Berlin, Jakarta, Geneva, Paris, and Cancun.[72] Momentum quickly grew. An international working group was formed at a Networking Conference organized by the Bertrand Russell Peace Foundation in Brussels in June 2003.[73] Some groups had already begun to independently organize tribunals,[74] so it was decided that a series of preliminary sessions would be held around the world, with the culminating session in Istanbul. The structure was non-hierarchical and coordination largely took place through an internet forum.[75]

In October 2003, a Platform Text was adopted at a three-day coordinating meeting in Istanbul, in order to provide guidance to participating groups.[76] Four aims, very similar to those of the Russell Tribunal, were identified: to gather evidence to inform the public of the illegality of the Iraq War; to

strengthen the mobilizations of people against the war; to challenge the failure of international institutions to fulfill their obligations under international
law to hold the US and its allies accountable; and to "bring a moral, political
and judicial judgment that contributes to build a world of peace and justice."[77]
In the face of institutional inaction, the Tribunal claimed that its authority
derived "from universal morals and human rights principles [which] can
speak for the world."[78] As Richard Falk, long-time advocate of global people's
power and one of the organizers, described it, the World Tribunal on Iraq
aimed to "*confirm* the law, and [enable citizens to] draw the appropriate political and legal consequences."[79]

Ultimately over twenty hearings and associated events were held in fifteen
countries, including several outside the European axis – India, Japan, South
Korea, and Turkey. Each session examined different aspects of the legality
of the intervention, including the use of depleted uranium (Hiroshima),
destruction of cultural heritage (Istanbul), privatization of Iraqi resources
(Copenhagen), commission of war crimes during the invasion and military
occupation (London), and the novel concept of violating the will of the
global antiwar movement (New York).[80] Hundreds of people volunteered
time, expertise, funds, and resources.[81] At the culminating session in Istanbul,
June 23–27, 2005, many well-known peace activists and international lawyers presented expert testimonies[82] and, in the by now well-established tradition of people's tribunals, personal testimony was given by several Iraqi
civilians and former US soldiers.[83] Arundhati Roy, spokesperson for the "Jury
of Conscience" comprised of fourteen highly respected public figures,[84] gave
the closing speech, and the jury's *Declaration of Conscience* was released in
the following weeks, which set out the findings, charges, and recommendations of the jury in detail.[85]

The *Declaration* was in many ways reminiscent of the findings of the
Russell Tribunal. The invasion and occupation of Iraq was condemned as
illegal and the US and UK governments were charged with sixteen breaches
of international law including the crime of aggression (*jus ad bellum*) and a
large number of *jus in bello* offences: targeting the civilian population and
infrastructure, using illegal weapons, creating conditions under which the
status of Iraqi women was seriously degraded, the use of torture, illegally
rewriting Iraqi laws, widely devastating the environment, failing to protect
Iraq's cultural heritage, and obstructing the right to freedom of information
in Iraq.[86] Supporting states were also charged with complicity in war crimes.
Unlike the Russell Tribunal, a number of other actors were also charged: the
Security Council for failing to protect the Iraqi people; private corporations
for profiting from complicity in war crimes; and major corporate media for

spreading deliberate falsehoods.[87] The *Declaration* recognized the right of the
Iraqi people to resist the illegal occupation, and recommended, *inter alia*,
immediate withdrawal of coalition forces and the payment of compensation
to Iraq. With respect to individual criminal responsibility, an exhaustive investigation was recommended, beginning with US President George W. Bush
and UK Prime Minister Tony Blair.[88] Thirty-eight of the "most obvious" other
individuals were also listed for investigation.

As illustrated by these three examples, people's judgment tribunals have
much in common with the recent anti-impunity focus in international
human rights advocacy and activism. Indeed, the Tokyo Women's Tribunal
was inspired by related developments in international criminal law and seen
by many involved as making a further contribution to them.[89] Centrally concerned with the failures of existing international institutions to apply the law to
powerful actors, people's judgment tribunals, in keeping with developments in
the formal law, are now also likely to provide a platform for assessing individual
criminal responsibility, in addition to state responsibility. Implicitly (explicitly
in the case of the Tokyo Women's Tribunal) the idea of amnesty for international crimes is rejected. Also in step with the current focus of the international
human rights movement, the issue of the criminal responsibility of non-state
actors, such as multinational corporations and international institutions is
likely to be raised, as by the World Tribunal on Iraq. Perhaps the most striking
similarity is the focus on giving voice to the victims of human rights abuses,
which is a departure from the earlier concern of human rights advocates with
the rights of defendants to a fair trial, as Karen Engle has argued.[90] A major
achievement of people's judgment tribunals has been the creation of substantial archives of injustice that would not otherwise have existed, which include
the personal testimonies of many people whose suffering is not recognized by
formal systems of law. These archives provide continuing opportunities for
ordinary people to revise their judgments of the past and present. The legalistic
focus of people's judgment tribunals presents a challenge to legal and political
institutions, on their own terms, from within the existing framework of law,
to end the exceptionalism that grants impunity to the most powerful actors.
Although this challenge has yet to bear much fruit – the Japanese government
continues to deny legal responsibility for the comfort system and the US and its
allies continue to enjoy impunity for the wars in Vietnam and Iraq – people's
judgment tribunals nevertheless help to foster the hope that criminal courts
might one day address the injustices that are being highlighted.

Yet, despite the confidence expressed by people's judgment tribunals in
the justice of the existing law, if only it were impartially and consistently

applied, they also implore people to make a judgment based not only on law, but also on conscience. There is thus a tension between legal and ethical aspirations in the work of these tribunals that is an ever-present reminder that law alone is not sufficient for justice to be realized. This tension surfaced during the discussion of the aims of the World Tribunal on Iraq, at the October 2003 coordinating meeting in Istanbul. Participants Ayça Çubuçu and Jayan Nayar were both struck by the competing "grammars of justice and legitimacy"[91] that emerged between the "legalist" and "political"/"politico-ethicist" perspectives.[92] The legalists wanted the tribunal to speak in the "impartial" grammar of international law, arguing that following legal procedures as closely as possible would maximize its legitimacy and make it difficult for even the most conservative ideologues to disagree.[93] Whereas those in the politico-ethicist camp thought that imitating official tribunals would "belittle" and "undermine" the project[94] and, instead, wanted to speak in the multiple grammars of activism – including the political, ethical, artistic, and poetic – as well as the legal.[95] In the end, some sessions relied heavily on legal experts, following closely the form of a trial and reaching a "verdict" (as in Japan), while others emphasized broader notions of justice emanating from the ethical frameworks embraced by the antiwar movement (as in New York and Istanbul).[96]

The uneasy alliance in the World Tribunal on Iraq, between legalist and politico/ethicist frameworks for judgment, is evident from the International Law Explanatory Note appended to the jury's *Declaration of Conscience*, which identifies the specific customs, principles, and treaty rules of international law that have been violated, and describes its purpose as "back[ing] up the Jury Statement that rests its assessments primarily on a moral and political appraisal of the Iraq war."[97] This tension was also apparent in the Russell Tribunal, which, despite its focus on demonstrating the illegality of US actions in Vietnam, was described by Sartre as examining the facts "in our hearts and consciences."[98] Even the *Charter of the Tokyo Women's Tribunal*, the most legalistic of my three examples, identified "the principles of law, human conscience, humanity and gender justice" as providing guidance for the Tribunal's deliberations and it ultimately highlighted the question of the international community's moral responsibility to victims of war crimes who do not have access to a mechanism that can provide them with justice.[99] The productive engagement of people's judgment tribunals with the tensions between legal and ethical frames of justice is an important reminder, especially to those seeking to end impunity, of the limits of the justice provided by law.

B. *People's Law Tribunals: Recognizing New Sources of Law*

This second category of people's tribunals is considerably more critical of the law than people's judgment tribunals. They proceed from the conviction that the law itself needs to change before justice is possible.[100] People's testimonies are understood as the source of a more inclusive and liberatory law, capable of disrupting the hierarchies of power constituted and supported by the law that emanates from states. In this paradigm, "the people" may refer to a diversity of oppressed or marginalized groups, such as workers, women, poor people, ethnic minorities, and indigenous or colonized peoples. While people's law tribunals may also call for the judgment of the people, and thus overlap with my first category, the primary aspiration is to identify, apply, and promote new or alternative legal principles and rules that address the issues raised by victim and expert testimonies. For these tribunals, a broader contextual analysis of the inequitable distribution of resources and power provides a backdrop to their deliberations, enabling a structural analysis of injustice. Two examples will suffice for present purposes: the Permanent Peoples' Tribunal established in 1979 by Italian lawyer and socialist politician Lelio Basso, who had been one of the Russell Tribunal Members, and the International Tribunal on Crimes against Women held in Brussels in 1976 (Brussels Women's Tribunal), organized by feminist activists.

The Permanent Peoples' Tribunal understands the "needs of public conscience" as an alternative source of law[101] – the law of peoples. Deliberations in its sessions are guided by the *Universal Declaration on the Rights of Peoples*,[102] which was "proclaimed" at an international non-governmental conference in Algiers, convened by the Lelio Basso Foundation in 1976,[103] at the height of hopefulness about the emergence of a new and more equitable international economic order in the wake of decolonization. Nayar describes the *Universal Declaration on the Rights of Peoples* as "a manifesto of struggle, a demand for the recognition of the *right*, the legitimacy, of struggles against the *wrongs* of violence, oppression and exploitation."[104] To this end, a range of collective rights are declared, including the right of peoples to fight for their liberation, to existence, to political self-determination, to equal and just terms in international trade, and to their artistic, historical, and cultural wealth.[105] Some of these rights have since been more formally recognized in General Assembly Declarations[106] and the 1981 *African Charter on Human and Peoples' Rights*.[107] However, official enthusiasm for peoples' rights waned in the wake of the Cold War.[108] Despite, or perhaps because of the cooling of official support, the idea of peoples' rights has continued to be embraced by an expanding assortment of peoples' movements, as a means of identifying the structural nature of the injustices they seek to highlight, which a focus on individual human rights tends to conceal.

There have been over forty Permanent Peoples' Tribunal sessions since the first in 1979, which considered the plight of the peoples of the Western Sahara.[109] While primarily concerned in the early years with *jus in bello* relating to foreign invasions, genocide, the self-determination struggles of colonized peoples, and abuses by repressive governments,[110] the focus has since broadened to address other injustices not adequately acknowledged by formal law, such as those resulting from environmental destruction, industrial disasters, and economic globalization.[111] The entities held responsible for the violations of peoples' rights have also expanded from an exclusive focus on states to consideration of the legal responsibility of international institutions, such as the World Bank and IMF, and transnational corporations, such as those involved in the agro-chemical and garment industries.[112] The Permanent Peoples' Tribunal, based in Rome, is international in its ambitions, although it has particularly strong links with peoples' movements in Latin America.[113] A standing roster of potential jurists is maintained, which includes well-known international lawyers, scientists, political figures, and artists – several of whom are Nobel laureates.[114] The Permanent Peoples' Tribunal works in cooperation with national liberation movements, NGOs, political groups, trade unions, and other groups of people, as well as sometimes governments and intergovernmental organizations, and is largely reliant on the energies and resources of these groups to organize its sessions.[115]

Women constitute another variation of "the people," as already seen with the Tokyo Women's Tribunal. The idea that women's experience of gendered oppression might be the source of more emancipatory law resonates strongly with feminist methodologies that draw on women's experience as a form of knowledge, making people's law tribunals particularly attractive as a feminist form of protest. The proposal to organize an international women's tribunal first surfaced in 1974 at an International Feminist Strategy workshop in Denmark, and was discussed in more detail later that year at an International Feminist Conference in Frankfurt.[116] What was to become the 1976 Brussels Women's Tribunal was planned as a "counter-action" to the equality goals of International Women's Year (1975), which were seen as a hypocritical effort to "integrat[e] women into the existing patriarchal structures."[117] Ultimately, women from forty countries participated in the Brussels Women's Tribunal.[118] In her opening remarks (*in absentia* as she was ill), Simone de Beauvoir described it as "the start of a radical decolonization of women,"[119] indicating that the crimes identified by the tribunal were to be understood in the context of the patriarchal oppression of women as a group, rather than as crimes for which individual perpetrators were primarily responsible. Unlike the people's judgment tribunals, this tribunal sought to "indict the [patriarchal] system" rather than states or individual defendants.[120]

The people's law for the Brussels Women's Tribunal emerged from the testimonies of women's everyday experience of patriarchal violence and exploitation. The organizers sought to "expose crimes unrecognized as such by the legal system and question the sincerity of a number of laws which pretend to defend the rights of women."[121] They reasoned that "oppressed peoples have the right to disassociate themselves from those definitions of crimes which have been developed by their oppressors to serve their own interests."[122] Curiously, at least in retrospect, the laws of war were not considered – not as laws of questionable sincerity or as a body of law that fails to recognize crimes against women as such. The laws whose sincerity was questioned included laws criminalizing abortion and contraception, the law of homicide (which concealed the prevalence of femicide), and laws against rape and family violence (which were seldom enforced). The new crimes that emerged from women's testimonies included forced/compulsory motherhood, female castration, compulsory heterosexuality, the persecution of non-virgins, unmarried mothers and lesbians, women's enforced economic dependency on men, no wages for housework, and the double oppression of Third World, immigrant, and religious minority women. In short, *"all man-made forms of women's oppression* were seen as crimes against women."[123]

Not only did the Brussels Women's Tribunal destabilize the individualized concept of a crime, but it also subverted the tribunal form, performing a deeper critique of law's assumptions and procedures. There was no panel of judges as "the verdict is in our hands"[124] and no expert witnesses as "our analyses … must be informed by feelings, not just intellect."[125] While an order of proceedings had been organized, it was continually disrupted by participants who wanted to play a more active role. Some wanted to give spontaneous testimony, while others wanted more analysis and discussion of follow-up action.[126] Although this was chaotic, it meant the Tribunal had "come alive" and was "deeply emotionally involving" for everyone.[127] Unprecedented media attention was generated by the policy to ban all men from attending the tribunal, including journalists. While most of this publicity was negative, it drew attention to feminist issues that had hitherto received little public exposure.[128] An assessment of achievements four months later, relying on reports from Italy, Norway, Germany, Ireland, Israel, France, Austria, Belgium, Holland, South Africa, and the US, found that local feminist movements had been strengthened, some of the specific complaints of testifiers had been addressed, refuges and rape crisis centers had been established, other women's tribunals had been held or were planned, a women's journalist association had been formed, publicity about the tribunal had been widely disseminated, and international networks were expanding and consolidating[129] — a significant impact by any calculation.

As both the Permanent Peoples' Tribunal and Brussels Women's Tribunal illustrate, people's law tribunals have less in common with the recent anti-impunity focus in international human rights law than people's judgment tribunals because the focus of their critique is state made law, rather than the failure of states to apply the law. Yet there remain some commonalities. Foremost among them is the focus on victim testimonies as the foundation for development of the law, with even less space given over to adversarial argumentation than afforded by people's judgment tribunals. The emphasis on victims' experiences of injustice is consistent with the shift in concern of human rights advocates from the rights of the accused to those of victims. Permanent Peoples' Tribunal sessions have also kept in step with formal legal developments by examining the responsibility of non-state actors, including multinational corporations and international institutions, while the Brussels Women's Tribunal was ahead of its time with its recognition of crimes in the private sphere of the family. Among their achievements, the creation of valuable archival resources would surely be counted, as well as their challenge to the grip that states have on the sources of law and the means of its development. This challenge has, in some respects, borne some fruit, with the law of peoples continuing to enjoy some standing in the lexicon of the formal law, albeit heavily contested, and developments in the criminal law aimed at addressing some of the silences in law that people's movements have highlighted, particularly in response to feminist critiques. In their appeals for substantive legal change, therefore, people's law tribunals do lend some support to the hope that formal law may yet provide remedies for the injustices they highlight.

However, people's law tribunals are a considerably more paradoxical space to negotiate than that of people's judgment tribunals, because the tension between legalist and ethico-political goals is even more pronounced. On the one hand, they lend legitimacy to the existing categories and authority of the law by assuming a tribunal form, even as protest, by using legal languages of "crimes" and "rights," and ultimately by calling on states to adopt and enforce newly identified people's law. Yet they also mount a fundamental critique of the law, seeking to change the relations of power that are deeply embedded in the existing law, its institutions and practices. Their efforts to produce a more emancipatory system of law, by insisting that its development must be centrally informed by and respond to people's experiences of subjugation and oppression, presents a cautionary reminder to human rights advocacy that has suspended its critique of the state and lost sight of the violence of the law itself. In addition, people's law tribunals remind us of the structural causes of injustice and the dangers of conceiving responsibility only or primarily in individual terms, whether individual people, states, or multinational corporations. They remind us that there is also the need to challenge the structures of neo-imperial and patriarchal power, which trivialize so many injustices or dismiss them as quotidian inevitability – and that this challenge is a task that lies largely outside the law, in the politics of the everyday in which we all share some responsibility.

C. People's Responsibility Tribunals: Imagining Transformative Justice

The idea of shared responsibility for injustice is at the heart of the mission of my third category of people's tribunals – people's responsibility tribunals. They offer an even more robust critique of law's inability to acknowledge and address the structural causes of injustice and fundamentally challenge those who think that imposing individual criminal responsibility offers the primary route to ending impunity. In various ways, people's responsibility tribunals seek to extricate law and conceptions of justice from the control of states. Their aspirations are avowedly utopian, working toward the transformation of the entire system of law as we know it, which is seen as deeply complicit in maintaining injustice. At the heart of their transformative vision is the idea that we, the people, share the responsibility for injustice and need to find ways to acknowledge and act on it. People's responsibility tribunals have in many respects abandoned the hope that the existing law, and its enforcement practices, might be amenable to the deep change they believe is necessary – although they may also engage with the politics of the present by promoting law enforcement and/or law reform. Two examples that illustrate these tribunals are the World Courts of Women, which aim to "find new visions for our times" by making visible the everyday violence suffered by women on the peripheries of the current world order,[130] and Tribunal 12, which accused "Europe" of systematic mistreatment of refugees, migrants, and asylum seekers.

The World Courts of Women project, initiated in 1992 by two NGO networks, the Asian Women's Rights Association and El Taller International,[131] works closely with local activist groups, primarily in the Global South, broadly defined. To date, over forty Courts of Women have been convened in Asia, the Middle East, Southeastern Europe, Africa, and, more recently, Latin America and the US.[132] The goals, somewhat reminiscent of the Brussels Women's Tribunal, are to protest violence against women, not as an individual crime, but as embedded in other systemic forms of violence.[133] As a result, the subject matter ranges much more broadly than that covered by the earlier tribunal, examining not only violence against women as a specific topic,[134] but also linking it to the violence of development,[135] population policies,[136] nuclear testing,[137] war,[138] racism,[139] neo-liberal economic policies,[140] poverty,[141] dowry,[142] and so on. There is a consistent focus on the structural underpinnings of violence and, thus, the need for systemic change. As with other people's tribunals, the World Courts of Women hold public hearings that are grounded in personal and expert testimonies and a "jury" of wise women and men respond in ways that will enhance the collective search for new visions and practices of justice.[143] However, they also consciously set out to be subversive of conventional courtroom practices by incorporating multiple grammars of protest, including the artistic and lyrical so as to engage the imagination and expand the world of the possible. Participants are engaged in a performance that uses various ways of speaking, learning, and relating to each other through the incorporation of poetry, song, and dance into the proceedings and the use of art and other visual forms of testimony.[144]

While the World Courts of Women are skeptical about appealing to the existing law for justice, many of them nevertheless make demands on law in the present in response to the evidence presented, adopting some elements of both people's judgment and people's law tribunals. For example, the Court of Women on Crimes against Dalit Women called on the Indian government to establish specialized courts to enforce existing laws,[145] and the World Court of Women on Poverty in the US adopted a resolution, outlining the "extreme violence perpetrated by poverty and the capitalist system," to be presented to UN human rights mechanisms and bodies to inform their work in developing the law.[146] However, their main goals are to embark on what is often described as a quest or journey: "to challenge the master narratives of our times," including "the dominant human rights discourse, whose frames have excluded the knowledges of women," to define a "new politics" and open "new imaginaries."[147] Regularly making reference to Audre Lord's admonition that "the master's tools will never destroy the master's house,"[148] the World Courts of Women hope to incubate "a new generation" of women's human rights and initiate "alternative institutions" whereby women's reconceived human rights violations will be redressed.[149] So although the language of women's human rights is used repeatedly, it is deployed as a language of popular justice that will engender a new feminist ethics of solidarity and mutuality in both politics and law.

However, the most salient features that locate the World Courts of Women in my third category is their emphasis on testimonies of protest and survival, not just suffering and pain, which are linked to a politics of collective responsibility. A session of each court is routinely devoted to testimonies of resistance, evocatively referred to as the "Gathering of the Spirit,"[150] the "Time of the Wind,"[151] "In the Eye of the Storm,"[152] or, more simply, "Aren't We All Testifiers."[153] These sessions give participants the opportunity to share their stories of courage and rebellion, both in their personal lives and through involvement in larger social and political movements. The testimonies speak to shared responsibility for justice and the need for new forms of inclusive political community to achieve it, based on women's creativity, courage, and strength. All testifiers, as Margot Waller explains, "speak as members, to members, of community" and new relationships are forged between them and listeners, which prompt everyone to take responsibility for unlearning old ways of thinking and promoting transformative change, wherever and however they can.[154]

The idea that responsibility for injustice is shared was also promoted by Tribunal 12, which was held in Stockholm on May 12, 2012. Organized by Shaharazad, an organization of exiled and diasporic writers based in Europe,[155] Tribunal 12 put "Europe" on trial for the inhumanity of the political economy of its border controls.[156] As Sara Dehm has observed, the concept of Europe was left deliberately undefined in order to open the question of responsibility, rather than limit it to governments and state-based institutions.[157] The organizers included themselves amongst those accused.[158] They used the format of a tribunal to perform their protest, utilizing many grammars of protest but particularly the literary and artistic, in solidarity with the struggles for justice of unauthorized migrants across Europe. Their performance of a tribunal enabled them to raise questions of responsibility within and beyond the framework of law. A team of prosecutors outlined the "charges" against Europe. Actors presented the stories of people who could not safely attend in person, describing punitive border protection practices, harsh punishments, violent detention practices, exploitative working conditions, homelessness, lack of access to basic services and resources, and living with the constant fear of deportation.[159] No "defense" was offered because organizers felt that this would require identification of those responsible and unduly limit the field of obligation.[160] The proceedings, which also included expert testimonies that drew a larger picture of abuse and mistreatment, were streamed live to twenty European cities, where people could watch in public venues, such as parks and libraries, and were later replayed on Swedish television. The jury, primarily made up of activist-writers and critical thinkers, offered their individual reflections, as well as a joint verdict.[161] In their reflections, Europe was described as "a post-modern slave system" by Egyptian writer Nawal El Saadawi and as "a monster, a beast" by Swedish author Henning Mankell.[162]

In its joint verdict, the jury condemned European governments for violating existing asylum, detention, and irregular migration laws, and urged them to immediately reverse the privatization practices that placed many at the mercy of the multinational corporations employed to police the borders and run detention centers.[163] They also promoted people's law as a popular expression of justice, urging governments to respect universal norms of humanity that "go beyond existing law," such as the principle of equal human worth regardless of status,[164] directly challenging the notion of fixed territorial borders and the power of states to exclude. The jury also took full advantage of the openness of the concept of Europe to address Europe's civil society in their verdict as "a critical Europe-wide force for addressing these abuses," noting that the issue was "too important" to leave in the hands of governments and their agents This observation was an acknowledgment that law can itself be part of the problem and that change must come from outside state-based political and legal communities. In an important gesture of inclusivity, the jury identified immigrant struggles for justice as constituting "in good part" Europe's civil society, concretely disrupting the idea of state boundaries. By addressing itself to "Europe," Tribunal 12 called on all European subjects, including citizens and irregular migrants, to speak out against the inhuman border policies and to take responsibility for forging inclusive practices in their local communities and daily lives, as well as in the broader polity. Their goal was to produce more open and inclusive narratives and practices of Europe and thereby foster alternative foundations for European community.

While people's responsibility tribunals may share some of the aims of people's judgment and people's law tribunals, their ambitions go well beyond mobilizing people's movements to insist that the law be universally applied and/or that popular justice be recognized as a source of new law. They consciously mount a searing critique of the existing state-based legal framework, setting out to challenge its boundaries and reshape the associated ideas of community and responsibility. The failure to address injustice and end impunity for human rights violations is a charge not only directed to states and their agents, although this is certainly recognized as a part of the problem. Impunity for injustice is understood as implicating everyone who might be considered to be among its beneficiaries. People's responsibility tribunals therefore present a fundamental challenge to those who focus on individual criminal responsibility as the primary means to tackle the problem of impunity. Their message is that the law itself may be deeply implicated in maintaining and naturalizing the systems of impunity that it claims to address, and that responsibility lies, in some respects, with everyone. People's responsibility tribunals aspire to give form and voice to political communities that are not bound or divided by national loyalties and identities, which work in solidarity with the struggles of those whose experiences of injustice are not recognized by state-based politics and therefore remain without legal remedy. They are a prescient reminder that to cast the gaze of anti-impunity struggles too narrowly is to betray the hope of justice that they arouse. Seeking an end to impunity for gross human rights violations requires, as Dehm has observed, "a different account of political belonging and accountability";[165] a redrawing of the boundaries of law and a remaking of political community.

II. THE POLITICS OF LISTENING AND COLLECTIVE RESPONSIBILITY

This journey, through a condensed history of the challenges that people's tribunals present to legal justice, brings me now to reflect on my own experience of the Phnom Penh Hearing, where the question of responsibility hung heavily over the proceedings, along with the intense humidity of the Cambodian climate, although the question was not clearly articulated in the way of a people's responsibility tribunal. As we "listened with our hearts," the testifiers told us of their traumatic experiences of sexual violence during conflicts in Bangladesh, Cambodia, Timor-Leste, and Nepal, which had been ignored, denied, trivialized, or inadequately addressed by official efforts to promote post-conflict justice. The official refusal to recognize legal and/or political responsibility – Russell's "crime of silence" – had consigned them to the margins of their communities, variously marking them as unmarriageable, shameful, and blameworthy. The warmth with which they embraced each other in their shared experiences, despite barriers of language and culture, and their eagerness to tell their stories publicly, was deeply hopeful. In speaking of events that had taken place a long time ago – more than thirty or forty years in the case of the Bangladeshi and Cambodian testifiers – they also bore witness to their courage and tenacity. The testimonies were not just of suffering, but of resistance and dogged survival, although it would have been good if this aspect had been highlighted by devoting a particular session to stories of protest and courage, as the Courts of Women do. Nevertheless, the Phnom Penh Hearing was, in the words of the Courts of Women project, "writ[ing] a counter-history, by creating a space where we can listen with care to the voices speaking in their own centre."[166]

The aims of the Phnom Penh Hearing encompassed, to some extent, all three of the legal aspirations of people's tribunals discussed above. The foremost goal was to draw attention to the "inability or unwillingness of judi-cial transitional justice mechanisms" to apply the law so as to provide justice for survivors of gender-based violence;[167] a goal that was particularly com-pelling in the context of the decision by the co-investigative judges in the Extraordinary Chambers in the Courts of Cambodia (ECCC) to not include charges relating to rapes that occurred in security centers and work coopera-tives because they could not see a link between the evidence and the accused Khmer Rouge leaders.[168] To the extent that its emphasis was on law enforce-ment, the Phnom Penh Hearing sat firmly in the tradition of people's judg-ment tribunals, focused primarily on condemning international and domestic institutions for failing to hold states and individual perpetrators to account. However, the hearing also aimed to promote "acknowledgment of the gen-der-based atrocities inflicted on women during conflict," which echoes the aspirations of people's law tribunals to promote more inclusive interpretations of the existing law and/or show how it should be developed or reformed. Other aims were to provide survivors with the opportunity to "break the silence" that has attended gender-based violence during conflict and foster a "regional dia-logue" on the best ways to deliver justice for survivors, which invite a rethink-ing of received notions of justice, looking both in and beyond the law, like people's responsibility tribunals. Although the question of the responsibility of those of us who attended the hearing – to do something more than listen supportively – was not explicitly addressed, I found myself wondering, as I lis-tened to painful testimonies, about our collective responsibility, including my own, to act on these stories and support the struggles for justice being related to us.

In my subsequent thinking about this question of collective responsibility, I have found Iris Marion Young's thoughts on responsibility for justice help-ful. While Young does not deny the importance of attributing direct causal responsibility to blameworthy states, international institutions, corporations, and individuals, she is concerned that this type of responsibility is too often the exclusive focus[169] – a concern that I think lies at the heart of people's respon-sibility tribunals. Young builds on the distinction that Hannah Arendt makes between "guilt" and "political responsibility": the former attributes moral or legal fault, based usually on blameworthy intent, while the latter attaches to everyone as a result of their membership in a political community in rela-tion to things done in the name of their nation or polity.[170] Both Young and Arendt believe, like the Tribunal 12 organizers, that focusing just on guilt (the *raison d'être* of the law) works to absolve others, including ourselves, and also deflects attention from background conditions of structural inequality and oppression. The imperative to take political responsibility, as Young describes it, arises when we see injustices being committed by the institutions of which we are a part. We then "have the responsibility to try to speak out against [those injustices] with the intention of mobilizing others to oppose them, and to act together to transform the institutions to promote better ends."[171] This type of responsibility is invoked by people's judgment tribunals.

However, Young argues that basing shared responsibility only on our membership in a political community is too limiting. She proposes a "social connection" model for thinking about responsibility, which is not restricted to political communities, but extends across national borders to include people who are globally dispersed.[172] In her social connection model, responsibility in relation to injustice derives from "belonging together with others in a system of interdependent processes of cooperation and competition through which we seek benefits and aim to realize projects."[173] Although Young's primary focus is on responsibility for structural conditions of economic and social inequality, her paradigm also translates into thinking about responsibility for the devastating and continuing effects of armed conflict. Young offers a number of "parameters" for thinking more specifically about the responsibility that arises from our social connectedness, which she sees as more open and discretionary than a duty.[174] These parameters include a person's power to influence the situation; their relative privilege in relation to unjust structures; their interest in change (the strongest interests lying with those who are victims of the injustice); and their collective ability to draw on and activate existing resources, group affiliations, and networks.[175]

Applying Young's parameters to my own case makes it clear that my responsibility did not end with fulfilling the specific tasks I had assumed as a Panel Member in Phnom Penh, which included taking responsibility for the Panel Statement of findings and recommendations. Acquitting these responsibilities was only a start. My location in the legal academy gives me particular powers of influence through my teaching and research, grants me a privileged platform for dissemination of ideas about justice and the law, and enables me to tap into many formal networks of power. My personal situation as a feminist and queer activist strongly informs my interest in and commitment to change, and links me into more marginalized community networks and forms of solidarity. Young's model of social connectedness suggests many ways that I can and must take responsibility for my part in the failure to recognize and redress the testimonies of injustice that I witnessed in Phnom Penh. Participating in this collection, as part of a critical re-examination of contemporary anti-impunity discourse and practice, is but one contribution that I am able to make.

During the Phnom Penh Hearing, there were moments when the international language of anti-impunity as "guilt" asserted itself in a way that left no room for local conceptions of responsibility and justice, let alone broader notions of collective responsibility. The opening video message from Zainab Bangura, the Special Representative of the UN Secretary-General on Sexual Violence in Conflict, set the scene by speaking of impunity only in terms of individual criminal prosecutions, as if this covered the field, and congratulating testifiers on the contributions they were making to putting an end to the impunity of perpetrators, as if this were the primary goal of the hearing.[176] Her limited account of responsibility was reinforced by her assertion that "every resource of the international community must be devoted to finding perpetrators and ending impunity,"[177] as if this was the sum total of justice. The expert testimonies presented by international law experts Silke Studinsky[178] and Susana SáCouto[179] also focused on the need to strengthen legal accountability for perpetrators of sexual violence during armed conflict. Studinsky's testimony was primarily concerned with broadening the legal definitions of sexual and gender-based violence and understanding it as a threat to international peace and security (and thus a trigger for Security Council enforcement measures), rather than drawing links to the testimonies of victims and the responsibilities of those of us listening.[180] Curiously, SáCouto's survey of lessons learned from judicial and non-judicial approaches to gender justice made no mention of people's tribunals, despite her location within one, and therefore did not discuss the limitations of state-based transitional justice mechanisms. Recognizing disillusionment with such mechanisms as one of the drivers of people's tribunals would have opened the question of responsibility, beyond the frame of law.

The exception to this pattern of presenting the fight against impunity in terms of criminal justice was the testimony of Anne-Marie Goetz, as representative of UN Women. Speaking in the language of politics rather than law, she stressed the importance of women's empowerment and participation in ending sexual violence during armed conflict and in its aftermath,[181] emphasizing that advancing gender justice is not a technocratic process, but about power and politics.[182] Yet even she failed to draw those of us listening to the proceedings, in the electrifying atmosphere of the Phnom Penh Ecumenical Center, directly into the frame of responsibility. Although the experts spoke with passion and commitment, there was very little real resonance between what they had to say and the survivors' testimonies of their quotidian struggles for survival in the present realities of post-conflict injustice. For me, it was an object lesson in how agendas, understood as universal, can not only fail to connect with the local, but can also dictate how the problem is understood and addressed at the local level. This power of the international to control the terms of justice, and the scope of responsibility, was demonstrated in the final

Panel Statement, in which I have to admit to having had an influential hand. Like the expert testimonies and in the tradition of people's judgment tribunals, the Panel Statement invokes impunity in the narrow sense of the failures of criminal justice mechanisms, locating responsibility with governments and international institutions. While some recommendations are also directed to civil society and NGOs – to raise awareness and mobilize their constituencies to demand justice for survivors and to recognize and celebrate their courage and resilience – the Statement falls short of invoking the sense of shared and collective responsibility that people's responsibility tribunals promote and Young outlines in greater detail.

Yet, in retrospect, making a connection between listening and responsibility seems so obvious. At the end of each session, the facilitator of the Phnom Penh proceedings invited everyone – panelists, testifiers, supporters, ECCC civil parties, translators, technicians, expert witnesses, activists, ECCC staff, and government officials – to rise up as one community to participate in relaxation exercises,[183] on the understanding that listening to the testimonies was upsetting and painful for us all. This created a stirring atmosphere of solidarity in recognition of our shared precarity and common humanity, despite our many differences. It required only a small step to make specific reference to this solidarity in our Panel Statement and acknowledge our shared responsibility to carry the new knowledge of survivors' testimonies into our workplaces, families, communities, and networks: to do whatever we can, in solidarity with survivors, to struggle for justice both in and beyond the law, as an imperative of the politics of listening. That we failed to take this small step is testament to the powerful grip that legal justice has on our imaginings and hopes for justice.

III. CONCLUSION

People's tribunals give expression to popular dreams of justice. They assume a people's jurisdiction that operates outside the state and, in some respects, beyond the framework of the present international legal order. It is a jurisdiction that provides victims with the opportunity for their voices to be heard and valued, and enables the creation of an archive of their suffering and courage into the present, which would not otherwise exist. It is also a jurisdiction that seeks to attribute responsibility for widespread human rights abuses and systemic inequality, not only to states and individual perpetrators, but also more broadly to the people. The responsibility of the people for (in)justice can be understood in at least three different ways. First, people's judgment tribunals draw attention to the duty of the people to mobilize in protest at the failure of the existing legal and political institutions to hold powerful actors to account. Second, people's law tribunals enable marginalized people to speak out about law's failure to recognize their experiences of injustice and oppression as such, and urge their participation in the articulation of alternative people's law, which will be capable of challenging the systemic injustices ignored by formal law. Third, people's responsibility tribunals invoke a collective responsibility, challenging everyone to recognize the part we play in enabling the formal systems of law to operate without protest, to acknowledge the benefits we may enjoy as a result of the system, and to accept that we all have some responsibility for ensuring that change occurs.

Presenting a number of powerful challenges to the contemporary faith in criminalization as providing the primary route to justice, people's tribunals remind us that legal institutions may themselves be a part of the problem in their failure to apply the law to powerful actors, their focus on individual rights and responsibilities, and their inability to address systemic forms of violence and inequality. However, it is the idea of shared responsibility for injustice that most fundamentally challenges the turn to individualized criminal accountability as the dominant response to injustice. While often seeking to promote change that would renew confidence in law's potential to deliver justice, people's tribunals also remind us of the infinity of possible claims for justice and the need for expansive ideas of responsibility for injustice, both within and beyond the confines of the law.[184] This responsibility includes working together to resist the many failures of law and legal institutions to apply the law, to interpret the law so that all lives are valued equally, and to treat structural violence as unacceptable rather than inevitable. People's tribunals point to the need for transformative change, to a much larger justice than legal mechanisms can deliver, and to the responsibility of us all to play our part in bringing this justice into being.

While it will always be important to struggle to achieve the maximum justice that is possible in the existing social order,[185] and international criminal law has a role to play in this, people's tribunals are a means of exploring possible future conditions and frames of justice, because they enable us to imagine justice beyond the limited forms offered by state-based legal recognition and rights. However, pursuing these possibilities relies on those who listen to painful testimonies moving beyond expressions of sympathy and empathy to reflect on the ways that they (we) may be implicated in the violence and the structural conditions that make justice impossible. As Susan Sontag suggests, in her meditation on the thoughts and emotions that are provoked by looking at photos of war, it is important to also see how "[western] privileges are located on the same map as [non-western] suffering, and may – in ways we prefer not to imagine – be linked to their suffering."[186] I would add that injustice is not always neatly distributed along a North/South grid, but is present everywhere because of the many intersecting hierarchies of power and privilege that we are all complicit in maintaining if we fail to protest and act to disable them. I would also reject the implication of "us" and "them" in Sontag's reflections and focus instead on our social connectedness and shared vulnerabilities. To move toward the inclusive justice that is reached for by people's tribunals, sharing testimonies of suffering and survival against the odds provides only an initial spark of solidarity. Those of us who listen (whether in person or virtually) need to discover how to turn that spark of recognition into the fire of solidarity and resistance, and find better ways to assume our shared responsibility for injustice in all its multiple dimensions, whether the context is armed conflict and its aftermath, state (in)security, or quotidian violence and oppression.

NOTES

1 Theresa de Langis, *Asia-Pacific Women's Hearing on Gender-Based Violence in Conflict: Report on the Proceedings* (Phnom Penh: Cambodian Defenders Project, 2012). The other panel members were Vahida Nainar, Aurora Javate De Dios, and Vichuta Ly (*in absentia*).
2 See "Cambodian Defenders Project," *cdpcambodia.org*, accessed February 4, 2014, www.cdpcambodia.org/.
3 de Langis, *Women's Hearing Report*, 31.
4 Dianne Otto et al., *Panel Statement for Asia-Pacific Regional Women's Hearing on Gender-Based Violence in Conflict* (Phnom Penh: Cambodian Defenders Project, October 11, 2012).
5 Wendy Brown, "Suffering Rights as Paradoxes," *Constellations* 7, no. 2 (2000): 208–229.
6 "Introduction by Bertrand Russell," *Against the Crime of Silence: Proceedings of the Russell International War Crimes Tribunal, Stockholm, Copenhagen,* ed. John Duffett (New York: Bertrand Russell Peace Foundation, 1968), 3–5, 5. Two sessions were held, in Stockholm (May 7– 10, 1967) and Roskilde near Copenhagen (November 20–December 1, 1967).
7 For example, the International Sakharov Committee, based in Copenhagen, organized a number of public hearings on human rights abuses in the USSR, Eastern Europe, Afghanistan, and Cuba between 1975 and 1986. See Arthur W. Blaser, "How to Advance Human Rights without Really Trying: An Analysis of Nongovernmental Tribunals," *Human Rights Quarterly* 14, no. 3 (1992): 339–370, 348–349.
8 Craig Borowiak, "The World Tribunal on Iraq: Citizens' Tribunals and the Struggle for Accountability," *New Political Science* 30, no. 2 (2008): 161–186, 165.
9 See, e.g., Philip Alston, ed., *Peoples' Rights* (Oxford: Oxford University Press, 2001).
10 Andrew Byrnes and Gabrielle Simm, "Peoples' Tribunals, International Law and the Use of Force," *University of New South Wales Law Journal* 36, no. 2 (2013): 711–744.

See also Tribunal on the Legality of Nuclear Weapons, Madrid (1983); London Nuclear Warfare Tribunal organized by Lawyers for Nuclear Disarmament and British Campaign for Nuclear Disarmament (January 3–6, 1985); Tribunal on the Legality of Nuclear Weapons, Los Angeles (1987).

11 Permanent People's Tribunal, *Permanent Peoples' Tribunal on Industrial Hazards and Human Rights, Bhopal I*, Bhopal (October 19–23, 1992); Permanent People's Tribunal, *Bhopal II*, London (November 28–December 2, 1994). See also Bard College, "The Bhopal Memory Project," *bhopal.bard.edu*, accessed February 4, 2014, http://bhopal.bard.edu; Permanent Peoples' Tribunal, *Session on Chernobyl and Its Consequences for the Environment, Health and Human Rights*, Vienna (April 12–15, 1996).

12 Concerned Citizens Tribunal, *An Inquiry into the Carnage in Gujarat: Crime against Humanity*, vols. 1–3 (Gujarat: Citizens for Justice and Peace, 2002), see "Concerned Citizens Tribunal – Gujarat 2002," *sabrang.com*, accessed February 4, 2014, www.sabrang.com/tribunal/.

13 The Courts of Women, established in 1992, co-organized by El Taller and the Asian Women's Human Rights Council: see Marguerite Waller, "The Courts of Women," *weap.org*, April 17, 2011, accessed February 4, 2014, http://weap.org/news/386/17/The-Courts-of-Women.html.

14 Tribunal 12, "Report from Tribunal 12," Stockholm, May 12, 2012, accessed February 4, 2014, http://tribunal12.org/wp-content/uploads/2011/02/Tribunal12_Report1.pdf.

15 *Kānaka Maoli Nation, Plaintiff v United States of America, Defendant* (Ka Ho'okolokolonui Kānaka Maoli, People's International Tribunal, Hawai'i, August 12–21, 1993. See also Sally Engle Merry, "Resistance and the Cultural Power of Law," *Law and Society Review* 29, no. 1 (1995) 11–26, 20–23.

16 Permanent Peoples' Tribunal on the Human Wrongs Committed by the International Monetary Fund and the World Bank, Berlin (1998) and Madrid (1994); Independent Tribunal on the World Bank Group in India, New Delhi (September 21–24, 2007): see "Independent Tribunal on the World Bank Group in India," worldbanktribunal.org, accessed February 4, 2014, www.worldbanktribunal.org/index.html.

17 Permanent Peoples' Tribunal, *Session on Workers' and Consumers' Rights in the Garment Industry*, Brussels (April 30-May 5, 1998); Permanent Peoples' Tribunal on Global Corporations and Human Wrongs, University of Warwick (March 22–25, 2000): see "Permanent Peoples' Tribunal on Global Corporations and Human Wrongs, University of Warwick, 22–25 March 2000, Findings and Recommended Action," *Law, Social Justice & Global Development* 1 (2001), accessed February 4, 2014, www2.warwick.ac.uk/fac/soc/law/elj/lgd/2001_1/ppt/; Permanent Peoples' Tribunal, *Session on Agrochemical Transnational Corporations*, Bangalore (December 3–6, 2011), see Pesticide Action Network International, "Agrochemical Transnational Corporations and Human Rights Violations," agricorporateaccountability.net, accessed February 4, 2014, www.agricorporateaccountability.net/.

18 Peter De Waal, ed., *Review of the 1976 Tribunal on Homosexuals and Discrimination* (Sydney: Tribunal Working Group, 1994).

19 *Russell Tribunal on Human Rights in Psychiatry*, Berlin (June 30–July 2, 2001), see "June 30 to July 2, 2001 in the Urania-Haus, An der Urania 17 in Berlian," freedom-of-thought.de, accessed February 4, 2014, www.freedom-of-thought.de/.

20 Gérard Chaliand, "The Crime of Silence," A *Crime of Silence: The Armenian Genocide*, ed. Gerard J. Libaridian, 243–246 (London: Zed Books, 1985).

21 Jayan Nayar, "A People's Tribunal against the Crime of Silence? The Politics of Judgment and an Agenda for People's Law," *Law, Social Justice & Global Development* 2 (2001), accessed February 4, 2014, http://www2.warwick.ac.uk/fac/soc/law/elj/lgd/2001_2/nayar/.

22 See, e.g., Christine Chinkin, "People's Tribunals: Legitimate or Rough Justice?" *Windsor Yearbook of Access to Justice* 24, no. 2 (2006): 201–220.

23 Iris Marion Young, *Responsibility for Justice* (New York: Oxford University Press, 2011).

24 See also Judith Butler, *Precarious Life: The Powers of Mourning and Violence* (London: Verso 2003).

25 "Women's Court: Feminist Approach to Justice – Report on Implementation Activities January–December 2011," zenskisud.org, 23–26, 5, accessed February 4, 2014, www.zenskisud.org/en/pdf/Report%20on%20implemented%20activities%20January%20-%20December%202011 pdf.

26 Ibid., 5.

27 Zenski Sud (Women's Court) – Feminist Approach to Justice, Sarajevo, May 7–10, 2015. I was a member of the Judicial Council at this event. See further www.zenskisud.org/en/index.html; www.huffingtonpost.com/jasmina-tesanovic/womens-tribunal-sarajevo-_b_7222604.html, accessed June 3, 2015,

28 "Exchanges of Correspondence with Heads of State: Letter from De Gaulle to Sartre," *Against the Crime of Silence: Proceedings of the Russell International War Crimes Tribunal, Stockholm, Copenhagen*, ed. John Duffett, 27–28 (New York: Bertrand Russell Peace Foundation, 1968), 28 (Paris: April 19, 1967).

29 Jean-Paul Sartre, "Answer and Commentary to De Gaulle's Letter Banning the Tribunal from France," in *Against the Crime of Silence: Proceedings of the Russell International War Crimes Tribunal, Stockholm, Copenhagen*, ed. John Duffett (New York: Bertrand Russell Peace Foundation, 1968), 29–36, 32–34 (originally published in *Nouvel Observateur*).

30 Carol Smart, *Feminism and the Power of Law* (London: Routledge, 1989).

31 Nayar, "A People's Tribunal against the Crime of Silence?" 2–3.

32 The Bertrand Russell Peace Foundation was established in 1963 to carry forward Russell's work for peace, human rights, and social justice, see "Bertrand Russell Peace Foundation," *russfound.org*, accessed February 4, 2014, www.russfound.org/about/about.htm.

33 "Aims and Objectives of the International War Crimes Tribunal," *Against the Crime of Silence: Proceedings of the Russell International War Crimes Tribunal, Stockholm, Copenhagen*, ed. John Duffett (New York: Bertrand Russell Peace Foundation, 1968), 14–16, 14–15 (issued publicly November 15, 1966).

34 Borowiak, "The World Tribunal on Iraq," 170.

35 Jean Paul Sartre, "Inaugural Statement to the 1967 Russell Tribunal," *Against the Crime of Silence: Proceedings of the Russell International War Crimes Tribunal, Stockholm, Copenhagen*, ed. John Duffett (New York: Bertrand Russell Peace Foundation, 1968), 40–45, 43–44.

36 Bertrand Russell, "Opening Statement to the First Tribunal Session," *Against the Crime of Silence: Proceedings of the Russell International War Crimes Tribunal,*

Stockholm, Copenhagen, ed. John Duffett (New York: Bertrand Russell Peace Foundation, 1968), 49–51, 49.

37 The Swedish session was held in Stockholm (May 2–10, 1967), and the Danish session in Roskilde (November 20–December 1, 1967).

38 The Japanese session was held in Tokyo (August 28–30, 1967). See also Arthur Jay Klinghoffer and Judith Apter Klinghoffer, *International Citizens' Tribunals: Mobilizing Public Opinion to Advance Human Rights* (New York: Palgrave, 2002) 149–152.

39 "Introduction by Bertrand Russell," 13.

40 See generally the evidence documented in *Against the Crime of Silence: Proceedings of the Russell International War Crimes Tribunal, Stockholm, Copenhagen*, ed. John Duffett (New York: Bertrand Russell Peace Foundation, 1968).

41 "Foreword by Ralph Schoenman," *Against the Crime of Silence: Proceedings of the Russell International War Crimes Tribunal, Stockholm, Copenhagen*, ed. John Duffett (New York: Bertrand Russell Peace Foundation, 1968), 6–10, 9.

42 "The International War Crimes Tribunal: Tribunal Members," *Against the Crime of Silence: Proceedings of the Russell International War Crimes Tribunal, Stockholm, Copenhagen*, ed. John Duffett (New York: Bertrand Russell Peace Foundation, 1968), 17.

43 "Foreword by Ralph Schoenman," 8.

44 "Aims and Objectives of the International War Crimes Tribunal," *Against the Crime of Silence: Proceedings of the Russell International War Crimes Tribunal, Stockholm, Copenhagen*, ed. John Duffett (New York: Bertrand Russell Peace Foundation, 1968), 14–16, 15.

45 Samuel Moyn, "From Antiwar Politics to Antitorture Politics," *Law and War*, eds. Austin Sarat, Lawrence Douglas, and Martha Umphrey (Stanford: Stanford University Press, 2014).

46 "Verdict of the Stockholm Session," *Against the Crime of Silence: Proceedings of the Russell International War Crimes Tribunal, Stockholm, Copenhagen*, ed. John Duffett, 302–309 (New York: Bertrand Russell Peace Foundation, 1968) (the verdict was handed down on May 10, 1967); "Summary and Verdict of the Second Session (Roskilde, Denmark)," *Against the Crime of Silence: Proceedings of the Russell International War Crimes Tribunal, Stockholm, Copenhagen*, ed. John Duffett, (New York: Bertrand Russell Peace Foundation, 1968), 643–650.

47 Ibid.

48 Klinghoffer and Klinghoffer, *International Citizens' Tribunals*, 115–117.

49 "Foreword by Ralph Schoenman," 7–8.

50 Anthony D'Amato, "Book Review: Against the Crime of Silence; On Genocide," *California Law Review* 57, no. 4 (1969): 1033–1038, 1035.

51 Women's International War Crimes Tribunal for the Trial of Japan's Military Sexual Slavery, Tokyo (December 8–12, 2000): see "Violence against Women in War – Network Japan," jca.apc.org, accessed February 4, 2014, http://www1.jca.apc.org/vaww-net-japan/english/.

52 *World Tribunal on Iraq: Making the Case against War*, ed. Müge Gürso'y So'kmen (Northampton, Massachusetts: Olive Branch Press, 2008).

53 Despite its inaccuracy, survivors have continued to use the term "comfort women" as it is in common usage.

54 Karen Knop, "The Tokyo Women's Tribunal and the Turn to Fiction," *Events: The Force of International Law*, eds. Fleur Johns, Richard Joyce, and Sundhya Pahuja (New York: Routledge, 2011), 145.

55 Christine M. Chinkin, "Women's International Tribunal on Japanese Military Sexual Slavery," *American Journal of International Law* 95, no. 2 (2001): 335–341, 338.

56 Three organizations that played key roles were the Korean Council for Women drafted into Military Sexual Slavery, ASCENT (Asia Centre for Women's Human Rights, based in the Philippines), and VAWW-Net Japan (Violence against Women in War Network, Japan). An International Organizing Committee took overall responsibility for research, investigations, drafting the Charter of the Tribunal, and preparing the hearing in Tokyo.

57 Ustinia Dolgopol, "The Judgment of the Tokyo Women's Tribunal," *Alternative Law Journal* 28, no. 5 (2003): 242–249, 243.

58 Samuel Moyn, "From Antiwar Politics to Antitorture Politics."

59 Ustinia Dolgopol, "The Judgment of the Tokyo Women's Tribunal," 243.

60 Prosecution teams from ten countries (including East Timor and Taiwan) presented indictments, which were joined into a common indictment by the two lead prosecutors, Patricia Viseur Sellers (former Legal Adviser for Gender-Related Crimes, to Office of the Prosecutor, International Criminal Tribunal for the Former Yugoslavia (ICTY)) and Ustinia Dolgopol (Senior Lecturer, Flinders Law School, South Australia).

61 Yayori Matsui, "Women's International War Crimes Tribunal on Japan's Military Sexual Slavery: Memory, Identity and Society," *East Asia: An International Quarterly* 19, no. 4 (2001): 119, 123–125.

62 Chinkin, "Women's International Tribunal," 338.

63 Alexis Dudden, "'We Came to Tell the Truth: Reflections on the Tokyo Women's Tribunal," *Critical Asian Studies* 33, no. 4 (2001): 591–602, 595.

64 Gabrielle Kirk McDonald (former president of the International Criminal Tribunal for the Former Yugoslavia (ICTY)), Carmen Mari Arguibay (president of the International Women's Association of Judges and former ad hoc judge at the ICTY), Christine Chinkin (Professor of International Law, London School of Economics), and Willy Mutunga (Professor of Law, University of Kenya, and president of NGO, Human Rights Commission of Kenya).

65 *The Prosecutors and the Peoples of the Asia-Pacific Region v. Hirohito et al; The Prosecutors and the Peoples of the Asia-Pacific Region v. Japan*, Summary of Findings and Preliminary Judgment (December 12, 2000), at para. 6. See Women's International War Crimes Tribunal, "Summary of Findings," koreanp.co.jp, accessed February 4, 2014, http://www1.korea-np.co.jp/pk/153th_issue/2000122304.htm.

66 *The Prosecutors and the Peoples of the Asia-Pacific Region* Summary of Findings and Preliminary Judgment, at para. 24.

67 Ibid., at paras. 27–30.

68 Ibid., at paras. 31–37.

69 Ibid., at para. 4.

70 The Women's International War Crimes Tribunal for the Trial of Japan's Military Sexual Slavery, *The Prosecutors and the Peoples of the Asia-Pacific Region v. Hirohito Emperor Showa et al. and the Government of Japan* (Judgment, Case

No. PT-2000-1-T, December 4, 2001), *internationalcrimesdatabase.org*, accessed February 4, 2014, www.internationalcrimesdatabase.org/Case/981.

71 Richard Falk, "Opening Speech on Behalf of the Panel of Advocates," *World Tribunal on Iraq: Making the Case against War*, ed. Müge Gürsöy Sökmen, 5–11 (Northampton, Massachusetts: Olive Branch Press, 2008).

72 Borowiak, "The World Tribunal on Iraq," 176.

73 Coordinating Committee for World Tribunal on Iraq, "World Tribunal on Iraq: Platform Text," Istanbul, October 29, 2003, 1–2 ("Origins of the Project"), accessed February 4, 2014 www.wagingpeace.org/articles/2003/10/29_iraq-tribunal_istanbul.pdf.

74 Borowiak, "The World Tribunal on Iraq," 176.

75 Jayan Nayar, "Empire's Law, Peoples' Law and the World Tribunal on Iraq," *Empire's Law: The American Imperial Project and the "War to Remake the World,"* ed. Amy Bartholomew, 313–339 (London and Ann Arbor: Pluto Press, 2006).

76 Coordinating Committee for World Tribunal on Iraq, "World Tribunal on Iraq: Platform Text".

77 Ibid.

78 Ibid.

79 Richard A. Falk, *The Costs of War: International Law, the UN, and World Order after Iraq* (New York: Routledge, 2008) 171 (emphasis added).

80 "List of WTI Sessions held Worldwide," *World Tribunal on Iraq: Making the Case against War*, ed. Müge Gürsöy Sökmen (Northampton, Massachusetts: Olive Branch Press, 2008) 512–514.

81 Müge Gürsöy Sökmen, "Preface," *World Tribunal on Iraq: Making the Case against War*, ed. Müge Gürsöy Sökmen, ix–xi (Northampton, Massachusetts: Olive Branch Press, 2008) x–xi.

82 They included Walden Bello (University of the Philippines), Christine Chinkin (London School of Economics), Ken Coates (Bertrand Russell Peace Foundation), Richard Falk (University of California, Santa Barbara), Johan Galtung (Universidad de Alicante, Spain), Ahmad Mohamed al-Jaradat (Palestinian peace activist), Corrine Kumar (World Courts of Women, India/Tunisia), Ömer Madra (Independent Radio, Turkey), Akira Maeda (Tokyo Zokei University), and Abdul Wahab al-Obeidi (Iraqi human rights activist).

83 Nermin al-Mufti, "The Occupation as Prison," *World Tribunal on Iraq: Making the Case against War*, ed. Müge Gürsöy Sökmen (Northampton, Massachusetts: Olive Branch Press, 2008), 302–307; Rana M. Mustafa, "Testimony on Falluja," *World Tribunal on Iraq: Making the Case against War*, ed. Müge Gürsöy Sökmen (Northampton, Massachusetts: Olive Branch Press, 2008), 314–316; Tim Goodrich (former US Air Force pilot), "The Conduct of the US Army," *World Tribunal on Iraq: Making the Case against War*, ed. Müge Gürsöy Sökmen (Northampton, Massachusetts: Olive Branch Press, 2008), 228–234.

84 "Biographies of the Jury of Conscience," *World Tribunal on Iraq: Making the Case against War*, ed. Müge Gürsöy Sökmen (Northampton, Massachusetts: Olive Branch Press, 2008), 559–562.

85 "Declaration of the Jury of Conscience," *World Tribunal on Iraq: Making the Case against War*, ed. Müge Gürsöy Sökmen (Northampton, Massachusetts: Olive Branch Press, 2008), 492–501.

86 Ibid., 494–497.
87 Ibid., 497–499.
88 Ibid., 500.
89 Matsui, "Women's International War Crimes Tribunal," 132–133; Dolgopol, "The Judgment of the Tokyo Women's Tribunal," 247.
90 See Karen Engle, "A Genealogy of the Criminal Law Turn in Human Rights", this volume [Chapter 1].
91 Ayça Çubuçu, "On Cosmopolitan Occupations: The Case of the World Tribunal on Iraq," *Interventions* 13, no. 3 (2011): 422–442, 434–35.
92 Nayar, "Empire's Law, Peoples' Law," 324.
93 Çubuçu, "On Cosmopolitan Occupations," 435.
94 Ibid.
95 Ibid., 437.
96 Borowiak, "The World Tribunal on Iraq,"178.
97 "Declaration of the Jury of Conscience, *Appendix I: International Law,*" Müge Gürsöy Sökmen, ed., *World Tribunal on Iraq: Making the Case against War* (Northampton, Massachusetts: Olive Branch Press, 2008), 502–509.
98 Sartre, "Inaugural Statement to the 1967 Russell Tribunal," 43.
99 See Dolgopol, "The Judgment of the Tokyo Women's Tribunal," 247.
100 Blaser, "How to Advance Human Rights without Really Trying," 365, argues that non-governmental human rights tribunals all contribute in some way to the creation of new legal norms.
101 Lelio and Lisli Basso Foundation, "Permanent Peoples' Tribunal Introduction," internazionaleleliobasso.it, accessed February 4, 2014, www.internazionaleleliobasso.it/?page_id=207&lang=en.
102 Unrepresented Nations and Peoples Organization, *Universal Declaration of the Rights of Peoples* (July 4, 1976), accessed February 4, 2014, www.unpo.org/article/105.
103 François Rigaux, "Postscript: The Genocide of the Armenians and the Permanent Peoples' Tribunal," *A Crime of Silence: The Armenian Genocide,* ed. Gerard J. Libaridian, 240–241. See also Janine Odink, "The Permanent Peoples' Tribunal," *Netherlands Quarterly of Human Rights* 11, no. 2 (1993): 229–232.
104 Nayar, "A People's Tribunal against the Crime of Silence?" 12 (emphasis original).
105 *Universal Declaration of the Rights of Peoples,* at preamble para. 3, arts. 1, 5, 10, and 14.
106 See, e.g., United Nations General Assembly, *Declaration on the Granting of Independence to Colonial Countries and Peoples* (A/RES/1514(XV), December 14, 1960), accessed February 4, 2014, www.un.org/en/ga/search/view_doc.asp?symbol=A/RES/1514(XV)&Lang=E&Area=RESOLUTION; United Nations General Assembly, *Declaration of the Right of Peoples to Peace,* annex (A/RES/39/11, November 12, 1984), accessed February 4, 2014, www.un.org/en/ga/search/view_doc.asp?symbol=A/RES/39/11&Lang=E&Area=RESOLUTION; United Nations General Assembly, *Declaration on the Right to Development,* annex (A/RES/41/128, December 4, 1986), accessed February 4, 2014, www.un.org/en/ga/search/view_doc.asp?symbol=A/RES/41/128&Lang=E&Area=RESOLUTION; United Nations General Assembly, *Declaration on the Rights of Indigenous Peoples,* annex

(A/RES/61/295, September 13, 2007), accessed February 4, 2014, www.un.org/en/ga/search/view_doc.asp?symbol=A/RES/61/295&Lang=E.

107 *African Charter on Human and Peoples' Rights,* opened for signature June 27, 1981, 1520 U.N.T.S. 217 (entered into force October 21, 1986).

108 Philip Alston, "Peoples' Rights: Their Rise and Fall," *Peoples' Rights,* ed. Philip Alston (Oxford: Oxford University Press, 2001), 259–293, 269.

109 Permanent Peoples' Tribunal, *Session on Western Sahara,* Brussels (November 10–11, 1979).

110 See, e.g., Permanent Peoples' Tribunal, *Session on the Role of the Soviet Military in Afghanistan,* Stockholm (May 1–3, 1981) and Paris (December 16–20, 1982); Permanent Peoples' Tribunal, *Session on Allegations of Genocide Committed by Turkey on the Armenian People,* Paris (April 13–16, 1984); Permanent Peoples' Tribunal, *Session on the US Intervention in Nicaragua,* Brussels (October 5–8, 1984); Permanent Peoples' Tribunal, *Session on Suppression of the Bangsa Moro People in the Philippines during the Marcos Regime,* Antwerp (October 30–November 3, 1980); Permanent Peoples' Tribunal, *Session on the use of force by Indonesia in East Timor,* Lisbon (June 19–21, 1981); Permanent Peoples' Tribunal, *Session on the Mobutu regime in Zaire,* Rotterdam (September 18–20, 1982).

111 See, e.g., Permanent Peoples' Tribunal, *Session on Industrial Hazards and Human Rights–Bhopal,* Bhopal (October 19–23, 1992), and London (November 28–December 2, 1994); Permanent Peoples' Tribunal, *Session on Chernobyl, Consequences for the Environment, Health and Human Rights,* Vienna (April 12–15, 1995).

112 Permanent Peoples' Tribunal, *Session on Multinationals and Human "Wrongs,"* Warwick (March 22–23, 2000); Permanent Peoples' Tribunal, *Session on Agrochemical Transnational Corporations,* Bangalore (December 3–6, 2011).

113 Odink, "The Permanent Peoples' Tribunal," 231.

114 Borowiak, "The World Tribunal on Iraq," 174.

115 Odink, "The Permanent Peoples' Tribunal," 230–231.

116 Diana E.H. Russell and Nicole Van de Ven, *Crimes against Women. Proceedings of the International Tribunal* (California: Les Femmes, 1976) 218–219.

117 Ibid.

118 Ibid., 230.

119 Ibid., xiii.

120 Ibid., 240.

121 Ibid.

122 Ibid., 219.

123 Ibid. (emphasis in original)

124 Ibid., 240.

125 Ibid., 220.

126 Ibid., 249–51.

127 Ibid., 267.

128 Ibid., 268.

129 Ibid., 284–294.

130 The Women's Economic Agenda Project, "The History and Present of the World Courts of Women," *weap.org,* accessed February 4, 2014, http://weap.org/WCW/WCWAbout.htm.

131 Feminist activists Corinne Kumar (India) and Nelia Sanchez (Philippines) cofounded the Asian Women's Human Rights Council in 1989 and, in 1990, Kumar became Secretary General of El Taller, an NGO based in Tunis: see "Eltaller," eltaller.in, accessed February 4, 2014, www.eltaller.in.

132 See generally, El Taller International, "Courts of Women," eltaller.in, accessed February 4, 2014, www.eltaller.in.

133 Waller, "The Courts of Women."

134 The Lahore Tribunal on Violence against Women, Pakistan (December 29, 1993–January 7, 1994); See Simorgh Women's Collective and Asian Women's Human Rights Council, *In the Court of Women: The Lahore Tribunal on Violence against Women, 1993–94* (Lahore: Simorgh Women's Resource and Publication Centre, 1995); The Court of Women on Women against Violence, Huairou, Beijing (September 1995); The Mediterranean Forum on Violence against Women, Casablanca (November 1999); The African Court of Women: Lives, Livelihoods, Lifeworlds, Africa Social Forum, Lusaka (December 2004).

135 The Court of Women on Crimes against Women related to the Violence of Development, Bangalore (January 1995). See *Speaking Tree, Womenspeak: Asia-Pacific Public Hearing on Crimes against Women related to the Violence of Development* (Bangalore: Asian Women's Human Rights Council and Vimochana, 1995).

136 Asia-Pacific Public Hearing on Crimes against Women related to Population Policies, Cairo (September 1994).

137 Nga Wahine Pacifika: The Pacific Court of Women on Uranium Mining, Nuclear Testing and the Land, Auckland (September 1999).

138 The World Court of Women against War, for Peace, Cape Town (March 2–9, 2001). See Corinne Kumar, "The World Court of Women against War, For Peace," archive.is, accessed February 4, 2014, http://archive.is/BKz8B; The World Court of Women on US War Crimes, World Social Forum, Mumbai (January 18, 2004). See Asian Women's Human Rights Council and El Taller International, "World Court of Women on US War Crimes," *iraktribunal.de*, accessed February 4, 2014, www.iraktribunal.de/internat/wcw_mumbai_final.htm.

139 The World Court of Women against Racism, Durban (August 30, 2001). See Human Rights Education Associates, "World Court of Women against Racism," hrea.org, accessed February 4, 2014, www.hrea.org/lists/wcar/markup/msg00028.html.

140 The International Court of Women against Neoliberal Policies in Latin America, Havana (2005).

141 The African Court of Women on Poverty, World Social Forum, New York (January 22, 2007); The World Courts of Women on Poverty in the US, Oakland, California (May 10–13, 2012), Philadelphia (October 2013), Louisville Kentucky, and Detroit (still to be held). See "World Courts of Women on Poverty in the US," worldcourtsofwomen.wordpress.com, accessed February 4, 2014, http://worldcourtsofwomen.wordpress.com/.

142 *Daughters of Fire*: Indian Court of Women on Dowry and Related Forms of Violence against Women, Bangalore (July 27–29, 2009).

143 El Taller International, "Courts of Women."

144 For example, the World Court of Women against War, for Peace included an exhibition entitled "Testimony through Art," which included quilts and tapestries, paintings, photographs, drawings, poetry, and narratives from thirty-five countries; an art installation called "Lines of Violation" using images of the hands of "comfort women"; and their voices. The preparatory process included "Caravans of Women" which traveled to different countries and regions in order to connect with local issues and ongoing campaigns relating to war, conflict, and violence.

145 The Court of Women on Crimes against Dalit Women, Bangalore (March 1994).

146 Jenny Castillo, "US Courts of Women on Poverty, Western Region – The Contours of a New Political Imaginary," http://weap.org, accessed February 4, 2014, http://weap.org/WCW/wcw-summary.htm.

147 El Taller International, "Courts of Women."

148 See, e.g., The Women's Economic Agenda Project, "The Vision, AWHRC and El Taller International, The Courts of Women," weap.org, February 4, 2014, http://weap.org/WCW/wcw-achived-pages/WCWAbout/the-vision-awhrc-and-el-taller.

149 Ibid.

150 The World Court of Women against War, For Peace, Session 5; The African Court of Women: Lives, Livelihoods, Lifeworlds, Session 3.

151 The World Court of Women on Crimes against Women, Beijing, Session 3

152 The World Court of Women on US War Crimes, Session V.

153 Mediterranean Forum on Violence against Women, Session 5.

154 Waller, "The Courts of Women."

155 "Shaharazad: Stories for Life," www.shahrazadeu.org/, accessed February 4, 2014. Tribunal 12 was organized by Shaharazad in collaboration with the Swedish Forum for Human Rights and Kulturhuset (Stockholm's cultural centre).

156 Tribunal 12, "Report from Tribunal 12."

157 Sara Dehm, "Judging 'Europe': Articulations of Migrant Justice and a Popular International Law?" Paper presented at the *Expert Seminar on Peoples' Tribunals and International Law*, Rome (September 27–28, 2013).

158 Ibid.

159 Tribunal 12, "Report from Tribunal 12," 2–5.

160 Dehm, "Judging 'Europe,'" 15.

161 The seven-member jury included one international lawyer, B.S. Chimni, Professor and Chair of the Centre for Legal Studies at Jawaharlal Nehru University, Delhi.

162 Dehm, "Judging 'Europe,'" 5–6.

163 Ibid.

164 Tribunal 12, "Report from Tribunal 12."

165 Dehm, "Judging 'Europe,'" 3.

166 El Taller International, "Courts of Women."

167 "Concept Note," Asia-Pacific Regional Women's Hearing on Gender-Based Violence in Conflict, in *Material Package for International Guests* 31–32 Cambodian Defenders Project, 2012).

168 *Closing Order*, Case File No. 002/19-09-2007-ECCC-OCIJ, para. 1429 (Extra-ordinary Chambers in the Courts of Cambodia, 2011) Further, the co-investigative judges found that "rape did not exist as a crime against humanity in its own right

in 1975–1979," Decision on Appeals by Nuon Chea and Ieng Thirith against the Closing Order 11.2, February 15, 2011. Therefore, in relation to rapes that occurred in the context of forced marriage, the former Khmer Rouge leaders were charged with sexual violence as other inhumane acts as crimes against humanity. Thanks to Melbourne Law School PhD candidate Maria Elander for explaining this point to me.

169 Young, *Responsibility for Justice*, 97–104.
170 Ibid., 75–93.
171 Ibid., 92.
172 Ibid., 105.
173 Ibid.
174 Ibid., 144.
175 Ibid., 144–151.
176 de Langis, *Women's Hearing Report*, 8.
177 Quote from my own notes, taken during the hearing.
178 Silke Studzinsky, International Counsel for Civil Parties before the ECCC and German lawyer.
179 Susana SáCouto, Professor and Director of the War Crimes Research Office, American University Washington College of Law.
180 de Langis, *Women's Hearing Report*, 9.
181 Ibid., 11–12.
182 Sourced from my own notes, taken during the hearing.
183 A psychosocial support team of seven psychologists provided support to testifiers and audience members throughout the Hearing, organized by the Transcultural Psychosocial Organization Cambodia (TPO), one of the convening non-governmental organizations.
184 Wendy Brown, "Suffering Rights as Paradoxes," *Constellations* 7 (2000): 230–241.
185 Karl Marx, "On the Jewish Question," *Selected Writings*, ed. Lawrence H. Simon, trans. Lloyd D. Easton and Kurt H. Guddat (Indianapolis: Hackett, 1994), 1–26.
186 Susan Sontag, *Regarding the Pain of Others* (Great Britain: Penguin, 2004).

10

Beyond Nuremberg: The Historical Significance of the Post-Apartheid Transition in South Africa

Mahmood Mamdani[*]

A dominant tendency in the contemporary human rights movement holds up Nuremberg as a template with which to define responsibility for mass violence. This same tendency tends to narrow the meaning of justice to criminal justice, thereby individualizing the notion of justice in neo-liberal fashion.

As it moved away from a call for structural reform to accent individual criminal responsibility, the human rights movement came to ideologize Nuremberg. There is no consensus on the timing of this move: some date it to the late 1970s with the crisis of nationalism, others to the 1990s with the end of the Cold War. More recently, this same movement has tended to exceptionalize the South African transition from apartheid by center-staging the process known as "truth and reconciliation" and sidelining the political process that led to the larger agreement of which the decision to constitute a Truth and Reconciliation Commission (TRC) was but one part. I suggest a critical appreciation of the post-apartheid transition in South Africa, one that focuses on the political process known as Convention for a Democratic South Africa (CODESA), both to rethink the centrality of and to suggest a move beyond the logic of Nuremberg.

The human rights movement that gathered steam in the late 1970s anchored itself ideologically in the lessons of the Holocaust and presented itself as a post-Nuremberg movement. What connected this movement of the 1970s and beyond to Nuremberg was less historical chronology than its apolitical thrust. Samuel Moyn has argued that human rights were "born as an alternative to grand political mission," as "a moral criticism of politics."[1] In this essay, I seek to connect the moral and the political, the ethical and the historical, through a discussion of two responses to crimes against humanity: the criminal trials

* This chapter was first published in *Politics & Society*, 43(1) 61–88 (2015).

known as Nuremberg; and CODESA, the political talks that led to the end
of apartheid.

The contemporary human rights movement anchors itself ideologically in
the lessons of defeat, not of revolution – the lessons of the Nazi Holocaust, not
of the French Revolution.[2] Whereas the movement organized around the revolutionary banner – Rights of Man – was highly political, the contemporary
human rights movement is consciously antipolitical, which is the meaning
it gives to the notion of "human" and "humanitarian." Nuremberg is said
to redefine the problem and the solution. The problem is extreme violence
– radical evil – and the question it poses is responsibility for the violence. The
solution encapsulated as "lessons of Nuremberg" is to think of violence as
criminal, and of responsibility for it as individual – state orders cannot absolve
officials of individual responsibility. Above all, this responsibility is said to be
ethical, not political.

Could one argue that the lesson of the transition from apartheid is the
opposite? Should extreme violence be thought of more as political than criminal? I was part of the audience one gray morning in Cape Town when the
TRC questioned F.W. de Klerk. De Klerk had read out a statement enu-
merating the wrongs of apartheid and concluded by taking responsibility for
apartheid. But the TRC was not interested. Its interest was narrowly focused
on specific human rights violations such as murder, torture, and kidnapping:
did de Klerk know of these? Had he authorized any of these? It was striking
how different this was from what we know of Nuremberg. At Nuremberg, the
greatest responsibility lay with those in positions of power, those who had
planned and strategized, not those with boots on the ground. At the TRC, the
responsibility lay with the one who pulled the trigger. The greatest responsibility seemed to lie with the one closest to the scene of the crime. *Why was
the leadership of apartheid not held responsible for it?* The answer is political,
not ethical.

The negotiations that ended apartheid provide raw material for a critique of
universalist claims made by the current human rights movement. To reflect
on the lessons of apartheid, we need to begin with two questions: How shall
we think of extreme violence, of mass violence – as criminal or political? And
how shall we define responsibility for large-scale violence – as criminal or
political? I suggest that the present rush for courtroom solutions advocated by
the human rights community is the result of a double failure: analytical and
political. Analytically, it confuses political with criminal violence. Politically,
the focus on perpetrators is at the expense of a focus on the issues that drive
the violence. As such, it is likely to magnify rather than mitigate violence in
the public sphere.

What distinguishes political from criminal violence? The key distinction is *qualitative*.[3] Political violence requires more than just criminal agency; it needs a political constituency. More than just perpetrators, it needs supporters. That constituency, in turn, is held together and mobilized by an issue. More than criminal violence, political violence is issue driven.

For a start, I suggest two ways of thinking of political violence, one born in the aftermath of the Holocaust and the other in the aftermath of apartheid, two great crimes against humanity. We tend to identify the first with Nuremberg and the latter with the TRC and think of the TRC as a departure from Nuremberg, as displacing punishment with forgiveness. Not crime and punishment, but crime and forgiveness. I suggest that this is a mistake for a number of reasons. To begin with, the TRC was less an alternative to Nuremberg than an attempt at a surrogate Nuremberg. It shared a critical premise with Nuremberg, the assumption that all violence is criminal and responsibility for it is individual. It is not the TRC but CODESA that provides the real alternative to Nuremberg. It is CODESA that signifies the larger political project that chartered the terms that ended legal and political apartheid and provided the constitutional foundation to forge a post-apartheid political order. The TRC followed from CODESA, and not the other way around. Nuremberg and CODESA have radically different implications for how we think of human wrongs, and thus of human rights. Whereas Nuremberg shaped a notion of justice as criminal justice, CODESA calls on us to think of justice primarily as political justice. Whereas Nuremberg has become the basis of a notion of *victims' justice* – as a complement rather than an alternative to *victors' justice* – CODESA provides the basis for an alternative notion of justice, which I call *survivors' justice*.[4]

I. NUREMBERG

Nuremberg was one of two tribunals at the conclusion of World War II. The second was the Tokyo tribunal. Nuremberg was an innovation for at least three reasons. The judges at Nuremberg rejected the claim that individual officials were not responsible for an "act of state." Nuremberg established the principle of *individual* responsibility for the violation of human rights. The judges at Nuremberg also established *criminal* responsibility for these crimes. Finally, Nuremberg stood for a universalism whereby "the international community" would "be able to reach back through the boundaries of state sovereignty to protect individuals or impose norms," thereby holding these individuals directly accountable to "the international community."[5] The "international community," as Elizabeth Borgwardt noted, was a euphemism for "a group of 'civilized nations,' to which otherwise sovereign polities were ultimately answerable."[6]

Nuremberg was born of a debate among victorious powers on how they should deal with defeated Nazis.[7] Winston Churchill argued that "Hitler and his gang had forfeited any right to legal procedure" and so should be summarily shot. Henry Morgenthau, Jr., US Secretary of the Treasury and a close friend of Franklin D. Roosevelt agreed. Morgenthau went further and called for a destruction of German industry so Germany would never again rise as a power. Henry Stimson, Roosevelt's Secretary of War, led the opposition. Stimson wanted a trial, not just a show trial, but a trial with due process.[8] In a speech that is said to have persuaded Truman to appoint him the Chief Prosecutor at Nuremberg, Robert Jackson had argued only three weeks before his appointment: "You must put no man on trial under forms of a judicial proceeding if you are not willing to see him freed if not proven guilty ... the world yields no respect for courts that are organized merely to convict."[9]

Even if based on due process, Nuremberg needs to be understood as symbolic and performative. For a start, only the losers were put on trial. The victors appointed not only the prosecutor, but the judges too. For their part, the accused preferred to be tried by the United States rather than by anyone else. They expected a fairer trial from Americans who, unlike the victims – Jews, Russians, French, British – had the privilege of pavilion seats during the war. They also expected softer treatment from the Americans, who were most likely to be German allies in the brewing Cold War. For official America, Nuremberg was an excellent opportunity to inaugurate the new world order by showcasing a performance of how a civilized liberal state conducts itself. At a time when the air was full of cries for revenge, Robert Jackson told the audience at Church House in London: "A fair trial for every defendant. A competent attorney for every defendant."[10]

Nuremberg combined elements of both victors' justice and victims' justice. Victors' justice followed from the outcome of the war: victorious powers established a rule of law under which alleged perpetrators were tried. The notion that justice would follow victory was not new. It followed a long established tradition of how we think of justice in the aftermath of victory, be that victory the result of war between states or revolution between classes or a civil war of a different type. In every case, the assumption is that once the conflict has ended, there is a clear victor under whose power justice can be administered. This overall frame marks Nuremberg as a model for victors' justice.[11]

The accused at Nuremberg were charged with four crimes: (1) Conspiracy to wage aggressive war; (2) Waging aggressive war counts (1) and (2) were together called Crimes against Peace); (3) War crimes (violations of the laws and customs of war, such as mistreatment of prisoners of war and abuse of enemy civilians); (4) Crimes against humanity (including the torture and slaughter of millions on racial grounds).[12] Striking about this list is the fact that conspiracy to wage war and its actual waging were defined as the principal crimes ((1) and (2)), whereas genocide and mass slaughter came last in this series of four crimes.

The Allies were divided on this order. The French disagreed that waging war was a crime in law; it is what states did.[13] At the Tokyo trial, which took twice as long, partly because of long and substantial dissenting opinions, Justice Radhabinod Pal of India argued that the charge of crime against peace (both (1) and (2)) was a case of *ex post facto* legislation which "served only to protect an unjust international order, if there were no other workable provisions for peaceful adjustment of the status quo."[14] Much later, in 1992, Telford Taylor, who had replaced Jackson as the Chief Prosecutor in the twelve remaining US-conducted trials in Germany, and who then had a distinguished career as professor of law at Columbia Law School, conceded that the court's judgment on counts (1) and (2) did indeed rely on *ex post facto* law.[15]

An even more serious problem arose from the fact that the victors' court was not likely to put the victors on trial. Would not Truman's order to fire-bomb Tokyo and to drop atom bombs on Hiroshima and Nagasaki, leading to untold civilian deaths at a time when the war was already ending, qualify as "gratuitous human suffering" and a "crime against humanity," to use the language of the court? Had not Winston Churchill committed a "crime against humanity" when he ordered the bombing of residential, working-class sections of German cities, particularly Dresden, in the last months of the war? Most agreed that the British policy of terror bombing of civilian areas killed some 300,000 and seriously injured another 780,000 German civilians.[16]

Nuremberg is also identified with victims' justice, often thought of as an alternative to victors' justice, but in fact a complement to it. One of the charges against the accused was that they had committed "crimes against humanity." The charge was first formulated in 1890 by George Washington Williams, a historian, a Baptist minister, a lawyer, and the first black member of the Ohio state legislature, in a letter to the US Secretary of State in which he documented atrocities committed by King Leopold's colonial regime in Congo, concluding that this was a "crime against humanity."[17] I have already pointed out that crime against humanity was last of the four charges against the accused at Nuremberg. As the trial proceeded, the emphasis on victims' justice began to diminish. The reason was political: as the Cold War developed, US policy toward Germany moved from a demand for justice to a call for accenting accommodation over punishment. The effect was most evident in the trial of Alfried Krupp, the leading German industrial magnate. The Krupp family had been manufacturers of steel since the early nineteenth century, and Europe's leading manufacturers and suppliers of guns and munitions by World War I. They had armed Germany in three major wars. During World War II, Krupp managed 138 concentration camps. Ranged throughout Europe, all were privately owned by Krupp. Alfried Krupp used slave labor from the camps and prisoners of war to build his factories, and provided Hitler's wars with money and weapons, as a combination of investment and commitment. One of those charged at Nuremberg, Krupp was released in 1951, his fortune restored.[18] There was little justice for victims at Nuremberg. When it came, it was political and it was obtained outside the court.

To understand the particular form that victims' justice took, we need to appreciate the political context that framed Nuremberg. Nuremberg functioned as part of a larger political logic shared by the victorious Allied powers. This was that winners and losers, victims and perpetrators, must be physically separated into different political communities. As they redrew boundaries and transferred millions across borders, Allied Powers carried out or sanctioned the most extreme ethnic cleansing in modern history. By 1950, between 12 and 14 million Germans had fled or were expelled from east-central Europe. Historians consider this the largest forcible movement of any population in modern European history. This, in turn, was part of a larger forced transfer of populations from Central and Eastern Europe, estimated at more than 20 million. German federal agencies and the German Red Cross estimate that between 2 and 2.5 million civilians died in the course of expulsions. Some writers have described this forced movement of populations as "population transfer," others as "ethnic cleansing," and yet others as "genocide."[19]

The possibility of victims' justice flowed from the assumption that there would be no need for winners and losers to live together after victory. Perpetrators would remain in Germany and victims would depart for another homeland. Yesterday's perpetrators and victims will not have to live together, for there would be a separate state – Israel – for survivors. The process culminated in the period after Nuremberg with the creation of the State of Israel, seen as a state for victims. Indeed, post-Holocaust language reserves the identity "survivors" only for yesterday's victims. As in Israel, this is also the case in contemporary Rwanda. In both cases, the state governs in the name of victims.

II. THE TRANSITION FROM APARTHEID

The post-apartheid transition in South Africa is popularly identified with the work of the Truth and Reconciliation Commission (TRC). This work is presumed to have been guided by the dictum that perpetrators are forgiven past crimes in return for acknowledging the past (truth). It is said that the TRC created a new precedent: immunity from prosecution (some may say, impunity) in return for acknowledging the truth: forgiveness in return for an honest confession. In a few words: Forgive, but not forget. This claim is central to the contemporary ideologization of the TRC.

I shall discuss the TRC in greater detail in a later section, but it should suffice to point out the problem with this widely accepted notion: it is not quite true. Key to the post-apartheid transition was not an exchange of amnesty for truth, but amnesty for the willingness to reform. That reform was the dismantling of juridical and political apartheid. The real breakthrough represented by the South African case is not contained in the TRC but in the talks that preceded it, CODESA, which have so far been dismissed as nothing but hard-nosed pragmatism.

The ground for CODESA was prepared by a double acknowledgment by both sides of the conflict. To begin with, both recognized that there was little prospect of ending the conflict in the short run. For farsighted leaders, this was equivalent to a recognition that their preferred option was no longer within reach: neither revolution (for liberation movements) nor military victory (for the apartheid regime) were on the cards. If South Africa is a model for solving intractable conflicts, it is an argument for moving from the best to the second-best alternative. That second–best alternative was political reform. The quest for reform, for an alternative short of victory, led to the realization that if you threaten to put the leadership from either side in the dock they will have no interest in reform. This change in perspective led to a shift away from criminalizing or demonizing the other side to treating it as a political adversary. Its consequence was to displace the paradigm of criminal justice identified with Nuremberg.

I suggest that we think of CODESA less as an alternative to Nuremberg than as a response to a different set of circumstances. As such, it is also a statement that Nuremberg cannot be turned into a universally applicable formula. CODESA was born of the realization that the conditions that obtained in apartheid South Africa were different from those that led to Nuremberg. The difference was twofold. First, whereas Nuremberg followed a military victory, the conflict in South Africa had not ended. How do you stop a conflict that has not ended? How do you convince adversaries that it is in their interest to stop an ongoing conflict? Surely, this could not be done by prioritizing criminal justice and threatening to take the political leadership on either side – the apartheid state or the anti-apartheid movement – to court, because the people you would want to take to court are the very people you would need to stop the conflict. Second, whereas Nuremberg was informed by a larger logic that drove the postwar settlement, that of ethnic cleansing, one that called for a physical separation of yesterday's victims and yesterday's perpetrators into separate political communities, in South Africa there was no question of creating an Israel for victims of apartheid.[20] Instead, it was clear that victims and perpetrators, blacks and whites, would have to live in the same country.

Rather than put justice in the back seat, CODESA presents us with a radically new way of thinking about justice. It presents a double breakthrough. To begin with, CODESA distinguished between different forms of justice – criminal, political, and social. It prioritized political justice, the reform of the political system, over the other two. The difference between political and criminal justice is twofold. One, political justice affects groups, whereas criminal justice targets individuals. Two, the object of criminal justice is punishment; that of political justice is political reform. A shift of logic from the criminal to the political led to decriminalizing and legitimizing both sides to the conflict. The liberation movements – the African National Congress (ANC), the Pan Africanist Congress (PAC), and the Communist Party – were all unbanned. The apartheid regime, the National Party, and the highly secretive underground network known as the Broederbond, also ceased to be treated as pariahs by anti-apartheid activists. In decriminalizing and legitimizing opponents, CODESA turned enemies into political adversaries. In the process, CODESA also moved the goalposts. The goal was no longer the internment and punishment of individuals charged with so many crimes, but a change of rules that would bring them and their constituencies into a reformed political community. CODESA's achievement was to bring adversaries to agree on a political reform that dismantled legal and political apartheid and redefined an inclusive citizenship.

The full impact of this change in perspective was no less than a shift of paradigmatic significance. Whereas Nuremberg was backward-looking, preoccupied with justice as punishment, CODESA sought a balance between the past and the future, between redress for the past and reconciliation for the future. The paradigm shifted from one of victims' justice to that of survivors' justice – where the meaning of survivors changed to include all those who had survived apartheid: yesterday's victims, yesterday's perpetrators, and yesterday's beneficiaries (presumed to be bystanders), all were treated as "survivors."

III. CODESA

The political reform defined the challenge faced by the negotiators at CODESA: to forge a transition from a white minority regime to a government elected by an enfranchised population. As an interim measure, the parties to the negotiation agreed to lay down a set of Constitutional Principles that would define the parameters of the Interim Constitution. The Declaration of Intent stated: "South Africa will be a united, democratic, non-racial and non-sexist state in which sovereign authority is exercised over the whole of its territory."[21] The Declaration notwithstanding, the negotiations at CODESA were testimony to so much horse-trading, with each side strengthening its negotiating hand using a variety of means, including violence, outside the negotiating chambers.

CODESA assembled in December 1991 and broke up in May 1992. During that period, each side tried to muster a consensus and, failing that, a clear majority within its ranks. In the tussle of political wills that ensued, both sides employed an array of resources, from mass mobilization to targeted violence. When the ultra-right white Conservative Party won a by-election in Potchestrom after the start of CODESA, the National Party government called for a whites-only referendum in March 1992. The government interpreted that victory as a mandate from the white population to continue to negotiate a political end to apartheid. The ANC responded to the whites-only referendum with "rolling mass action" in May and a mass stayaway on June 12, which turned out to be a massive withholding of labor. Both mobilized in the face of political violence and the threat of more. Thus, when police responded to the June 12 stayaway with the massacre at Bapoteng, the Congress of South African Trade Unions (COSATU) led yet another stayaway on August 3, and the ANC organized a march on Ciskei on September 7.

Sporadic violence triggered heightened mobilization, in turn underlining the urgency of further negotiations. The two sides came together to draft a Record of Understanding on September 26, 1992. The agreement stipulated that a democratically elected assembly would draft the final constitution within a fixed time frame and within the framework of constitutional principles agreed upon by a meeting of negotiators appointed by all parties; but in reality, it was driven by the principals: the National Party and the ANC.

The ANC cleared the ground for agreement with historic concessions, famously known as the "sunset clauses." Floated by the General Secretary of the Communist Party, Joe Slovo, in an article in the party journal, *The African Communist*, these undoubtedly represented a consensus position shared by the leadership of both the South African Communist Party and the ANC. The sunset clauses called for power-sharing between the two sides, retention of the old bureaucracy (and presumably other organs of the state: police, military, and the intelligence services) and, finally, a general amnesty in return for full disclosure. The different elements that comprised the sunset clauses – such as the introduction of a political democracy but a retention of all other structures of the apartheid state, and an amnesty in return for full disclosure – had been in the air for some time, but this was the first time they were presented as parts of a single package.[22]

Much has been written on the amnesty component of the proposal that came to inform the work of the TRC. In a brilliant study on the genealogy of the TRC, Adam Sitze has argued for the need to locate both the idea and the provisions of amnesty in the colonial history of South Africa, in particular the practice of granting state indemnity following periods of martial law and brutal suppression of popular protest. Sitze offers this approach as an explicit alternative to the approach that has come to be favored by the transitional justice industry, connecting the establishment of the TRC with influences ranging from Nuremberg-style prosecutions to Latin American-style blanket amnesties. Instead, Sitze calls for locating both the TRC and prior state-sponsored indemnities in the larger history of anticolonial protest and colonial repression.[23]

Following the Sharpeville Massacre of 1960 and the suppression of the Soweto Uprising of 1976, the South African parliament "passed extremely wide indemnity acts that protected not only South African police officers but also a large number of state officials from prosecution for the civil and criminal wrongs they inflicted" during these times. As a result, "SADF members were already indemnified in advance for any illegal acts they might commit in honest and good faith service to the public good." This already existing protection from prosecution was "widened even more by the indemnity acts passed by the South African Parliament in 1990 and 1992." Even though the Sharpeville Massacre and the Soweto Uprising "fell within the TRC's juridical and investigative mandate," Sitze argues that "the indemnity provisions of the [1957] Defence Act, in combination with the specific indemnity acts passed in 1961 and 1977, decreased or even nullified the power of the TRC's 'carrots and sticks' approach." To put it bluntly, "it is unclear why any state official, member of the SADF or officer of the South African Police would feel obliged to run the risk of trading truth for amnesty when he or she was already expressly protected from prosecution by prior indemnity legislation."[24] Indeed, "the South African Defence Force chose to coordinate its contributions to the Truth and Reconciliation Commission by way of a centralized 'Nodal Point,' a single point, suggesting a clenched sphincter, through which all information is meant to pass."[25]

My purpose here is not to trace the genealogy of the legislation that set up the TRC, but to underline its political prerequisite: the simple fact was that the establishment of the TRC was not an independent development but followed the political agreement arrived at CODESA. Joe Slovo did not need to state what was clear to one and all: that the real *quid pro quo* for the sunset clauses was the dismantling of juridical and political apartheid and the introduction of electoral reforms that would enfranchise the majority and pave the way for majority rule. An acceptance of the sunset clauses would mean that South Africa would not have its own version of Nuremberg.

The Multi-Party Negotiating Process began on March 5 at Kempton Park, but it was sluggish.[26] It took another political crisis to generate momentum. That crisis was the assassination of Chris Hani on April 10, 1993. The parties agreed on June 1 that elections would be held ten months later, on April 27, 1994. The shared sense that storm clouds were indeed gathering on the horizon made it possible to truncate discussions, especially on fundamentals such as the "constitutional principles" and the constitution itself. Power was ceded to technical committees (with further technical assistance from the Harvard Negotiation Project), in the name of preventing and breaking deadlocks in the negotiations. Agreement was driven forward by a procedure known as "sufficient consensus." It allowed the two principals, the ANC and the National Party, to meet outside the formal discussion and define agreement on key issues. There was also agreement that the process that led to the drafting of Namibia's 1982 Constitutional Principles and that gave the Interim Constitution a weight more enduring than that of an interim political agreement be duplicated in South Africa. The combination of binding principles agreed upon by unelected negotiators and the adjudicating power of the Constitutional Court, which was given powers to throw out a constitution drafted by an elected assembly, was acknowledged by many as a blatant curb on majority rule; but, at the same time, it was seen as necessary to attaining that same majority rule.

The Constitutional Principles included a number of key provisions.[27] The central provision was the inclusion of a Bill of Rights as part of a set of constitutional checks and balances. The Bill of Rights included protection of private property as a fundamental human right. At the same time, and without a stated rationale, the clause providing the restoration of land to the majority population was placed outside the Bill of Rights. Where property rights clashed, as in the case of white settlers and black natives, the former received Constitutional protection, the latter no more than a formal acknowledgment in law.[28]

This disparity was reinforced at the local level, through the coming together of two political forces that found common ground in the negotiations: white settlers and Native Authorities in Bantustans. For the Native Authorities, there was Act 3 of 1994, which gave constitutional recognition to the Zulu monarchy, and Schedule 6, which recognized "indigenous and customary law." For the settlers, the prize was the passage of the Local Government Transition Act of 1993. The Act entrenched consociational government at the local level – in contrast to the national and provincial levels. Local government elections were structured in such a way that they precluded black voters from obtaining two-thirds majority on a local government council. The operative principle was known as the "ward limitation system." Section 245(3) stipulated that only 40 percent of seats on a council be elected by proportional representation. The remaining 60 percent would be elected from ward-based constituencies with the proviso that no more than half the seats be drawn from historically black areas. This provision guaranteed non-blacks 30 percent of the seats. Section 176(a) required a local authority to muster a two-thirds majority to pass its budget. Furthermore, Section 177 required that the executive committee of a local government be composed in proportion to party representation on the local government council; even more, it stipulated that all decisions be made by consensus. Where consensus could not be reached, a two-thirds majority was required for executive committee decisions. The combined effect of these provisions was that local authorities in former white areas could not make any significant decision without the agreement of councilors representing its white residents.

Two further measures had the effect of entrenching – not just protecting – white privilege in small towns. When it came to establishing a transitional (town) council in the pre-interim phase, a negotiating forum had to get 80 percent support from its delegates. Because it controlled most of the (white) local government councils in the Transvaal and thus the Transvaal Municipal Association, consensus decision-making processes fit in with the agenda of the white supremacist Conservative Party. The requirement for consensus-based decision-making had the effect of vesting elected representatives of white residents with an effective veto over local government decisions.[29]

The second measure concerned powers of taxation, putting practically insurmountable legal obstacles in the way of any popular project to redistribute income through taxation. Clause 17 required that local government taxes and levies had to be based on a uniform structure for its area of jurisdiction. This prevented new local governments from taxing white areas so they could spend more revenue in black areas. Thus did CODESA entrench white privilege, both in the constitution and in the law that established the framework for local government.

IV. THE TRC

There are two debates in South Africa today. The first focuses on the perpetrator, and thus on criminal justice. The second focuses on the beneficiary,

and thus on social justice. Whereas there is hardly a popular demand in contemporary South Africa calling for perpetrators of apartheid to be tried and
punished, it is the debate around social justice that more and more drives
the critique of the post-apartheid transition, in particular the downplaying
of social justice in the agreements concluded at CODESA. I have a mixed
response to this critique. The demand that the end of apartheid should have
delivered social justice ignores the political reality that defined the context
in which CODESA was negotiated. The political prerequisite for attaining
social justice would have been a social revolution, but there was no revolution
in South Africa. If apartheid was not defeated, neither was it victorious. The
most one can say is that there was a stalemate. Even if social justice could not
have been part of the package negotiated at CODESA, it is not unreasonable
to expect that it would have figured prominently on the agenda for a post-
apartheid South Africa. Instead, a lid was put on both legislative endeavors
for social justice and narrative attempts to underline its necessity. We have
already seen that the constitution negotiated at CODESA defended the integrity of property accumulated during the apartheid era as part of a constitutionally sanctified Bill of Rights. At the same time, the semi-official narrative
crafted by the TRC described apartheid not as a system in which a racialized
power disenfranchised and dispossessed a racialized majority, but as a set of
human rights violations of a minority of individual victims carried out by an
even smaller minority of individual perpetrators.

Did the beneficiaries of apartheid win at the negotiating table what its
authors and perpetrators could not win on the battlefield? If so, what set
of political conditions made this possible? The main condition was to play
off two wings of the anti-apartheid movement, reinforcing the leadership
of the external wing and sidelining the internal wing. The anti-apartheid
camp comprised two very different kinds of force: on the one hand, exiled
"liberation movements," principally the ANC, whose scanty presence on the
ground contrasted with its enormous popular prestige; and, on the other, an
internally organized anti-apartheid resistance that knit together dozens of
community and shop-floor level organizations into a single archetypal network, called the United Democratic Front (UDF), which was responsible
for the stalemate in which apartheid found itself. The "sufficient consensus"
crafted by the ANC and the National Party stretched and strained the relation between the exile and the internal wings of the anti-apartheid opposition. In marginalizing the forces identified with the internal opposition, the
sufficient consensus also sidelined the agenda for social justice. This is, however, not the place to elaborate on this political outcome. My purpose here
is to focus on the double closure – constitutional and narrative – that was

the result of the political alliance between reform forces within the ruling National Party and the ANC-based exile wing, the alliance that ushered in the post-apartheid transition.

The basic elements of the new constitution were crafted in CODESA, whereas the outlines of a narrative for the "new" South Africa were crafted by the TRC. In contrast to CODESA, the process guided by the TRC was designed as a civic educational process. The TRC was comprised of three committees, of which the decisions of only the Amnesty Committee had the force of law. The other two committees – the Human Rights Committee and the Reparations (compensation) committee – functioned in an advisory capacity. Though set up by legislation and resourced by the state, the TRC was not subject to control by any state authority. It was free to define its own agenda within the framework of the legislation that set it up. This gave it a double freedom: the power to craft a semi-official narrative of apartheid; and guaranteed daily access to prime time media to communicate this narrative to a wider public.

The legislation that set up the TRC gave it the freedom to define "the victim."[30] In interpreting the legislation, the TRC made three key decisions. First, the TRC individualized the victim. To do so was to ignore precisely what was distinctive about apartheid, that it was a system based on group oppression. Second, the TRC defined a human rights violation narrowly, as violating the "bodily integrity" of an individual. This distinction too proved problematic in a context where the vast majority of the population suffered violence as extra-economic. The violence of apartheid did not target the "bodily integrity" of a population group defined as "Bantu" but their means of livelihood, land, and labor. Finally, there was the question of defining the perpetrator. When it came to measures that directly affected the vast majority of the oppressed population, measures such as the *forced removal* of millions from land gazetted as "white areas" or *pass laws* that tracked the movement of all black people, extra-economic coercion was the work of apartheid authorities, and not the initiative of individual operatives. Just as victims were defined and targeted as racialized groups and not as individuals, perpetrators too were part of a racialized power and did not for the most part function as individuals.

The TRC had the legislative freedom to define the victim, whether as an individual or a group. Whereas apartheid legislation classified the subject population as so many races defined in law – and governed them as groups and not as individuals – the TRC remained adamant that victims had to be individuals. When it came to "gross violation of human rights," this is how Section 1(1)(ix) of the Act defined its meaning:[31]

"Gross violation of human rights" means the violation of human rights through – (a) the killing, abduction, torture or *severe ill-treatment* of any person; or (b) any attempt, conspiracy, incitement, instigation, command or procurement to commit an act referred to in paragraph (a), which emanated from conflicts of the past and which was committed during the period 1 March 1960 to 10 May 1994 within or outside the Republic, and the commission of which was advised, planned, directed, commanded or ordered, by any person acting *with a political motive.* (emphasis mine)

The debate focused on the meaning of "severe ill-treatment" and the definition of "political motive."

In 1959, the apartheid government passed the Promotion of Bantu Self-Government Act. The Act was to provide the legal umbrella for a far-reaching ethnic and racial cleansing of 87 percent of the land that was defined as "white" South Africa. A widely distributed and cited investigation by The Surplus People Project documented that 3.5 million had indeed been moved forcibly by South African authorities between 1960 and 1982 as part of the project to create ethnic homelands. The Commission accepted the estimate and acknowledged that the process involved "collective expulsions, forced migration, bulldozing, gutting or seizure of homes, the mandatory carrying of passes, forced removals into rural ghettos, and increased poverty and desperation."[32] Did these practices constitute "severe ill-treatment"? After noting that "forced removals" were "an assault on the rights and dignity of millions of South Africans," the Commission claimed it could not acknowledge them since these violations "may not have been 'gross' as defined by the Act."[33]

The distinction between "bodily integrity rights" and "subsistence rights" echoes a familiar distinction in social theory between the realm of the political and that of the economic, that of the state and that of the market, the former the source of oppressive practices that directly deny rights and the latter the source of inequalities that indirectly limit the means to exercise these rights. But practices such as coerced labor and forced removals could neither be classified as just economic or political; they were both. Where a command economy was obtained, the familiar distinction between the political and the economic obscured practices where political power directly intervenes in the sphere of economic relations. Like slavery, coerced labor and forced removals required the direct and continued use of force. Neither could be dismissed as structural outcomes lacking in agency and, therefore, not signifying a violation of civil rights. Rather than an outcome of "the dull compulsion of market forces," to use a formulation of Marx, these practices were characteristic of extra-economic forms of coercion. Rather than illuminate the divide between the economic and the political, they tended to articulate the relation between the two.

Then there was the question of distinguishing a "political" from a "non-political" motive. Were pass laws – the backbone of a legal regime that targeted every black South African – political? Were arrests under pass laws political? According to estimates made by the South African Institute of Race Relations, over a million people had been administratively ordered to leave urban areas by 1972.[34] "From the early sixties," the Commission noted, "the pass laws were the primary instrument used by the state to arrest and charge its political opponents."[35] Indeed, the Commission found that the proportion of pass law offenders was "as high as one in every four inmates during the 1960s and 1970s."[36] The Commission accepted that "the treatment of pass law offenders could well be interpreted as a human rights violation," but it still refused to include the category of pass law prisoners in the institutional hearings on prisons. In spite of the fact that "a strong argument was made for the inclusion of this category of common law prisoners in the hearings," the Commission refused on the grounds that these were common law prisoners and not "political prisoners". Yet the only "common law" these prisoners had violated was the pass law, the law that criminalized the exercise of a basic human right, the right of free movement.

Another category that raised questions about how the Commission distinguished political from non-political motives was that of *farm prisoners*. The notorious farm prisons system was directly connected to the pass law system. Failure by a black person to produce a pass resulted in an arrest. As the number of arrests grew, so did the financial burden on the state. The Department of Native Affairs proposed a solution in General Circular 23 of 1954: "It is common knowledge that large numbers of natives are daily being arrested for contraventions of a purely technical nature. These arrests cost the state large sums of money and serve no useful purpose. The Department of Justice, the South African Police and this Department have therefore held consultations on the problem and have evolved a scheme, the object of which is to induce unemployed natives roaming about the streets in the various urban areas to accept employment outside such urban areas."[37] This is how the scheme was to work: henceforth, when black persons failed to produce a pass, they "were not taken to court but to labor bureaux where they would be induced or forced to volunteer." In theory, they were to be told that if they "volunteered" for farm labor, charges against them would be dropped as an exchange. The result, the Commission noted, was that "arrests for failure to produce a pass became a rich source of labor for the farms," ensuring the farmers "a cheap supply of labor." But the category farm prisoners did not feature in the prison hearings. Why not? Because, said the Commission, "nobody came forward to give evidence."[38] "Nobody" here presumably refers to the victims of the farm labor system; it could not possibly refer to its institutional managers since the Commission had the legal right to subpoena reluctant or even unwilling witnesses, and had done so in other instances but obviously chose not to do so in this and related cases.

Perhaps the most blatant exclusion from prison hearings was that of *prisoners detained without trial*. The number so detained between 1960 and 1990 was estimated at some 80,000 South Africans by the Human Rights Committee, whose reports were made available to the Commission. In the words of the Human Rights Committee, as cited by the Commission: "There can be little doubt that the security police regard their ability to torture detainees with total impunity as the cornerstone of the detention system."[39] The most notorious instance of death in detention was that of Steve Biko. The Commission acknowledged the detention (and murder) of Steve Biko as a gross violation of human rights, but did not acknowledge others. The Commission gave no legal reasons for excluding the category of detainees from prison hearings. It simply did not have the time: "There were practical rather than legal reasons for excluding detention from the prison hearings."[40]

Anyone familiar with the contents of the five-volume Commission Report will testify that these volumes are a rich source of information on everyday apartheid and its practices. This was the work of the research staff of the Commission, which comprised mainly historians and social scientists. The evidence they accumulated, however, had to be filtered through legislated categories as interpreted by members of the Commission. Unlike researchers, these were drawn from two very different groups: religious leaders and members of the psychological profession. As a group, they were determined that both the confession and the reprieve had to be individual to be meaningful.

When the public outcry grew against the Commission's decision to exclude from its hearings all violence that had targeted groups and communities, the TRC responded by holding institutional hearings, but then specified that these were to clarify the background, the context, against which specific violations were committed. The Commission thus distinguished between structural and willed outcomes; the former reduced to "context" and "background" and the latter highlighted as evidence of agency. To make the point, it distinguished between "bodily integrity rights" and "subsistence rights," individual and group rights, and political and non-political motivations – ruling that only politically motivated violations of bodily integrity (but not subsistence) rights and individual (but not group) rights fell within its legislative purview.[41]

Why was the "enforced transfer of a person from one area to another" a violation of a right over one's person, but not the migrant labor system that involved both coerced movement and coerced labor? If arson was defined as a gross violation, then why did not a similar destruction through bulldozing, a practice characteristic of forced removals, also count as a gross rights violation? Pass laws and forced removals, both targeting communities and not individuals, had been at the heart of the claim that apartheid was indeed a "crime against humanity." But in the report of the Commission, both were reduced to "background" and "context."

At the end, the Commission came up with three truly bizarre conclusions. The first was a list of more than 20,000 names of individuals it acknowledged as victims of gross violations of human rights. The TRC recommended only those – and not the millions of victims of pass law, forced removals, and forced labor – to receive reparations from the post-apartheid state. Second, the Commission compiled a time series of violations over its mandate, which began with the Sharpeville Massacre in 1960 and closed with the first democratic elections in 1994. "Most violations," the Commission concluded, "took place in the period after the unbanning of political parties (1990–1994)"[42] and were the result of conflict between anti-apartheid groups, especially the ANC and the Inkatha Freedom Party (IFP) in Natal. The Commission then compiled a list of "perpetrator organisations." From this followed the Commission's most scandalous conclusion. It identified the IFP as the top "perpetrator organization" and the ANC as the third in that notorious list of perpetrators. In contrast, the state security services came as runners-up: the South African Police (SAP) second and the South African Defense Forces (SADF) trailing in fourth place.[43]

How could the Commission arrive at these bizarre conclusions? To begin with, the Commission saw itself as working within the framework of the agreement reached at CODESA, which included respecting the legality of apartheid. Second, the Commission did not even question the legitimacy of apartheid legislation that indemnified state operatives already indemnified by the apartheid parliament through a series of laws, stretching from the Sharpeville Massacre through the Soweto Uprising to the end of apartheid. Scholars who have studied these indemnities estimate that the numbers indemnified between only 1990 and 1994 range anywhere between 13,000 and 21,000. Contrast this with the 7,094 individuals identified as perpetrators, "the majority of whom were, in concrete terms, drawn from the ranks of liberation movements."[44] If the TRC honored the indemnification granted by a whole series of indemnity jurisprudence, which unfailingly followed on the heels of each human rights catastrophe under apartheid, then was the TRC left with no more than to complete the indemnification begun under apartheid, by granting amnesty mainly to those in the liberation movements alleged to have committed human rights violations?

There were many debates inside the Commission, but only one minority view was appended to the Commission's Report as a formal expression of dissent. This was penned under the name of Commissioner Wynand Malan. This is how Malan put his "main reservation": "The Act does not put apartheid on trial. It accepts that apartheid has been convicted by the negotiations at Kempton Park and executed by the adoption of our new Constitution. The Act charges the Commission to deal with gross human rights violations, with crimes both *under apartheid law and present law*"[45] (italics mine). At the same time, Malan insisted that the Commission stay away from any reference to international law: "international law does not provide for the granting of amnesty for a crime against humanity."[46] Malan was the only one to state forthrightly the assumptions that made sense of the Commission's work. My only critique is that he ascribed these flaws to the Act, and not to the Commission's interpretation of it.

Malan called for a shift from the plane of morality to that of history, and from a focus on the personal and the individual to one on community. In Malan's words: "Slavery is a crime against humanity. Yet Paul, in his letters to the Ephesians and Colossians, is uncritical of the institution and discusses the duties of slaves and their masters. Given a different international balance of power, colonialism too might have been found a crime against humanity."[47] Malan called on the Commission to put together a narrative that would provide a foundation for national reconciliation: "If we can reframe our history to include both perpetrators and victims as victims of the ultimate perpetrator – namely the conflict of the past – we will have fully achieved unity and reconciliation."[48] Malan was right that recognizing victims and perpetrators of apartheid can only be the first step to reconciliation. The next step would be to recognize both as *survivors* who must together shape a *common* future. Reconciliation cannot be between perpetrators and victims; it can only be between survivors.

The narrative the TRC crafted also had its political effects. Because the TRC focused on perpetrators and kept out of sight the beneficiaries of mass violations of rights – such as pass laws and forced expulsions – it allowed the vast majority of white South Africans to go away thinking that they had little to do with these atrocities. Indeed, most learned nothing new. The alternative would have been for the TRC to educate white South Africans that no matter their political views   whether they were for, against, or indifferent to apartheid, aware of its actions or not – they were all, without exception, its beneficiaries when it came to residential areas where they lived, the jobs they held, the schools they went to, the taxes they did or did not pay, the cheap labor they employed, and so on. Because the TRC was not a legislative organ, because its decisions – except on amnesty – did not have the force of law, the TRC did not face the same political restrictions as did the negotiators at Kempton Park. At the same time, the TRC had access to state resources and could reach right into South African living rooms at prime time. It needed to educate ordinary South Africans, black and white, about everyday apartheid and its impact on the life chances and circumstances of generations of South Africans. Such an education would have brought home to one and all the morality and the necessity of social justice. It would at least have educated them as to why the political reform that had brought them an end to juridical and political apartheid was unlikely to hold in the absence of social justice.

In the end, the TRC addressed itself to a tiny minority of South Africans, perpetrators and their victims, the former state operatives and the latter political activists. It ignored lived apartheid, which would have made sense of the lived experience of the vast majority of South Africans. When it came to reconciliation, it addressed a small minority, the old and the new elite, but ignored the vast majority of the population.

In sum, the TRC set aside the distinctive everyday violence of apartheid, the violence that targeted entire groups and that was central to realizing its political agenda. This is because the TRC understood violence as criminal, not political; as driven by individual perpetrators, and not groups of beneficiaries; as targeting identifiable, individual victims, and not entire groups. It focused on violence as excess, not as norm. It thus limited the criminal responsibility of individual operatives to actions that exceeded political orders – actions that would have been defined as crimes under apartheid law. In doing so, the TRC distinguished between the violence of apartheid – pass laws, forced removals, and so on – and the excess violence of its operatives. Because it did so, it was unable to achieve even that which Nuremberg did: to compile a comprehensive record of the atrocities committed by the apartheid regime. This is why the TRC should be seen as a special court within the framework of apartheid law.

The TRC hoped to function as a surrogate Nuremberg by displacing the logic of crime and punishment with that of crime and confession. By linking confession to amnesty, the TRC attempted to subordinate the logic of criminal justice to that of political justice, but the attempt was not successful. The TRC ended up trying to hold individual state officials criminally responsible – but only for those actions that would have been defined as crimes under apartheid law. Put differently, it held them accountable for violence that infringed apartheid law, but not for violence that was enabled by apartheid law. It limited criminal responsibility to actions that would have been crimes under apartheid law. In doing so, it both upheld apartheid as a rule of law and the law that undergirded apartheid.

What could the TRC have done differently in light of the fact that its work followed the agreement arrived at during the political negotiations known as CODESA? Instead of claiming to be laying the groundwork for "reconciliation," it would, first of all, have openly acknowledged that the basis of reconciliation was arrived at in the political and legislative processes that preceded and made possible its creation. To do so would be to acknowledge the possibilities open before it. Second, it could have turned its privileged and daily access to public resources and mass media to turn its public performance into a public educational campaign. The point of this campaign would have been to frame the terms of post-apartheid discourse by center-staging the question of social justice, and thus going beyond identifying individual perpetrators and individual victims to highlighting both beneficiaries and victims of apartheid as groups. That would have educated the white population about the structural horrors and social outcomes of apartheid as a mode of governing society – to make the argument that the political reconciliation of adversarial elites could only be made durable if followed by social reconciliation of the population at large.

The TRC shared with Nuremberg an understanding of justice that individualized it, a tendency that many now understand as part of a neoliberal orientation. Both were oriented to individual guilt even though one prioritized reconciliation, and the other prosecution. To stop here and to accent reconciliation over prosecution would be to accent impunity and lack of accountability. When it comes to reconciliation, it is not the TRC, but CODESA that shows the way forward. Unless it is combined with reform, reconciliation is unlikely to last. To be durable, it needs to be joined to a protracted process of reform, not only political as with CODESA, but social, as the TRC had the opportunity to underline – but did not.

V. LESSONS FOR AFRICA

Like the violence that marked apartheid South Africa, mass violence in African countries is not the outcome of inter-state conflict; it is in most cases the product of civil wars. Does the end of apartheid offer a lesson for the rest of Africa?

Both the TRC and CODESA were born of the internal situation in South Africa. If the TRC failed, it was not because of internal factors; rather, its shortcomings flowed from emulating a model defined by the global human rights regime: even if the TRC offered amnesty in place of punishment, it identified criminal responsibility with individual agents ("perpetrators") and presumed that they should be held individually accountable ("criminal justice"). The choice is between a criminal process – whether in its mock version performed by the TRC or in the strict version promised by the International Criminal Court (ICC) – and a CODESA-style political process. It is neither the mock court-style process of the TRC, which organized informal hearings and offered amnesty in return for "truth," nor criminal trials offered by the ICC, with the inevitable consequence that alleged perpetrators be politically disenfranchised, but the creation of a CODESA-type inclusive political process focusing on the most contentious issues that offers a way forward for conflict-ridden African countries. What distinguished the political process was that its focus was neither perpetrators nor victims, but the contentious issues that have driven different cycles of violence. The process aimed to be inclusive of all, whether perpetrators, victims, beneficiaries, or bystanders. The object, too, was not to identify and punish (or forgive) perpetrators, but to reform the political community and make it more inclusive. If South Africa has a lesson to offer the rest of Africa, that lesson is not contained in the practices of the TRC, but rather in those of CODESA.

The South African transition was not unique. It was preceded by the political settlement in Uganda at the end of the 1980–86 civil war, and followed by the settlement in Mozambique. The outcome of the civil war in Uganda made for a political stalemate in a situation in which one side (the National Resistance Army) had "won" militarily in a war waged in the Luwero Triangle (a small part of the country), but lacked an organized political presence in large sections of the country. Its political resolution was a power-sharing arrangement called the "broad base," which gave positions in the cabinet to those opposition groups that agreed to renounce the use of arms even if not their political objectives.

In Mozambique, six months after the South African elections in 1994, there was another impressive settlement, which followed a fifteen-year civil war. Like CODESA, this settlement also renounced both the battlefield and the courts as two versions of a winner-take-all approach, unsuited to a conflict in which there was no winner. The peace process in Mozambique decriminalized Renamo, an insurgency aided and advised by the apartheid regime, whose practices included the recruitment of child soldiers and the mutilation of civilians. A retribution process in Mozambique would have meant no settlement at all; instead, individuals from Renamo's leadership were brought into the political process and invited to run in national and local elections. The "broad base" deal in Uganda, the South African transition, and the postwar resolution in Mozambique were all achieved before the ICC came into existence.

Contrast this with the Ugandan government's response to a post-1986 insurgency by a string of groups, the last of these being the Lord's Resistance Army (LRA).[49] Like Renamo in Mozambique, the LRA kidnapped children and forced them to become child soldiers, and mutilated civilians as a regular practice. When the Ugandan parliament passed a resolution calling for a full amnesty for the leadership of the LRA, as a prelude to their participation in the political process, the presidency looked for a way to undercut it. Bent on punishing the civilian population he saw as having supported a string of insurgencies, the president turned to the ICC. The ICC willingly issued warrants against the leadership of the LRA in 2005, a fact that effectively sabotaged both the democratic process within the country and the overall peace process. The LRA moved across the border, at first to Congo and then to Central African Republic. Although it is a pale semblance of its earlier self, the LRA continues to flicker as an insurgent force.

It is not accidental that all the examples I have cited above – the "broad base" in Uganda, the end of apartheid, and the end of the civil war in Mozambique – happened before the ICC was set up. In all three cases, the accent was on the "survivor," not the "victim." From this point of view, the survivor is not the victim who survived, but all who survived the civil war, whether victim, perpetrator, or bystander. The way forward, I argue, lies not with "victims' justice," but with a more inclusive notion of "survivors' justice."

As with Nuremberg, victors' justice and victims' justice are not alternatives; they are two sides of the same coin. Victims' justice is not possible without a victor who can set up a rule of law under which victims may obtain justice. Criminal justice, like the military battlefield, is a place where there can only be winners and losers. It risks setting up the ground for the next war. As I shall argue in the next section, the pursuit of victims' justice risks perpetuating the cycle of violence. For a more inclusive notion of justice – survivors' justice – to be possible, the focus needs to shift from perpetrators to issues that drive the conflict.

VI. NUREMBERG AND THE CONTEMPORARY HUMAN RIGHTS MOVEMENT

As interpreted by the human rights movement, the lesson of Nuremberg is twofold: one, that responsibility for mass violence must be ascribed to individual agents; and, two, that criminal justice is the only politically viable and morally acceptable response to mass violence. Turned into the founding moment of the new human rights movement, Nuremberg is today the model for the ICC and is held as the fitting antidote to every incident of mass violence.[50]

To de-ideologize Nuremberg is to recognize that the logic of Nuremberg flowed from the context of inter-state war, one that ended in victory for one side, which then put the losers on trial. The logic of a court trial is zero sum: you are either innocent or guilty. This kind of logic ill-fits the context of a civil war. Victims and perpetrators in civil wars often trade places in ongoing cycles of violence. No one is wholly innocent and no one wholly guilty. Each side has a narrative of victimhood. Victims' justice is the flip side of victors' justice: both demonize the other side, and exclude it from participation in the new political order. A civil war can end up either as a renegotiated union or as a separation between states. The logic of Nuremberg drives parties in the civil war to the latter conclusion: military victory and the separation of yesterday's perpetrators and victims into two separate political communities. It is fitting to recall that the founding moment of the South African transition is not a criminal trial, but political negotiations, CODESA, reflecting a radically different context: not a war between states, but civil war.

The contemporary human rights movement is permeated with the logic of Nuremberg. Human rights groups focus on atrocities for which they seek individual criminal responsibility. Their method of work has a formalized name: Naming and Shaming. The methodology involves a succession of clearly defined steps: catalog atrocities, identify victims and perpetrators, name and shame the perpetrators, and demand that they be held criminally accountable. The underside of the focus on perpetrators is to downplay issues. Read the field reports of Human Rights Watch and you will find that, except for a *pro forma* one- or two-page introduction on history and context, the focus is on "naming and shaming." Indeed, context is considered a distraction from establishing the universality of human rights.[51]

This is problematic if one recognizes that political violence is often not a standalone incident but part of a *cycle of violence* – a fact obscured by the absence of a historical context. In a previous book on the Rwandan genocide,[52] I set about constructing an historical account of the violence: the more I did so, the more I realized that victims and perpetrators tended to trade places. Where victims and perpetrators have traded places, each side has a narrative of victimhood. The more you downplay context, the more you tend to locate the motivation for violence in either the individual psychology of the perpetrator or the culture of a group of perpetrators. The tendency to portray the perpetrator as the driving force behind the violence leads to freezing the two identities, perpetrator and victim, leading to the assumption that the perpetrator is always the perpetrator and the victim is always the victim. The result is to demonize the agency of the perpetrator – and diminish the agency of the victim. Demonizing goes along with branding, and reinforces the assumption that you can easily and eternally separate the bad from the good. The more depoliticized our notion of violence, the more the temptation to think of violence as its own explanation. Indeed, the tendency is to seek the explanation for violence in the person of the perpetrator. From being a problem, violence also becomes the solution. The temptation is to think that eliminating the perpetrator will solve the problem. But instead of showing a way out of the dilemma, violence introduces us to a quagmire. It feeds the cycle of violence.

Violence is not its own explanation. This much becomes clear with a shift of focus from human rights to human wrongs. Human rights may be universal, but human wrongs are specific. To focus on human wrongs is, first, to highlight context. It is, second, to underline issues. And it is, third, to produce a narrative that highlights the cycle of violence. To break out of the cycle of violence, we need to displace the victim narrative with that of the survivor. A survivor narrative is less perpetrator-driven, more issue-driven. Atrocities become part of a historical narrative, no longer seen as so many stand-alone acts but as parts of an ongoing cycle of violence. To acknowledge that victim and perpetrator have traded places is to accept that neither can be marked as a permanent identity. The consequence is to de-demonize – and thus to humanize – the perpetrator.

If Nuremberg has been ideologized as a paradigm, the end of apartheid has been exceptionalized as an improbable outcome produced by the extraordinary personality of Nelson Mandela. But the lesson of South Africa is to look for the solution within the problem and not outside it. The point is to strive for internal reform, not external intervention. CODESA has a double significance. CODESA focused on the cycle of violence as threatening the very foundation of a political community. It dared to reimagine the political community by recognizing in the after effects of violence an opportunity to re-found the political community. In doing so, it underlines the need to return to an older tradition in political theory, one that stretches from Hobbes to Arendt and recognizes political violence – conquest, civil war – as potentially foundational to the creation of an inclusive political order.

On the negative side, CODESA – and the TRC – failed to acknowledge that this same violence has also been foundational to the establishment of a liberal socio-economic order. In the words of Marx, this extra-economic violence was key to primitive accumulation. To imagine a socio-economic order beyond liberalism is to focus on the question of social justice. The downside of the South African transition was its attempt to put a political lid on a public conversation about social justice in post-apartheid South Africa. It is arguable that the political balance of forces that shaped the post-apartheid transition also defined its limits, a limitation reflected in the fact that the transition was more political than social. This should have been all the more reason to expect a non-binding process like the TRC to make room for a discussion on social justice.

Neither victors' justice nor victims' justice, CODESA shed the zero-sum logic of criminal justice for the inclusive nature of political justice, inclusion through the reform of the political community in which yesterday's victims, perpetrators, bystanders, and beneficiaries may participate as today's survivors. Political reform targets entire groups, not isolated individuals. Its object is not punishment, but a change of rules; not state creation, but state reform. By turning its back on revenge, it offers the possibility of creating new communities of survivors. By focusing on the link between creating an inclusive political order and an inclusive rule of law, it calls for a deep reflection on the relation between politics and law. The point of it all was not to avenge the dead, but to give the living a second chance.

NOTES

1 Samuel Moyn, *The Last Utopia: Human Rights in History* (Cambridge: Belknap Press, 2012), 8–9.
2 For an extended discussion, see Robert Meister, *After Evil: A Politics of Human Rights* (New York: Columbia University Press, 2012).
3 There is also a *quantitative* distinction – that of *sheer scale*. The larger its scale, the more the likelihood that the violence is either unleashed by the state or is part of an anti-state mobilization, i.e., a civil war or an insurgency, or both. When it comes to extreme violence, one needs to reflect on the question: can we afford a punishment that even approximates the enormity of the crime? For an analogy, what rationale do policymakers give for not applying the same rules to large-scale theft, say by the banks in the period preceding the recent collapse, as we do to petty crime? The only explanation that makes any sense is the fear of unintended consequences – collateral damage is sure to outweigh the intended punishment. Critics claim that such a context calls for a systemic solution.
4 I have developed the notion of "survivor" and "survivors' justice" as a way to sublate the distinction between "victims" and "perpetrators" that drives contemporary human rights activism. My own thinking has been strongly influenced by an engagement with Robert Meister that has lasted over four decades, ever since we were graduate students at Harvard. Meister's point of view is best summed up in his latest book, *After Evil*. Whereas Meister approaches the South African transition from the standpoint of what was not achieved (social justice), my concern is to underline what was achieved (political justice).

5 Elizabeth Borgwardt, *A New Deal for the World: America's Vision for Human Rights* (Cambridge: Harvard University Press, 2005), 8, 74, 191. The question of sovereignty remains a bone of contention in international law. Article 2 of the UN Charter, for example, opens with the blanket assurance that "nothing contained in the present Charter shall authorize the United Nations to intervene in matters which are essentially within the domestic jurisdiction of any state," only to follow with a claw-back qualifier that "the exemption did not apply to matters affecting threats to international peace." See United Nations General Assembly, *Charter of the United Nations and Statute of the International Court of Justice*, art. 2(7) (1945).

6 Borgwardt, *A New Deal for the World*, 69.

7 The hardline policy as advocated by the Secretary of the Treasury, Henry Morgenthau, Jr. who argued that any attempt to reconstruct Germany industrially – even if to pay back reparations – would have the unintended effect of making Europe dependent on Germany without making Germany similarly dependent on Europe. This would leave the more basic political problem unsolved: what would prevent Germany from making a third attempt in as many generations to dominate Europe? In public speeches, Morgenthau compared Germany to "a mental patient, a problem child ... a case of retarded development, a young girl led astray, a slab of molten metal ready for the molder and much else besides," concluding that "the hard facts of defeat and of the need for political, economic and social reorientation must be the teachers of the German people." Secretary of War Henry Stimson disagreed, privately complaining of "Semitism gone wild for vengeance" in a reference to Morgenthau's German Jewish heritage. George Kennan opposed "even the mildest denazification program" as eliminating "the people upon whom Germany had to depend for future leadership" and as likely to lead to "disharmony." American public opinion – with 34 percent wanting to destroy Germany as a political entity, 32 percent wanting supervision and control over Germany, and only 12 percent wanting to rehabilitate Germany – was in support of a Morgenthau-type approach. A public statement released at the Yalta Conference took the hard line: "It is our inflexible purpose to destroy German militarism and Nazism and to ensure that Germany will never again be able to disturb the peace of the world.... We are determined to disarm and disband all German armed forces; break up for all time the German General Staff that has repeatedly contrived the resurgence of German militarism; remove or destroy all German military equipment; eliminate or control all German industry that could be used for military production; bring all war criminals to just and swift punishment and exact reparation in kind for the destruction wrought by the Germans; wipe out the Nazi party, Nazi laws, organizations and institutions, remove all Nazi and militarist influences from public office and from the cultural and economic life of the German people; and to take in harmony such other measures in Germany as may be necessary to the future peace and safety of the world." Borgwardt, *A New Deal for the World*, 207, 210.

8 Norbert Ehrenfreund, *The Nuremberg Legacy: How the Nazi War Crimes Trials Changed the Course of History* (New York: Palgrave Macmillan, 2007), 7.

9 Ibid., 10.

10 There were some obvious lags. The biggest deficiency was the failure to provide the defendant with the right to appeal convictions to a higher court. Article 26 of the London Charter spelled out that the judgment of the tribunal as to guilt or

innocence "shall be final and not subject to review." Ehrenfreund, *The Nuremberg Legacy*, 12, 16.

11 Nazi officers at Nuremberg were charged with waging aggressive war, with conspiracy to wage it, and "crimes against humanity." At the time, there were plenty of criticisms of the hypocrisy of charging defeated states with violence against civilians when victorious states were known to have carpet-bombed and firebombed enemy cities, and even targeted them with atomic weapons.

12 Ehrenfreund, *The Nuremberg Legacy*, 16–17.

13 Ibid., 14.

14 Ibid., 234.

15 Ibid., 56–57.

16 Michael Walzer, *Just and Unjust Wars: A Moral Argument with Historical illustrations*, 2nd ed. (New York: Basic Books, 1992), 250. Cited in Ehrenfreund, *The Nuremberg Legacy*, 59. The socialist leader Norman Thomas wrote in 1947 of the hypocrisy of charging the German General Staff with the crime of waging "aggressive war": "Aggressive war is a moral crime but this will not be established in the conscience of mankind by proceedings such as those at Nuremberg, where Russians sit on the bench and exclude evidence of Hitler's deal with Stalin. What was the latter's war against Finland, Poland and the Baltic states but aggression? Indeed, what major power had not in comparative recent years been guilty of acts of aggression?" Borgwardt, *A New Deal for the World*, 225, 231.

17 George Washington Williams, a veteran of the US Civil War, arrived in Congo in 1890 as a journalist. Expecting to see the paradise of enlightened rule that Leopold had described to him in Brussels, Williams instead found what he called "the Siberia of the African Continent." Traveling a thousand miles up the Congo River, Williams interviewed the Congolese about their experience of the regime, taking extensive notes. He then wrote an open letter to King Leopold that Adam Hochschild has described as "one of the greatest documents in human rights literature." Published in many American and European newspapers, it was the first comprehensive, detailed indictment of the regime and its slave labor system. In a subsequent letter to the US Secretary of State, Williams declared Leopold II guilty of "crimes against humanity" and appealed to the international community of the day to "call and create an International Commission to investigate the charges herein preferred in the name of Humanity ...." A century later, Hochschild's historical study concluded that a third of the Congolese population had died during Leopold's rule. Adam Hochschild, *King Leopold's Ghost: A Story of Greed, Terror and Heroism in Colonial Africa* (Boston: Houghton Mifflin, 1998).

18 Ehrenfreund, *The Nuremberg Legacy*, 23, 25.

19 Here I cite some important works from what is a huge and growing literature on the subject. Mette Zølner, *Re-Imagining The Nation: Debates on Immigrants, Identities and Memories* (New York: P.I.E.-Peter Lang, 2000); Peter H. Schuck and Rainer Münz, *Paths to Inclusion: The Integration of Migrants in the United States and Germany* (New York: Berghahn Books, 1997); Anna Bramwell, *Refugees in the Age of Total War* (New York: Routledge, 1988); Piotr Eberhardt, *Political Migrations in Poland 1939–1948* (Warsaw: Przegląd Wschodni, 2006);

Myron Weiner, *Migration and Refugees: Politics and Policies in the United States and Germany* (Brooklyn: Berghahn Books, 1998); Steffen Prauser and Arfon Rees, "The Expulsion of 'German' Communities from Eastern Europe at the end of the Second World War," *European University Institute* HEC No. 2004/1 (2004); Jan Owsinski and Piotr Eberhardt, *Ethnic Groups and Population Changes in Twentieth-Century Central-Eastern Europe: History, Data, Analysis* (Armonk: M.E. Sharpe, 2002); Alfred M. De Zayas, *A Terrible Revenge* (New York: Palgrave Macmillan, 1994).

20 It is true that the relatively poor and powerless among the beneficiaries of apartheid feared reprisals after the end of apartheid and agitated for a separate autonomous (though not independent) political community, the Afrikaaner *Volkstaat*, to defend themselves.

21 Richard Spitz and Mathew Chaskelson, *The Politics of Transition: A Hidden History of South Africa's Negotiated Settlement* (Oxford: Hart Publishing, 2000), 3, 21, 22.

22 Kader Asmal, Louise Asmal, and Ronald Suresh Roberts, *Reconciliation Through Truth: A Reckoning of Apartheid's Criminal Governance* (Cape Town: David Philip Publishers, 1997); Alex Boraine, *A Country Unmasked: Inside South Africa's Truth and Reconciliation Commission* (New York: Oxford University Press, 2001); Priscilla B. Hayner, *Unspeakable Truths: Transitional Justice and the Challenge of Truth Commissions* (New York: Routledge, 2010); Mahmood Mamdani, "Reconciliation without Justice," *Southern African Review of Books*, no. 46 (1996).

23 "What might we learn if, instead of viewing it as a variation on transitional mechanisms in Germany and Latin America, we were to view it instead as a variation on the theory and practice of indemnity in South African law?" Adam Sitze, *The Impossible Machine: A Genealogy of South Africa's Truth and Reconciliation Commission* (Ann Arbor: University of Michigan Press, 2013), 4.

24 Ibid., 25.

25 Ibid., 207 (citation omitted).

26 This paragraph and the rest of this section, are based on Spitz and Chaskelson, *The Politics of Transition*, 30, 38, 48, 57, 78–80, 84–85, 337–338, 322, 86, 159. Specific page numbers are indicated following the citation in the main body of the text above.

27 The first was the independence of key central institutions: the Public Service Commission, the Reserve Bank, the Public Prosecutor, and the Auditor General. The Constitutional Court refused to certify the first draft of the final Constitution on the grounds that it did not provide sufficient protection for the autonomy of the Auditor General and the Prosecutor. This was remedied. Schools and universities also retained autonomy.

28 The scholarly debate focuses on the tensions between the constitutional protection of private property in the Bill and the commitment to land reform. The final constitution contains contradictory elements on this point. It does indeed protect private property, and existing property relations in the property clause (Section 25, see below), which sets out the conditions under which expropriation can take place. In the interim constitution, land expropriation could take place based on, among other things, "public purpose," but this later changed in

the final constitution to also say in the "public interest." This opened the existing Constitutional framework to contradictory undertakings – on the one hand
the protection of existing property rights, entrenching settler-acquired land, and
on the other, opening the door for restitution and expropriation based on the
expressed commitment to "citizens to gain access to land on an equitable basis"
(Subsection 5). Compensation, however, had to be considered equitable; in policy the willing seller/willing buyer approach was agreed upon – thereby leaving
property owners with an effective veto on the question, until legal and political
dispute decide otherwise on what is in the public interest, what is fair compensation, and so on.

This goes back to 1913 only, and deals with existing legal ownership, and therefore does not deal with the political and historical question of conquest and land
dispossession that inaugurates a legal regime of private property that privileges set-
tler claims to ownership.

Here are the relevant sections of the constitution:

25. Property

1. No one may be deprived of property except in terms of law of general application, and no law may permit arbitrary deprivation of property.
2. Property may be expropriated only in terms of law of general application –
   a. for a public purpose or in the public interest; and
   b. subject to compensation, the amount of which and the time and manner of
      payment of which have either been agreed to by those affected or decided or
      approved by a court.
3. The amount of the compensation and the time and manner of payment must be
   just and equitable, reflecting an equitable balance between the public interest
   and the interests of those affected, having regard to all relevant circumstances,
   including:
   a. the current use of the property;
   b. the history of the acquisition and use of the property;
   c. the market value of the property;
   d. the extent of direct state investment and subsidy in the acquisition and ben-
      eficial capital improvement of the property; and
   e. the purpose of the expropriation.
4. For the purposes of this section:
   a. the public interest includes the nation's commitment to land reform, and to
      reforms to bring about equitable access to all South Africa's natural resources;
      and
   b. property is not limited to land.
5. The state must take reasonable legislative and other measures, within its available resources, to foster conditions which enable citizens to gain access to land
   on an equitable basis.
6. A person or community whose tenure of land is legally insecure as a result of
   past racially discriminatory laws or practices is entitled, to the extent provided by
   an Act of Parliament, either to tenure which is legally secure or to comparable
   redress.

7. A person or community dispossessed of property after 19 June 1913 as a result of past racially discriminatory laws or practices is entitled, to the extent provided by an Act of Parliament, either to restitution of that property or to equitable redress.
8. No provision of this section may impede the state from taking legislative and other measures to achieve land, water and related reform, in order to redress the results of past racial discrimination, provided that any departure from the provisions of this section is in accordance with the provisions of section 36(1).

I am thankful to Suren Pillay of the University of Western Cape for this clarification.

29 The consensus-building process was marked by three phases: councils in the pre-interim phase were appointed by local negotiation forums in which statutory and non-statutory delegates were equally represented; then came the interim phase with a "government of local unity"; majority decision-making would come into play only in the final phase, after the first local government elections under the new constitution. Spitz and Chaskelson, *The Politics of Transition*, 186.

30 Mahmood Mamdani, "Amnesty or Impunity? A Preliminary Critique of the Report of the Truth and Reconciliation Commission of South Africa (TRC)," *Identities, Affiliations, and Allegiances*, eds. Seyla Benhabib, Ian Shapiro, and Danilo Petranovic (New York: Cambridge University Press, 2007).

31 Truth and Reconciliation Commission, *The Truth and Reconciliation Commission of South Africa Report – Volume 1* (1998), 60 [hereinafter *TRC Report – Volume* [#]].

32 *TRC Report – Volume 1*, 34; *TRC Report – Volume 2* (1998), 409.

33 *TRC Report – Volume 1*, 34.

34 *TRC Report – Volume 3* (1998), 528.

35 Ibid., 163.

36 *TRC Report – Volume 4* (1998), 200.

37 Cited in *TRC Report – Volume 4*, 202.

38 Ibid.

39 This from a March 1983 paper by the Committee, cited in Human Rights Committee, *A Crime Against Humanity*, ed. Max Coleman (1998) (quoted in *TRC Report – Volume 4*, 201).

40 *TRC Report – Volume 4*, 201.

41 *TRC Report – Volume 1*, 64.

42 Ibid., 172.

43 *TRC Report – Volume 3*, 3, 162.

44 Sitze, *The Impossible Machine*, 27.

45 *TRC Report – Volume 5* (1998), 440.

46 Ibid., 449.

47 Ibid., 448.

48 Ibid., 443; it is for survivors to "succeed in integrating, through political engagement, all our histories, in order to discontinue the battles of the past."

49 For an analysis of the human rights regime in relation to the LRA and the Uganda government, see Adam Branch, *Displacing Human Rights: War and Intervention in Northern Uganda* (New York: Oxford University Press, 2011).

50 The International Criminal Court, founded after the Cold War, adopted Nuremberg as precedent when it came to trial procedure. Ehrenfreund, *The Nuremberg Legacy*, xvii.

51 I have elaborated the argument in Mahmood Mamdani, *Saviors and Survivors: Darfur, Politics and the War on Terror* (New York: Pantheon, 2010).

52 Mahmood Mamdani, *When Victims Become Killers: Nativism, Colonialism and Genocide in Rwanda* (Princeton: Princeton University Press, 2006).

Index

.